Themes for Writers

Themes for Writers

Paul Eschholz
Alfred Rosa

University of Vermont

St. Martin's Press
New York

Senior editor: Karen J. Allanson
Managing editor: Patricia Mansfield-Phelan
Project editor: Alda D. Trabucchi
Production supervisor: Alan Fischer
Cover and text design: Sheree Goodman
Cover painting: Augustus Vincent Tack, *Aspirations*, 1928.
  The Phillips Collection, Washington, D.C.

Library of Congress Catalog Card Number: 92-62770
Copyright © 1994 by St. Martin's Press, Inc.
8 7 6 5 4
f e d c b a

For information, write:
St. Martin's Press, Inc.
175 Fifth Avenue
New York, NY 10010

ISBN: 0-312-09204-0

Acknowledgments

Ascher, Barbara Lazear, "The Box Man." From *Playing after Dark* by Barbara Lazear
  Ascher. Copyright © 1982, 1983, 1984, 1985, and 1986 by Barbara Lazear Ascher.
  Used by permission of Doubleday, a division of Bantam Doubleday Dell Publish-
  ing Group, Inc.
Adler, Mortimer J., "How to Mark a Book," *Saturday Review of Literature*, July 6, 1940.
  Copyright © by Mortimer J. Adler; Copyright © 1967 renewed by Mortimer J.
  Adler. Reprinted by permission of the author.
Alvarez, Julia, "Snow." From *How the Garcia Girls Lost Their Accents.* Copyright © by
  Julia Alvarez 1991. Published by Plume, an imprint of New American Library, a
  division of Penguin Books USA Inc. Originally published in hardcover by Algon-
  quin Books of Chapel Hill. First publication: *Warnings: An Anthology on the Nu-
  clear Peril*, Northwest Review Books, 1984. Reprinted by permission of Susan
  Bergholz Literary Services, New York.
Asimov, Isaac, "The Difference Between a Brain and a Computer." From *Please Explain*
  by Isaac Asimov. Copyright © 1973 by Isaac Asimov. Reprinted by permission of
  Houghton Mifflin Co. All rights reserved.
Asimov, Isaac, "Intelligence." Published by permission of the Asimov Estate c/o Ralph
  M. Vicinanza, Ltd.

Acknowledgments and copyrights are continued at the back of the book on pages
527–529, which constitute an extension of the copyright page.

Preface

Themes for Writers offers sixty-five short, lively essays that have been selected for their appropriateness for use by beginning college writers. Most of the selections are shorter than one thousand words, like the essays the students themselves are commonly asked to write. The essays have been grouped by themes that we know from our own classroom experience are of interest to college students. The essays invite students to engage the issues raised within each thematic grouping, and they stimulate discussion and written responses. We have sought a level of readability that is neither so easy as to be condescending nor so difficult as to distract the reader's attention from the theme under study. Although we have included a few classics, the majority of the essays have been written in the last ten years. Over 50 percent of the essays are written by women and 25 percent by minority writers. They are drawn from a wide range of sources, represent a variety of contemporary prose styles, and illustrate basic rhetorical principles and patterns.

The essays are grouped in seventeen chapters. In Part I (Chapters 1–12) we present the following themes: Sense of Self; Family Ties; Everyday Heroes and Role Models; Relationships; Friends; Education; Work; A Multicultural Society; Language and Diversity; Addictions; The Natural World; and Life and Death. Each of these thematic chapters contains four essays introduced by a brief statement and rationale for the relevance of the theme. To get students started with each essay we include a brief statement about the author as well as a brief introduction to the essay that we have called Preparing to Read. Here we locate the reading within its larger thematic context and ask the students to reflect on their own thoughts and attitudes toward it.

Each essay is followed by study materials in three parts: Vocabulary, Understanding the Essay, and Exploring the Theme: Discussion and Writing. The Vocabulary exercise draws from each reading a number of words that students will find worth adding to their active vocabularies. The exercise asks students to see how the word is used in the context of the selection and then to write a sentence of their own using the word. Understanding the Essay provides a set of questions for checking comprehension and for guiding students through the content and rhetorical features of the reading. The questions in Exploring the Theme: Discussion and Writing reach beyond the confines of the essay to raise some central issues for classroom discussion and paper topics. Most questions are designed to stimulate critical analysis and to promote the lively exchange of ideas. Finally, at the end of each thematic chapter in the text, we give Writing Suggestions that ask students to write about the theme using one or more of the readings in that chapter.

In Part II, *On Becoming a Better Writer* (Chapters 13–17), we address matters of writing. In Chapter 13, Writers on Writing, we present five essays by highly respected teachers of writing on important aspects of the writing process. In reading what these teachers have to say about the writing process, students will become more conscious of their own habits as writers. Chapters 14–17 focus on four essential elements of a good essay: Thesis, Organization, Paragraphs, and Effective Sentences. These chapters all follow a similar pattern. Each opens with an explanation of the element or principle to be considered. We then present three essays, each of which has its own brief introduction providing information about the author and directing the student's attention to the rhetorical feature. Every essay is followed by study materials in three parts: Vocabulary, Understanding the Essay (these are similar to those found in the thematic chapters) and Writing Activities which provide an in-class opportunity for students to practice the various rhetorical strategies and techniques.

The arrangement of the chapters suggests a logical teaching sequence, moving from self-oriented themes to broader social and universal concerns. In this approach the chapters on writing can be used as needed while students are working with themes. An alternative teaching strategy is to start with the chapter Writers on Writing and any of the other chapters in Part II, before embarking on the themes themselves. Each chapter is self-contained, so that instructors may easily devise their own sequences, omitting or emphasizing particular chapters according to the needs of a particular group of students. The Rhetorical Table of Contents (pp. xvii–xxi) classifies all of the readings in this book according to rhetorical organizational patterns.

We wish to express our appreciation to the many reviewers who helped us with their constructive comments and suggestions as we prepared *Themes for Writers*. We are especially grateful to Ron Leiber,

Nassau Community College; Beverly J. Slaughter, Brevard Community College; Janine Reed, Ohio Wesleyan University; Robbie Pinter, Belmont University; and A. J. Dasher, Palm Beach Community College–Central Campus.

We wish to thank Karen Allanson, our editor at St. Martin's Press, for believing in us and this project. Bill Soeltz, our St. Martin's college representative, confirmed our belief that beginning writers could profit from a thematically arranged collection of brief essays and encouraged us to compile one. Thanks also go to Mark Wanner and Susan Palmer for their cheerful and prompt editorial assistance. Our greatest debt, as always, is to our students for all that they have taught us.

Paul Eschholz
Alfred Rosa

Contents

Rhetorical Table of Contents

Cause and Effect

Comparison and Contrast

Process Analysis

Themes for Writers

INTRODUCTION

Themes for Writers is designed to help you become a better writer by presenting a collection of essays on a wide variety of themes, or subjects, that will cause you to think, to question, and to respond. We begin with twelve themes of interest to the college student ranging from personal to broader issues—from a Sense of Self and Family Ties, to Everyday Heroes and Role Models, Relationships and Friends, Education, Work, a Multicultural Society, Language and Diversity, and Addictions to the broader concerns of The Natural World and the issues of Life and Death. By reading and understanding these essays you will become knowledgeable about these subjects, more current in your thinking about them, and more thoughtful about the implications of events in our rapidly evolving society—characteristics that will in themselves make you a better writer.

Themes for Writers, as its title implies, is also about writing. By encouraging you to become a careful, analytical reader, one who understands the structures and strategies by which meanings are conveyed in prose, *Themes for Writers* will also help you become a better writer. To assist you further in achieving this goal, we provide additional writing instruction in a section entitled "On Becoming a Better Writer" that includes "Writers on Writing," a chapter of five essays offering practical advice by leading teachers of writing, as well as chapters that focus on four important features of all essays—Thesis, Organization, Paragraphs, and Effective Sentences.

Working with Themes

Reading can be a major source of ideas for writing. On a basic level our reading compels us to respond to what we've read, to agree with or argue against the issues, ideas, attitudes, and perspectives of other writers. We take up our pens to de-

1

scribe our own experiences with the topic under discussion or to elaborate on or extend what another has written, to agree with the examples of others or to generate better ones of our own, to qualify what we read or simply to oppose its wrongheadedness. Reading, then, allows us to engage in a dialogue on the issues. It brings us into conversation with someone who is present but on our terms—a voice that is providing subjects and topics, issues and ideas that we can listen to, consider, question, reflect upon, applaud, disagree with, or even turn away from, as we please.

Reading is also provocative in somewhat more mysterious ways. Your imagination can be so sensitized or stimulated by an image, the description of a person or object, that it clings to your memory, and you are encouraged to write and create similar effects in your readers. For example, after reading Barbara Huttmann's "A Crime of Compassion," an essay about a nurse's refusal to let a cancer patient be resuscitated yet again, Erin Tremblay, one of our students, wrote a moving essay about her own experience with a cancer patient from whom she ironically learned what happiness is all about. After reading several essays in the section on Family Ties about the new family configurations that result from death, divorce, or remarriage, Kate Clark, another student, turned to her own family situation. She remembered a time when she was eight years old, four years after her parents' divorce, and how she went out alone on a "date" with her father, an experience that was for her the beginning of a new relationship with him. Sometimes, for no apparent reason, a sentence triggers a special insight. This happened to Caitlin Florschultz, for example, when she read Randall Williams's discussion in "Daddy Tucked the Blanket," in which he reminisces about the houses his family lived in as poor Southerners. Caitlin was moved to write an essay in which she tried to come to grips with what "home" meant for her. In still other cases, the tone, humor, irony, organization, or details that an author uses may excite a response in us that leads to writing.

Getting the Most
Out of Your Reading

To get the most out of your reading, you need to commit yourself to the task. This means that you bring a level of dedication and seriousness to your reading. You may think that you can read with the radio or television on, for example, or with friends holding a conversation nearby, or by quickly glancing through a piece of writing, reading sentences here and there and getting the general idea. You need, instead, to create an environment, or remove yourself to one, that is right for reading because it is quiet and free of distractions. You need as well to push other thoughts and pressures that you may be experiencing out of your mind for a time. The reading you are attempting to do in psychology will not go well if you are still thinking about what you did on your calculus test earlier in the day.

It's perhaps inevitable that not all the essays in *Themes for Writers* will be equally appealing to you. What if essays on nature, drugs in China, or eating disorders, say, do not hold as much interest for you as some others included here? That's only natural. It's worth remembering, however, that you can be pleasantly surprised by reading about subjects you thought had little interest for you. If you open yourself to your reading, to the possibility of new experiences, you will soon find yourself richly rewarded by the knowledge, ideas, and emotions that can come only from reading.

Reading and Rereading

We begin each chapter with a brief introduction to the theme in which we set a general context for reading the essays that follow. Each selection begins with a brief biographical note on the author, often explaining the author's authority for writing about the subject. The section entitled Preparing to Read provides a detailed introduction to the reading and a context for the essay. Preparing to Read is intended to guide your reading by raising questions and pointing out features you should not miss. Frequently these questions get you to think about the subject and to examine your own attitudes about it before your first reading.

Read the selection at least twice, regardless of its length. It takes two readings, at least, because you are too concerned in the first reading with the meaning of the selection, how it unfolds, where it begins, and how it concludes. In these readings you will become familiar with the selection, its subject and topic, its length, how easy or difficult it is to follow the author's line of reasoning, and what ideas it starts with and how it ends up. You may even decide that you like this author, or that you do not really have a sense of the author but have found the information useful and the ideas somewhat stimulating. The first reading, then, allows you to become familiar with the essay.

The second reading is like watching a movie for the second time. You know how everything turns out and are now better able to pay attention to the finer points of how it was composed, to how the parts work together to achieve the writer's goals. You understand better the writer's purpose, the thesis and its implications, the development of the paragraphs, the kinds of sentences used and the appropriateness of the author's choice of words. The second reading, consequently, is very important for the kinds of information it yields for improving your own writing.

Ask Yourself Questions About the Selection

As you study the text of an essay, ask yourself some basic questions about its content and form. The following questions will get you started:

1. What is the author trying to say? What is his or her main point or thesis? Remember that a thesis is a one- or two-sentence statement that makes an assertion about something.

2. Why is the author trying to say it? What is his or her purpose: to narrate? to describe? to explain? to argue?

3. What strategies of organization or techniques of development does the author use?

4. How do these strategies suit the author's subject and purpose?

5. How effectively does the essay achieve its purpose?

These important questions can be asked about any piece of writing, but they are not the only ones. Answers to these questions will lead you to yet other questions as the exciting process of critical reading unfolds.

You will notice that each reading is followed by a list of useful words together with their definitions, which you will need to know for a complete understanding of the reading. The Vocabulary section asks you to demonstrate your newly gained knowledge of these words by using them in your own sentences in the spaces provided.

Finally, we provide Understanding the Essay, a set of questions that tests your comprehension of the essay, as well as Exploring the Theme: Discussion and Writing, practical discussion/writing exercises related to the essay. At the end of each chapter, we give Writing Suggestions that grow out of either individual readings or groupings of readings, or that encourage writing on the overarching concerns of the themes themselves.

Mark Your Text

As you read, use a pencil. Mark the selection's main point when you find it stated directly. Look for supporting arguments or examples that illustrate the author's main argument. Label the parts and aspects of the essay. If you read a particularly well-developed paragraph, bracket it and write, "Well-developed paragraph." If you like an idea that the author has presented, write "Good idea." Do the same when the author uses a variety of sentence patterns or strong transitions. On the other hand, if you feel the need to be critical, some reasonable responses might be "No" or "How can you say that?" or "Maybe" or "Weak ending." In short, carry on a dialogue with the author, and try always to get inside the content of the essay while observing the author's writing techniques. As the noted philosopher and educator Mortimer Adler has written in his essay, "How to Mark a Book" (pp. 481–88), full ownership of a book occurs not with its purchase, but instead "comes only when you have made it a part of yourself, and the best way to make yourself a part of it is by writing in it."

When annotating a text, don't be timid. Mark up the book as much as you need to. Underline key passages and use check marks, asterisks, bold vertical lines in the margins, or, if you like, a commercial highlighter. It's probably best to be consistent so you don't have to spend time and effort interpreting your own notation system. Also, do not let the task of annotating become burdensome or assume a greater importance than what you are trying to achieve. Annotations are the visible evidence of your attempt to achieve a greater understanding of an essay, or book, by interaction with it.

Getting to Know Yourself as a Writer

Have you ever thought about what you do when you write, the process that you follow in writing a composition? Do you try to write a finished essay in one writing or draft? Or do you need to revise a number of times? Do you start to write immediately or do you need to gather information and ideas first? Do you worry about your grammar and punctuation at every stage of your writing, especially if you are writing for your English instructor? It is helpful to think about the way you write and to learn how others go about it. You may find ways of refining or improving the steps that you take or of even learning a new approach to writing.

Most writers follow what is known as "the writing process" when they write. The following is a list of the steps in that process, along with a detailed description of the various activities that are undertaken in each step developed by Professor Donald M. Murray of the University of New Hampshire.

THE WRITING PROCESS

Prewriting

1. *Collect*   Writers know effective writing requires an abundant inventory of specific, accurate information. The information is collected through reading, interviewing, observing, and remembering.

2. *Connect*   Meaning begins to be discovered as pieces of information connect and evolve into patterns of potential meaning. The writer plays with the relationships between pieces of information to discover as many patterns of meaning as possible.

3. *Rehearse*   In the mind and on paper, the writer follows language toward meaning. The writer will rehearse titles, leads, partial drafts, and sections of a potential piece of

writing to discover the voice and the form which lead to meaning and communicate that meaning.

Writing

4. *Draft*   The writer completes a discovery draft, usually written as fast as possible, often without notes, to find out what the writer knows and does not know, what works and does not work. The writer is particularly interested in what works, because most effective writing is built from extending and reinforcing the strongest elements in a piece of writing.

Rewriting

5. *Develop*   The writer explores the subject by developing each point through definition, description, and, especially, documentation that shows as well as tells the writer, and then the reader, what the piece of writing means. The writer usually has to add information to understand the potential meaning of the drafts and often has to restructure them.

6. *Clarify*   The writer anticipates and answers all the readers' questions. At this stage the writer cuts everything that is unnecessary and often adds those spontaneous touches we call style. They produce the illusion of easy writing that means easy reading.

Editing

7. *Edit*   The writer goes over the piece line by line, often reading aloud, to make sure that each word, each mark of punctuation, each space between words contributes to the effectiveness of the piece of writing. The writer uses the simplest words appropriate to the meaning, writes primarily with verbs and nouns, respects the subject-verb-object sentence, builds paragraphs that carry a full load of meaning to the reader, and continues to use specific, accurate information as the raw material of vigorous, effective writing. The writer avoids any breaks with the customs of spelling and language that do not clarify meaning.

Sharing

8. *Final Copy*   The writer shares his or her writing with an audience.

Themes for Writers provides you with readings that are sure to stimulate your thinking on twelve contemporary themes and presents information, instruction, and practice in writing essays. By reading carefully and thoughtfully and by becoming more sensitive to your own writing process, you can begin to have more control over your own writing. Erin Tremblay, Caitlin Florshultz, and Kip Turner, three of our own writing students at the University of Vermont, found this to be true, and their work is a good example of what can be achieved by using the writing process to develop both thinking and writing skills.

Three Model Student Essays

After reading several of the essays in the Life and Death section—namely, Barbara Huttmann's "A Crime of Compassion" and Ellen Goodman's "Whose Life Is It Anyway?"—Erin Tremblay decided to write about her unusual encounter with a terminally ill person while working in her hometown hospital the summer before coming to college. In her first draft Erin got caught up in a detailed description of her job as a receptionist in the radiology department. She remembered being overwhelmed—especially during her first two weeks on the job—by all the different routines she had to learn and the difficult, often demanding people whom she had to greet and work with each day. And she remembered meeting Mary Alice Collins, a cancer patient who had come in for her CAT scan appointment.

After sharing her rough draft with classmates, Erin realized she had given far too many details about her job as a receptionist and not enough details about Mary Alice Collins. As she revised, Erin tried to show her readers more about Mary Alice. She wanted to create a dominant impression of a wonderfully warm and happy older woman. Erin wasn't as interested in capturing Mary Alice's physical appearance as she was her spirit, her energy, and her positive attitude about life even in the face of death. The more she focused on Mary Alice, the more Erin discovered just what their meeting had meant to her. She found herself dropping long passages in which she simply described her work routines. Later she added dialogue both to let Mary Alice speak for herself and to enliven the narrative. By the time she produced her final draft Erin was satisfied that she had captured the essence of her meeting with Mary Alice Collins. Here's Erin's story.

Mary Alice Collins

Erin Tremblay

I sat staring down at the six orange lights blinking in unison. My heart beat fast, my forehead got hot, and I knew I would soon be in a sweat. I made a futile attempt to remember who was on hold, for what, and on which line. As my throat choked up, and tears swelled in my eyes, I became aware of a presence in front of my desk. Unwillingly, I looked up and saw a petite, elderly woman smiling at me.

Beginning Sets Context: who, what, where, to whom

"Can I help you?" I asked, somewhat annoyed.

"Good morning, dear. My name is Mary Alice Collins, and I have an appointment for a CAT scan today."

Dialogue: lets characters speak for themselves

Her words, CAT scan, echoed in my ears. I quickly thumbed through the disarrayed schedule, knowing that the technologists in CAT scan insisted that their patients take priority over all other patients. I found her name scribbled next to a time box marked 11:00 a.m. To the right of her name was the exam that she was having and her clinical history. A bold CA told her whole

Organization: chronological sequence of events

Selection of Details: emphasizes Mary Alice Collins' personality and the seriousness of her illness

story. I looked back at Mary Alice, who was patiently smiling.

"You're scheduled for eleven o'clock. I'll let them know that you're here. Please have a seat in the waiting area behind you."

"Thank you, dear," she replied, winking as she turned away.

CA meant cancer. This good-natured woman had cancer, yet one would never be able to tell from watching her. Maybe she did not know? When I brought her name up in the computer, ten different exams appeared in her billing history under the title ONCOLOGY. This was her fifth visit to the hospital in just the last week. She had to have known. I sat staring blankly at the screen thinking how unfair life had been to this admirable lady.

Selection of Details: job setting contrasts with Mary Alice Collins' personality/ patience

"Erin," the other receptionist snapped, "I told you that you can't keep putting people on hold, and forgetting about them. You left a doctor on hold for over five minutes!"

"Sorry."

I wanted to scream! It was only my second week working in the radiology department; nevertheless, everyone expected miracles. How was I supposed to handle this hectic array of duties that even the most experienced receptionist would not be expected to perform? No one ever made any attempt to help or ease me into the job. Feeling absolutely abused, I went about my business counting the minutes until my lunch break.

When I reluctantly returned from my lunch break, I noticed that the department heads were running around in an uproar. I immediately became worried. While I prayed to God that the problem had nothing to do with me, I saw her, Mary Alice Collins. It was now one thirty, two and a half hours after her original exam was scheduled, and she was still in the waiting room. I learned that a car accident victim required an emergency CAT scan, so her appointment was delayed.

I found myself walking away from my duties at the front desk to offer my apologies and assistance to Mrs. Collins. I surveyed the crowded lounge. The room was full of anxious stares. An elderly man barked at me, complaining,

Contrast: of other patients with Mary Alice Collins

"Where's my wife?"

"She'll be out in ten more minutes, Mr. Goldstein. You must be patient."

I walked farther into the dimmed room. Two young mothers sat in the corner gossiping while their toddlers played on the floor. They were making quite a spectacle of themselves, screeching and laughing

Selection of Details: creates dominant impression of Mary Alice Collins

loudly. But everyone else in there looked like zombies watching television. Mary Alice Collins was the only person not oblivious to the children's enjoyment. As I approached, I could see this warm woman sharing each laugh and thrill that the children experienced, as if she were on the floor playing with the toys as well. I sat beside her, absorbing the vibrancy that generated about her.

Dialogue: shows instead of tells

"Mrs. Collins," I interrupted, "I wanted to thank you for being so patient . . ."

"Oh dear, I truly don't mind waiting. I enjoy meeting all these nice people that come in here."

Her sweet reply compelled me to offer words of encouragement. I knew that I was not supposed to discuss a patient's personal health, but an inner voice told me not to care about the hospital's rule.

"I hope I don't offend you, but I've read your clinical history, and I know why you're here. I think you're remarkable for being so pleasant and patient." Instantly she laughed and replied,

"I know that I have cancer. I'm not putting up an act. I am happy! I'm grateful that I've lived long enough to enjoy my first grandchild. I'm lucky to have seen all of New England and its beauty. I've lived a very full life!" She went on telling me about her battle with cancer. She had been fighting it for two long years. Six months prior, the doctors thought that all the cancer cells were killed. But now she returned to the hospital because the malignancy had spread after all. I admired how she remained confident and optimistic, despite knowing that death was so near.

The front desk got busy once again, so I wished Mary Alice to take care, and returned to the chaos. The afternoon was as active as the morning was, yet it went much smoother. Time that usually dragged by had picked up a faster pace. I relaxed and found myself actually joking with some of the other receptionists. I did not allow anything to bother me.

Contrast: Erin's attitude changes

At three thirty, transport brought down a wheelchair for the patient in CAT scan who was being admitted to the hospital. At three forty-five, Mary Alice Collins was wheeled by the front desk. She asked the boy pushing her chair to stop.

"Don't feel sorry for me, I want you to be happy," she said to me with a smile before waving and saying good-bye.

Ending: moment of truth

Caitlin Florschultz's paper grew out of her reading the essays in the Family Ties chapter. Her assignment was to explain something on which she was a "minor authority" and, like Erin and Kip, she was free to choose her own topic. She knew from past experience that to write a good essay she would have to write on a topic she cared about. She also knew she should allow herself a reasonable amount of time to decide on a topic, gather her ideas and examples, and focus on a thesis. At the outset she latched on to something her mother had told her as a child, that a "home is where you hang your hat." Caitlin was fascinated by the idea of "home" and what it meant. As a high schooler she remembered being confident in knowing what a home was, but now that she is living in an apartment at college and her divorced mother is in California, and her stepfather and his new wife are in the Vermont house, she's not so sure anymore. After some discussion, Caitlin decided that she wanted to explore the concept of home and try to tie down what it meant to her.

Caitlin began by brainstorming about her topic. She made lists of everything she could remember about the houses she'd lived in as a child growing up in Marlboro, Vermont, and the feelings that she had for each. She recalled one in particular, the first house that her family owned, the house that she lived in from age twelve until she departed for college. She listed all the physical details that were important to her about these houses and the people she associated with them. And she tried to remember what other members of her family had said about home. When she was confident that she had amassed enough information to begin writing, she made a rough outline, using a simple chronological organization pattern that she felt would reflect and capture the maturing of her idea of a home. Keeping this pattern in mind, Caitlin wrote a first draft of her essay.

After sharing her draft with several classmates and getting their responses, she reread it carefully herself, assessing how it could be improved. Caitlin realized that she had spent too much time talking about the ten different places she'd lived before the age of twelve and had not given enough information about the house that she had come to think of as home while she was in high school. By stressing those characteristics that the first ten houses had in common, Caitlin found that she could eliminate much of what she'd written about them. Next, she expanded her treatment of the one house she had lived in for eight years, paying particular attention to developing her reasons for thinking that this house was somehow special. She also found places where phrases and even whole sentences could be added to clarify her meaning. She repositioned some sentences, added some key transitions, and changed a number of words to create a more powerful effect.

The final draft of Caitlin's paper illustrates that she learned how the parts of a well-written essay fit together and how to revise a paper so that it emulates the qualities of the model essays that she read and studied in class. The following is the final draft of Caitlin's essay.

Home

Caitlin Florschultz

"Home is where you hang your hat." That's what my mother has always told me.

"But what if I leave my hat at school, and it gets lost?" I asked her one day many years ago.

She smiled and said, "Then home is where I am."

For as long as I can remember, my hat, my mother, and my home have been together in the same small New England town, that is, until I went away to college. Now my hat is packed away in an unmarked box in the closet of my Burlington apartment. My mother is on the other side of the country trying out life in California. And home? I'm still not quite sure where that is these days.

Introduction: anecdote sets up central question about "home"

Organization: chronological sequence of events

Comparision: glosses over first ten houses, emphasizing similarities

Focus: emphasis on house where feelings of permanence and stability first appeared

I grew up in Marlboro, Vermont. By the time I was twelve I had lived in about ten different locations, but they were all within the boundaries of Marlboro. Because I was young and flexible, I perceived each move as an exciting change and not a time of stress. And now that I think about it, very little did change with each move. My friends and family all stayed the same, and I was able to bring all of my belongings with me. While Marlboro covers a fairly large area, it has a population of only about five hundred. Therefore, each new place we moved to was guaranteed to have a lot in common with the last. All of my homes during that time were secluded and surrounded by acres of undeveloped land creating individual forests waiting to be explored. Each move presented me a new part of Marlboro that I had yet to discover.

Finally, when I was twelve, my family settled down and we built our own house, on our own land, in our own secluded part of Marlboro. It was a great feeling to have an actual physical structure that I could always return to and find my mother and the rest of my family, as well as a permanent place to hang my hat.

Because we all helped to design the house and actually watched its daily progression, when we moved in it immediately felt more permanent than any other place that we had ever lived. My mother grew brilliant flower gardens and various bushes around the perimeter of the house, and my stepfather planted tiny apple trees. And each spring as the pilings of snow melted, we marveled at their growth.

Description: creates dominant impression of house

I believe that the setting of the house also increased its value and made it even more our own. Set back off of a road that is barely traveled upon itself, the house can neither see nor be seen by another house. The rocky driveway winds upward through the dense trees and could almost be mistaken for a dry riverbed. Within a year of living there, I knew the house inside and out, as well as every inch of land that we owned. I knew where to find the best sledding hills in the winter. I knew where to walk so as to avoid disturbing the underground yellow jackets' nests or getting scratched up by the pricker bushes.

The house eventually molded to each of us and began to bear the marks of a home that is not rented or borrowed but clearly lived in by

Selection of Details: used to convey intimacy

its owners. By the time I left for college it was no longer new. The walls showed my little brother's progression through the years with little stick figures, then large backward letters, and eventually short mispelled words, all scratched on with crayon or permanent marker. There were a scattering of half-moons etched into the kitchen floorboards from my leaning back on the stools while incessantly talking on the phone in my high school years. There are probably millions of these scars and bruises covering the entire house, even after most of its creators and abusers are long gone. We all left a mark just as the house has left a mark on each of us.

Contrast: old feelings for house contrasted with new ones

Obviously, over the years I developed a strong emotional attachment to my house, this physical structure and its solid surroundings. It became undoubtedly my home, in every sense of the word. Somewhere along the line, between then and now things have changed. The house itself still exists, and the rose bushes and apple trees in the yard continue to grow even without the aid of my watchful eye. The sledding hills and climbing trees are now void of climbers and sledders, as they were before we came,

unasked, to share their lives. Of
the creators and worshippers of the
house only one remains. My once
stepfather is not enough to maintain the traditional feelings of
hominess that always went along
with the house.

    I returned just last weekend
and I was amazed by the changes
that were neither visual nor physical. As I turned up the driveway, I
felt the excitement that always accompanies returning home after being away for a while. I had been
gone for over two months. As the
car drew closer to the opening in
the woods where I had spent the
last eight years of my life my stomach tightened. My own car sat in
the driveway, covered by colorful
leaves and pine needles, with a For
Sale sign in the window. I glanced
secretly toward the kitchen window
looking for my mother and realized
that the feeling that I had felt
when we turned into the driveway
was gone. After a friendly but
brief greeting from my stepfather
and his new wife, I went directly
to my bedroom. I was thankful to
find it in the same state of disar-
ray that I had left it when I was
last there. But looking around I realized that although it was almost
as cluttered and full of junk as it

Selection of Details: emphasizes the absense of a sense of home now

had always been, very few of the
things that remained were of much
importance to me. I came to realize
that this was true of the whole
house. The living room was filled
with plants, as it had been since
we moved in. But after a moment of
inspection I realized that none of
the plants were familiar to me.
These foreign intruders appeared in
various forms throughout each of
the rooms that I entered, subtly
taking the place of the traditional
objects that I was used to. I tore
the house apart with my eyes,
searching perhaps for the sense of
home that I always thought would be
there. Compared to how strong the
feeling was just a year or two before, I found nothing.

Analogy: helps to explain feelings associated with house

Upon leaving I suddenly remembered a time when I felt similar to
the way that I did at that moment.
Just a couple of months before, our
dog of twelve years died, lying
peacefully on the front lawn. I remember staring at her body from ten
feet away. And although she looked
perfectly fine and could very well
have been sleeping, there was no
life or energy generating from her
body. Her physical body was there,
her physical appearance was the
same, but the feeling was gone. And
as I looked back at the house one

more time, I realized that it
wasn't much different from my dog.
The most that either of them had to
offer me now was a bundle of valuable memories.

Although it has taken over
twenty years, I believe that I have
finally come to a partial understanding of what home is. In the
past, I have thought of it as an accumulation of physical objects, people, and places that were safe and
represented little change. In a
sense, I think that that is still
accurate, but now I realize that it
is more than that. Most important,
it is a feeling that comes from
within.

Conclusion: a house is not necessarily a 'home'—new extended definition of home

When I visit my mother in California, I easily feel at home, even
though I have spent less than a
week of my life there. Even though
the house and city themselves are
of no great value to me, my mother
alone is capable of generating a
welcome that makes me feel as if I
have returned home. A large part of
my home right now is here in Burlington with my cat, my friends,
and my ever-growing collection of
hats. Although this house is a tem-
porary one, the people and objects
within it create that important
feeling of hominess. When I enter
the house these comfortable sur-

> roundings welcome me, and when I
> move to a new location I will be
> sure to bring them with me. And if
> I lose my hat, then I will always
> have others.

For one of his essays in College Writing, Kip Turner was asked to select a magazine or newspaper advertisement that was in some way related to one of the themes in *Themes for Writers*. His task was to analyze and interpret the advertisement, then to explain how the ad worked to sell the product. In the context of the theme of "work," Kip decided to focus on the public images that companies create for themselves while trying to sell their products. The automobile industry in particular interested Kip. As a result he scoured magazines for innovative or different car ads. An ad for the Saturn SC in *Newsweek* caught his eye, and it became the subject of his essay (see p. 23).

In his first draft Kip carefully described the ad that he had selected, ever mindful not to overlook any details that might be significant. In a sense he pretended that he was describing the ad to a person who hadn't seen it so that person could reproduce it. Next Kip answered a series of questions about his ad in his journal. These questions included: How do your ad and product compare and contrast with other ads for similar products? What else besides the product is being sold? How does the language work in your ad? How does the verbal message interact with the visual one? What is your emotional response to the ad or to the product? What are some of the themes that emerge when you look at your ad? What stands out most to you, and why? How does this ad work to sell the product? Kip's answers to these questions, especially the last one, helped him identify his interpretive approach and develop a thesis statement.

Armed with a thesis or controlling idea, Kip made a scratch outline of the main points he wanted to cover in his essay:

Thesis: The Saturn advertisement is not so much an ad to sell the car itself, but an attempt to convince potential consumers that the Saturn company's number one priority is dedication to the consumer and, therefore, the manufacture of a safe and quality automobile.

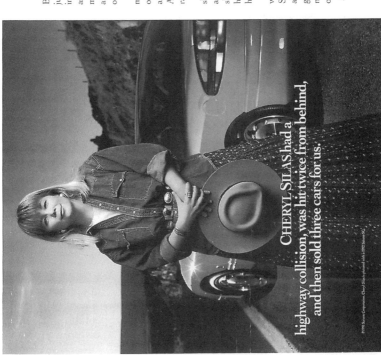

CHERYL SILAS had a
highway collision, was hit twice from behind,
and then sold three cars for us.

A policeman at the accident, Officer Jimmie Boylan, thought, "She's lucky to be alive." Cheryl had just stepped out of her totalled Saturn coupe. Upon impact, her shoulder harness and lap belt held her right as the spaceframe of her car absorbed most of the collision. He watched as Cheryl's sport coupe and the other cars were towed away.

The following week, Cheryl made the return trip to Saturn of Albuquerque and ordered another SC, just like her first. And then we started noticing some rather unconventional "referrals."

A few days later, Officer Boylan came into the showroom and ordered a grey sedan for himself. Then a buddy of his, also a policeman, did the same. And shortly thereafter, Cheryl's brother, more than a little happy that he still had a sister, and needing a new car himself, bought yet another Saturn in Illinois.

But the topper came when a very nice young woman walked into the showroom to test drive a sedan. She said she just wanted to know a little more about what our cars were like. Not that she was going to buy one right away, or anything. She'd just never seen a Saturn up close until she'd rear-ended one out on the highway several weeks earlier.

A DIFFERENT KIND OF COMPANY. A DIFFERENT KIND OF CAR.
If you'd like to know more about Saturn, and our new sedans and coupe, please call us at 1-800-522-5000.

Reproduced with permission of Saturn Corporation.

1. Introduction
2. Description of ad's prominent features
3. Contrast of Saturn ad to ads of other automakers
4. Analysis/interpretation of Cheryl Silas, Saturn owner
5. Conclusion

In writing his next draft, Kip followed his outline, drawing upon those portions of his ad that best supported his interpretation. His essay went through one additional draft before he felt satisfied that he had made his point as effectively as he wished. Although we present only his final version here, you should be aware that his essay is the result of a number of revisions made over the course of three or four weeks.

A Different Kind of Advertisement . . .

Kip Turner

What is really distinct about the two-page advertisement for Saturn automobiles in *Newsweek* is that it appears to be not so much an advertisement to sell the car itself, but an attempt to convince you, the potential consumer, that the Saturn company's number one priority is dedication to the consumer and, therefore, the manufacture of a safe and quality automobile.

Thesis Statement

The left-hand page is a picture, while the right-hand one is occupied by gray and black text on a white background. The picture depicts a pleasant-looking woman, roughly 35 years old, named Cheryl Silas. She stands at the side of a windy road near dusk, her sparkling

Details: prominent features of ad's picture

clean red Saturn SC parked behind
her, slightly out of focus.

Superimposed in white letter-
ing over the bottom of the picture,
the headline reads, "Cheryl Silas
had a highway collision, was hit
twice from behind, and then sold
three cars for us." On the opposite
page are four short paragraphs of
very casual-sounding text, the
first explaining that, although her
Saturn coupe was "totalled," Cheryl
was unhurt in the accident. In the
second paragraph, we are told that
Cheryl "ordered another SC just
like her first." In the third paragraph we learn that Officer Boylan,
the policeman at the accident, was
so impressed with the fact that she
was unhurt that he bought a Saturn
automobile just like Cheryl's. Another policeman and Cheryl's
brother followed suit. And in the
final paragraph we are told that a
woman who had rear-ended a Saturn—
perhaps Cheryl's car—had come in
for a test drive. Below this, Saturn's motto appears in black text:
"A Different Kind of Company. A Different Kind of Car."

Upon examination of the advertisement, one first notices that
Saturn does not show a picture of
their new SC and list of all of the
fantastic options they offer, as do

**Details:
prominent
features of ad's
text**

Contrast: other carmakers emphasize product over customer

the Chrysler and Ford advertisements located pages away. Instead, they choose to focus on Cheryl and, by emphasizing her and not their product, they present an example of how they truly are different. They are showing us that their reputation and dedication speak for themselves, as if to suggest that their cars are good enough so that they don't need to show them off. More

analysis/ interpretation

important, they are presenting an example of how they appreciate their own customers so much that they would actually dedicate a two-page ad to profiling one of them.

Selection of Details: creates dominant impression of customer Cheryl Silas

It's a refreshing and effective approach, yet it wouldn't work with just anybody; Cheryl herself is the real key to this ad's effectiveness. Cheryl is not a model; she does not display a trendy haircut, or the newest fashions from *Cosmopolitan,* thereby alienating the common public. Dressed in a sun dress, a plain white T-shirt, and a denim button-up shirt with both sleeves rolled up, she comes across as very genuine and unobtrusive. Her straight blonde hair hangs at shoulder length and her hands are crossed in front of her. Looking the camera directly in "the eye," Cheryl immediately impresses you with the fact that she seems very straightforward and honest. She displays a reserved smile which communicates the message, "Don't underestimate me; I'm no dummy."

Quite simply, she is intriguing, especially in light of the surrounding material found in *Newsweek*. Flipping through pages of feature stories, pictures of politicians, and slick advertisements, I find Ms. Silas standing out as indisputably authentic. You read the ad and you say to yourself, "Yeah, I'd believe her. She's for real."

Saturn's advertisement is innovative in many ways. To the analyst, it symbolizes a company which is clever and resourceful. By using a new "profile" approach and an extremely persuasive spokesperson, Saturn successfully relates to the people of today. To the public, the ad is a sign of the times. Today's consumer is tired of supporting big business, only to be left behind to become another number after the sale is complete. Consumers want the respect they believe they deserve as patrons: they want to be "Cheryl Silas," not "service claim number 9,345B." By turning down an opportunity to brag about their accomplishments and, instead, paying tribute to their customers, Saturn has shown us that their main con-

analysis/ interpretation

Conclusion: returns to point made in thesis

cern is indeed the consumer. This
attitude, coupled with the confidence in their products they ex-
hibit by not profiling the car, illustrate to the potential consumer
the level of consideration and personal regard they can expect to receive as owners of Saturn automobiles.

I
THEMES
FOR
WRITERS

1

SENSE OF SELF

One of life's great journeys is the search for self. Each of us wants to know who we are, how we perceive ourselves, and how we are regarded by others. The search is fascinating, filled by turns with both the expected and the unanticipated. Sometimes we are surprised at what we find, sometimes bored. The journey can bring great happiness and fulfillment as we realize that we are all we hoped to be and more. But it can be risky, too. We may discover that we are somehow other than we thought we were.

As we attempt to get a sense of who we are, we naturally try to take a personality snapshot. We freeze an image of ourselves in time. "There I am. That's me," we say. It's a natural urge to want to frame ourselves; after all, it simplifies matters, but we may be doing ourselves a disservice, too. Just as there is great diversity among the peoples of this planet, there is great diversity in each of us. A person is an American, an American of mixed heritage, Chinese and white, a woman, a graduate of UCLA, a product of the 1960s generation, a teacher who lives in California, a wife, a mother, a tennis player, and a lover of hard rock. Add to this growing mosaic a deep religious commitment, a sense of civic responsibility, a concern for events beyond her circle of friends and even her country, and you begin to see why a snapshot just won't do. But consider, as well, that she is not today who she was yesterday and will be tomorrow. She is changing and growing. She is not married to the same man, has given up jogging for tennis, has shunned meat for a vegetable diet, has been afflicted by severe migraine headaches in recent years, and is now trying to get along better with her teenage children. Not a snapshot but a movie.

No sense of ourselves, it seems, can be arrived at without taking into account our immense complexity as humans and our mutability, our power to change and re-create ourselves. Each of

31

us is of many ever-changing parts, organically intertwined and, we hope, evolving for the better. Perhaps the best we can do is to recognize that we are not one self but many and realize that the journey to discover who we are can be exciting indeed.

WHO SHALL I BE?

Jennifer Crichton

Jennifer Crichton was born in 1957 in New York City. She attended Brown University and Barnard College, and spent a brief time in the Pacific Northwest. Crichton has written a novel, Delivery: A Nurse-Midwife's Story, *and has contributed to several publications including* Ms., Mademoiselle, Outside, *and* Seventeen. *She is currently working on a book about family therapy.*

Preparing to Read

Think of the person you are. How do you think you are perceived by your current friends and acquaintances? Now think of who you'd *like* to be. Could you change yourself into that person if you were able to make a fresh start? Crichton ponders a time when many people are able to make a fresh start if they want to—when they first go to college. They have no history with their new friends, and their life is, in a way, starting over. As you read the selection, think about how much you *can* change before you stop being yourself. How much "baggage" do we bring with us, even to a situation where we start with a clean slate?

The student is a soul in transit, coming from one place en 1
route to someplace else. Moving is the American way, after all. Our guiding principle is the fresh start, our foundation the big move, and nothing seduces like the promise of a clean slate.

"Do you realize how many people saw me throw up at Bob 2
Stonehill's party in tenth grade? A lot of people," says my friend Anne. "How many forgot about it? Maybe two or three. Do you know how much I wanted to go someplace where nobody knew I threw up all over Bob Stonehill's living room in tenth grade? Very much. This may not seem like much of a justification for

going away to college, but it was for me." Going away to college gives us a chance to rinse off part of our past, to shake off our burdensome reputations.

3   We've already survived the crises of being known, allowing how American high schools are as notoriously well-organized as totalitarian regimes, complete with secret police, punishment without trial, and banishment. High school society loves a label, cruelly infatuated with pinning down every species of student. Hilary is a klutz, Julie is a slut, and Michele a gossiping bitch who eats like a pig.

4   No wonder so many of us can't wait to be free of our old identities and climb inside a new skin in college. Even flattering reputations can be as confining as a pair of too-tight shoes. But identity is tricky stuff, constructed with mirrors. How you see yourself is a composite reflection of how you appear to friends, family, and lovers. In college, the fact that familiar mirrors aren't throwing back a familiar picture is both liberating and disorienting (maybe that's why so many colleges have freshman "orientation week").

5   "I guess you could call it an identity crisis," Andrea, a junior now, says of her freshman year. "It was the first time nobody knew who I was. I wasn't even anybody's daughter any more. I had always been the best and brightest—what was I going to do now, walk around the dorm with a sign around my neck saying 'Former High School Valedictorian'?"

6   For most of my college years, I was in hot pursuit of an identity crisis, especially after a Comparative Literature major informed me that the Chinese definition of "crisis" was "dangerous opportunity," with the emphasis on opportunity. On college applications, where there were blanks for your nickname, I carefully wrote "Rusty," although none of my friends (despite the fact that I have red hair) had ever, even for a whimsical moment, considered calling me that. I was the high-strung, sensitive, acne-blemished, antiauthoritarian, would-be writer. If I went through a day without some bizarre mood swing, people asked me what was wrong. I didn't even have the leeway to be the cheerful, smiling sort of girl I thought I might have it in me to be. My reputation seemed etched in stone, and I was pretty damn sick of it. As I pictured her, Rusty was the blithe spirit who would laugh everything off, shrug at perils as various as freshman mixers, bad grades, and cafeterias jammed with aloof strangers, and in general pass through a room with all the vitality and appeal of a cool gust of wind.

But when I arrived at college, Rusty had vaporized. She was   7
simply not in the station wagon that drove me up to campus.
Much of college had to do with filling in the blanks, but changing myself would not be so easy, so predictable, so clichéd.

My parents, acting as anxious overseers on the hot, humid   8
day I took my new self to college, seemed bound by a demonic
ESP to sabotage my scarcely budding new identity. After a summer planning how I would metamorphose into the great American ideal, the normal teenage girl, I heard my mother tell my
roommate, "I think you'll like Jenny—she's quite the oddball."
Luckily, my roommate was saturated with all kinds of information the first day of college had flung at her, and the last thing
she was paying attention to were the off-the-cuff remarks this
oddball's mother was making. My unmarked reputation kept its
sheen as it waited for me to cautiously build it up according to
plan. My parents left without any further blunders, except to
brush my bangs from my eyes ("You'll get a headache, Sweet-
heart") and foist on what had been a blissfully bare dormitory
room an excruciatingly ugly lamp from home. As soon as the
station wagon became a distant mote of dust on the highway, I
pulled my bangs back over my eyes in my New Wave fashion of
choice, tossed the ugly lamp in the nearest trash can, and did
what I came to college to do. Anonymous, alone, without even a
name, I would start over and become the kind of person I was
meant to be: like myself, but better, with all my failures, rejec-
tions, and sexual indiscretions relegated to a history I hoped
none of my new acquaintances would ever hear of.

Why was it, I wondered, when *any* change seemed possible   9
that year, had it been so impossible in high school? For one
thing, people know us well enough to see when we're attempting
a change, and change can look embarrassingly like a public admission of weakness. Our secret desires, and the fact that we're
not entirely pleased with ourselves, are on display. To change in
public under the scrutiny of the most hypercritical witnesses in
the world—other high school students—is to risk failure ("Look
how cool she's trying to be, the jerk!") or succeeding but betray-
ing friends in the process ("I don't understand her any more,"
they say, hurt and angry) or feeling so much like a fraud that
you're forced to back down. And while we live at home, parental
expectations, from the lovingly hopeful to the intolerably ambitious, apply the pressure of an invisible but very effective mold.

10   Jacki dressed in nothing but baggy Levi's and flannel shirts
for what seemed to be the endless duration of high school, even
though she came to a sort of truce with her developing woman's
body in eleventh grade and wasn't averse any longer to looking
pretty. Looking good in college was a fantasy she savored because
in high school, "I didn't want to make the attempt in public and
then fail," she explains now, looking pulled together and chic. "I
thought everyone would think I was trying to look good but I only
managed to look weird. And I didn't want a certain group of girls
who were very image-conscious to think they'd won some kind of
victory either, that I was changing to please them.

11   "So I waited for college, and wore nice, new clothes right off
the bat so nobody would know me any other way. I had set my
expectations too high, though—I sort of thought that I'd be transformed into a kind of femme fatale or something. When I wasn't
measuring up to what I'd imagined, I almost ditched the whole
thing until I realized that at least I wasn't sabotaging myself any
more. When I ran into a friend from high school, even though I
had gotten used to the nice way I looked, I was scared that she
could see right through my disguise. That's how I felt for a long
time: a slobby girl just pretending to be pulled together."

12   At first, any change can feel uncomfortably like a pretense,
an affectation. Dana had been a punked-out druggy in high
school, so worried about being considered a grind that she
didn't use a fraction of her considerable vocabulary when she
was around her anti-intellectual friends. She promised herself to
get serious academically in college, but the first night she spent
studying in the science library, she recalls, "I half-expected the
other kids to look twice at me, as if my fish-out-of-water feeling
was showing. Of course, it wasn't. But it was schizophrenic at
first, as if I were an impostor only playing at being smart. But
when you do something long enough that thing becomes *you*. It's
not playing any more. It's what you are."

13   Wanting to change yourself finds its source in two well-
springs: self-hatred and self-affirmation. Self-affirmation takes
what already exists in your personality (even if slightly stunted
or twisted) and encourages its growth. Where self-affirmation is
expansive, self-hatred is reductive, negating one's own personality while appropriating qualities external to it and applying
them like thick pancake makeup.

14   Joan's thing was to hang out with rich kids with what can

only be described as a vengeance. She dressed in Ralph Lauren, forayed to town for $75 haircuts, and complained about the tackiness of mutual friends. But after a late night of studying, Joan allowed her self-control to slip long enough to tell me of her upbringing. Her mother was a cocktail waitress and Joan had never even found out her father's name. She and her mother had trucked about from one Western trailer park to another, and Joan always went to school dogged by her wrong-side-of-the-tracks background. That Joan had come through her hard-scrabble life with such strong intellectual achievement seemed a lot more creditable—not to mention interesting—than the effort-less achievements of many of our more privileged classmates. Joan didn't think so, and, I suppose in fear I'd blow her cover (I never did), she cut me dead after her moment's indulgence in self-revelation. Joan was rootless and anxious, alienated not only from her background but, by extension, from herself, and paid a heavy psychic price. This wasn't change: this was lies. She scared me. But we learn a lot about friends from the kinds of masks they choose to wear.

After all, role-playing to some degree is the prerogative of   15
youth. A woman of romance, rigorous academic, trendy New Waver, intense politico, unsentimental jock, by turn—we have the chance to experiment as we decide the kind of person we want to become. And a stereotypical role, adopted temporarily, can offer a refuge from the swirl of confusing choices available to us, by confining us to the limits of a type. Returning to my old self after playing a role, I find I'm slightly different, a little bit more than what I was. To contradict one's self is to transcend it.

As occasional fugitives from our families, we all sometimes   16
do what Joan did. Sometimes you need a radical change in order to form an identity independent of your family, even if that change is a weird but transient reaction. My friend Lisa came from a family of feminists and academics. When she returned home from school for Thanksgiving, dressed as a "ditsy dame" straight out of a beach-blanket-bingo movie, she asked me, "How do you think I look? I've been planning this since tenth grade. Isn't it great?" Well, er, yes, it was great—not because she looked like a Barbie doll incarnate but because nobody would ever auto-matically connect her life with that of her parents again.

Another friend, Dan, went from a Southern military academy   17
to a Quaker college in the North to execute his scheme of becom-

ing a serious intellectual. The transformation went awry after a few months, partly because his own self was too likably irrepressible. It wouldn't lie down and play dead. "I kept running into myself like a serpent chasing its tail," as he puts it. But his openness to change resulted in a peculiar amalgamation of cultures whose charm lies in his realizing that, while he's of his background, he's not identical to it. Most of our personalities and bodies are just as stubbornly averse to being extinguished, even if the fantasy of a symbolic suicide and a renaissance from the ashes takes its obsessive toll on our thoughts now and again. But a blank slate isn't the same as a blank self, and the point of the blank slate that college provides is not to erase the past, but to sketch out a new history with a revisionist's perspective and an optimist's acts.

18   And what of my changes? Well, when I was friendly and happy in college, nobody gaped as though I had sprouted a tail. I learned to laugh things off as Rusty might have done, and there was one particular counterman at the corner luncheonette who called me Red, which was the closest I came to being known as Rusty.

19   What became of Rusty? Senior year, I stared at an announcement stating the dates that banks would be recruiting on campus, and Rusty materialized for the first time since freshman year. Rusty was a Yuppie now, and I pictured her dressed in a navy-blue suit, looking uneasily like Mary Cunningham, setting her sights on Citibank. I was still the high-strung, oversensitive, would-be writer (I'm happy to report my skin did clear up), but a little better, who left the corporate world to Rusty. For myself, I have the slate of the rest of my life to write on.

Vocabulary

To get the most out of reading this essay, you should have a working understanding of the words listed on the next page. Following each word is a parenthetical reference, indicating the paragraph in which the word is used, as well as a definition for the word. Go back and look at the sentence in which the word appears, and see how the definition applies. To help you make this word a part of your active vocabulary, write a sentence of your own using the word in the space provided.

totalitarian (3): exercising absolute power

_____

_____

whimsical (6): lighthearted

_____

_____

aloof (6): apart, not caring

_____

_____

metamorphose (8): change shape

_____

_____

femme fatale (11): dangerously attractive woman

_____

_____

schizophrenic (12): having a mental disorder with more than one personality or identity

_____

_____

amalgamation (17): combination

_____

_____

Understanding the Essay

1. According to Crichton, why is being known such a burden, especially in high school? In what way is not being known disorienting?

2. Crichton says that "For most of my college years, I was in hot pursuit of an identity crisis." What does she mean? What does she do to pursue her "crisis"?

3. How can change be difficult, even during the first few days of college?

4. Why does Joan hang out with the rich kids? How did she scare Crichton?

5. What does Crichton mean when she says "a blank slate isn't the same as a blank self"?

6. What became of Rusty?

Exploring the Theme: Discussion and Writing

1. If you could create a new you, your own version of Crichton's Rusty, how would you change? Why?

2. The saying "No matter where you go, there you are" implies that change is difficult because we can't ever start over with what Crichton calls a blank self. How much of our self-identity and self-knowledge do you think is established by the end of high school? How much do you think a person can change in college?

MY GENERATION?

Jason Cooley

Jason Cooley, who graduated at nineteen from Burlington (Vermont) High School in 1992, wrote the following commentary on his generation for "The Edge," the teen page of The Burlington Free Press.

Preparing to Read

People often talk about "generations." There is the World War II generation, the baby boomer generation, and so on. Cooley offers a rather concise—dark and angry—definition of his generation. For Cooley, modern culture is anything but cultured—the primary influences on young people are shallow and accessible media images. As you read the selection, think about what a generation is. What defines a generation? What influences it as a group?

M y generation was born in the early-to-mid-'70s, which   1
means we have images of "Happy Days" and KISS
lodged somewhere in our subconscious. Our conscious
upbringing belongs to the '80s, a blur of Republican family values and Bill Cosby.

My generation has a deep contempt for the word "genera-   2
tion," and all other generations. We are a cynical bunch, possibly jealous because instead of being able to look back to the days of John F. Kennedy or the Beatles, we can only remember Michael Jackson, E.T. and the Smurfs. Cable television was our god and MTV our bible, or at least our etiquette book. We are a product of nuclear paranoia and experimental trends that failed embarrassingly.

My generation is violent. It began very much with the shoot-   3
ing of Ronald Reagan. I remember my mother explaining to me that the man who shot him was "crazy, like the man who shot

John Lennon." I think my generation can be explained by the fact that I was (and still am) more affected by the loss of the Walrus than the near-loss of our president. My generation was born with cable television, which is synonymous with violence. A decapitation has about as much effect on me as a feather; it makes me giggle, not vomit.

4   My generation is dysfunctional. We are bored, angry, tired and self-serving. Our motivation is greed. We fake concern for our own needs. The only people we really listen to are celebrities. We have just spent nearly a decade watching Madonna take her clothes off, year by year. Now that she's finally done, we can focus on something else, maybe college.

5   My generation is full of murderous psychos. When I was 6, my Luke Skywalker action figure was stolen from me. I was so angry, yet so afraid, because I never wanted to kill someone before. I very well may have carried this anger to now, where I could very believably hunt the thief down and destroy him. I'm not going to, but I *could*. So could a lot of other people my age. We all have this feeling that we've been wronged somehow, some way, by someone, even if we don't know who or what it is.

6   We are trend mongers. We devour catchphrases and clothing styles like M&Ms. "Not" was lame years ago. The new trend catching on is to cite Saturday morning cartoons as disturbing childhood memories. Example: "He-Man really freaked me out, man. Like, he was two different people, right? Wow, what a schizophrenic! He scared the hell out of me, man. Every time he said 'By the power of Grayskull,' I would cry my eyes out."

7   It sometimes seems like the goal of my generation is to capture the essence of who we are and what we mean and exploit the hell out of it in a book, or a movie, or even a single word. We all know that whoever does this accurately will be the first billionaire our generation will spawn. We read books like "Generation X" and see movies like "Slacker," hoping to find something we can identify with. And if not, who cares? It's almost better not to identify with anything, to be completely alone.

8   Not everyone my age is like this; I'm just telling you what I've seen. We were given images of He-Man and Mr. T and we were told to deal. We were confused. I don't think anyone my age can forget the trauma felt when Michael Jackson's hair caught on fire in 1984. We fear things like work, turning 30, having

children and being in prison. We are fast. No style lasts too long. We are "slackers."

I'm 19 years old. I'm not really a teen-ager, yet I'm not at all   9 an adult. I don't want to work, think or do anything I don't have to. I have no direction, no promise and no future. What happens to me will happen. My life is very much like the words to "It's The End Of The World As We Know It (And I Feel Fine)": just a haze of images, some coherent, most not. I lack concentration. I rarely can do one thing for too long. Hell, I could hardly sustain the interest required to finish *this.*

Vocabulary

To get the most out of reading this essay, you should have a working understanding of the words listed below. Following each word is a parenthetical reference, indicating the paragraph in which the word is used, as well as a definition for the word. Go back and look at the sentence in which the word appears, and see how the definition applies. To help you make this word a part of your active vocabulary, write a sentence of your own using the word in the space provided.

subconscious (1):   not in the conscious mind

_____

_____

cynical (2):   jaded, distrustful

_____

_____

etiquette (2):   proper way of interacting, manners

_____

_____

paranoia (2):   excessive fear

_____

_____

synonymous (3):   has the same meaning as

_____

_____

dysfunctional (4):   unable to function correctly, damaged

_____

_____

trauma (8):   injury, difficult experience

_____

_____

Understanding the Essay

1. According to the selection, what are five characteristics of Cooley's generation?
2. What influence has cable TV had on Cooley?
3. Why does Cooley say that his generation is "full of murderous psychos"?
4. What is the new trend for people of Cooley's age? What would you identify as the latest trend, according to your own experience?
5. What is a "slacker"?
6. What does Cooley think his life resembles? What future does he see for himself?

Exploring the Theme: Discussion and Writing

1. What five characteristics would you use to define your own generation? Explain your choices. What common experiences have done the most to shape you and your peers into an identifiable "generation"?

2. Do you think Cooley's pessimism is warranted? Has modern society with its MTV and He-Man turned out a dysfunctional generation? Or do you think that, with a few more years and more experience, Cooley and his peers will overcome their cynicism and fatalism and move on to a productive adulthood?

GROWING UP ASIAN
IN AMERICA

Kesaya Noda

Kesaya Noda teaches at Lesley College in Cambridge, Massachusetts. She was born in California but moved to New Hampshire at a young age. She visited Japan for the first time after she graduated from high school and has spent several years working and traveling in Japan since then.

Preparing to Read

One of the most difficult questions to ask yourself is "Who am I?" Most of us spend a lifetime asking that question in hopes we can better define ourselves from within. At the same time, other people are asking "Who are you?" and seeking to define us from the outside. In the following essay, Noda attempts the complex task of defining herself from both the inside and the outside in terms of her race, nationality, and gender.

1   Sometimes when I was growing up, my identity seemed to hurtle toward me and paste itself right to my face. I felt that way, encountering the stereotypes of my race perpetuated by non-Japanese people (primarily white) who may or may not have had contact with other Japanese in America. "You don't like cheese, do you?" someone would ask. "I know your people don't like cheese." Sometimes questions came making allusions to history. That was another aspect of the identity. Events that had happened quite apart from the me who stood silent in that moment connected my face with an incomprehensible past. "Your parents were in California? Were they in those camps during the war?" And sometimes there were phrases or nicknames: "Lotus Blossom." I was sometimes addressed or referred to as

racially Japanese, sometimes as Japanese American, and sometimes as an Asian woman. Confusions and distortions abounded.

How is one to know and define oneself? From the inside— within a context that is self defined, from a grounding in community and a connection with culture and history that are comfortably accepted? Or from the outside—in terms of messages received from the media and people who are often ignorant? Even as an adult I can still see two sides of my face and past. I can see from the inside out, in freedom. And I can see from the outside in, driven by the old voices of childhood and lost in anger and fear.   2

I Am Racially Japanese

A voice from my childhood says: "You are other. You are less than. You are unalterably alien." This voice has its own history. We have indeed been seen as other and alien since the early years of our arrival in the United States. The very first immigrants were welcomed and sought as laborers to replace the dwindling numbers of Chinese, whose influx had been cut off by the Chinese Exclusion Act of 1882. The Japanese fell natural heir to the same anti-Asian prejudice that had arisen against the Chinese. As soon as they began striking for better wages, they were no longer welcomed.   3

I can see myself today as a person historically defined by law and custom as being forever alien. Being neither "free white," nor "African," our people in California were deemed "aliens, ineligible for citizenship," no matter how long they intended to stay here. Aliens ineligible for citizenship were prohibited from owning, buying, or leasing land. They did not and could not belong here. The voice in me remembers that I am always a *Japanese* American in the eyes of many. A third-generation German American is an American. A third-generation Japanese American is a Japanese American. Being Japanese means being a danger to the country during the war and knowing how to use chopsticks. I wear this history on my face.   4

I move to the other side. I see a different light and claim a different context. My race is a line that stretches across ocean and time to link me to the shrine where my grandmother was raised. Two high, white banners lift in the wind at the top of the stone steps leading to the shrine. It is time for the summer festival. Black characters are written against the sky as boldly as the   5 clouds, as lightly as kites, as sharply as the big black crows I used to see above the fields in New Hampshire. At festival time there is liquor and food, ritual, discipline, and abandonment. There is music and drunkenness and invocation. There is hope. Another season has come. Another season has gone.

6   I am racially Japanese. I have a certain claim to this crazy place where the prayers intoned by a neighboring Shinto priest (standing in for my grandmother's nephew who is sick) are drowned out by the rehearsals for the pop singing contest in which most of the villagers will compete later that night. The village elders, the priest, and I stand respectfully upon the immaculate, shining wooden floor of the outer shrine, bowing our heads before the hidden powers. During the patchy intervals when I can hear him, I notice the priest has a stutter. His voice flutters up to my ears only occasionally because two men and a woman are singing gustily into a microphone in the compound, testing the sound system. A prerecorded tape of guitars, samisens, and drums accompanies them. Rock music and Shinto prayers. That night, to loud applause and cheers, a young man is given the award for the most *netsuretsu*—passionate, burning— rendition of a song. We roar our approval of the reward. Never mind that his voice had wandered and slid, now slightly above, now slightly below the given line of the melody. Netsuretsu. Netsuretsu.

7   In the morning, my grandmother's sister kneels at the foot of the stone stairs to offer her morning prayers. She is too crippled to climb the stairs, so each morning she kneels here upon the path. She shuts her eyes for a few seconds, her motions as matter of fact as when she washes rice. I linger longer than she does, so reluctant to leave, savoring the connection I feel with my grandmother in America, the past, and the power that lives and shines in the morning sun.

8   Our family has served this shrine for generations. The family's need to protect this claim to identity and place outweighs any individual claim to any individual hope. I am Japanese.

I Am a Japanese American

9   "Weak." I hear the voice from my childhood years. "Passive," I hear. Our parents and grandparents were the ones who were put into those camps. They went without resistance; they of-

fered cooperation as proof of loyalty to America. "Victim," I hear. And, "Silent."

Our parents are painted as hard workers who were socially uncomfortable and had difficulty expressing even the smallest opinion. Clean, quiet, motivated, and determined to match the American way; that is us, and that is the story of our time here.

"Why did you go into those camps," I raged at my parents, frightened by my own inner silence and timidity. "Why didn't you do anything to resist? Why didn't you name it the injustice it was?" Couldn't our parents even think? Couldn't they? Why were we so passive?

I shift my vision and my stance. I am in California. My uncle is in the midst of the sweet potato harvest. He is pressed, trying to get the harvesting crews onto the field as quickly as possible, worried about the flow of equipment and people. His big pickup is pulled off to the side, motor running, door ajar. I see two tractors in the yard in front of an old shed; the flat bed harvesting platform on which the workers will stand has already been brought over from the other field. It's early morning. The workers stand loosely grouped and at ease, but my uncle looks as harried and tense as a police officer trying to unsnarl a New York City traffic jam. Driving toward the shed, I pull my car off the road to make way for an approaching tractor. The front wheels of the car sink luxuriously into the soft, white sand by the roadside and the car slides to a dreamy halt, tail still on the road. I try to move forward. I try to move back. The front bites contentedly into the sand, the back lifts at a jaunty angle. My uncle sees me and storms down the road, running. He is shouting before he is even near me.

"What's the matter with you," he screams. "What the hell are you doing?" In his frenzy, he grabs his hat off his head and slashes it through the air across his knee. He is beside himself. "Don't you know how to drive in sand? What's the matter with you? You've blocked the whole roadway. How am I supposed to get my tractors out of here? Can't you use your head? You've cut off the whole roadway, and we've got to get out of here."

I stand on the road before him helplessly thinking, "No, I don't know how to drive in sand. I've never driven in sand."

"I'm sorry, uncle," I say, burying a smile beneath a look of sincere apology. I notice my deep amusement and my affection for him with great curiosity. I am usually devastated by anger. Not this time.

16   During the several years that follow I learn about the people and the place, and much more about what has happened in this California village where my parents grew up. The issei, our grandparents, made this settlement in the desert. Their first crops were eaten by rabbits and ravaged by insects. The land was so barren that men walking from house to house sometimes got lost. Women came here too. They bore children in 114 degree heat, then carried the babies with them into the fields to nurse when they reached the end of each row of grapes or other truck farm crops.

17   I had had no idea what it meant to buy this kind of land and make it grow green. Or how, when the war came, there was no space at all for the subtlety of being who we were—Japanese Americans. Either/or was the way. I hadn't understood that people were literally afraid for their lives then, that their money had been frozen in banks; that there was a five-mile travel limit; that when the early evening curfew came and they were inside their houses, some of them watched helplessly as people they knew went into their barns to steal their belongings. The police were patrolling the road, interested only in violators of curfew. There was no help for them in the face of thievery. I had not been able to imagine before what it must have felt like to be an American—to know absolutely that one is an American—and yet to have almost everyone else deny it. Not only deny it, but challenge that identity with machine guns and troops of white American soldiers. In those circumstances it was difficult to say, "I'm a Japanese American." "American" had to do.

18   But now I can say that I am a Japanese American. It means I have a place here in this country, too. I have a place here on the East Coast, where our neighbor is so much a part of our family that my mother never passes her house at night without glancing at the lights to see if she is home and safe; where my parents have hauled hundreds of pounds of rocks from fields and arduously planted Christmas trees and blueberries, lilacs, asparagus, and crab apples; where my father still dreams of angling a stream to a new bed so that he can dig a pond in the field and fill it with water and fish. "The neighbors already came for their Christmas tree?" he asks in December. "Did they like it? Did they like it?"

19   I have a place on the West Coast where my relatives still farm, where I heard the stories of feuds and backbiting, and

where I saw that people survived and flourished because fundamentally they trusted and relied upon one another. A death in the family is not just a death in a family; it is a death in the community. I saw people help each other with money, materials, labor, attention, and time. I saw men gather once a year, without fail, to clean the grounds of a ninety-year-old woman who had helped the community before, during, and after the war. I saw her remembering them with birthday cards sent to each of their children.

I come from a people with a long memory and a distinctive 20 grace. We live our thanks. And we are Americans. Japanese Americans.

I Am a Japanese American Woman

Woman. The last piece of my identity. It has been easier by far 21 for me to know myself in Japan and to see my place in America than it has been to accept my line of connection with my own mother. She was my dark self, a figure in whom I thought I saw all that I feared most in myself. Growing into womanhood and looking for some model of strength, I turned away from her. Of course, I could not find what I sought. I was looking for a black feminist or a white feminist. My mother is neither white nor black.

My mother is a woman who speaks with her life as much as 22 with her tongue. I think of her with her own mother. Grandmother had Parkinson's disease and it had frozen her gait and set her fingers, tongue, and feet jerking and trembling in a terrible dance. My aunts and uncles wanted her to be able to live in her own home. They fed her, bathed her, dressed her, awoke at midnight to take her for one last trip to the bathroom. My aunts (her daughters-in-law) did most of the care, but my mother went from New Hampshire to California each summer to spend a month living with grandmother, because she wanted to and because she wanted to give my aunts at least a small rest. During those hot summer days, mother lay on the couch watching the television or reading, cooking foods that grandmother liked, and speaking little. Grandmother thrived under her care.

The time finally came when it was too dangerous for grand- 23 mother to live alone. My relatives kept finding her on the floor beside her bed when they went to wake her in the mornings. My mother flew to California to help clean the house and make arrangements for grandmother to enter a local nursing home. On her last day at home, while grandmother was sitting in her big, overstuffed armchair, hair combed and wearing a green summer dress, my mother went to her and knelt at her feet. "Here, Mamma," she said. "I've polished your shoes." She lifted grandmother's legs and helped her into the shiny black shoes. My grandmother looked down and smiled slightly. She left her house walking, supported by her children, carrying her pocket book, and wearing her polished black shoes. "Look, Mamma," my mom had said, kneeling. "I've polished your shoes."

24   Just the other day, my mother came to Boston to visit. She had recently lost a lot of weight and was pleased with her new shape and her feeling of good health. "Look at me, Kes," she exclaimed, turning toward me, front and back, as naked as the day she was born. I saw her small breasts and the wide, brown scar, belly button to pubic hair, that marked her because my brother and I were both born by Caesarean section. Her hips were small. I was not a large baby, but there was so little room for me in her that when she was carrying me she could not even begin to bend over toward the floor. She hated it, she said.

25   "Don't I look good? Don't you think I look good?"

26   I looked at my mother, smiling and as happy as she, thinking of all the times I have seen her naked. I have seen both my parents naked throughout my life, as they have seen me. From childhood through adulthood we've had our naked moments, sharing baths, idle conversations picked up as we moved between showers and closets, hurried moments at the beginning of days, quiet moments at the end of days.

27   I know this to be Japanese, this ease with the physical, and it makes me think of an old, Japanese folk song. A young nursemaid, a fifteen-year-old girl, is singing a lullaby to a baby who is strapped to her back. The nursemaid has been sent as a servant to a place far from her own home. "We're the beggars," she says, "and they are the nice people. Nice people wear fine sashes. Nice clothes."

28   If I should drop dead,
        bury me by the roadside!
        I'll give a flower
        to everyone who passes.

What kind of flower?
The cam-cam-camellia (tsun-tsun-tsubaki)
watered by Heaven:
alms water.

The nursemaid is the intersection of heaven and earth, the   29
intersection of the human, the natural world, the body, and the
soul. In this song, with clear eyes, she looks steadily at life,
which is sometimes so very terrible and sad. I think of her while
looking at my mother, who is standing on the red and purple
carpet before me, laughing, without any clothes.

> I am my mother's daughter. And I am myself.   30
> I am a Japanese American woman.

Epilogue

I recently heard a man from West Africa share some memories of   31
his childhood. He was raised Muslim, but when he was a young
man, he found himself deeply drawn to Christianity. He struggled against this inner impulse for years, trying to avoid the
church yet feeling pushed to return to it again and again. "I
would have done *anything* to avoid the change," he said. At last,
he became Christian. Afterwards he was afraid to go home, fearing that he would not be accepted. The fear was groundless, he
discovered, when at last he returned—he had separated himself,
but his family and friends (all Muslim) had not separated themselves from him.

The man, who is now a professor of religion, said that in the   32
Africa he knew as a child and a young man, pluralism was em-
braced rather than feared. There was "a kind of tolerance that
did not deny your particularity," he said. He alluded to zestful,
spontaneous debates that would sometimes loudly erupt between Muslims and Christians in the village's public spaces. His
memories of an atheist who harangued the villagers when he
came to visit them once a week moved me deeply. Perhaps the
man was an agricultural advisor or inspector. He harassed the
women. He would say:

> "Don't go to the fields! Don't even bother to go to the fields. Let   33
> God take care of you. He'll send you the food. If you believe in
> God, why do you need to work? You don't need to work! Let
> God put the seeds in the ground. Stay home."

34   The professor said, "The women laughed, you know? They just laughed. Their attitude was, 'Here is a child of God. When will he come home?' "

35   The storyteller, the professor of religion, smiled the most fantastic, tender smile as he told this story. "In my country, there is a deep affirmation of the oneness of God," he said. "The atheist and the women were having quite different experiences in their encounter, though the atheist did not know this. He saw himself as quite separate from the women. But the women did not see themselves as being separate from him. 'Here is a child of God,' they said. 'When will he come home?' "

Vocabulary

To get the most out of reading this essay, you should have a working understanding of the words listed below. Following each word is a parenthetical reference, indicating the paragraph in which the word is used, as well as a definition for the word. Go back and look at the sentence in which the word appears, and see how the definition applies. To help you make this word a part of your active vocabulary, write a sentence of your own using the word in the space provided.

perpetuated (1):   continued, kept alive

_____

_____

allusions (1):   references to

_____

_____

influx (3):   coming in

_____

_____

Shinto (6):   a Japanese religion

_____

_____

arduously (18):   accomplishing with hard work

---

pluralism (32):   acceptance of two or more points of view

---

harangued (32):   yelled at

Understanding the Essay

1. Why does Noda say that her identity "seemed to hurtle toward [her] and paste itself right to [her] face"?
2. What is Noda's family's claim to identity and place in Japan? Why does the need to protect it outweigh individual desires and hopes?
3. What does Noda do to better understand her parents' lack of resistance to their incarceration in detention camps during World War II? What does she learn?
4. Why do you think Noda says her mother is her dark self, "a figure in whom I thought I saw all that I feared most in myself"?
5. What is the meaning of the folk song?
6. How does the epilogue relate to the rest of the essay? What point is Noda making with the story of the atheist and the village women?

Exploring the Theme: Discussion and Writing

1. How would you define yourself? What elements of your heritage, upbringing, and experience play the largest roles in forming your identity?

2. The United States contains members of nearly every ethnic group on earth, but some groups—as Noda points out in her essay—are made to feel less American than others. When and from where did your family arrive in the United States? How do you feel you fit into American society? How much of a role has being an American played in establishing your identity?

How It Feels to Be Colored Me

Zora Neale Hurston

Born and raised in the rural South, Zora Neale Hurston grew up to become one of the stars of the celebration of African-American culture known as the Harlem Renaissance. Her work as an anthropologist, folklorist, and novelist centered on maintaining and sharing her cultural heritage. To her credit she has a collection of folktales, an autobiography, numerous short stories and magazine articles, and five novels, most notable among them her masterwork, Their Eyes Were Watching God.

Preparing to Read

Imagine growing up in a world where you are *different*. What would you feel not being like everyone else? What would it take to maintain a positive self-image, not to feel like an outsider? In the following essay, taken from *I Love Myself When I Am Laughing*, Hurston expresses an enthusiastic pride in having grown up "colored" in a white world. Hurston confesses that discrimination "does not make me angry. It merely astonishes me. How *can* any deny themselves the pleasure of my company? It's beyond me." And after reading the following selection, we're confident that you would like to meet this wonderful woman if she were still living.

I am colored but I offer nothing in the way of extenuating   1
circumstances except the fact that I am the only Negro in
the United States whose grandfather on the mother's side
was *not* an Indian chief.

I remember the very day that I became colored. Up to my   2
thirteenth year I lived in the little Negro town of Eatonville,
Florida. It is exclusively a colored town. The only white people I

knew passed through the town going to or coming from Orlando. The native whites rode dusty horses, the Northern tourists chugged down the sandy village road in automobiles. The town knew the Southerners and never stopped cane chewing when they passed. But the Northerners were something else again. They were peered at cautiously from behind curtains by the timid. The more venturesome would come out on the porch to watch them go past and got just as much pleasure out of the tourists as the tourists got out of the village.

3   The front porch might seem a daring place for the rest of the town, but it was a gallery seat for me. My favorite place was atop the gate-post. Proscenium box for a born first-nighter. Not only did I enjoy the show, but I didn't mind the actors knowing that I liked it. I usually spoke to them in passing. I'd wave at them and when they returned my salute, I would say something like this: "Howdy-do-well-I-thank-you-where-you-goin'?" Usually automobile or the horse paused at this, and after a queer exchange of compliments, I would probably "go a piece of the way" with them, as we say in farthest Florida. If one of my family happened to come to the front in time to see me, of course negotiations would be rudely broken off. But even so, it is clear that I was the first "welcome-to-our-state" Floridian, and I hope the Miami Chamber of Commerce will please take notice.

4   During this period, white people differed from colored to me only in that they rode through town and never lived there. They liked to hear me "speak pieces" and sing and wanted to see me dance the parse-me-la, and gave me generously of their small silver for doing these things, which seemed strange to me for I wanted to do them so much that I needed bribing to stop. Only they didn't know it. The colored people gave no dimes. They deplored any joyful tendencies in me, but I was their Zora nevertheless. I belonged to them, to the nearby hotels, to the county— everybody's Zora.

5   But changes came in the family when I was thirteen, and I was sent to school in Jacksonville. I left Eatonville, the town of the oleanders, as Zora. When I disembarked from the river-boat at Jacksonville, she was no more. It seemed that I had suffered a sea change. I was not Zora of Orange County any more, I was now a little colored girl. I found it out in certain ways. In my heart as well as in the mirror, I became a fast brown—warranted not to rub nor run.

But I am not tragically colored. There is no great sorrow 6
dammed up in my soul, nor lurking behind my eyes. I do not
mind at all. I do not belong to the sobbing school of Negrohood
who hold that nature somehow has given them a lowdown dirty
deal and whose feelings are all hurt about it. Even in the helter-
skelter skirmish that is my life, I have seen that the world is to
the strong regardless of a little pigmentation more or less. No, I
do not weep at the world—I am too busy sharpening my oyster
knife.

Someone is always at my elbow reminding me that I am the 7
granddaughter of slaves. It fails to register depression with me.
Slavery is sixty years in the past. The operation was successful
and the patient is doing well, thank you. The terrible struggle
that made me an American out of a potential slave said "On the
line!" The Reconstruction said "Get set!"; and the generation
before said "Go!" I am off to a flying start and I must not halt in
the stretch to look behind and weep. Slavery is the price I paid
for civilization, and the choice was not with me. It is a bully
adventure and worth all that I have paid through my ancestors
for it. No one on earth ever had a greater chance for glory. The
world to be won and nothing to be lost. It is thrilling to think—
to know that for any act of mine, I shall get twice as much praise
or twice as much blame. It is quite exciting to hold the center of
the national stage, with the spectators not knowing whether to
laugh or to weep.

The position of my white neighbor is much more difficult. 8
No brown specter pulls up a chair beside me when I sit down to
eat. No dark ghost thrusts its leg against mine in bed. The game
of keeping what one has is never so exciting as the game of
getting.

I do not always feel colored. Even now I often achieve the 9
unconscious Zora of Eatonville before the Hegira. I feel most
colored when I am thrown against a sharp white background.

For instance at Barnard. "Beside the waters of the Hudson" I 10
feel my race. Among the thousand white persons, I am a dark
rock surged upon, and overswept, but through it all, I remain
myself. When covered by the waters, I am; and the ebb but
reveals me again.

Sometimes it is the other way around. A white person is set 11
down in our midst, but the contrast is just as sharp for me. For

instance, when I sit in the drafty basement that is The New World Cabaret with a white person, my color comes. We enter chatting about any little nothing that we have in common and are seated by the jazz waiters. In the abrupt way that jazz orchestras have, this one plunges into a number. It loses no time in circumlocutions, but gets right down to business. It constricts the thorax and splits the heart with its tempo and narcotic harmonies. This orchestra grows rambunctious, rears on its hind legs and attacks the tonal veil with primitive fury, rending it, clawing it until it breaks through to the jungle beyond. I follow those heathen—follow them exultingly. I dance wildly inside myself; I yell within, I whoop; I shake my assegai above my head, I hurl it true to the mark *yeeeeooww!* I am in the jungle and living in the jungle way. My face is painted red and yellow and my body is painted blue. My pulse is throbbing like a war drum, I want to slaughter something—give pain, give death to what, I do not know. But the piece ends. The men of the orchestra wipe their lips and rest their fingers. I creep back slowly to the veneer we call civilization with the last tone and find the white friend sitting motionless in his seat, smoking calmly.

12   "Good music they have here," he remarks, drumming the table with his fingertips.

13   Music. The great blobs of purple and red emotion have not touched him. He has only heard what I felt. He is far away and I see him but dimly across the ocean and the continent that have fallen between us. He is so pale with his whiteness then and I am *so* colored.

14   At certain times I have no race, I am *me*. When I set my hat at a certain angle and saunter down Seventh Avenue, Harlem City, feeling as snooty as the lions in front of the Forty-Second Street Library, for instance. So far as my feelings are concerned, Peggy Hopkins Joyce on the Boule Mich with her gorgeous raiment, stately carriage, knees knocking together in a most aristocratic manner, has nothing on me. The cosmic Zora emerges. I belong to no race nor time. I am the eternal feminine with its string of beads.

15   I have no separate feeling about being an American citizen and colored. I am merely a fragment of the Great Soul that surges within the boundaries. My country, right or wrong.

Sometimes, I feel discriminated against, but it does not   16
make me angry. It merely astonishes me. How *can* any deny
themselves the pleasure of my company? It's beyond me.

But in the main, I feel like a brown bag of miscellany   17
propped against a wall. Against a wall in company with other
bags, white, red and yellow. Pour out the contents, and there is
discovered a jumble of small things priceless and worthless. A
first-water diamond, an empty spool, bits of broken glass,
lengths of string, a key to a door long since crumbled away, a
rusty knife-blade, old shoes saved for a road that never was and
never will be, a nail bent under the weight of things too heavy
for any nail, a dried flower or two still a little fragrant. In your
hand is the brown bag. On the ground before you is the jumble it
held—so much like the jumble in the bags, could they be emptied, that all might be dumped in a single heap and the bags
refilled without altering the content of any greatly. A bit of colored glass more or less would not matter. Perhaps that is how
the Great Stuffer of Bags filled them in the first place—who
knows?

Vocabulary

To get the most out of reading this essay, you should have a
working understanding of the words listed below. Following
each word is a parenthetical reference, indicating the paragraph
in which the word is used, as well as a definition for the word.
Go back and look at the sentence in which the word appears, and
see how the definition applies. To help you make this word a
part of your active vocabulary, write a sentence of your own
using the word in the space provided.

extenuating (1):   lessening the magnitude or seriousness

_____

_____

venturesome (2):   bold, disposed to taking risks

_____

_____

deplored (4):   expressed strong disapproval, censure

_____

_____

lurking (6):   existing unobserved or unsuspected

_____

_____

specter (8):   a phantom, apparition

_____

_____

plunges (11):   throws oneself wholeheartedly into an activity

_____

_____

rambunctious (11):   boisterous, disorderly

_____

_____

raiment (14):   clothing, garments

_____

_____

fragrant (17):   having a pleasant odor

_____

_____

Understanding the Essay

1. What does Hurston mean when she says she remembers the day she "became colored"?
2. As a child, how aware of racial differences was Hurston? How do you know this?

3. What does Hurston mean when she says, "I do not weep at the world—I am too busy sharpening my oyster knife"?
4. In paragraph 8, Hurston mentions a "brown specter" and a "dark ghost." To what is she referring?
5. What cultural stereotype does Hurston embrace in paragraph 11? Does her contrasting of blacks and whites strike you as fair? Explain.
6. Hurston concludes her essay with the analogy of the colored bags. Explain how the analogy works. Do you find it effective?
7. Many African-American and other minority writers convey attitudes ranging from rage, to despair, to resignation at the way whites have treated them. Hurston's attitude is obviously different. How would you describe it? What does this tell you about the kind of person she is?

Exploring the Theme: Discussion and Writing

1. Although Hurston herself was able to rise above the oppression that African-Americans endured as slaves, what can the millions of African-Americans who may still feel they are living in the shadow of their slave beginnings do for themselves? What help might they need to achieve a positive self-image and a sense of racial equality?
2. In paragraph 8 Hurston states, "The game of keeping what one has is never so exciting as the game of getting." In the context of her life in the years following the abolition of slavery, what does this statement mean? Does your own experience tend to confirm or argue against Hurston's observation on human nature? Explain.

WRITING SUGGESTIONS
FOR "SENSE OF SELF"

1.   A recent Louis Harris poll revealed the not too startling fact that Americans are "close to being obsessed with their physical appearance." How do you like your own physical appearance? Ask your friends whether they have self-doubts about the way they look. Write an essay in which you discuss your feelings about the way you imagine you appear to others. Are you "obsessed" with your appearance? What about yourself would you like to keep? What would you like to change? In preparation for writing, you may want to review Hurston's "How It Feels to Be Colored Me."

2.   We begin to learn who we are as children, and sometimes events in our early years have a powerful influence in shaping or redirecting our sense of self. Our friends, relatives, parents, and teachers can say things, give subtle and not so subtle assessments, and can shape or reshape us in ways that, fairly or unfairly, lead to sobering conclusions about ourselves. Of course, each of these influences can also have the opposite effect on us. These same people can encourage, elevate, inspire, and liberate us. Write an essay on a person or experience from your past that was very influential in forming your character.

3.   We all seek to define ourselves, to be all that we can be, to echo the army's recruiting advertisement. Society, however, may define us more definitively than we define ourselves. Discuss this problem in an essay and suggest how one might not only confront it but overcome it.

4.   Kesaya Noda defines herself in part by the cultural group of Asian-Americans she belongs to. If you also belong to a cultural group that has had a big role in shaping your personality and character, write an essay about that influence. First of all, explain how much you know about your ancestry. Do you prize or resent its influence? Is it a mixed blessing? How are you a product of that culture? a contradiction to it?

5.   Traveling can change your thinking, your viewpoint, your tolerance for differences, and your character. If you have traveled extensively, think about how your experiences abroad have changed your sense of self. Write an essay in which you get close to the details—the actual causes and effects—of those changes.

2

FAMILY TIES

The simple family unit of a man, a woman, and their children is found in almost all societies. Its purpose in the past has been to provide mutual support, to nurture, and to transmit personal, cultural, religious, political, economic, intellectual, and ethical values. Most important, however, the family has been the single most significant social unit for fostering and providing love. Within the family we learn, or should learn, unconditional love, caring and affection that needs neither justification nor explanation.

A touching example of this kind of love is found in the essay "Daddy Tucked the Blanket" by Randall Williams. After a "violent argument" over a broken washing machine, when everyone except his father had gone to bed, Williams sees his father approach his mother: "He was standing right over Mama and she was already asleep. He pulled the blanket up and tucked it around her shoulders and just stood there and tears were dropping off his cheeks and I thought I could faintly hear them splashing against the linoleum rug."

In recent years, it has become almost a cliché to say the American family is in trouble. To be sure, it is changing. It may not look like it used to, may not be made up of one's biological relations as much as it once was, may go through disintegration and reconstruction, and may have as many sad and happy moments as it ever did. It is certain, however, that something like the family will continue to exist.

The essays in this section seem to point to a new honesty with respect to the family. Revealing and surprisingly candid reflections on divorce, the naming of children, the special relationship between a mother and daughter, the question of who one's "real" father is, and the admission of the devastating impact of economic deprivation on the family—topics dealt with in this section—are good examples of that honesty.

ONE SON, THREE FATHERS

Steven O'Brien

Steven O'Brien is a teacher and writer. At the time he wrote this essay, he was pursuing his doctorate at the Harvard Graduate School of Education. "One Son, Three Fathers" explores the variety of emotions O'Brien experienced as one of a boy's three father figures, and ultimately makes some broader observations about contemporary definitions of "family." This essay originally appeared in the New York Times *on December 28, 1986.*

Preparing to Read

How many of your friends belong to what was once a "typical" family: Mom, Dad, and siblings living together in one house or apartment? Chances are that some of your friends go back and forth between their parents' homes, and some may even have—like Sebastian in the following article—three fathers. Societal acceptance of divorce has made it easier for adults to choose new directions in their lives, but it can be difficult and confusing for children. Biological parents, stepparents—just who are Mom and Dad? Think about your own family situation as you read the essay. How do you think you would react if you were in Seb's shoes?

The first time I met him, he fell asleep in his spaghetti. It 1 didn't matter. I was in love. Not with him, but with his mother. She had kept Sebastian from napping so that we wouldn't be interrupted after dinner. He was only 18 months old, a tiny little body topped off by a big head covered with blond hair.

His divorced mother and I, both 25, dated for a month, lived 2 together nine more, and then married. It was Karen I wanted, not Sebastian, but they were a package deal. Ironically, he turned out to be the best part of the bargain.

3   Because my teaching schedule matched Sebastian's pre-school schedule, I spent more time with him than his mother did. On the way home after school in the afternoon, he loved to sit on his Scooby-Doo lunch box in the back seat of my car and sing hit pop tunes like "Fly, Robin, Fly" and "SOS."

4   His biological father wasn't as available as I was to deal with the unscheduled traumas of childhood. I slowly began to fill his role. Seb turned to me for comfort the night before he had to face a bully who had promised to hurt him. At age 4, he didn't understand, and I couldn't explain, why the world needed bullies. I could only repeat what my father had said: fight back as best you can and don't let anyone know that he can push you around, or it will never end. He cried at breakfast, regained his composure before school, stood up for his rights and got thoroughly trounced. When he couldn't fall asleep that night, he asked to borrow my wool knit sailor cap. "Tomorrow," he said, "with this on, I won't be afraid. I'll be 100 times stronger." The bully ignored him the next day, in order to torment someone else.

5   Brian, Sebastian's father, and I had been trained as teachers. Perhaps this was why both of us wanted to help the boy. Then, too, I had been raised with a stepsister and had seen the psychological damage that loss of contact with a parent could cause. In any case, Seb continued to spend time with me and with his father even after Brian remarried. Seb never had any problem distinguishing between the two of us, although other people were often confused because he referred to us as Daddy Steve and Daddy Brian. We all benefited from the arrangement. Sebastian shared things with Brian that I couldn't give him. For instance, I never followed sports, but Brian had studied to be a sports announcer.

6   After eight years of marriage, my wife and I separated. At first, Seb stayed with me and visited his mother, but after her remarriage, she missed him too much. He was moved to her new home nearby. Legally, of course, I had no rights. A child counselor I consulted suggested that I fade out of the picture as soon as possible. Instead, I maintained my home, with a bedroom for Seb, within walking distance of his. With his mother's consent, he started spending one night a week at my place. He loved to show off his second home to his friends by bringing them around, unannounced, for snacks.

Seb's grandparents had died years before. My place in his   7
life gradually changed to resemble the role my favorite uncle
and grandparents played in mine. It was hard at first, relinquishing my old relationship with him, but I grew to like the new one.
I had the fun of seeing him without the frustration of trying to
live with and discipline him.

Although we talked about it, and he understood after the   8
divorce that we were no longer legally connected, Seb insisted
on continuing to call me dad and using my last name as his own.
I asked, "What's in a name, anyway?" He responded, "It says
whose son I am." I told him that wasn't the issue. That I didn't
have any choice. Neither biology nor law gave me the right to
claim such a role; but he shattered my logic in a quavering voice
with the question, "Don't you want to be my father anymore?"
We hugged; I said: "Of course I want to. As long as you want me
to be your father, I will be." That was five years ago.

Because Sebastian and I live in the same community, I often   9
learn details about him I would otherwise miss. My neighbor,
Sebastian's eighth-grade social-studies teacher, told me that he
was going up and down the aisles asking each student at the end
of the year if they had any brothers or sisters who would be
going to the junior high the next fall. When he got to Seb, he
said, "Oh, that's O.K. Seb, I used to live next door to you, and I
know that you are an only child." Sebastian answered with a
smile, "That's right, Mr. Tulley, there are so many parents in my
family that there isn't room for any more kids."

After the laughter died down, several fellow students asked   10
Seb how many parents he had. He said three fathers and two
mothers. Another said, "Wow, Christmas must be great." Seb
hesitated and then explained, "Christmas is about a 7, but birth-
days are a definite 10."

Still, I wonder how he and his generation will view marriage.   11
One night, we were talking about girls, the next-most-important
issue on his mind, after driving. I said, "Well, someday, you'll find
the right young woman and you won't be satisfied until you
marry her." I wasn't prepared for his reply: "No, dad, I don't think
so. It never works for long, and divorce hurts too much." Taken
aback, I assured him that marriage did work, and that just because his parents' marriages hadn't, it was no reason to give up on
the institution. He looked at me patiently and said: "Dad, none of
my friends' parents are still together. Everybody gets divorced

sooner or later. Don't worry, I'm all right. I can take care of myself. Love 'em and leave 'em. Right?"

12   I don't think I had realized until that moment that, since my divorce from Sebastian's mother, "love 'em and leave 'em" exactly described the way I had been living and handling my own relationships with women. What could I say to Seb?

Vocabulary

To get the most out of reading this essay, you should have a working understanding of the words listed below. Following each word is a parenthetical reference, indicating the paragraph in which the word is used, as well as a definition for the word. Go back and look at the sentence in which the word appears, and see how the definition applies. To help you make this word a part of your active vocabulary, write a sentence of your own using the word in the space provided.

ironically (2):   unexpectedly

_____

_____

traumas (4):   injuries, difficult experiences

_____

_____

composure (4):   control over emotions, calmness

_____

_____

trounced (4):   thoroughly beaten

_____

_____

relinquishing (7):   giving up, letting go

_____

_____

biology (8):   study of living things, blood (as opposed to step) relationships

---

quavering (8):   shaking, unsteady

---

institution (11):   part of the framework of a society

Understanding the Essay

1. Why did O'Brien get to spend so much time with Seb?
2. Why did O'Brien want to help Seb? Why did O'Brien think it was good for Seb to see Brian, his natural father, regularly?
3. What kind of relationship does O'Brien have with Seb after the divorce? Why do you think he ignored the child counselor's advice?
4. Why doesn't O'Brien have any right to call himself Seb's "father"? Why does Seb keep his last name anyway?
5. What does the scene in school where Seb jokes about why he's an only child tell you about how Seb handles his complicated parental situation? How does O'Brien learn about Seb's activities?
6. What have the divorces done to Seb's view of marriage?

Exploring the Theme: Discussion and Writing

1. Seb says that marriage "never works for long, and divorce hurts too much." What is your view of marriage? How has your view been influenced by your parents' experiences?

2. How does divorce affect children? If your parents are divorced, draw upon your own experiences; if not, describe how you think a divorce has affected a child that you know or once knew.

How We Named Our Baby

Sarah Pattee

*Sarah Pattee wrote feature articles for several newspa-
pers for almost ten years. She now has two children,
Harley Mack Pattee Henigson and Emma Lincoln Pattee, and she writes part-time for the* Los Angeles Times.
The following selection appeared in M.O.M. *(Spring
1989), a magazine published by Mothers & Others for
Midwives.*

Preparing to Read

Do you know the story of how you were named? Did your
parents choose the name of a relative or friend, or did they just
like the way your name sounded? Whatever discussions or arguments your parents had about your name, it's likely that they
pale in comparison with what Pattee and her husband went
through in naming their son Harley Mack Pattee Henigson. Pattee thinks that names carry a lot of meaning, and she was unwill-
ing to follow the traditional pattern of giving the children their
father's surname. But how should they be named to indicate
that they are the children of a Pattee and a Henigson? Pattee
offers a solution here, as well as the questions and issues raised
when one doesn't name a child the traditional way.

It wasn't easy naming Harley Mack Pattee Henigson. Our   1
son isn't even four months old and there's been enough
debate and emotional upheaval about his name to last a
lifetime.

When my husband and I married five years ago we hardly   2
talked about names. We both assumed I'd keep mine and he'd
keep his.

Then we had a child. That's when I realized how deeply   3
emotional the issue of naming can be, when I began asking myself how deep my convictions run, when I began questioning just

how equal my "equal marriage" was.

4   Naming Harley has involved not only my husband and me, but both our families and, in a sense, society at large. I found out you can't question society's way of naming without bumping up against deeply embedded sexism under the guise of "It's always been done this way."

5   I quickly learned not to ask anyone emotionally attached to us for advice, especially relatives. This is truly an issue where parents have to look inside themselves and choose what feels best for them, no matter what child psychologists and mothers-in-law say.

6   We thought carefully about each of these choices:

.   Giving the father's name to the children seems to be the most common choice among two-name couples. One friend told me she took this route because "The fight with relatives over keeping my own name was bad enough; I didn't have enough energy to fight about the children."

7   A lot of people told me that giving children different surnames would undermine the strength of the family. I always respond by saying love, attention, and acceptance make a family, not sharing the same last name, especially in this age of blended families.

8   I sympathized with my friends who were tired of the struggle and the criticism from family members. But I asked myself, What was the use of keeping my own name only to lose it through our children? And because I really believe children learn from what we do, not from what we say, I was afraid he would think his parents were hypocrites. If we say, "Your mom and dad are equal partners" but push aside Mom's name for Dad's, what does that say about our brand of equality?

9   We thought about giving our son my last name. At first I liked this idea, but after thinking about it, I wondered if it was fair to favor my name over my husband's. I didn't want to name our son just to make a statement, either.

10   We thought about hyphenating the name, but we never felt comfortable with that option. It seemed unfair to give a child something as bulky as Pattee-Henigson. Whose name would come first? That's a serious issue; in 1982 the Nebraska Su-

preme Court ruled the father's surname has to precede the mother's surname in the case of hyphenating children's names. Putting aside the scary implications of the state telling parents how to name their children, I also wonder what happens when the last name gets dropped in school or off legal documents that only have so much space for names? And can hyphenated names be sustained across generations? It seems, once again, women's names would get lost.

We thought—very briefly—about making up a new surname   11
or combining our names into "Henigtee" or "Patson." We didn't like the idea at all. I really like my name—first, middle, and last. My husband really likes his name—first, middle, and last. Even as a child, I liked having an unusual surname.

The last option we considered was giving our children alter-   12
nate surnames. Our boys would be named after my husband; girls would be named after me. And boys would get my surname as a middle name; girls would get my husband's surname as their middle name.

I found out there's even a name for this method of naming   13
children. It's called the "bilineal solution," a new way of naming created by Sharon Lebell, author of a newly published book, *Naming Ourselves, Naming Our Children* (The Crossing Press, $6.95). I called Lebell in San Francisco, where she lives with her husband, John Loudon, and two daughters, who both bear her surname. She believes society's way of naming children after their fathers—she calls it "patronomy"—is so entrenched that a simple and solid alternative is needed. Naming boys for their fathers and girls for their mothers is one way of ensuring both parents' names get passed through the generations, she said. And it will change society slowly but surely.

"So much will change when women stop naming themselves   14
in reference to men," she said.

We chose Lebell's solution. So, three months after his birth,   15
Harley Mack Pattee Henigson had his name. I plan to use those four names all the time and to write all four whenever I have to fill out a form; it's already on his passport. And I plan to tell my son why naming him meant so much to us.

We adapted Lebell's idea a little by adding on an extra middle   16
name, Mack, in honor of an uncle who died suddenly two years

ago. Some friends added their own twist: They named their daughters after the father and sons after the mother. They told me they did it as protection against a "worst-case scenario," meaning in case their daughter gives up her name upon marrying.

17   Through this struggle to name Harley, I've realized how important names are. Names hold power. Names are your history. Names have spiritual meaning.

18   And I think I see why this issue makes a lot of people uncomfortable, because it forces them to confront their own decisions in life. I've tried to remember that and balance my philosophy with a good dose of humor and compassion. Of course, some people will never understand our reasons, and I have to accept that, too.

19   Of course, we had a boy this first time so what we've decided so far doesn't seem so radical. When we have a girl, that will be the true test of our commitment to change.

20   And if we don't have girls? Already, we're considering naming at least one boy after me, although Lebell told me it's best not to do this as it dilutes the strength of her "bilineal solution." Part of the charm of her solution, she believes, is the "roll of the dice" aspect. We may still decide to alternate names if we have boys, though.

21   Whatever we decide the next time around, this self-searching has been a gift for my huband and me. Naming Harley encouraged us to re-examine our marriage partnership (how equal are we?), our reasons for wanting children (to make a statement to society?), and our ideas about what it means to be a family. (In the end, love and acceptance of your children count the most.)

22   We have grown and changed through naming Harley Mack Pattee Henigson. I hope the same happens to him when it's his turn to name his own children.

Vocabulary

To get the most out of reading this essay, you should have a working understanding of the words listed on the next page. Following each word is a parenthetical reference, indicating the paragraph in which the word is used, as well as a definition for the word. Go back and look at the sentence in which the word appears, and see how the definition applies. To help you make

this word a part of your active vocabulary, write a sentence of your own using the word in the space provided.

upheaval (1):   disturbance

_____

_____

convictions (3):   beliefs

_____

_____

embedded (4):   stuck in, difficult to pull out

_____

_____

sexism (4):   discrimination against a gender

_____

_____

undermine (7):   sabotage, work against

_____

_____

hypocrites (8):   those who say one thing but do another

_____

_____

surname (11):   last name

_____

_____

bilineal (13):   having two lines of heritage, from both parents

_____

_____

entrenched (13):   firmly in place, well established

_____

_____

Understanding the Essay

1. Explain the significance of each of Harley Mack Pattee Henigson's names. How did his parents decide on the order of the two last names?
2. How did the naming of Harley involve society at large?
3. What options did Pattee consider in naming Harley?
4. According to Lebell, what should parents do if they have all sons or all daughters? What does Pattee think of Lebell's solution?
5. Why is naming Harley so important to Pattee? What do names mean to her?
6. What did naming Harley make Pattee and her husband re-examine about their marriage?

Exploring the Theme: Discussion and Writing

1. Pattee says that naming a child "is truly an issue where parents have to look inside themselves and choose what feels best for them, no matter what child psychologists and mothers-in-law say." Do you agree with this statement? Do you think that it's all right for parents to use the names of their children to make a statement about broader issues?
2. Do you think the compromise Pattee and her husband arrived at to name Harley was reasonable? What is your response to Lebell's statement that using her naming system "will change society slowly but surely"?
3. What method do you think you will use to name your own child(ren)? Why?

Daddy Tucked
the Blanket

Randall Williams

Randall Williams wrote the following essay when he worked as a reporter for The Alabama Journal. *He used a college scholarship to launch himself into a successful career in journalism, but the pain he endured as a result of his deprived upbringing has remained with him.*

Preparing to Read

A child living in poverty has to deal not only with material deprivation—shabby clothes, poor housing, and a lack of nonessential items—but with psychological stress as well. In the following article Williams eloquently describes what it was like to grow up poor; for him, it involved shame, frustration, and anger. For his parents, poverty was a trap they were unable to escape. It has been said that having money isn't as important as avoiding the state of *not* having it. How important is money to you?

About the time I turned 16, my folks began to wonder why I didn't stay home any more. I always had an excuse for them, but what I didn't say was that I had found my freedom and I was getting out. 1

I went through four years of high school in semirural Alabama and became active in clubs and sports; I made a lot of friends and became a regular guy, if you know what I mean. But one thing was irregular about me: I managed those four years without ever having a friend visit at my house. 2

I was ashamed of where I lived. I had been ashamed for as long as I had been conscious of class. 3

We had a big family. There were several of us sleeping in one room, but that's not so bad if you get along, and we always did. As you get older, though, it gets worse. 4

5   Being poor is a humiliating experience for a young person trying hard to be accepted. Even now—several years removed—it is hard to talk about. And I resent the weakness of these words to make you feel what it was really like.

6   We lived in a lot of old houses. We moved a lot because we were always looking for something just a little better than what we had. You have to understand that my folks worked harder than most people. My mother was always at home, but for her that was a full-time job—and no fun, either. But my father worked his head off from the time I can remember in construction and shops. It was hard, physical work.

7   I tell you this to show that we weren't shiftless. No matter how much money Daddy made, we never made much progress up the social ladder. I got out thanks to a college scholarship and because I was a little more articulate than the average.

8   I have seen my Daddy wrap copper wire through the soles of his boots to keep them together in the wintertime. He couldn't buy new boots because he had used the money for food and shoes for us. We lived like hell, but we went to school well-clothed and with a full stomach.

9   It really is hell to live in a house that was in bad shape 10 years before you moved in. And a big family puts a lot of wear and tear on a new house, too, so you can imagine how one goes downhill if it is teetering when you move in. But we lived in houses that were sweltering in summer and freezing in winter. I woke up every morning for a year and a half with plaster on my face where it had fallen out of the ceiling during the night.

10   This wasn't during the Depression; this was in the late 60's and early 70's.

11   When we boys got old enough to learn trades in school, we would try to fix up the old houses we lived in. But have you ever tried to paint a wall that crumbled when the roller went across it? And bright paint emphasized the holes in the wall. You end up more frustrated than when you began, especially when you know that at best you might come up with only enough money to improve one of the six rooms in the house. And we might move out soon after, anyway.

12   The same goes for keeping a house like that clean. If you have a house full of kids and the house is deteriorating, you'll never keep it clean. Daddy used to yell at Mama about that, but

she couldn't do anything. I think Daddy knew it inside, but he had to have an outlet for his rage somewhere, and at least yelling isn't as bad as hitting, which they never did to each other.

But you have a kitchen which has no counter space and no hot water, and you will have dirty dishes stacked up. That sounds like an excuse, but try it. You'll go mad from the sheer sense of futility. It's the same thing in a house with no closets. You can't keep clothes clean and rooms in order if they have to be stacked up with things. 13

Living in a bad house is generally worse on girls. For one thing, they traditionally help their mother with the housework. We boys could get outside and work in the field or cut wood or even play ball and forget about living conditions. The sky was still pretty. 14

But the girls got the pressure, and as they got older it became worse. Would they accept dates knowing they had to "receive" the young man in a dirty hallway with broken windows, peeling wallpaper and a cracked ceiling? You have to live it to understand it, but it creates a shame which drives the soul of a young person inward. 15

I'm thankful none of us ever blamed our parents for this, because it would have crippled our relationships. As it worked out, only the relationship between our parents was damaged. And I think the harshness which they expressed to each other was just an outlet to get rid of their anger at the trap their lives were in. It ruined their marriage because they had no one to yell at but each other. I knew other families where the kids got the abuse, but we were too much loved for that. 16

Once I was about 16 and Mama and Daddy had had a particularly violent argument about the washing machine, which had broken down. Daddy was on the back porch—that's where the only water faucet was—trying to fix it and Mama had a washtub out there washing school clothes for the next day and they were screaming at each other. 17

Later that night everyone was in bed and I heard Daddy get up from the couch where he was reading. I looked out from my bed across the hall into their room. He was standing right over Mama and she was already asleep. He pulled the blanket up and tucked it around her shoulders and just stood there and tears 18 were dropping off his cheeks and I thought I could faintly hear them splashing against the linoleum rug.

19   Now they're divorced.

20   I had courses in college where housing was discussed, but the sociologists never put enough emphasis on the impact living in substandard housing has on a person's psyche. Especially children's.

21   Small children have a hard time understanding poverty. They want the same things children from more affluent families have. They want the same things they see advertised on television, and they don't understand why they can't have them.

22   Other children can be incredibly cruel. I was in elementary school in Georgia—and this is interesting because it is the only thing I remember about that particular school—when I was about eight or nine.

23   After Christmas vacation had ended, my teacher made each student describe all his or her Christmas presents. I became more and more uncomfortable as the privilege passed around the room toward me. Other children were reciting the names of the dolls they had been given, the kinds of bicycles and the grandeur of their games and toys. Some had lists which seemed to go on and on for hours.

24   It took me only a few seconds to tell the class that I had gotten for Christmas a belt and a pair of gloves. And then I was laughed at—because I cried—by a roomful of children and a teacher. I never forgave them, and that night I made my mother cry when I told her about it.

25   In retrospect, I am grateful for that moment, but I remember wanting to die at the time.

Vocabulary

To get the most out of reading this essay, you should have a working understanding of the words listed on the next page. Following each word is a parenthetical reference, indicating the paragraph in which the word is used, as well as a definition for the word. Go back and look at the sentence in which the word appears, and see how the definition applies. To help you make this word a part of your active vocabulary, write a sentence of your own using the word in the space provided.

class (3):   social/economic group

_____

_____

humiliating (5):   embarrassing, hurting one's pride

_____

_____

articulate (7):   effective at communicating

_____

_____

sweltering (9):   very hot and stuffy

_____

_____

futility (13):   uselessness

_____

_____

affluent (21):   wealthy

_____

_____

Understanding the Essay

1. What was "irregular" about Williams during his high-school days?
2. Why is poverty more difficult for a child to deal with as he or she gets older?
3. What factors kept the Williams family poor even though Mr. Williams "worked his head off"?
4. Why didn't the Williams boys spend more time and effort trying to fix up their houses?

5. Which relationship in the family was damaged by poverty? How was it damaged?

6. Why were Williams and his brothers and sisters spared abuse from their parents? Who was cruel to them?

Exploring the Theme: Discussion and Writing

1. Describe the house(s) you grew up in. What were you particularly proud of in them? Were you ashamed of anything?

2. Why do you think Williams is grateful for the moment when his classmates and teacher laughed at his short Christmas list? What do you think that moment taught him?

MOTHER LOVE

Nancy Friday

?? J̶ How can she be both

Nancy Friday, a (pop) psychologist and writer, is best known for her groundbreaking book My Mother/My Self: The Daughter's Search for Identity. *She has also researched and written extensively about women's and men's sexual fantasies, and about the effects of jealousy on intimate relationships. Friday, who attended Wellesley College, resides in Key West, Florida.*

Preparing to Read

The bond between mothers and their children is depicted as the purest kind of love—Mother Love, as Friday calls it. Yet it involves sacrifice on the part of the woman; of all the roles she can fill, she is reduced to one: mother. Of all the people she can share her life with, only one, her child, can demand so much of her time and attention. In "Mother Love," Friday challenges the notion of easy, instinctual Mother Love. Think about your relationship with your mother. Did she hide some of her painful emotions from you? How do you think her life might have been different if she hadn't been a "mother"?

We are raised to believe that mother love is different from other kinds of love. It is not open to error, doubt, or the ambivalence of ordinary affections. This is an illusion.   1

Mothers may love their children, but they sometimes do not like them. The same woman who may be willing to put her body between her child and a runaway truck will often resent the day-by-day sacrifice the child unknowingly demands of her time, sexuality, and self-development.   2

A woman without a daughter may try to explore life's infinite possibilities. Her own mother left out so much. But when a daughter is born, fears she thought she had conquered long ago   3

are re-aroused. Now there is another person, not simply dependent on her, but(like)her, and therefore subject to all the dangers
she has fought all her life. The mother's progress into a larger
sexuality is halted. Ground gained that she could have held
alone is abandoned. She retreats and entrenches herself in the
cramped female stance of security and defense. The position is
fondly hailed as mother protector. It is the position of fear. She
may be only half alive but she is safe, and so is her daughter. She
now defines herself not as a woman but primarily as a mother.
Sex is left out, hidden from the girl who must never think of her
mother in danger: in sex. It is only with the greatest effort that
the girl will be able to think of herself that way.

4   When women's lives were more predictable, we could more
easily afford this enigmatic picture of womanhood. When we
had no alternative but to repeat our mother's life, our mistakes
and disappointments were pretty much confined to her space,
her margin of error and unhappiness. I do believe our grandmothers, even our mothers, were happier; not knowing as much
as we do and not having our options, there was less to be unhappy about. A woman might give up her sexuality, hate being a
housewife, not like children, but if every woman was doing it,
how could she articulate her frustration? She could feel it certainly, but you can't want what you don't know about. Television, for instance, gave them no sense of thwarted expectations.
Today women's lives are changing at a rate and by a necessity
we couldn't control if we wanted to; we need all the energy that
suppression consumes. If we are going to fill more than women's
traditional role, we can't afford the exhaustion that goes with
constant emotional denial. There are pressures on women other
than the 'maternal instinct."There are the new economic and
social demands. Even if we decide to lead our mothers' lives the
fact is that our daughter may not. We may continue, through
denial and repression, to keep alive the idealization of motherhood for another generation, but where will that leave her?

5   If women are going to be lawyers as well as mothers, they
must differentiate between the two, and then differentiate once
again about their sexuality. That is the third—and *not* mutually
exclusive—option. As the world changes, and women's place in it,
mothers must consciously present this choice to their daughters.
A woman may incorporate all three choices within herself—and
even more—but at any given moment she must be able to say to

herself and her daughter, "I chose to have you because I wanted to be a mother. I chose to work—to have a career, to be in politics, to play the piano—because that gives me a different feeling of value about myself, a value that is not greater nor lesser than motherhood, only different. Whether you choose to work or not, to be a mother or not, it will have nothing to do with your sexuality. Sexuality is the third option—as meaningful as either of the other two."

The truth is that the woman and the mother are often at war 6
with one another—in the same body. Like so many women since the world began, my mother could not believe in this opposition of the two desires. Tradition, society, her parents, religion itself told her that there was no conflict; that motherhood was the logical and natural end product of sex. Instead of believing what every woman's body tells every woman's mind, that sexuality and eroticism are a fundamentally different and opposite drive to motherhood, my mother accepted the lie. She took as her act of faith the proposition that if she were a real woman, she would be a good mother and I would grow up the same. If I repeated her path and pattern of motherhood, it would justify and place the final stamp of value on what she had done. It would say her attitude, behavior, and deepest feelings were not split, but were in fact in harmony, a woman in unison with nature.

Some women do make this choice gladly. They may be the 7
majority, but my mother was not one of them. As I am not—her daughter in this too. Even in a good marriage, many women resent the matronly, nonsexual role their children force them to play. My mother didn't even have a good marriage; she was a young widow.

Frightened as she was, as much in need of my father as my 8
sister and I were of her, mother had no choice but to pretend that my sister and I were the most important part of her life; that neither fear, youth and inexperience, loss, loneliness or her own needs could shake the unqualified and invincible love she felt for us. My mother had no body of woman-to-woman honesty and shared experience to use in her fight against the folk wisdom that said just being a woman carried all the inherent wisdom needed to be a mother—that it was either "natural" to her, or she was a failure as a woman.

In all the years we lived together, it is a shame we never 9
talked honestly about our feelings. What neither of us knew then

was that I could have stood honesty, no matter how frightening. Her angers, disillusionments, fears of failure, rage—emotions I seldom saw—I could have come to terms with them if she had been able to speak to me. I would have grown used to the idea that while mother loved me, at times other emotions impaired that love, and developed trust that in time her love for me would always return. Instead, I was left trying to believe in some perfect love she said she had for me, but in which I could not believe. I did not understand why I couldn't feel it no matter what her words said. I grew to believe that love itself, from her or anybody else, was a will-o'-the-wisp, coming or going for reasons I could not control. Never knowing when or why I was loved, I grew afraid to depend on it.

10   The older I get, the more of my mother I see in myself. The more opposite my life and my thinking grow from hers, the more of her I hear in my voice, see in my facial expression, feel in the emotional reactions I have come to recognize as my own. It is almost as if in extending myself, the circle closes in to completion. She was my first and most lasting model. To say her image is not still a touchstone in my life—and mine in hers—would be another lie. I am tired of lies. They have stood in the way of my understanding myself all my life. I have always known that what my husband loves most in me is that I have my own life. I have always felt that I had partially deceived him in this; I am very clever at pretense. My work, my marriage, and my new relationships with other women are beginning to make his assumptions about me true—that I am an independent, separate individual. They have allowed me to respect myself, and admire my own sex. What still stands between me and the person I would like to be is this illusion of perfect love between my mother and me. It is a lie I can no longer afford.

Vocabulary

To get the most out of reading this essay, you should have a working understanding of the words listed below. Following each word is a parenthetical reference, indicating the paragraph in which the word is used, as well as a definition for the word. Go back and look at the sentence in which the word appears, and see how the definition applies. To help you make this word a part of your active vocabulary, write a sentence of your own using the word in the space provided.

ambivalence (1):   contradictory strong feelings

_____

_____

enigmatic (4):   puzzling, mysterious

_____

_____

thwarted (4):   stymied, denied

_____

_____

eroticism (6):   sexuality, sexual pleasure

_____

_____

proposition (6):   statement presented as fact

_____

_____

inherent (8):   born with, natural

_____

_____

will-o'-the-wisp (9):   unrealistic or deceptive goal

_____

_____

Understanding the Essay

1. What fears are rearoused in a woman when she gives birth to a daughter? Why do those fears emerge only when a daughter is born, not a son?

2. The position of mother protector is applauded by society, but why do women adopt it?

3. Why were women happier in past generations?

4. According to Friday, what are the three options for women? Why does Friday believe they're not mutually exclusive?

5. "The truth is that the woman and the mother are often at war with one another—in the same body." What does Friday mean by this statement?

6. Why is it a shame that Friday and her mother never spoke honestly about their feelings?

7. What still stands between Friday and the person she'd really like to be?

Exploring the Theme: Discussion and Writing

1. Friday, speaking from a woman's viewpoint, equates sex with danger. What do you think she means by this? Why is the mother protector, in seeking safety and security for her daughter, forced to abandon sex and hide her sexuality from her daughter?

2. Friday says, "I do believe our grandmothers, even our mothers, were happier; not knowing as much as we do and not having our options, there was less to be unhappy about." Do you agree with this statement? Explain why or why not.

WRITING SUGGESTIONS
FOR "FAMILY TIES"

1. Randall Williams thinks that poverty had a tremendous impact on his early family life. Write an essay in which you assess the impact, for better or worse, of your family's economic status on you as a child. Think in terms of the psychological implications, not merely the material.

2. How would you define "family"? Should the definition include the requirement of marriage? Do an unwed mother and child constitute a family? What about divorced parents? Gay and lesbian adoptions? People living in communal arrangements without legal ties?

3. How important is it to you that both parents' names be reflected in the name of their child? Would you use the "bilineal solution" discussed by Pattee? Write an essay expressing your current thinking on this subject.

4. Many discussions concerning the fascination and importance of names come under the title "What's in a Name?" Write an essay in which you explore what names signify, what they suggest, and how they can affect one's sense of self as well as one's impression of others.

5. Randall Williams writes that his family's poverty shamed him. Did he blame his parents for their poverty? Was he ashamed of his parents? Did the family's poverty ruin his relationship with his parents? Is it possible to be ashamed of one's parents? Write an essay in which you examine some aspect of your relationship with your parents.

6. Did your mother try to display a perfect love for you, as Friday's mother did for her? How do you think her communication of her fears and struggles—or lack thereof—has influenced you? Write an essay on your relationship with your mother.

3

EVERYDAY HEROES AND ROLE MODELS

It's fashionable today to say that what's wrong with society is that we have no heroes or the wrong ones. If we mean by heroes those who are larger than life, who are courageous and risk life and limb to do the impossible, and who think of the public good rather than personal reward, perhaps there is more than a little truth in this point of view. Still, every so often we ourselves experience or read accounts of just such a hero, and we are awestruck by his or her wonderful deeds.

It's important to realize, also, that our view of heroes and heroic action is symbolic. Our heroes reflect our values, what we most cherish in society. So when we talk about whether or not our concept of the hero has changed, we should realize that we are talking about ourselves and the evolution of our beliefs and values.

We see our heroes today as being less like Superman and more like our friends and neighbors—people whose miracles seem only slightly beyond our grasp, whose deeds are not so much otherworldly as they are uncommon. Some of our every-day heroes and role models are parents who go the extra distance, doctors who demonstrate not only their skill but their compassion, those quietly nursing AIDS patients, big brothers and sisters who take up the slack, foster parents with love to share, and all those who selflessly offer opportunities to others. Could it be we share a belief that society needs not so much a knight on a white horse as just a bit more concern, a bit more effort, to turn the uncommon into the everyday?

In this section, we offer four views of everyday heroes and role models. Two essays discuss the influence of special teachers, Miss Duling for Eudora Welty and Miss Hurd for Nicholas Gage, and one suggests that we might profit from looking back through our ancestry for role models within our own families. Another essay, written by an African-American admissions officer at Harvard University, criticizes the media for creating black sports and entertainment heroes, especially male role models, and for misleading our black youth.

THE HEROES WE KNOW

David and Barbara Bjorklund

David and Barbara Bjorklund wrote the following article for Parents *magazine in September 1989 in response to parents' concerns that their children don't have good heroes to look up to these days. They both work in the psychology department at Florida Atlantic University.*

Preparing to Read

Children's heroes are thought of as larger-than-life figures. Star athletes, movie stars, or even comic book crime fighters can be inspirational, but they are also remote, and it has been difficult to find one with an untarnished image in recent years. The Bjorklunds argue that children should be able to find their heroes closer to home—perhaps *in* their homes. Who were your heroes when you were a child? Why were they heroic to you?

1   We heard a good story recently from Aunt Ellen. While visiting her grandchildren in Chicago, Aunt Ellen was invited by her nine-year-old granddaughter to come to the girl's school to visit her third-grade class. Aunt Ellen asked why—was there a special program planned, or was it Grandparents' Day? "No," her granddaughter explained, "it's just that we are studying the Statue of Liberty, and I wanted the other kids to see what a real *immigrant* looks like!"

2   It's a good story on several levels: first, because Aunt Ellen is a stylish, suntanned lady who spends winters in Florida and summers traveling the four corners of the world—hardly the stereotypical image of an immigrant with tattered luggage, wearing native clothing. And it's also a good story because Aunt Ellen really *is* an immigrant. She came to this country as a young child with her parents and her sister, Gulli, sailing from Sweden to New York, past the Statue of Liberty. The family had

relatives here to sponsor them, so they didn't have to go through immigration on Ellis Island, but her story of leaving her home and adjusting to a new culture is an exciting saga of Bjorklund family history, and of American history as well.

Aunt Ellen did go to her granddaughter's class and spent the   3
afternoon telling the story of her trip to America to a group of spellbound third graders. They asked her questions and added accounts of their own grandparents' histories, and a good time was had by all.

In an age when we parents lament the lack of heroes for our   4
children to admire, we would be wise to look to our own family tree. Not many of us had forefathers who sailed over on the *Mayflower* or whose names would appear in history books, but we all have our share of Aunt Ellens, who were participants in or witnesses to important chapters in history.

The children in our family have two grandfathers who were   5
World War II combat veterans, one who served in Europe and one in the Pacific. It is interesting for us to hear our children ask them questions about the war and to hear the old stories that were too new to tell when we were children. Then there was Great-aunt May, who retired after teaching kindergarten for 45 years and spent the next several decades of her life developing new strains of amaryllis lilies, registering each one with the name of a child in our family. And in a younger generation there is Aunt Marcia, who was one of the first women to graduate from the U.S. Military Academy at West Point. Her experiences have made a good story for the girls in the family, and her success and determination have made it easier for them to follow in her footsteps if they, too, decide to pursue a military career.

Stories about heroes help make history interesting and real   6
for school-age kids. They are good topics for imaginary play. They give kids someone to emulate when they grow up and something to talk about when they compare family backgrounds with their friends. When children's heroes are members of their family, it elevates their self-esteem and sense of family pride. When we tell our children about interesting family members, we spell out our values and our expectations for them. We make them feel that they are part of an important group, even though the family may be scattered across the country.

It's not necessary to become expert genealogists to find he-   7
roes in our family tree. Everyone has stories about where they

were when big events occurred. Maybe we should ask some questions the next time the relatives get together. We could write down the stories or turn on a tape recorder while they answer. We could retell the stories to our children at bedtime. And maybe, at other times, we could just turn off the TV and talk.

Vocabulary

To get the most out of reading this essay, you should have a working understanding of the words listed below. Following each word is a parenthetical reference, indicating the paragraph in which the word is used, as well as a definition for the word. Go back and look at the sentence in which the word appears, and see how the definition applies. To help you make this word a part of your active vocabulary, write a sentence of your own using the word in the space provided.

lament (4):   mourn, complain

_____

_____

emulate (6):   imitate, follow

_____

_____

genealogists (7):   those who study family trees

_____

_____

Understanding the Essay

1. Why was Aunt Ellen a good guest for her granddaughter's class while they studied the Statue of Liberty?
2. What was Aunt Ellen's "exciting saga"?
3. Why should we look to our own family tree for heroes?
4. Why is it good for children to learn more about their families' heroes?

5. What national or world event had an impact on you? Describe where you were and what you were doing when it happened, as if your child had asked you to.

Exploring the Theme: Discussion and Writing

1. Think about a relative who, like the Bjorklunds' Great-aunt May, is interesting but not apparently heroic. Describe this relative and explain what makes him or her a hero.

2. The Bjorklunds say that positive family stories should be told but, along with heroes, most families have their share of "black sheep." Should these people be ignored in family stories? Why or why not?

THE TEACHER WHO CHANGED MY LIFE

Nicholas Gage

Nicholas Gage was born in Greece in 1939, but he came to America when he was nine to escape civil war in his homeland. His mother didn't get out of Greece—she was captured and shot by Communist guerrillas. Gage is now a successful journalist and the author of Eleni, *a book about his mother, and* A Place for Us, *which tells how he adapted to life in the United States.*

Preparing to Read

The title of Gage's essay says it all—it's a fond tribute to the teacher who set him on the road to a happy and successful career. Such direct influence is rare, but for most of us, someone— a teacher, a friend, or a relative—has helped us begin to sort out what we want to do or has helped develop our abilities. Although it may be too early for you to be sure, do you think any of your teachers or friends have changed your life? How have they influenced you?

1   The person who set the course of my life in the new land I entered as a young war refugee—who, in fact, nearly dragged me onto the path that would bring all the blessings I've received in America—was a salty-tongued, no-nonsense schoolteacher named Marjorie Hurd. When I entered her classroom in 1953, I had been to six schools in five years, starting in the Greek village where I was born in 1939.

2   When I stepped off a ship in New York Harbor on a gray March day in 1949, I was an undersized 9-year-old in short pants who had lost his mother and was coming to live with the father he didn't know. My mother, Eleni Gatzoyiannis, had been imprisoned, tortured and shot by Communist guerrillas for sending me

and three of my four sisters to freedom. She died so that her children could go to their father in the United States.

The portly, bald, well-dressed man who met me and my sisters seemed a foreign, authoritarian figure. I secretly resented him for not getting the whole family out of Greece early enough to save my mother. Ultimately, I would grow to love him and appreciate how he dealt with becoming a single parent at the age of 56, but at first our relationship was prickly, full of hostility.   3

As Father drove us to our new home—a tenement in Worcester, Mass.—and pointed out the huge brick building that would be our first school in America, I clutched my Greek notebooks from the refugee camp, hoping that my few years of schooling would impress my teachers in this cold, crowded country. They didn't. When my father led me and my 11-year-old sister to Greendale Elementary School, the grim-faced Yankee principal put the two of us in a class for the mentally retarded. There was no facility in those days for non–English-speaking children.   4

By the time I met Marjorie Hurd four years later, I had learned English, been placed in a normal, graded class and had even been chosen for the college preparatory track in the Worcester public school system. I was 13 years old when our father moved us yet again, and I entered Chandler Junior High shortly after the beginning of seventh grade. I found myself surrounded by richer, smarter and better-dressed classmates who looked askance at my strange clothes and heavy accent. Shortly after I arrived, we were told to select a hobby to pursue during "club hour" on Fridays. The idea of hobbies and clubs made no sense to my immigrant ears, but I decided to follow the prettiest girl in my class—the blue-eyed daughter of the local Lutheran minister. She led me through the door marked "Newspaper Club" and into the presence of Miss Hurd, the newspaper adviser and English teacher who would become my mentor and my muse.   5

A formidable, solidly built woman with salt-and-pepper hair, a steely eye and a flat Boston accent, Miss Hurd had no patience with layabouts. "What are all you goof-offs doing here?" she bellowed at the would-be journalists. "This is the Newspaper Club! We're going to put out a *newspaper.* So if there's anybody in this room who doesn't like work, I suggest you go across to the Glee Club now, because you're going to work your tails off here!"   6

7   I was soon under Miss Hurd's spell. She did indeed teach us
to put out a newspaper, skills I honed during my next 25 years as
a journalist. Soon I asked the principal to transfer me to her
English class as well. There, she drilled us on grammar until I
finally began to understand the logic and structure of the English language. She assigned stories for us to read and discuss;
not tales of heroes, like the Greek myths I knew, but stories of
underdogs—poor people, even immigrants, who seemed ordinary until a crisis drove them to do something extraordinary.
She also introduced us to the literary wealth of Greece—giving
me a new perspective on my war-ravaged, impoverished homeland. I began to be proud of my origins.

8   One day, after discussing how writers should write about
what they know, she assigned us to compose an essay from our
own experience. Fixing me with a stern look, she added, "Nick, I
want you to write about what happened to your family in
Greece." I had been trying to put those painful memories behind
me and left the assignment until the last moment. Then, on a
warm spring afternoon, I sat in my room with a yellow pad and
pencil and stared out the window at the buds on the trees. I
wrote that the coming of spring always reminded me of the last
time I said goodbye to my mother on a green and gold day in
1948.

9   I kept writing, one line after another, telling how the Communist guerrillas occupied our village, took our home and food,
how my mother started planning our escape when she learned
that the children were to be sent to re-education camps behind
the Iron Curtain and how, at the last moment, she couldn't escape with us because the guerrillas sent her with a group of
women to thresh wheat in a distant village. She promised she
would try to get away on her own, she told me to be brave and
hung a silver cross around my neck, and then she kissed me. I
watched the line of women being led down into the ravine and
up the other side, until they disappeared around the bend—my
mother a tiny brown figure at the end who stopped for an instant to raise her hand in one last farewell.

10   I wrote about our nighttime escape down the mountain,
across the minefields and into the lines of the Nationalist soldiers, who sent us to a refugee camp. It was there that we
learned of our mother's execution. I felt very lucky to have come
to America, I concluded, but every year, the coming of spring

made me feel sad because it reminded me of the last time I saw my mother.

I handed in the essay, hoping never to see it again, but Miss Hurd had it published in the school paper. This mortified me at first, until I saw that my classmates reacted with sympathy and tact to my family's story. Without telling me, Miss Hurd also submitted the essay to a contest sponsored by the Freedoms Foundation at Valley Forge, Pa., and it won a medal. The Worcester paper wrote about the award and quoted my essay at length. My father, by then a "five-and-dime-store chef," as the paper described him, was ecstatic with pride, and the Worcester Greek community celebrated the honor to one of its own.

For the first time I began to understand the power of the written word. A secret ambition took root in me. One day, I vowed, I would go back to Greece, find out the details of my mother's death and write about her life, so her grandchildren would know of her courage. Perhaps I would even track down the men who killed her and write of their crimes. Fulfilling that ambition would take me 30 years.

Meanwhile, I followed the literary path that Miss Hurd had so forcefully set me on. After junior high, I became the editor of my school paper at Classical High School and got a part-time job at the Worcester *Telegram and Gazette*. Although my father could only give me $50 and encouragement toward a college education, I managed to finance four years at Boston University with scholarships and part-time jobs in journalism. During my last year of college, an article I wrote about a friend who had died in the Philippines—the first person to lose his life working for the Peace Corps—led to my winning the Hearst Award for College Journalism. And the plaque was given to me in the White House by President John F. Kennedy.

For a refugee who had never seen a motorized vehicle or indoor plumbing until he was 9, this was an unimaginable honor. When the Worcester paper ran a picture of me standing next to President Kennedy, my father rushed out to buy a new suit in order to be properly dressed to receive the congratulations of the Worcester Greeks. He clipped out the photograph, had it laminated in plastic and carried it in his breast pocket for the rest of his life to show everyone he met. I found the much-worn photo in his pocket on the day he died 20 years later.

15   In our isolated Greek village, my mother had bribed a cousin to teach her to read, for girls were not supposed to attend school beyond a certain age. She had always dreamed of her children receiving an education. She couldn't be there when I graduated from Boston University, but the person who came with my father and shared our joy was my former teacher, Marjorie Hurd. We celebrated not only my bachelor's degree but also the scholarships that paid my way to Columbia's Graduate School of Journalism. There, I met the woman who would eventually become my wife. At our wedding and at the baptisms of our three children, Marjorie Hurd was always there, dancing alongside the Greeks.

16   By then, she was Mrs. Rabidou, for she had married a widower when she was in her early 40s. That didn't distract her from her vocation of introducing young minds to English literature, however. She taught for a total of 41 years and continually would make a "project" of some balky student in whom she spied a spark of potential. Often these were students from the most troubled homes, yet she would alternately bully and charm each one with her own special brand of tough love until the spark caught fire. She retired in 1981 at the age of 62 but still avidly follows the lives and careers of former students while overseeing her adult stepchildren and driving her husband on camping trips to New Hampshire.

17   Miss Hurd was one of the first to call me on Dec. 10, 1987, when President Reagan, in his television address after the summit meeting with Gorbachev, told the nation that Eleni Gatzoyiannis' dying cry, "My children!" had helped inspire him to seek an arms agreement "for all the children of the world."

18   "I can't imagine a better monument for your mother," Miss Hurd said with an uncharacteristic catch in her voice.

19   Although a bad hip makes it impossible for her to join in the Greek dancing, Marjorie Hurd Rabidou is still an honored and enthusiastic guest at all family celebrations, including my 50th birthday picnic last summer, where the shish kebab was cooked on spits, clarinets and *bouzoukis* wailed, and costumed dancers led the guests in a serpentine line around our Colonial farmhouse, only 20 minutes from my first home in Worcester.

20   My sisters and I felt an aching void because my father was not there to lead the line, balancing a glass of wine on his head while he danced, the way he did at every celebration during his

92 years. But Miss Hurd was there, surveying the scene with quiet satisfaction. Although my parents are gone, her presence was a consolation, because I owe her so much.

This is truly the land of opportunity, and I would have enjoyed 21 its bounty even if I hadn't walked into Miss Hurd's classroom in 1953. But she was the one who directed my grief and pain into writing, and if it weren't for her I wouldn't have become an investigative reporter and foreign correspondent, recorded the story of my mother's life and death in *Eleni* and now my father's story in *A Place for Us*, which is also a testament to the country that took us in. She was the catalyst that sent me into journalism and indirectly caused all the good things that came after. But Miss Hurd would probably deny this emphatically.

A few years ago, I answered the telephone and heard my 22 former teacher's voice telling me, in that won't-take-no-for-an-answer tone of hers, that she had decided I was to write and deliver the eulogy at her funeral. I agreed (she didn't leave me any choice), but that's one assignment I never want to do. I hope, Miss Hurd, that you'll accept this remembrance instead.

Vocabulary

To get the most out of reading this essay, you should have a working understanding of the words listed below. Following each word is a parenthetical reference, indicating the paragraph in which the word is used, as well as a definition for the word. Go back and look at the sentence in which the word appears, and see how the definition applies. To help you make this word a part of your active vocabulary, write a sentence of your own using the word in the space provided.

refugee (1): person displaced by war or other hardship

_____

_____

guerrillas (2): soldiers who are not part of an official army

_____

_____

authoritarian (3): ruling by force

_____

_____

tenement (4): building with many apartments, one usually occupied by poorer families in a city

_____

_____

mentor (5): special teacher

_____

_____

mortified (11): horrified, embarrassed

_____

_____

vocation (16): job, career

_____

_____

eulogy (22): speech of praise at a person's funeral

_____

_____

Understanding the Essay

1. When Gage first arrives in the United States, why does he resent his father?
2. Why does Gage join the Newspaper Club? Why does he stay?
3. How do the stories Gage reads in Miss Hurd's class differ from the Greek myths he knows?
4. How does Gage come to understand the power of the written word? Why wouldn't he have discovered it as quickly without Miss Hurd's help?

5. How did Gage's father react to his writing accomplish-ments? From what is written about him, what image do you have of Gage's father?

6. What did Miss Hurd do, specifically, to start Gage on his journalistic and literary career?

Exploring the Theme: Discussion and Writing

1. It could be said that Nicholas Gage began his career at age thirteen in Miss Hurd's Newspaper Club. He was lucky to find a career for which he had both the talent and desire at such an early age, and to be encouraged to pursue it by a respected teacher. Even though you may not have been as lucky in finding a career as early as Gage, what career path would you like to pursue at this time? Why?

2. Identify someone who has taught you something of impor-tance in your life—a teacher, a coach, a friend, a family member, and the like. What were you taught? Why was it important to you? What made this person an effective teacher?

THE WRONG EXAMPLES
David L. Evans

Daivd L. Evans is a senior admissions officer at Harvard University. He is alarmed by the lack of qualified black male applicants to college and wrote the following article for Newsweek *(March 1, 1993) to suggest a possible reason for this lack.*

Preparing to Read

Whom do you look up to? Who helps you to decide how you should behave or what paths you can follow in life? A parent, a teacher, or a close older friend can have a powerful influence on you as a role model. For many of us, good role models are easy to find. Evans argues in the following article, however, that young black males lack good role models close to home. As a result, they try to follow their unrealistic dreams in the footsteps of TV heroes like athletes and comedians and don't prepare for success in less glamorous, but far more attainable, careers. As you read the article, think about the influence of TV and other media role models on you. How much impact do you think such messages as "I want to be like Mike [Michael Jordan]" have on the children Evans writes about?

1   As a college admissions officer I am alarmed at the dearth of qualified black male candidates. Often in high schools that are 90 percent black, *all* the African-American students who come to my presentation are female! This gender disparity persists to college matriculation where the black male population almost never equals that of the female.

2   What is happening to these young men? Who or what is influencing them? I submit that the absence of male role models and slanted television images of black males have something to do with it.

106

More than half of black children live in homes headed by   3
women, and almost all of the black teachers they encounter are
also women. This means that most African-American male children do not often meet black male role models in their daily
lives. They must look beyond their immediate surroundings for
exemplary black men to emulate. Lacking in-the-flesh models,
many look to TV for black heroes.

Unfortunately, TV images of black males are not particularly   4
diverse. Their usual roles are to display physical prowess, sing,
dance, play a musical instrument or make an audience laugh.
These roles are enticing and generously rewarded. But the reality is that success comes to only a few extraordinarily gifted
performers or athletes.

A foreigner watching American TV would probably conclude   5
that most successful black males are either athletes or entertainers. That image represents both success and failure. Success,
because the substantial presence of blacks in sports, music and
sitcoms is a milestone in the struggle begun almost 50 years ago
to penetrate the racial barriers of big-league athletics and television. It is a failure because the overwhelming success of a *few*
highly visible athletes, musicians and comedians has type-cast
black males. Millions see these televised roles as a definition of
black men. Nowhere is this more misleading than in the inner
city, where young males see it as "the way out."

Ask a random sample of Americans to identify Michael Jor-   6
dan, Bo Jackson, Magic Johnson, Hammer, Prince, Eddie Murphy or Mike Tyson. Correct responses would probably exceed
90 percent. Then ask them to identify Colin Powell, August
Wilson, Franklin Thomas, Mike Espy, Walter Massey, Earl
Graves or the late Reginald Lewis and I doubt that 10 percent
would respond correctly. The second group contains the chair-
man of the Joint Chiefs of Staff, a Pulitzer Prize-winning play-
wright, the president of the Ford Foundation, the secretary of
agriculture, the director of the National Science Foundation,
the publisher of *Black Enterprise* magazine and the former CEO
of a multimillion-dollar business.

The Democratic National Convention that nominated Bill   7
Clinton brought Ron Brown, Jesse Jackson, David Dinkins, Kurt
Schmoke and Bernard Shaw into living rooms as impressive
role models. Their relative numbers at the convention were in
noticeable contrast to the black baseball players who made up

nearly half of the All-Star teams on the Tuesday night of the convention.

8   This powerful medium has made the glamour of millionaire boxers, ballplayers, musicians and comedians appear so close, so tangible that, to naive young boys, it seems only a dribble or dance step away. In the hot glare of such surrealism, schoolwork and prudent personal behavior can become irrelevant.

9   Impressionable young black males are not the only Americans getting this potent message. *All* TV viewers are subtly told that blacks are "natural" athletes, they are "funny" and all of them have "rhythm." Such a thoroughly reinforced message doesn't lie dormant. A teacher who thinks every little black boy is a potential Bo Jackson or Eddie Murphy is likely to give his football practice a higher priority than his homework or to excuse his disruptive humor.

10   Television's influence is so pronounced that one seldom meets a young black man who isn't wearing paraphernalia normally worn by athletes and entertainers. Young white men wear similar attire but not in the same proportion. Whites have many more televised role models from which to choose. There are very few whites in comparison to the number of blacks in the NBA. Black males are 12½ percent of the American male population but constitute 75 percent of the NBA and are thereby six times overrepresented. That television presents poor role models for *all* kids doesn't wash.

11   These highly visible men's influence is so dominant that it has redefined the place of neck jewelry, sneakers and sports apparel in our society. The yearning to imitate the stars has sometimes had dire consequences. Young lives have been lost over sneakers, gold chains and jackets. I daresay that many black prison inmates are the flotsam and jetsam from dreamboats that never made it to the NBA or MTV.

12   Producers of TV sports, popular music and sitcoms should acknowledge these "side effects" of the American Dream. More important are the superstars themselves. To a man, they are similar to lottery winners and their presence on TV is cruelly deceptive to their electronic protégés. Surely they can spend some of their time and resources to convince their young followers that even incredible talent doesn't assure fame or fortune. An athlete or performer must also be amazingly lucky in his quest for Mount Olympus.

A well-trained mind is a surer, although less glamorous, 13
bet for success. Arthur Ashe spent his whole life teaching precisely this message. Bill Cosby and Jim Brown also come to
mind as African-American superstars who use their substantial influence to redirect young black males. At this time,
when black men are finally making some inroads into the upper echelons of American society, we need more than ever to
encourage the young to look beyond the stereotypes of popular
culture.

Vocabulary

To get the most out of reading this essay, you should have a
working understanding of the words listed below. Following
each word is a parenthetical reference, indicating the paragraph
in which the word is used, as well as a definition for the word.
Go back and look at the sentence in which the word appears, and
see how the definition applies.To help you make this word a part
of your active vocabulary, write a sentence of your own using the
word in the space provided.

disparity (1):   contrast

_____

_____

matriculation (1):   enrollment

_____

_____

emulate (3):   strive to imitate or to be like

_____

_____

surrealism (8):   altered reality, unreal

_____

_____

paraphernalia (10):   objects associated with a particular activity or theme

_____

_____

flotsam and jetsam (11):   material washed up on a beach, items that aren't noted or cared for

_____

_____

protégés (12):   those who attempt to follow in the footsteps of a particular person

_____

_____

echelons (13):   ranks, groups established by a certain criterion

_____

_____

Understanding the Essay

1. Why are more African-American female students interested in going to college than African-American male students, according to Evans?
2. What is wrong with the TV image of successful black males? Are such images helpful to young blacks in forming their identities? How are they harmful?,
3. Why do more people know what Bo Jackson's job is than Mike Espy's?
4. TV's image of black males as athletes or entertainers reaches everybody. Why does Evans think it can be harmful when people other than young blacks absorb the images' message?
5. Why don't young white males tend to wear as much jewelry and sports attire as young blacks, even though there are also many successful white athletes?

6. What does Evans think can be done about what he terms "the wrong examples"? What do you think can be done to create more realistic role models for young African-American males?

Exploring the Theme:
Discussion and Writing

1. How much do you think TV influences you? Your friends? What kinds of influence does it have?

2. Identify a role model for yourself. It can be anyone who has accomplished goals or lived and behaved in a manner that you admire. Explain the reasons why you chose this role model.

MISS DULING

Eudora Welty

Eudora Welty has had a long and successful writing career. She was born and raised in Jackson, Mississippi, and wrote the book excerpted here, One Writer's Beginnings, *in 1984. It's about how she became a writer, and this piece concerns a figure of authority from her childhood.*

Preparing to Read

An authority figure is someone who commands attention, respect, fear, and little affection. A person who wields authority can have a great impact—both positive and negative—on other people's lives. Miss Duling, as described by Welty, is the ultimate authority figure to her students, wielding her bell as a kind of weapon. Yet she commands respect and admiration from former students, as well as gratitude for her influence on them. Have you ever known an authority figure like Miss Duling? How did he or she affect your life?

1   From the first I was clamorous to learn—I wanted to know and begged to be told not so much what, or how, or why, or where, as when. How soon?

> Pear tree by the garden gate,
> How much longer must I wait?

This rhyme from one of my nursery books was the one that spoke for me. But I lived not at all unhappily in this craving, for my wild curiosity was in large part suspense, which carries its own secret pleasure. And so one of the godmothers of fiction was already bending over me.

2   When I was five years old, I knew the alphabet, I'd been vaccinated (for smallpox), and I could read. So my mother

walked across the street to Jefferson Davis Grammar School and asked the principal if she would allow me to enter the first grade after Christmas.

"Oh, all right," said Miss Duling. "Probably the best thing you could do with her."   3

Miss Duling, a lifelong subscriber to perfection, was a figure of authority, the most whole-souled I have ever come to know. She was a dedicated schoolteacher who denied herself all she might have done or whatever other way she might have lived (this possibility was the last that could have occurred to us, her subjects in school). I believe she came of well-off people, well-educated, in Kentucky, and certainly old photographs show she was a beautiful, high-spirited-looking young lady—and came down to Jackson to its new grammar school that was going begging for a principal. She must have earned next to nothing; Mississippi then as now was the nation's lowest-ranking state economically, and our legislature has always shown a painfully loud reluctance to give money to public education. That challenge *brought* her.   4

In the long run she came into touch, as teacher or principal, with three generations of Jacksonians. My parents had not, but everybody else's parents had gone to school to her. She'd taught most of our leaders somewhere along the line. When she wanted something done—some civic oversight corrected, some injustice made right overnight, or even a tree spared that the fool telephone people were about to cut down—she telephoned the mayor, or the chief of police, or the president of the power company, or the head doctor at the hospital, or the judge in charge of a case, or whoever, and calling them by their first names, *told* them. It is impossible to imagine her meeting with anything less than compliance. The ringing of her brass bell from their days at Davis School would still be in their ears. She also proposed a spelling match between the fourth grade at Davis School and the Mississippi Legislature, who went through with it; and that told the Legislature.   5

Her standards were very high and of course inflexible, her authority was total; why *wouldn't* this carry with it a brass bell that could be heard ringing for a block in all directions? That bell belonged to the figure of Miss Duling as though it grew directly out of her right arm, as wings grew out of an angel or a tail out of the devil. When we entered, marching, into her school,   6 by strictest teaching, surveillance, and order we learned grammar, arithmetic, spelling, reading, writing, and geography; and she, not the teachers, I believe, wrote out the examinations: need I tell you, they were "hard."

7   She's not the only teacher who has influenced me, but Miss Duling, in some fictional shape or form, has stridden into a larger part of my work than I'd realized until now. She emerges in my perhaps inordinate number of schoolteacher characters. I loved those characters in the writing. But I did not, in life, love Miss Duling. I was afraid of her high-arched bony nose, her eyebrows lifted in half-circles above her hooded, brilliant eyes, and of the Kentucky R's in her speech, and the long steps she took in her hightop shoes. I did nothing but fear her bearing-down authority, and did not connect this (as of course we were meant to) with our own need or desire to learn, perhaps because I already had this wish, and did not need to be driven.

8   She was impervious to lies or foolish excuses or the insufferable plea of not knowing any better. She wasn't going to have any frills, either, at Davis School. When a new governor moved into the mansion, he sent his daughter to Davis School; her name was Lady Rachel Conner. Miss Duling at once called the governor to the telephone and told him, "She'll be plain Rachel here."

9   Miss Duling dressed as plainly as a Pilgrim on a Thanksgiving poster we made in the schoolroom, in a longish black-and-white checked gingham dress, a bright thick wool sweater the red of a railroad lantern—she'd knitted it herself—black stockings and her narrow elegant feet in black hightop shoes with heels you could hear coming, rhythmical as a parade drum down the hall. Her silky black curly hair was drawn back out of curl, fastened by high combs, and knotted behind. She carried her spectacles on a gold chain hung around her neck. Her gaze was in general sweeping, then suddenly at the point of concentration upon you. With a swing of her bell that took her whole right arm and shoulder, she rang it, militant and impartial, from the head of the front steps of Davis School when it was time for us all to line up, girls on one side, boys on the other. We were to march past her into the school building, while the fourth-grader she nabbed played time on the piano, mostly to a tune we could have skipped to, but we didn't skip into Davis School.

10   Little recess (open-air exercises) and big recess (lunch-boxes

from home opened and eaten on the grass, on the girls' side and the boys' side of the yard) and dismissal were also regulated by Miss Duling's bell. The bell was also used to catch us off guard with fire drill.

It was examinations that drove my wits away, as all emergen-   11
cies do. Being expected to measure up was paralysing. I failed to make 100 on my spelling exam because I missed one word and that word was "uncle." Mother, as I knew she would, took it personally. "You couldn't spell *uncle?* When you've got those five perfectly splendid uncles in West Virginia? What would *they* say to that?"

It was never that Mother wanted me to beat my classmates   12
in grades; what she wanted was for me to have my answers right. It was unclouded perfection I was up against.

My father was much more tolerant of possible error. He only   13
said, as he steeply and impeccably sharpened my pencils on examination morning, "Now just keep remembering: the examinations were made out for the *average* student to pass. That's the majority. And if the majority can pass, think how much better *you* can do."

I looked to my mother, who had her own opinions about the   14
majority. My father wished to treat it with respect, she didn't. I'd been born left-handed, but the habit was broken when I entered the first grade in Davis School. My father had insisted. He pointed out that everything in life had been made for the convenience of right-handed people, because they were the majority, and he often used "what the majority wants" as a criterion for what was for the best. My mother said she could not promise him, could not promise him at all, that I wouldn't stutter as a consequence. Mother had been born left-handed too; her family consisted of five left-handed brothers, a left-handed mother, and a father who could write with both hands at the same time, also backwards and forwards and upside down, different words with each hand. She had been broken of it when she was young, and she said she used to stutter.

"But you still stutter," I'd remind her, only to hear her say   15
loftily, "You should have heard me when I was your age."

In my childhood days, a great deal of stock was put, in gen   16
eral, in the value of doing well in school. Both daily newspapers in Jackson saw the honor roll as news and published the lists,

and the grades, of all the honor students. The city fathers gave the children who made the honor roll free season tickets to the baseball games down at the grandstand. We all attended and all worshiped some player on the Jackson Senators: I offered up my 100's in arithmetic and spelling, reading and writing, attendance and, yes, deportment—I must have been a prig!—to Red McDermott, the third baseman. And our happiness matched that of knowing Miss Duling was on her summer vacation, far, far away in Kentucky.

Vocabulary

To get the most out of reading this essay, you should have a working understanding of the words listed below. Following each word is a parenthetical reference, indicating the paragraph in which the word is used, as well as a definition for the word. Go back and look at the sentence in which the word appears, and see how the definition applies. To help you make this word a part of your active vocabulary, write a sentence of your own using the word in the space provided.

craving (1):   strong desire

_____

_____

civic (5):   concerning a town or city

_____

_____

compliance (5):   submission, obeying a command

_____

_____

inordinate (7):   excessive

_____

_____

impervious (8):   unaffected by

_____

_____

militant (9):   combative

_____

_____

impartial (9):   fair, without favoritism

_____

_____

deportment (16):   conduct

_____

_____

Understanding the Essay

1. Why does Welty say that Miss Duling "was a dedicated schoolteacher who denied herself all she might have done or whatever other way she might have lived"? What brought Miss Duling into teaching?

2. What made Miss Duling such a figure of authority for Welty?

3. How has Miss Duling's influence carried beyond the walls of Davis School?

4. Describe Miss Duling's appearance. How might her appearance add to her authority?

5. Was Welty the kind of student that Miss Duling wanted in Davis School? How are Welty's mother and Miss Duling alike in their educational philosophies?

6. How were good students rewarded in Jackson?

Exploring the Theme:
Discussion and Writing

1. What do you want to achieve in education, beyond just passing classes? What influence have your parents had on your education? What influence have your early teachers and principals had on your education? Explain.

2. Describe a teacher or principal from your elementary school who was an authority figure for you. What made him or her an authority figure? How do you think he or she influenced your life?

WRITING SUGGESTIONS FOR "EVERYDAY HEROES AND ROLE MODELS"

1. Write an essay in which you define the term "everyday hero." How does the everyday hero differ from those heroes of classical mythology or ancient lore? Do you think "everyday hero" is a contradictory term? Is it a useful term? Explain.

2. Of what value is it to read about and discuss heroes and role models? What can our heroes and role models tell us, for better or worse, about ourselves and the society in which we live? Write an essay in which you discuss the relationship between ourselves and our society.

3. Write an essay discussing a hero or role model in your life. What specifically did this person do that won your admiration? How are you a different person because of the influence? Did this person figure prominently in an event or sequence of events that represent a turning point in your life or gave you a new outlook or goal?

4. For many of us, our parents were our greatest role models as we grew up, and they remain so today. If one or both of your parents fulfilled this role, write an essay explaining how.

5. Are you, or have you been, a hero of some kind? How and why? Was your heroism of the more traditional sort, or were you what you'd consider an everyday hero? Do you understand your heroism and what motivated it? Write an essay explaining the circumstances of your actions.

6. People who commit heroic acts (e.g., save a drowning person, come to the aid of a comrade in battle) often claim they are not heroes, that they did nothing out of the ordinary. Should we regard such responses as the truth or false modesty? Could it be that such people really lead extraordinary lives, that their act was a natural outgrowth of their concern for others? Write an essay in which you explore acts of uncommon valor for what they can tell us about our backgrounds, our upbringing, and our values.

7. Write an essay about a teacher or coach who made a difference in your life. How might you be different today if this person had not come into your life? You may want to review the essays by Welty and Gage before you begin to gather your information and develop your own essay.

4

RELATIONSHIPS

It is no exaggeration to say that the relationships that each of us has, from the casual to the intimate, define us. We regard our relationships with others as a fundamental part of our lives. If we can forge strong relationships, we feel good about ourselves; if not, we have self-doubts about our ability to get along and our larger motives and goals in life. Consequently, most of us work pretty hard at making our relationships better. We worry about our true feelings, as well as the honesty of those we encounter, the ways that we perceive those around us and, in turn, are perceived by them. When we talk about relationships, we most often speak about good, healthy, meaningful, and durable ones and what it takes to bring them about.

Most people would admit that at the center of any good relationship is good communication—people need to understand each other if they are to build friendship and intimacy. So often, however, try as we might to communicate effectively, we are blocked by obstacles and forces that we are neither aware of nor able to overcome. Most often these obstacles and forces are thought to arise from the differences in roles and perceptions we inherit from our culture. Consequently, it is necessary to understand those forces before we can make progress in developing relationships. The essays and short story in this section examine some of the reasons why it is difficult for people, especially opposite sexes, to communicate with each other. The authors of these selections discuss the changing dating scene and how it is now more acceptable for women to ask men out; the different ways that boys and girls play together and their objectives in playing; and how children's books institutionalize or fail to represent the reality of relationships between parents and their children. Finally, we turn to a tragic and ironic short story that reminds us of what can happen when communication between the sexes fails or is not allowed to flourish.

WILL YOU GO OUT WITH ME?

Laura Ullman

Laura Ullman was a single student when she wrote the following article for Newsweek. *She has since married and had a daughter, but her struggles, successes, and failures in the dating scene inspired the article. Ullman continues to write about the comic side of everyday life in Los Angeles, California.*

Preparing to Read

Dating is always a difficult exercise. Asking another person for a date is nerve-racking, and going on the actual date can be worse—especially if you don't get along with your date very well. For Ullman, dating was even more difficult because the rules were changing but no new guidelines had been established. Could she ask a young man for a date and still be considered respectable? This is just one of the issues she ponders in the following selection. While you're reading, think about the dating scene in your school. Are women comfortable asking men out? Has dating changed a lot since Ullman wrote her article?

1   Every day I anxiously wait for you to get to class. I can't wait for us to smile at each other and say good morning. Some days, when you arrive only seconds before the lecture begins, I'm incredibly impatient. Instead of reading the *Daily Cal*, I anticipate your footsteps from behind and listen for your voice. Today is one of your late days. But I don't mind, because after a month of desperately desiring to ask you out, today I'm going to. Encourage me, because letting you know I like you seems as risky to me as skydiving into the sea.

2   I know that dating has changed dramatically in the past few years, and for many women, asking men out is not at all daring.

But I was raised in a traditional European household where simply the thought of my asking you out spells "naughty." Growing up, I learned that men call, ask and pay for the date. During my three years at Berkeley, I have learned otherwise. Many Berkeley women have brightened their social lives by taking the initiative with men. My girlfriends insist that it's essential for women to participate more in the dating process. "I can't sit around and wait anymore," my former roommate once blurted out. "Hard as it is, I have to ask guys out—if I want to date at all!" Wonderful. More women are inviting men out, and men say they are delighted, often relieved, that dating no longer depends solely on their willingness and courage to take the first step. Then why am I digging my nails into my hand trying to muster up courage?

I keep telling myself to relax since dating is less stereotypical and more casual today. A college date means anything from studying together to sex. Most of my peers prefer casual dating anyway because it's cheaper and more comfortable. Students have fewer anxiety attacks when they ask somebody to play tennis than when they plan a formal dinner date. They enjoy last-minute "let's make dinner together" dates because they not only avoid hassling with attire and transportation but also don't have time to agonize.

Casual dating also encourages people to form healthy friendships prior to starting relationships. My roommate and her boyfriend were friends for four months before their chemistries clicked. They went to movies and meals and often got together with mutual friends. They alternated paying the dinner check. "He was like a girlfriend," my roommate once laughed—blushing. Men and women relax and get to know each other more easily through such friendships. Another friend of mine believes that casual dating is improving people's social lives. When she wants to let a guy know she is interested, she'll say, "Hey, let's go get a yogurt."

Who pays for it? My past dates have taught me some things: you don't know if I'll get the wrong idea if you treat me for dinner, and I don't know if I'll deny you pleasure or offend you by insisting on paying for myself. John whipped out his wallet on our first date before I could suggest we go Dutch. During our after-dinner stroll, he told me he was interested in dating me on a steady basis. After I explained I was more interested in a friendship, he told me he would have understood had I paid for my dinner. "I've practically stopped treating women on dates," he said defensively. "It's safer and more comfortable when we each pay for ourselves." John had assumed that because I graciously accepted his treat, I was in love. He was mad at himself for treating me, and I regretted allowing him to.

6   Larry, on the other hand, blushed when I offered to pay for my meal on our first date. I unzipped my purse and flung out my wallet, and he looked at me as if I had addressed him in a foreign language. Hesitant, I asked politely, "How much do I owe you?" Larry muttered, "Uh, uh, you really don't owe me anything, but if you insist . . ." Insist, I thought, I only offered. To Larry, my gesture was a suggestion of rejection.

7   Men and women alike are confused about who should ask whom out and who should pay. While I treasure my femininity, adore gentlemen and delight in a traditional formal date, I also believe in equality. I am grateful for casual dating because it has improved my social life immensely by making me an active participant in the process. Now I can not only receive roses but can also give them. Casual dating is a worthwhile adventure because it works. No magic formula guarantees "he" will say yes. I just have to relax, be Laura and ask him out in an unthreatening manner. If my friends are right, he'll be flattered.

8   Sliding into his desk, he taps my shoulder and says, "Hi, Laura, what's up?"

9   "Good morning," I answer with nervous chills. "Hey, how would you like to have lunch after class on Friday?"

10   "You mean after the midterm?" he says encouragingly. "I'd love to go to lunch with you."

11   "We have a date," I smile.

Vocabulary

To get the most out of reading this essay, you should have a working understanding of the words listed below. Following each word is a parenthetical reference, indicating the paragraph in which the word is used, as well as a definition for the word. Go back and look at the sentence in which the word appears, and see how the definition applies. To help you make this word a part of your active vocabulary, write a sentence of your own using the word in the space provided.

initiative (2): first step

_____

_____

blurted (2): spoke suddenly

_____

_____

muster (2): gather, build up

_____

_____

hassling (3): worrying, bothering

_____

_____

go Dutch (5): split the cost

_____

_____

femininity (7): female qualities

_____

_____

Understanding the Essay

1. Why do Ullman's girlfriends insist it's essential for women to participate in the dating process?
2. Why is Ullman digging her nails into her hand, trying to muster her courage?
3. What are some of the advantages of casual dating? What do you think are some of the disadvantages?
4. Ullman sends the wrong message to two men, once by not offering to go Dutch, once by offering to. Why was John angry at himself and not her? Why did Larry feel rejected?

5. Who should pay for Laura's lunch date with her friend? Explain your answer.

Exploring the Theme:
Discussion and Writing

1. How do you feel about casual dating, as opposed to what Ullman calls traditional formal dating? If you were asked out on a "casual" date, what would your expectations be?

2. Ullman writes, "While I treasure my femininity, adore gentlemen and delight in a traditional formal date, I also believe in equality." Does a traditional date, where the male pays for everything, have a place in a truly equal society?

NOT ALL MEN
ARE SLY FOXES

Armin A. Brott

Armin Brott is a freelance writer who lives in Berkeley, California. He has a small daughter, so he gets to read a lot of children's books. Some of the things he saw in her books disturbed him, so he wrote the following article for Newsweek.

Preparing to Read

A children's story usually has a moral that is easily understood. But the moral is only part of the story, and many people object to some of the other messages in "classic" stories like "Little Black Sambo" and "Mother Goose"—messages that imply women and minority groups are inferior. Brott, as a father, brings a different point of view to the debate. In the following selection he argues that most children's stories show fathers as poor parents, and though this negative image is usually overlooked, it can have a big impact on children's thinking. Think back to the books you read as a child—which ones do you remember the best? Why do you remember them? What kind of influence did they have on you?

If you thought your child's bookshelves were finally free of   1
openly (and not so openly) discriminatory materials, you'd
better check again. In recent years groups of concerned parents have persuaded textbook publishers to portray more accurately the roles that women and minorities play in shaping our country's history and culture. "Little Black Sambo" has all but disappeared from library and bookstore shelves; feminist fairy tales by such authors as Jack Zipes have, in many homes, replaced the more traditional (and obviously sexist) fairy tales. Richard Scarry, one of the most popular children's writers, has

reissued new versions of some of his classics; now female animals are pictured doing the same jobs as male animals. Even the terminology has changed: males and females are referred to as mail "carriers" or "firefighters."

2   There is, however, one very large group whose portrayal continues to follow the same stereotypical lines as always: fathers. The evolution of children's literature didn't end with "Goodnight Moon" and "Charlotte's Web." My local public library, for example, previews 203 new children's picture books (for the under-5 set) each *month*. Many of these books make a very conscious effort to take women characters out of the kitchen and the nursery and give them professional jobs and responsibilities.

3   Despite this shift, mothers are by and large still shown as the primary caregivers and, more important, as the primary nurturers of their children. Men in these books—if they're shown at all—still come home late after work and participate in the child rearing by bouncing baby around for five minutes before putting the child to bed.

4   In one of my 2-year-old daughter's favorite books, "Mother Goose and the Sly Fox," "retold" by Chris Conover, a single mother (Mother Goose) of seven tiny goslings is pitted against (and naturally outwits) the sly Fox. Fox, a neglectful and presumably unemployed single father, lives with his filthy, hungry pups in a grimy hovel littered with the bones of their previous meals. Mother Goose, a successful entrepreneur with a thriving lace business, still finds time to serve her goslings homemade soup in pretty porcelain cups. The story is funny and the illustrations marvelous, but the unwritten message is that women take better care of their kids and men have nothing else to do but hunt down and kill innocent, law-abiding geese.

5   The majority of other children's classics perpetuate the same negative stereotypes of fathers. Once in a great while, people complain about "Babar's" colonialist slant (little jungle-dweller finds happiness in the big city and brings civilization—and fine clothes—to his backyard village). But I've never heard anyone ask why, after his mother is killed by the evil hunter, Babar is automatically an "orphan." Why can he find comfort only in the arms of another female? Why do Arthur's and Celeste's mothers come alone to the city to fetch their children? Don't the fathers care? Do they even have fathers? I need my answers ready for when my daughter asks.

I recently spent an entire day on the children's floor of the 6
local library trying to find out whether these same negative
stereotypes are found in the more recent classics-to-be. The librarian gave me a list of the 20 most popular contemporary
picture books and I read every one of them. Of the 20, seven
don't mention a parent at all. Of the remaining 13, four portray
fathers as much less loving and caring than mothers. In "Little
Gorilla," we are told that the little gorilla's "mother loves him"
and we see Mama gorilla giving her little one a warm hug. On
the next page we're also told that his "father loves him," but in
the illustration, father and son aren't even touching. Six of the
remaining nine books mention or portray mothers as the only
parent, and only three of the 20 have what could be considered
"equal" treatment of mothers and fathers.

The same negative stereotypes also show up in literature 7
aimed at the *parents* of small children. In "What to Expect the
First Year," the authors answer almost every question the parents of a newborn or toddler could have in the first year of their
child's life. They are meticulous in alternating between references to boys and girls. At the same time, they refer almost
exclusively to "mother" or "mommy." Men, and their feelings
about parenting, are relegated to a nine-page chapter just before
the recipe section.

Unfortunately, it's still true that, in our society, women do 8
the bulk of the child care, and that thanks to men abandoning
their families, there are too many single mothers out there. Nevertheless, to say that portraying fathers as unnurturing or completely absent is simply "a reflection of reality" is unacceptable.
If children's literature only reflected reality, it would be like
prime-time TV and we'd have books filled with child abusers,
wife beaters and criminals.

Young children believe what they hear—especially from a 9
parent figure. And since, for the first few years of a child's life,
adults select the reading material, children's literature should be
held to a high standard. Ignoring men who share equally in raising their children, and continuing to show nothing but part-time
or no-time fathers is only going to create yet another generation
of men who have been told since boyhood—albeit subtly—that
mothers are the truer parents and that fathers play, at best, a
secondary role in the home. We've taken major steps to root out
discrimination in what our children read. Let's finish the job.

Vocabulary

To get the most out of reading this essay, you should have a working understanding of the words listed below. Following each word is a parenthetical reference, indicating the paragraph in which the word is used, as well as a definition for the word. Go back and look at the sentence in which the word appears, and see how the definition applies. To help you make this word a part of your active vocabulary, write a sentence of your own using the word in the space provided.

discriminatory (1): biased, bigoted

---

feminist (1): pro-woman

---

sexist (1): biased language based on gender

---

terminology (1): jargon, names of things

---

stereotypical (2): clichéd, conforming

---

nurturer (3): caregiver

---

hovel (4): shack

_____

_____

entrepreneur (4): businessperson

_____

_____

perpetuate (5): maintain, prolong

_____

_____

colonialist (5): implying that Western culture is better than native culture

_____

_____

meticulous (7): careful, exacting

_____

_____

albeit (9): although

_____

_____

subtly (9): not obviously

_____

_____

Understanding the Essay

1. Why did Richard Scarry reissue some of his classic children's books?
2. What does a typical father do with children in a new children's book? What does he do in a classic children's book?

3. What question is Brott's daughter likely to ask him about Babar?

4. What high standards does Brott think children's literature should be held to? Do you agree with his standards?

5. What will happen, according to Brott, if children's books continue failing to reflect that many fathers spend time with their children?

Exploring the Theme:
Discussion and Writing

1. Brott claims that "to say that portraying fathers as unnurturing or completely absent is simply a 'reflection of reality' is unacceptable. If children's literature only re-flected reality, it would be like prime-time TV and we'd have books filled with child abusers, wife beaters and criminals." Do you agree with this statement? Why or why not?

2. What is your favorite children's book? Do you remember any stereotypical characters or discrimination against the characters? If you were to rewrite the story, how would you eliminate the problems?

IT BEGINS
AT THE BEGINNING

Deborah Tannen

Deborah Tannen teaches linguistics at Georgetown University. She studies the ways people communicate with one another and recently wrote You Just Don't Understand: Women and Men in Conversation, *a book that explores the reasons why men and women have trouble understanding members of the opposite sex.*

Preparing to Read

Have you ever had a conversation with a member of the opposite sex who seemed to be speaking a different language? It's a common problem, but people tend to pass it off as a joke. In this excerpt, Tannen sets out to prove that such miscommunication isn't a joke—it's a fact that the sexes have difficulty understanding each other. Men and women speak, in effect, different languages. Think about how you communicate with others. Do you fit Tannen's description for your sex? How do you think understanding these differences will help men and women communicate?

Even if they grow up in the same neighborhood, on the same block, or in the same house, girls and boys grow up in different worlds of words. Others talk to them differently and expect and accept different ways of talking from them. Most important, children learn how to talk, how to have conversations, not only from their parents but from their peers. After all, if their parents have a foreign or regional accent, children do not emulate it: they learn to speak with the pronunciation of the region where they grow up. Anthropologists Daniel Maltz and Ruth Borker summarize research showing that boys and girls

1

have very different ways of talking to their friends. Although they often play together, boys and girls spend most of their time playing in same-sex groups. And, although some of the activities they play at are similar, their favorite games are different, and their ways of using language in their games are separated by a world of difference.

2   Boys tend to play outside, in large groups that are hierarchically structured. Their groups have a leader who tells others what to do and how to do it, and resists doing what other boys propose. It is by giving orders and making them stick that high status is negotiated. Another way boys achieve status is to take center stage by telling stories and jokes, and by sidetracking or challenging the stories and jokes of others. Boys' games have winners and losers and elaborate systems of rules that are frequently the subjects of arguments. Finally, boys are frequently heard to boast of their skill and argue about who is best at what.

3   Girls, on the other hand, play in small groups or in pairs; the center of a girl's social life is a best friend. Within the group, intimacy is key: Differentiation is measured by relative closeness. In their most frequent games, such as jump rope and hopscotch, everyone gets a turn. Many of their activities (such as playing house) do not have winners or losers. Though some girls are certainly more skilled than others, girls are expected not to boast about it, or show that they think they are better than others. Girls don't give orders; they express their preferences as suggestions, and suggestions are likely to be accepted. Whereas boys say, "Gimme that!" and "Get outta here!" girls say, "Let's do this," and "How about doing that?" Anything else is put down as "bossy." They don't grab center stage—they don't want it—so they don't challenge each other directly. And much of the time, they simply sit together and talk. Girls are not accustomed to jockeying for status in an obvious way; they are more concerned that they be liked.

4   Gender differences in ways of talking have been described by researchers observing children as young as three. Amy Sheldon videotaped three- to four-year-old boys and girls playing in threesomes at a day-care center. She compared two groups of three—one of boys, one of girls—that got into fights about the same play item: a plastic pickle. Though both groups fought over the same thing, the dynamics by which they negotiated their conflicts were different. In addition to illustrating some of

the patterns I have just described, Sheldon's study also demonstrates the complexity of these dynamics.

While playing in the kitchen area of the day-care center, a little girl named Sue wanted the pickle that Mary had, so she argued that Mary should give it up because Lisa, the third girl, wanted it. This led to a conflict about how to satisfy Lisa's (invented) need. Mary proposed a compromise, but Sue protested:

MARY: I cut it in half. One for Lisa, one for me, one for me.
SUE: But, Lisa wants a *whole* pickle!

Mary comes up with another creative compromise, which Sue also rejects:

MARY: Well, it's a whole *half* pickle.
SUE: No, it isn't.
MARY: Yes, it is, a whole *half* pickle.
SUE: *I'll* give her a whole half. I'll give her a *whole whole*. I gave her a whole one.

At this point, Lisa withdraws from the alliance with Sue, who satisfies herself by saying, "I'm pretending I gave you one."

On another occasion, Sheldon videotaped three boys playing in the same kitchen play area, and they too got into a fight about the plastic pickle. When Nick saw that Kevin had the pickle, he demanded it for himself:

NICK: [Screams] Kevin, but the, oh, I *have* to cut! I want to cut it! It's mine!

Like Sue, Nick involved the third child in his effort to get the pickle:

NICK: [Whining to Joe] Kevin is not letting me cut the pickle.
JOE: Oh, I know! I can pull it away from him and give it back to you. That's an idea!

The boys' conflict, which lasted two and a half times longer than the girls', then proceeded as a struggle between Nick and Joe on the one hand and Kevin on the other.

In comparing the boys' and girls' pickle fights, Sheldon points out that, for the most part, the girls mitigated the conflict and preserved harmony by compromise and evasion. Conflict was more prolonged among the boys, who used more insistence, appeals to rules, and threats of physical violence. However, to say that these little girls and boys used *more* of one strategy or another is not to say that they didn't use the other strategies at all. For example, the boys did attempt compromise, and the girls did attempt physical force. The girls, like the boys, were struggling for control of their play. When Sue says by mistake, "*I'll* give her a whole half," then quickly corrects herself to say, "I'll give her a *whole whole*," she reveals that it is not really the size of the portion that is important to her, but who gets to serve it.

8   While reading Sheldon's study, I noticed that whereas both Nick and Sue tried to get what they wanted by involving a third child, the alignments they created with the third child, and the dynamics they set in motion, were fundamentally different. Sue appealed to Mary to fulfill someone else's desire; rather than saying that *she* wanted the pickle, she claimed that Lisa wanted it. Nick asserted his own desire for the pickle, and when he couldn't get it on his own, he appealed to Joe to get it for him. Joe then tried to get the pickle by force. In both these scenarios, the children were enacting complex lines of affiliation.

9   Joe's strong-arm tactics were undertaken not on his own behalf but, chivalrously, on behalf of Nick. By making an appeal in a whining voice, Nick positioned himself as one-down in a hierarchical structure, framing himself as someone in need of protection. When Sue appealed to Mary to relinquish her pickle, she wanted to take the one-up position of serving food. She was fighting not for the right to *have* the pickle, but for the right to *serve* it. (This reminded me of the women who said they'd become professors in order to teach.) But to accomplish her goal, Sue was depending on Mary's desire to fulfill others' needs.

10   This study suggests that boys and girls both want to get their way, but they tend to do so differently. Though social norms encourage boys to be openly competitive and girls to be openly cooperative, different situations and activities can result in different ways of behaving. Marjorie Harness Goodwin compared boys and girls engaged in two task-oriented activities: The boys were making slingshots in preparation for a fight, and the girls were making rings. She found that the boys' group was hierarchical: The leader told the others what to do and how to do it. The girls' group was egalitarian: Everyone made suggestions and tended to accept the suggestions of others. But observing the girls in a different activity—playing house—Goodwin found that they too adopted hierarchical structures: The girls who

played mothers issued orders to the girls playing children, who in turn sought permission from their play-mothers. Moreover, a girl who was a play-mother was also a kind of manager of the game. This study shows that girls know how to issue orders and operate in a hierarchical structure, but they don't find that mode of behavior appropriate when they engage in task activities with their peers. They do find it appropriate in parent-child relationships, which they enjoy practicing in the form of play.

These worlds of play shed light on the world views of women   11
and men in relationships. The boys' play illuminates why men would be on the lookout for signs they are being put down or told what to do. The chief commodity that is bartered in the boys' hierarchical world is status, and the way to achieve and maintain status is to give orders and get others to follow them. A boy in a low-status position finds himself being pushed around. So boys monitor their relations for subtle shifts in status by keeping track of who's giving orders and who's taking them.

These dynamics are not the ones that drive girls' play. The   12
chief commodity that is bartered in the girls' community is intimacy. Girls monitor their friendships for subtle shifts in alliance, and they seek to be friends with popular girls. Popularity is a kind of status, but it is founded on connection. It also places popular girls in a bind. By doing field work in a junior high school, Donna Eder found that popular girls were paradoxically—and inevitably—disliked. Many girls want to befriend popular girls, but girls' friendships must necessarily be limited, since they entail intimacy rather than large group activities. So a popular girl must reject the overtures of most of the girls who seek her out—with the result that she is branded "stuck up."

The Key Is Understanding

If adults learn their ways of speaking as children growing up in   13
separate social worlds of peers, then conversation between women and men is cross-cultural communication. Although each style is valid on its own terms, misunderstandings arise because the styles are different. Taking a cross-cultural approach to male-female conversations makes it possible to explain why dissatisfactions are justified without accusing anyone of being wrong or crazy.

14   Learning about style differences won't make them go away, but it can banish mutual mystification and blame. Being able to understand why our partners, friends, and even strangers behave the way they do is a comfort, even if we still don't see things the same way. It makes the world into more familiar territory. And having others understand why we talk and act as we do protects us from the pain of their puzzlement and criticism.

15   In discussing her novel *The Temple of My Familiar,* Alice Walker explained that a woman in the novel falls in love with a man because she sees in him "a giant ear." Walker went on to remark that although people may think they are falling in love because of sexual attraction or some other force, "really what we're looking for is someone to be able to hear us."

16   We all want, above all, to be heard—but not merely to be heard. We want to be understood—heard for what we think we are saying, for what we know we meant. With increased understanding of the ways women and men use language should come a decrease in frequency of the complaint "You just don't understand."

Vocabulary

To get the most out of reading this essay, you should have a working understanding of the words listed below. Following each word is a parenthetical reference, indicating the paragraph in which the word is used, as well as a definition for the word. Go back and look at the sentence in which the word appears, and see how the definition applies. To help you make this word part of your active vocabulary, write a sentence of your own using the word in the space provided.

anthropologists (1): scientists who study humans

_____

_____

hierarchically (2): containing high and low ranks

_____

_____

differentiation (3): making different, distinct

_____

_____

dynamics (4): flow of action

_____

_____

mitigated (7): reduced

_____

_____

affiliation (8): association, relationship to

_____

_____

chivalrously (9): gallantly

_____

_____

relinquish (9): release, let go

_____

_____

egalitarian (10): composed of equally valued members

_____

_____

commodity (11): thing to be sold or traded

_____

_____

paradoxically (12): as opposed to what one would expect

_____

_____

Understanding the Essay

1. Why wouldn't a boy enjoy playing house? Why wouldn't a girl enjoy playing baseball?
2. If a girl told another girl, "Get outta here!" how would her meaning differ from a boy's telling another boy the same thing?
3. Why did Joe help Nick get the pickle?
4. A common saying—at least in years past—is "A man is king of his castle." Why, according to Tannen, do men take control of their "castle"? Why do women let them?
5. According to Donna Eder, popular girls become disliked by most of their peers. To put it simply, popular girls become unpopular. How does this happen? Why doesn't it happen to boys?
6. Why should we learn about style differences between men and women?

Exploring the Theme: Discussion and Writing

1. Recall things that you've heard boys and girls say at playgrounds, ball fields, play groups, or other places where children can choose how they play together. Or visit a playground and listen to the children. What do they say to each other? Do their conversations and activities support Tannen's analysis?
2. What did you like to do with your best friend(s) when you were a child? Did you play like Tannen says a boy or girl is likely to play? If not, how did your play behavior differ from her generalizations?

THE STORY OF AN HOUR

Kate Chopin

Kate Chopin (1851–1904) lived in Louisiana after her marriage and her writing was influenced by the local Creole-Cajun culture. Chopin was an early feminist whose work was controversial when it was published. Her first novel, The Awakening, *angered many people by describing a Southern woman's sexual awakening. It is only recently that she has been recognized for her literary talent.*

Preparing to Read

Kate Chopin lived in an era when marriage could be a trap because there were no options for escape. Women in particular had little control over their lives. Once they had married and started a family, their futures as wives and mothers were unalterably set. The situation described in "The Story of an Hour" contrasts sharply with today's society, where many people say that marriage and divorce are taken too lightly. Imagine a life where you had few, if any, options for your future. How do you think you would react?

K nowing that Mrs. Mallard was afflicted with a heart 1
trouble, great care was taken to break to her as gently
as possible the news of her husband's death.

It was her sister Josephine who told her, in broken sentences; 2
veiled hints that revealed in half concealing. Her husband's
friend Richards was there, too, near her. It was he who had been
in the newspaper office when intelligence of the railroad disaster was received, with Brently Mallard's name leading the list of
"killed." He had only taken the time to assure himself of its truth
by a second telegram, and had hastened to forestall any less
careful, less tender friend in bearing the sad message.

3   She did not hear the story as many women have heard the same, with a paralyzed inability to accept its significance. She wept at once, with sudden, wild abandonment, in her sister's arms. When the storm of grief had spent itself she went away to her room alone. She would have no one follow her.

4   There stood, facing the open window, a comfortable, roomy armchair. Into this she sank, pressed down by a physical exhaustion that haunted her body and seemed to reach into her soul.

5   She could see in the open square before her house the tops of trees that were all aquiver with the new spring life. The delicious breath of rain was in the air. In the street below a peddler was crying his wares. The notes of a distant song which some one was singing reached her faintly, and countless sparrows were twittering in the eaves.

6   There were patches of blue sky showing here and there through the clouds that had met and piled one above the other in the west facing her window.

7   She sat with her head thrown back upon the cushion of the chair, quite motionless, except when a sob came up into her throat and shook her, as a child who has cried itself to sleep continues to sob in its dreams.

8   She was young, with a fair, calm face, whose lines bespoke repression and even a certain strength. But now there was a dull stare in her eyes, whose gaze was fixed away off yonder on one of those patches of blue sky. It was not a glance of reflection, but rather indicated a suspension of intelligent thought.

9   There was something coming to her and she was waiting for it, fearfully. What was it? She did not know; it was too subtle and elusive to name. But she felt it, creeping out of the sky, reaching toward her through the sounds, the scents, the color that filled the air.

10   Now her bosom rose and fell tumultuously. She was beginning to recognize this thing that was approaching to possess her, and she was striving to beat it back with her will—as powerless as her two white slender hands would have been.

11   When she abandoned herself a little whispered word escaped her slightly parted lips. She said it over and over under her breath: "free, free, free!" The vacant stare and the look of terror that had followed it went from her eyes. They stayed keen and bright. Her pulses beat fast, and the coursing blood warmed and relaxed every inch of her body.

She did not stop to ask if it were or were not a monstrous joy   12
that held her. A clear and exalted perception enabled her to
dismiss the suggestion as trivial.

She knew that she would weep again when she saw the kind,   13
tender hands folded in death; the face that had never looked
save with love upon her, fixed and gray and dead. But she saw
beyond that bitter moment a long procession of years to come
that would belong to her absolutely. And she opened and spread
her arms out to them in welcome.

There would be no one to live for her during those coming   14
years; she would live for herself. There would be no powerful
will bending hers in that blind persistence with which men and
women believe they have a right to impose a private will upon a
fellow-creature. A kind intention or a cruel intention made the
act seem no less a crime as she looked upon it in that brief
moment of illumination.

And yet she had loved him—sometimes. Often she had not.   15
What did it matter! What could love, the unsolved mystery,
count for in face of this possession of self-assertion which she
suddenly recognized as the strongest impulse of her being!

"Free! Body and soul free!" she kept whispering.   16

Josephine was kneeling before the closed door with her lips   17
to the keyhole, imploring for admission. "Louise, open the door!
I beg; open the door—you will make yourself ill. What are you
doing, Louise? For heaven's sake open the door."

"Go away. I am not making myself ill." No; she was drinking   18
in a very elixir of life through that open window.

Her fancy was running riot along those days ahead of her.   19
Spring days, and summer days, and all sorts of days that would
be her own. She breathed a quick prayer that life might be long.
It was only yesterday she had thought with a shudder that life
might be long.

She arose at length and opened the door to her sister's impor-   20
tunities. There was a feverish triumph in her eyes, and she carried herself unwittingly like a goddess of Victory. She clasped
her sister's waist, and together they descended the stairs. Richards stood waiting for them at the bottom.

Some one was opening the front door with a latchkey. It was   21
Brently Mallard who entered, a little travel-stained, composedly
carrying his grip-sack and umbrella. He had been far from the
scene of the accident, and did not even know there had been one.

He stood amazed at Josephine's piercing cry; at Richards' quick motion to screen him from the view of his wife.

22 But Richards was too late.

23 When the doctors came they said she had died of heart disease—of joy that kills.

Vocabulary

To get the most out of reading this essay, you should have a working understanding of the words listed below. Following each word is a parenthetical reference, indicating the paragraph in which the word is used, as well as a definition for the word. Go back and look at the sentence in which the word appears, and see how the definition applies. To help you make this word a part of your active vocabulary, write a sentence of your own using the word in the space provided.

afflicted (1): troubled, made ill

_____

_____

veiled (2): hidden, obscured

_____

_____

paralyzed (3): unable to move

_____

_____

abandonment (3): freely, without inhibition

_____

_____

aquiver (5): quivering, shaking

_____

_____

bespoke (8): told of

_____

_____

tumultuously (10): rapidly, violently

_____

_____

coursing (11): flowing

_____

_____

elixir (18): potion

_____

_____

Understanding the Essay

1. How did Mrs. Mallard react to news of her husband's death?
2. What was approaching to possess Mrs. Mallard when she went up to her room alone?
3. How do you think other people viewed Brently and Louise's marriage? Why?
4. Why doesn't love matter to Mrs. Mallard anymore? Do you think it did matter to her once? Explain your answers.
5. Explain the irony in the last line of the story.

Exploring the Theme: Discussion and Writing

1. Delete the last three sentences from the story, and then re-write the ending using the following sentence as the first line in your new ending: "Richards shielded Brently from

view and pushed him out the door before Mrs. Mallard had even glanced downstairs." Justify your plot.

2. Some people today blame many of society's ills on the breakup of the traditional family. With divorce common, women in the work force, and unmarried people living together, today's marriages—and today's families—are very different from what they were in Chopin's time, and they often aren't as stable. Yet for Chopin, marriages were so stable as to be horribly confining. With this in mind, how would you balance family stability with freedom within a marriage? Is there a happy medium that society should strive for? How important do you think stable families are in our society?

WRITING SUGGESTIONS
FOR "RELATIONSHIPS"

1. Write an essay on dating attitudes and arrangements at your school. Is a woman comfortable asking a man out on a date at your school? How would it change the dating scene if only men were allowed to ask for dates?

2. Deborah Tannen refers to Alice Walker's *The Temple of My Familiar* and recalls a character in that novel as remarking that people mainly want to be heard, even in a romantic relationship. What are the broader implications of that remark? Do you agree with the statement? Write an essay on what you look for in a relationship and why.

3. When you meet someone you love, do you think you will want to marry? Why or why not? Or if you have married, why did you? How do you think you would have viewed marriage in Chopin's era, when the line "until death do us part" was taken quite literally? Write an essay in which you put forth your ideas on marriage.

4. People sometimes form relationships with others from different racial, ethnic, religious, social, economic, and political origins. If you have had such a relationship, what stresses, if any, did you or your partner experience? Did the problems originate between you, or were they imposed from outside the relationship? If all went smoothly, why do you think it did? Write an essay reflecting your experiences and your assessment of them.

5. Did the books you read as a child and young adult influence your understanding of relationships? How do you know? Is it possible that you were subtly or subconsciously influenced? If, on the other hand, you remember having been influenced by specific stories, characters, and situations, write an essay on the nature of the influence. Before writing, you may want to review the book that affected you.

5

FRIENDS

Just about everyone needs friends. As a child, teenager, college student, parent, professional, retiree, and elderly person, at all stages of our lives we need the love, support, understanding, and companionship of special individuals whom we trust. We make friends through circumstance, common interest, inexplicable attraction or connection, and sometimes simply by accident. Friends care for, sometimes hurt, listen to, nurture, challenge, and—above all—accept each other.

One of the most common settings where intimacies are developed is academe. People end up living with or at least spending a lot of time with one another, perhaps to a certain extent replacing families left behind with new systems of peer support. Because college life provides countless opportunities for learning, socializing, and exchanging personal as well as intellectual ideas, it is perfect for fostering profound, lasting attachments.

The following four essays address a variety of issues surrounding adult friendship. Jennifer Crichton and Howard Solomon, Jr., explore how and why friendships—sometimes desperate, sometimes very deliberate—are made in college. In "Death of a Friendship," Stephanie Mansfield takes a positive look at the healthy aspects of how women's adult friendships in particular evolve, mature, and end. Lastly, Elvira M. Franco describes her remarkable experience as an older woman going back to school and sharing with other women, of her depth and perspective, the ageless joy in rediscovering individual and collective self.

COLLEGE FRIENDS

Jennifer Crichton

Jennifer Crichton was born in 1957 in New York City. She attended Brown University and Barnard College, and spent a brief time in the Pacific Northwest. She has written a novel, Delivery: A Nurse-Midwife's Story, *and has contributed to several publications including* Ms., Mademoiselle, Outside, *and* Seventeen. *Crichton is currently working on a book about family therapy.*

Preparing to Read

Think back to the formation of some of your friendships. How did you meet your friends? What first interested you about them? When someone enters a new setting like college, such questions take on extra importance. To avoid a friendless existence, one must make friends—but how? Crichton gives a vivid account of the somewhat desperate loneliness that most people experience when they have no friends to fall back on, and she reveals the lessons she learned as her college friendships evolved and matured.

A s far as I'm concerned, the first semester away at college is possibly the single worst time to make friends. You'll make them, but you'll probably get it all wrong, through no fault of your own, for these are desperate hours.

Here's desperation: standing in a stadium-like cafeteria, I became convinced that a thousand students busy demolishing the contents of their trays were indifferent to me, and studying me with ill-disguised disdain at the same time. The ability to mentally grasp two opposing concepts is often thought of as the hallmark of genius. But I credit my mind's crazed elasticity to panic. Sitting alone at a table, I see the girl I'd met that morning in the showers. I was thrilled to see her. The need for a friend had become violent. Back at the dorm, I told her more about my family's peculiarities and my cataclysmic summer fling than I'd ever let slip before. All the right sympathetic looks crossed her face at all the right moments, whereupon I deduced that through the good graces of the housing department, I'd stumbled upon a soulmate. But what seemed like two minds mixing and matching on a cosmic plane was actually two lonely freshmen under the influence of unprecedented amounts of caffeine and emotional upheaval. This wasn't a meeting of souls. This was a talking jag of monumental proportions.

3   By February, my first friend and I passed each other in the hall with lame, bored smiles, and now I can't remember her name for the life of me. But that doesn't make me sad in the least.

4   Loneliness and the erosion of high school friendships through change and distance leave yawning gaps that beg to be filled. Yet, I never made a real friend by directly applying for the position of confidante or soulmate. I made my best friendships by accident, with instant intimacy marking none of them—it wasn't mutual loneliness that drew us together.

5   I met my best friend Jean in a film class when she said Alfred Hitchcock was overrated. I disagreed and we argued out of the building and into a lifelong friendship where we argue still. We became friends without meaning to, and took our intimacy step by step. Deliberate choice, not desperate need, moved us closer. Our friendship is so much a part of us now that it seems unavoidable that we should have become friends. But there was nothing inevitable about it. It's easy to imagine Jean saying to me in that classroom, "Hitchcock's a hack, you're a fool, and that's all I have to say." But that was not all she had to say. Which is why we're friends today. We always have more to say.

6   Friendship's value wasn't always clear to me. In the back of my mind, I believed that platonic friendships were a way of marking time until I struck the pay dirt of serious romance. I'd managed to digest many romantic notions by my first year of college, and chief among them was the idea that I'd meet the perfect lover who would be everything to me and make me complete. I saw plunging into a relationship as an advanced form of friendship, friendship plus sex. Lacking sex, platonic friendships seemed like a lower standard of living. As long as

my boyfriend offered me so much in one convenient package, women friends were superfluous. I thought I was the girl who had everything.

But what made that relationship more—the sex—made it a 7 bad replacement for friendship. Sexual tension charged the lines of communication between us. White noise crackled on the wire as desire and jealousy, fear of loss, and the need to be loved conspired to cloud and distort expression. Influenced by these powerful forces, I didn't always tell the truth. And on the most practical level, when my boyfriend and I broke up, I had lost more than my lover, I lost my best friend.

"You can't keep doing this," Suzanne told me later that same 8 year.

"What?" 9

"Start up our friendship every time your relationship falls 10 apart."

"I don't do that," I said. It was exactly what I did. 11

"Yes, you do, and I'm sick of it. I'm not second best. I'm 12 something entirely different."

Once you see that relationships and friendships are different 13 beasts, you'll never think of the two things as interchangeable again, with friendships as the inferior version. . . .

Friendships made in college set a standard for intimacy 14 other friendships are hard-pressed ever to approach. "I've become a narrow specialist in my friendships since graduation," says Pam. "With one friend I'll talk about work. With another, we're fitness fanatics together. But I don't really know much about them—how they live their lives, what they eat for breakfast, or if they eat breakfast at all, who their favorite uncle is, or when they got their contact lenses. I don't even know who they voted for for President. There will be a close connection in spots, but in general I feel as if I'm dealing with fractions of people. With my college friends, I feel I know them *whole*."

In college, there's time to reach that degree of intimacy. One 15 night, my best friend and I spent hours describing how our respective families celebrated Christmas. My family waited until everyone was awake and caffeinated before opening presents, hers charged out of bed to rip open the boxes before they could wipe the sleep out of their eyes. We were as self-righteous as religious fanatics, each convinced our own family was the only one that did Christmas right. Did we really spend an entire night on a subject like that? Did we really have that much time?

16 Operating on college time, my social life was unplanned and spontaneous. Keeping a light on in our rooms was a way of extending an invitation. We had time to hang out, to learn to tell the difference between ordinary crankiness and serious depressions in each other, and to follow the digressions that were at the heart of our friendships. But after college, we had to change, and in scheduling our free-form friendships we felt, at first, self-conscious and artificial.

17 When I had my first full-time job, I called my best friend to make a dinner date a week in advance. She was still in graduate school, and thought my planning was dire evidence that I'd tumbled into the pit of adult convention. "Why don't you have your girl call my girl and we'll set something up?" she asked. Heavy sarcasm. While the terms of the friendship have shifted from digressive, spontaneous socializing to a directed, scheduled style, and we all feel a certain sense of loss, the value of friendship has, if anything, increased.

18 If my college journals were ever published in the newspaper, the headline would most likely read, "FEM WRITER PENS GOO," but I did find something genuinely moving while reading through my hyper-perceptions the other day. Freshman year I'd written: "I am interested in everything. Nothing bores me. I hope I don't die before I can read everything, visit every place, and feel all there is to feel."

19 The sentiment would be a lot more poignant if I'd actually gone ahead and died young, but I find it moving anyway because it exemplifies what's good about being young: that you exist as the wide-eyed adventurer, fueled by the belief that you might amount to something and anything, and that your possibilities are endless. When I feel this way now, I'm usually half-dreaming in bed on a breezy Saturday morning. Or I'm with a college friend—someone with whom I'd pictured the future, back when the future was a dizzying haze viewed with the mind's eye from the vantage point of a smoky dorm room. Together we carved out life with words and hopes. When I'm with her now, I remember that feeling and experience it all over again, because there's still a lot of hazy future to imagine and life to carve. With my friend, I can look to my future and through my past and remember who I am.

Vocabulary

To get the most out of reading this essay, you should have a working understanding of the words listed below. Following each word is a parenthetical reference, indicating the paragraph in which the word is used, as well as a definition for the word. Go back and look at the sentence in which the word appears, and see how the definition applies. To help you make this word a part of your active vocabulary, write a sentence of your own using the word in the space provided.

disdain (2): contempt

_____

_____

cataclysmic (2): disastrous, destructive

_____

_____

talking jag (2): spree, unrestrained conversation

_____

_____

confidante (4): female person with whom one discusses problems or tells secrets

_____

_____

platonic (6): nonsexual, not romantic

_____

_____

superfluous (6): unneeded, unimportant

_____

_____

digressive (17): rambling, unorganized

_____

_____

poignant (19): intense, moving

_____

_____

Understanding the Essay

1. Why is the first semester at college the worst time to make friends?
2. Why did Crichton reveal such personal information so quickly to her new dorm friend? What happened to their friendship?
3. How did Crichton meet her best friend, Jean? Why does she say they might very well have ended up not befriending each other?
4. Why do lovers usually make lousy best friends?
5. How do college friendships differ from friendships made after college? Why are they different?
6. What feeling does Crichton relive when she visits college friends?

Exploring the Theme: Discussion and Writing

1. Crichton feels that the friendships she made in college were different from those she made at other times. Compare the friendships you made in school with friendships made in other circumstances, such as work or sports. How are the friendships different, if at all?
2. Describe how you met your closest friend. What first impressions did you have? How have your impressions changed as you've gotten to know him or her better?

DEATH OF A FRIENDSHIP

Stephanie Mansfield

Stephanie Mansfield was born in Philadelphia in 1950. She received her B.A. in English from Trinity College in Washington, D.C. As a newspaper journalist, Mansfield has written for the London Daily Mail, *the* London Daily Telegraph, *and the* Washington Post. *Her work has also appeared in the* Washington Post Magazine, Smithsonian, Esquire, Vogue, H.G., *and* Fame *magazine. In 1989, she took a leave of absence from the* Post *to write a biography commissioned by G. P. Putnam Sons on the life of tobacco heiress Doris Duke. Mansfield, who lives in Alexandria, Virginia, is a writer-at-large for* G.Q. *magazine.*

Preparing to Read

It's always heartwarming to hear or read about a senior citizen who has had a friend for decades. Whether the occasion is a bash thrown by one for the other's retirement, an annual fishing excursion that netted a huge fish, or whatever, the thought that a college, high school, or even childhood friendship can endure so well is comforting to us. Yet we know that most friendships don't last a lifetime—we change our priorities, our addresses, our interests—and a once close friend seems more distant all the time. In "Death of a Friendship," Mansfield emphasizes that ending friendships can be a positive as well as a negative experience. We may have regrets, but reevaluating or ending a friendship that's lost its closeness can be a productive step for both parties. Have you had a breakup with a friend that hurt you? What caused it?

F riendships, like love affairs, can run out of steam. As we   1
grow up, sometimes we grow apart. Recently, a good
friend and I parted company. There was no blowup, no

crashing dishes, no dramatic pie-in-the-face. Just a gradual loss of faith, compounded by geographical distance and the demands of our careers.

2   Women are often more prepared for the end of a love affair than for the demise of a friendship. We have endless advice books on how to recover when your lover's left you, but little seems to be said about *friends* who break each other's hearts. Maybe it's because we never think of our relationships with other women as being passionate or intense. But a woman can be as emotionally dependent on a friend as she is on a lover, and when the relationship ends, abruptly or not, it can leave both women hurt and angry, wondering what went wrong.

3   I've learned from experience that good friendships are based on a delicate balance. When friends are on a par, professionally and personally, it's easier for them to root for one another. It's taken me a long time to realize that not all my "friends" wish me well. Someone who wants what you have may not be able to handle your good fortune: If you find yourself apologizing for your hard-earned raise or soft-pedaling your long-awaited promotion, it's a sure sign that the friendship is off balance. Real friends are secure enough in their own lives to share each other's successes—not begrudge them.

4   On the other hand, that balance may be upset when two friends *do* become equals. A woman I know valued her friendship with an older mentor who saw her only in that subservient role. When my friend became increasingly successful, and ultimately reached the level of her mentor, the older woman abruptly ended the relationship. It was clear that she was not needed in the same capacity and could not make the adjustment.

5   Friend-shedding is a rite of passage and should be seen as a positive sign of growth. Certain life events tend to accelerate this process—say, the sudden appearance of a good-looking boyfriend or maybe even an engagement ring.

6   It's not uncommon for friends to try unconsciously to sabotage these new relationships if they feel threatened by them. But if that happens frequently, it may be time to reevaluate your friendship. A frank discussion can work wonders in this situation—in my case, I found out that my friend and I were not as close as we'd once been. My life had taken a different direction since we'd first met, and I'd expected her to follow with the same speed and enthusiasm. We finally agreed that we are not as

alike as we had once thought, nor should we be. We decided that it was time to take a leave of absence from each other.

Putting each other "on hold" indefinitely is hard, but some-   7
times it's the wisest thing to do. It never hurts to put some distance between friends if the relationship is strained, and it may even prevent a final, irrevocable break.

Sometimes, friendships can be renewed on their own: Unlike   8
love affairs, which demand a certain degree of commitment to stay alive, a little healthy neglect can be good for a friendship and may even lead to a reconciliation that might not otherwise have taken place. And if that happens, you'll likely find yourself in a more honest, and certainly more balanced, relationship. Laying a friendship out on the table like that isn't easy, but in the long run, it pays off. After all, knowing who *isn't* your friend is just as important as knowing who is.

Vocabulary

To get the most out of reading this essay, you should have a working understanding of the words listed below. Following each word is a parenthetical reference, indicating the paragraph in which the word is used, as well as a definition for the word. Go back and look at the sentence in which the word appears, and see how the definition applies. To help you make this word a part of your active vocabulary, write a sentence of your own using the word in the space provided.

demise (2): death, defeat

_____

_____

subservient (4): inferior, deferential

_____

_____

mentor (4): special teacher

_____

_____

sabotage (6): undermine, disrupt

_____

_____

irrevocable (7): final, irreversible

_____

_____

Understanding the Essay

1. What made Mansfield and her former good friend part company?
2. Why is a woman often brokenhearted about losing a friend?
3. Why is it usually important for good friends to be on a par with each other? When is an imbalance appropriate?
4. What is the best way to reevaluate a friendship?
5. According to Mansfield, how do friendships and love affairs differ?

Exploring the Theme: Discussion and Writing

1. Describe a friendship of yours that has either ended or become less important for you. Why did you first befriend the other person? What led to the breakup or the distance between you now?
2. "Death of a Friendship" was obviously written from a woman's point of view. From your own experiences, your friends' experiences, and what you learned in the article, how do you think the article would have been different written from a man's point of view? Are broken friendships as heartbreaking for men as for women? Do you think men would communicate in the way that Mansfield recommends?

BEST FRIENDS

Howard Solomon, Jr.

Howard Solomon, Jr., was born in New York City and now lives in Bristol, Vermont. While a student at the University of Vermont, he majored in French and pursued personal interests in foreign affairs, photography, and cycling. For the following essay, Howard began by interviewing students in his dormitory, collecting information and opinions that he eventually brought together with his own experiences to develop a definition of "best friends."

Preparing to Read

Among our swirl of acquaintances and friends through the years, we value and appreciate a select few more than anyone else. From childhood best friends to the adults we can count on in a pinch, we seem to need these special friends. But what defines a "best friend"? Can we have more than one? And why do we need to have best friends? Armed with these and other questions, Solomon interviewed his fellow college students to find out. In "Best Friends" he mixes the answers he received with his own experience. Think about your own best friends as you read the essay. How closely do they fit the profile of a best friend presented here?

Best friends, even when they are not a part of our day-to-day lives, are essential to our well-being. They supply the companionship, help, security, and love that we all need. It is not easy to put into words exactly what a best friend is, because the matter is so personal. From time to time, however, we may think about our best friends—who they are, what characteristics they share, and why they are so important to us—in order to gain a better understanding of ourselves and our relationships.

2   I recently asked several people for their opinions on the subject, beginning with the qualities they valued in their own best friends. They all agreed on three traits: reciprocity, honesty, and love. Reciprocity means that one can always rely on a best friend in times of need. A favor doesn't necessarily have to be returned; but best friends will return it anyway, because they want to. Best friends are willing to help each other for the sake of helping and not just for personal gain. One woman said that life seemed more secure because she knew her best friend was there if she ever needed help.

3   Honesty in a best friendship is the sharing of feelings openly and without reserve. The people I interviewed said they could rely on their best friends as confidants: they could share problems with their best friends and ask for advice. They also felt that, even if best friends were critical of each other, they would never be hurtful or spiteful.

4   Love is probably the most important quality of a best friend relationship, according to the people I interviewed. They very much prized the affection and enjoyment they felt in the company of their best friends. One man described it as a "gut reaction," and all said it was a different feeling from being with other friends. Private jokes, looks, and gestures create personal communication between best friends that is at a very high level—many times one person knows what the other is thinking without anything being said. The specifics differ, but most everyone I talked to agreed that a special feeling exists, which is best described as love.

5   I next asked who could be a best friend and who could not. My sources all felt it was impossible for parents, other relatives, and people of the opposite sex (especially husbands and wives) to be best friends. One woman said such people were "too inhibitive." Personally, I disagree—I have two best friends who are women. However, I may be an exception, and most best friends may fit the above requirements. There could be a good reason for this, too: most of the people I interviewed felt that their best friends were not demanding, while relatives and partners of the opposite sex can be very demanding.

6   To the question of how many best friends one can have, some in my sample responded that it is possible to have several best

friends, although very few people can do so; others said it was possible to have only a very few best friends; and still others felt they could have just one—that single friend who is most outstanding. It was interesting to see how ideas varied on this question. Although best friends may be no less special for one person than another, people do define the concept differently.

Regarding how long it takes to become best friends and how 7 long the relationship lasts, all were in agreement. "It is a long hard process which takes a lot of time," one woman explained. "It isn't something that can happen overnight," suggested another. One man said, "You usually know the person very well before you consider him your best friend. In fact you know everything about him, his bad points as well as his good points, so there is little likelihood you can come into conflict with him." In addition, everyone thought that once a person has become a best friend, he or she remains so for the rest of one's life.

During the course of the interviews I discovered one impor- 8 tant and unexpected difference between men and women regarding the qualities of their best friends. The men all said that a best friend usually possessed one quality that stood out above all others—an easygoing manner or humor or sympathy, for example. One of them told me that he looked not for loyalty but for honesty, for someone who was truthful, because it was so rare to find this quality in anyone. The women I surveyed, however, all responded that they looked for a well-rounded person who had many good qualities. One said that a person who had just one good quality and not several would be "too boring to associate with." Does this difference hold true beyond my sample? If so, it means that men and women have quite different definitions of their best friends.

I have always wondered why my own best friends were so 9 important to me; but it wasn't until recently that something happened to make me really understand my relationship with my best friends. My father died, and this was a crisis for me. Most of my friends gave me their condolences. But my best friends did more than that: they actually supported me. They called long distance to see how I was and what I needed, to try and help me work out my problems or simply to talk. Two of my best friends even took time from their spring break and, along with two other best friends, attended my father's memorial service; none of my other friends came. Since then, these are the only people who have continued to worry about me and talk to me about my father. I know that, whenever I need someone, they will be there and willing to help me. I know also that, whenever they need help, I will be ready to do the same for them.

10 Yet, I don't value my best friends so much just for what they do for me. I simply enjoy their company more than anyone else's. We talk, joke, play sports, and do all kinds of things when we are together. I never feel ill at ease, even after we've been apart for a while. However, the most important thing for me about best friends is the knowledge that I am never alone, that there are others in the world who care about my well-being as much as I do about theirs. Surely this is a comforting feeling for everyone.

Vocabulary

To get the most out of reading this essay, you should have a working understanding of the words listed below. Following each word is a parenthetical reference, indicating the paragraph in which the word is used, as well as a definition for the word. Go back and look at the sentence in which the word appears, and see how the definition applies. To help you make this word a part of your active vocabulary, write a sentence of your own using the word in the space provided.

confidants (3): people with whom one discusses problems and shares secrets

---
---

inhibitive (5): constraining

---

condolences (9): expressions of comfort, regrets

Understanding the Essay

1. What three qualities are valued most in a best friend?
2. Which quality is the most important? Why?
3. How many best friends can one have?
4. Why is it difficult to find a best friend quickly? How long do your relationships with best friends last?
5. How do men's and women's definitions of a best friend differ?
6. Why does Solomon think people value their best friends so highly?

Exploring the Theme:
Discussion and Writing

1. Describe your relationship with your best friends. What makes them your best friends? Do you agree with Solomon's conclusions about best friends? What other qualities do you think are important in a best friend?
2. Do you think that you can be best friends with a member of the opposite sex? Why or why not?

A MAGIC CIRCLE
OF FRIENDS

Elvira M. Franco

*Elvira Franco returned to school in her forties. She wrote
about the group of older students she met and befriended
there for the* New York Times *(January 28, 1990).*

Preparing to Read

School is a constant stream of challenges that can make even
the most academically gifted students feel insecure. Starting a
course of study after age forty—after about a twenty-year break
from classes—can be especially nerve-racking. For Franco, her
fears were silenced and her enthusiasm for school was kindled
with the help of a special group of contemporaries who were
making the same bold return to school as she was. "A Magic
Circle of Friends" describes how Franco and her friends were
able to use their age and their life experiences to forge a new
understanding of friendship, school, and the world around
them. As you read the essay, think of how Franco's experience
would have differed if she hadn't found her "magic circle of
friends" at her school.

1   Older than forty and starting from scratch: I thought I was
a unique item, but as soon as I peeked out of my shell I
found a sea of women in similar positions.

2   The little child in us has grown mature and middle-aged,
almost to our surprise. We share a fear that sits in the back of the
mind like a spider ready to pounce: but we've also developed
determination, almost like a religion.

3   We know we have friends; at least, I know my friends are
with me, if not always, at least most of the time. And most of the

time I need them, and they me. We reach over the phone lines for that word of comfort, the encouragement we need to go on when our own store of willpower has become depleted.

Returning to school, I found my friends were my best fans. 4 In spite of their own insecurities, they never failed to offer me the cheering I often needed to rewrite a paper one more time or to stay up one last half-hour to re-read a difficult chapter.

After classes we would go to a diner, a bunch of over-forty 5 classmates. Working together on a project that we felt strongly about ignited a part of us we did not know existed. While we were quite far from orthopedic shoes, bifocals were prominent. Underneath the artful makeup, we would measure the wrinkles on each other's cheeks across the table, almost as if these lines could form a cord to link us.

It was a good time. For years, in a locked-up corner of our 6 minds, we had held the unspoken fear that we might actually be brain-dead. We were finally giving ourselves permission to celebrate our minds.

For some, it was a return to the carefree years of college. 7 For others, a first-time discovery that learning can be both fun and exhilarating. Besides the intellectual surprises, we found joy in each other's company, and we delved in this new-found camaraderie with an intensity we did not know we could achieve outside of love and pregnancies. We were, and are, proud of our ages. The only woman in the group who was under thirty struck most of us as brash, angry, and, frankly, quite inappropriate. We were probably insensitive to her needs, but somehow we failed to find out how she felt in our midst and were almost relieved when she found excuses for not joining our study sessions.

We ended up treating her almost like a daughter, and doing 8 for her what most of us have been doing for our own daughters: that is, picking up the slack. The hidden bonus was that now we could continue to do things our way, which, we all knew, was the best anyway. Things were smoother when she was not around: the rest of us would always agree, and even our disagreements were somehow smooth and enjoyable.

We had, in fact, created a sort of bubble around us, a magic 9 circle that follows us still and says we are bright, successful, caring, ambitious, and, finally, ready to change the world. We will not do it, as we might have been ready to do at twenty, pushing and fighting and abrading.

10   We will do it instead at a slower pace, because, along the way, we have learned lessons both small and big: for example, that the world is in no hurry to be changed and that we will have a better shot at it after a good night's sleep. We may not complete our plans by tomorrow, or even by the end of the week, because the details of our lives may interfere, such as a child home from college, or a neighbor's emergency.

11   Our goals may not even be achieved exactly as originally planned, and that is fine, too, because time has also brought us a sense of flexibility and an appreciation for the serendipitous properties of practically any action. The end product could turn out to be infinitely more complex, and in its way more perfect, more multifaceted and rich, than what we had first envisioned. The process is in itself an achievement.

12   They call us "late bloomers," they call us "returnees." We are sought by schools, thanks to the sheer numbers we represent, not to mention the life experience and the common sense that even the least bright among us brings to the classroom. We feel flattered and surprised, and our ego is bolstered by the realization that we are indeed quite capable.

13   There are fears, too ("Will it all make sense at some point?" "What if I'll never be able to get a decent job?"), but they are kept for only a few pairs of ears, where we know we will find support and understanding.

14   Graduation comes: the last papers have been handed in with trepidation, the test booklets carrying in their pages the very essence of our knowledge closed for the last time. Goodbys, with promises and some tears, even a photograph to keep as souvenir. We've made it: watch out world, here come the mothers and the grandmothers, ready to push, cajole, smile and negotiate to achieve those goals we did not have a chance to effect the first time around.

15   We may just be beginning to feel a few arthritic pangs in our toes and fingers, but with our hair neatly streaked and some expensive dental work, we know we still look good. We know we are still strong, smart, vital, and, most especially, ready to work. This time around we will make a big difference. We know, because, for sure, we already are different.

Vocabulary

To get the most out of reading this essay, you should have a working understanding of the words listed below. Following each word is a parenthetical reference, indicating the paragraph in which the word is used, as well as a definition for the word. Go back and look at the sentence in which the word appears, and see how the definition applies. To help you make this word a part of your active vocabulary, write a sentence of your own using the word in the space provided.

depleted (3): emptied, run out

_____

_____

intellectual (7): mental, academic

_____

_____

camaraderie (7): friendship

_____

_____

abrading (9): scraping, irritating

_____

_____

multifaceted (11): composed of many pieces, many-sided

_____

_____

bolstered (12): boosted, strengthened

_____

_____

Understanding the Essay

1. In your opinion, what is the "fear that sits in the back of [Franco and her friends'] mind like a spider ready to pounce"?

2. How did Franco's circle of friends help one another? What did they have in common, besides their age?

3. How did the women react to their return to school?

4. Why was the one younger woman difficult for the group to get along with? What happened to her relationship with the other women?

5. What had experience taught Franco and her friends about the way the world works?

6. How will Franco's group reach the goals they didn't have a chance to achieve the first time around?

Exploring the Theme:
Discussion and Writing

1. Franco doesn't describe her friends' personalities or good points, yet she says she and her friends "delved into this new-found camaraderie with an intensity we did not know we could achieve outside of love and pregnancies." Why do you think their friendships were so intense? How do the friendships she describes differ from your friendships at school? How are they similar?

2. Franco found out that the pressures of a difficult situation can sometimes be the catalyst for bringing about new friendships. We find this to be true when we go off to school, start a new job, enroll in a difficult course, are involved in an accident or some other stressful event. In an essay, examine what it is about pressure or stress that works to bring people together in ways they never dreamed possible?

WRITING SUGGESTIONS
FOR "FRIENDS"

1. Write a descriptive essay about a close friend. Keep in mind that your readers probably will not know her or him. You must bring the friend to life through stories, anecdotes, quotations, or some other means. In preparing to write, consider what distinguishes that person from other people you know. How and why is this friend special to you?

2. Write an essay in which you present your own definition of "friend." What for you are the responsibilities of friendship? What do you expect from people who call themselves your friend? What obligations do you feel toward them? Like Howard Solomon, Jr., you might interview classmates for their views on the defining characteristics of a friend.

3. Aristotle once said, "Wishing to be friends is quick work, but friendship is a slow-ripening fruit." Write an essay in which you develop Aristotle's idea with your own experiences and observations.

4. Not all our friends are of equal importance to us. Into what categories might you put your friends? Write an essay in which you describe each of these categories and present examples to illustrate what you mean.

5. How do the friends you have made in college differ from those you have made up until this time? What accounts for the difference? How does being engaged in intellectual pursuits affect the friendships you have made in college? In an essay, explore the special characteristics of college friendships.

6. What were your strongest childhood friendships like? What needs did they fulfill? If they differ in any way from your present friendships, how? Are you still friends with the people you knew as a child?

7. Not all friendships last forever. After reading Stephanie Mansfield's essay, write one of your own in which you explain why an important friendship of yours did not last.

6

EDUCATION

When we hear the word *education*, we naturally think of aspects of our formal education—teachers, books, homework, reading, writing, arithmetic, and all the other traditional academic subjects. Our scariest memories are of tests, of course. Russell Baker, the columnist for the *New York Times*, has written, "During formal education, the child learns that life is for testing. This stage lasts twelve years, a period during which the child learns that success comes from telling testers what they want to hear." We do not think of education as also encompassing the many ways we learn outside the classroom. And we don't have a good label for this kind of learning, either. We speak of life's lessons, the socialization process, having common sense or street smarts, being savvy or clever, knowing the ropes, or being able to think on one's feet.

Life's lessons are, of course, wonderful. They come to us unannounced often, as surprises, really, and they can become unforgettable turning points in our lives. We also tend to think of them as events in which we teach ourselves or are taught by circumstance or nature. But as in most formal learning situations, another person usually acts as a catalyst if not a teacher. And sometimes, too, the teacher becomes the student.

The following essays deal with education both inside and outside the classroom, with unexpected teachers and students. The late, brilliant science fiction writer Isaac Asimov recounts what his automobile mechanic taught him about intelligence. Physics professor Alexander Calandra tells how a student demonstrated what was wrong with a physics test Calandra gave and how this test encouraged students to stop thinking. Sharon A. Sheehan teaches sex education, traditionally an extracurricular subject, and explains why it should not be offered as a value-free subject. Finally, Dorothy Canfield Fisher retells the story of how a celebrated American, bereft of life's most fundamental lessons, takes the first steps toward making his dreams come true.

INTELLIGENCE

Isaac Asimov

Isaac Asimov had a long, successful career as a scientist and as a writer. He is best known for his science fiction books, such as the Foundation *trilogy, but he also wrote about such diverse topics as Shakespeare, history, and the Bible. In the following essay, he ponders his own intelligence—and lack thereof.*

Preparing to Read

Who's the smartest person you know? Perhaps he or she is a professor, writer, scientist, or someone else considered to be well educated and very intelligent. You probably didn't even think of your school's basketball coach or the local mechanic. Yet would you expect your smartest person to effectively mesh ten temperamental basketball players into a team that can run a motion offense and use a box-and-one defense to shut down the other team's big scorer? Would you call on her or him to fix your rough-running car engine? Intelligence, as Asimov states in his essay, is not absolute. Our society defines the academically gifted as intelligent, but perhaps "book smart" would be a better term. IQ tests don't take into account common sense or experience, attributes that the academically gifted often lack outside of a scholarly setting. As you read Asimov's essay, think about other types of "intelligence" that we may not at first recognize.

What is intelligence, anyway? When I was in the army I   1
received a kind of aptitude test that all soldiers took and, against a normal of 100, scored 160. No one at the base had ever seen a figure like that, and for two hours they made a big fuss over me. (It didn't mean anything. The next day I was still a buck private with KP as my highest duty.)

2   All my life I've been registering scores like that, so that I have the complacent feeling that I'm highly intelligent, and I expect other people to think so, too. Actually, though, don't such scores simply mean that I am very good at answering the type of academic questions that are considered worthy of answers by the people who make up the intelligence tests—people with intellectual bents similar to mine?

3   For instance, I had an auto-repair man once, who, on these intelligence tests, could not possibly have scored more than 80, by my estimate. I always took it for granted that I was far more intelligent than he was. Yet, when anything went wrong with my car I hastened to him with it, watched him anxiously as he explored its vitals, and listened to his pronouncements as though they were divine oracles—and he always fixed my car.

4   Well, then, suppose my auto-repair man devised questions for an intelligence test. Or suppose a carpenter did, or a farmer, or, indeed, almost anyone but an academician. By every one of those tests, I'd prove myself a moron. And I'd *be* a moron, too. In a world where I could not use my academic training and my verbal talents but had to do something intricate or hard, working with my hands, I would do poorly. My intelligence, then, is not absolute but is a function of the society I live in and of the fact that a small subsection of that society has managed to foist itself on the rest as an arbiter of such matters.

5   Consider my auto-repair man, again. He had a habit of telling me jokes whenever he saw me. One time he raised his head from under the automobile hood to say: "Doc, a deaf-and-dumb guy went into a hardware store to ask for some nails. He put two fingers together on the counter and made hammering motions with the other hand. The clerk brought him a hammer. He shook his head and pointed to the two fingers he was hammering. The clerk brought him nails. He picked out the sizes he wanted, and left. Well, doc, the next guy who came in was a blind man. He wanted scissors. How do you suppose he asked for them?"

6   Indulgently, I lifted my right hand and made scissoring motions with my first two fingers. Whereupon my auto-repair man laughed raucously and said, "Why, you dumb jerk, he used his *voice* and asked for them." Then he said, smugly, "I've been trying that on all my customers today." "Did you catch many?" I asked. "Quite a few," he said, "but I knew for sure I'd catch *you*."

"Why is that?" I asked. "Because you're so goddamned educated, doc, I *knew* you couldn't be very smart."

And I have an uneasy feeling he had something there.   7

Vocabulary

To get the most out of reading this essay, you should have a working understanding of the words listed below. Following each word is a parenthetical reference, indicating the paragraph in which the word is used, as well as a definition for the word. Go back and look at the sentence in which the word appears, and see how the definition applies. To help you make this word a part of your active vocabulary, write a sentence of your own using the word in the space provided.

aptitude (1): ability, potential

_____

_____

complacent (2): self-satisfied, nonchalant

_____

_____

intellectual (2): mental, academic

_____

_____

oracles (3): prophecies

_____

_____

academician (4): someone whose career is in an academic field, such as a professor or researcher

_____

_____

foist (4): force upon

_____

_____

arbiter (4): decision maker, controller

_____

_____

raucously (6): loudly, stridently

_____

_____

Understanding the Essay

1. Why did Asimov's 160 score on the army's aptitude test mean little to him?
2. Describe Asimov's relationship with his mechanic.
3. How well would Asimov do if his mechanic made up the questions for the intelligence test? Why does society consider Asimov more intelligent than his mechanic?
4. Why was Asimov's mechanic so confident that Asimov would fall for his joke? Why did his confidence make Asimov uneasy?

Exploring the Theme: Discussion and Writing

1. Tell Asimov's mechanic's joke to some of your friends, and try to include both "book smart" and "street smart" people. How many fell for it? Did book smart people fall for it more? What do you think is the difference between being educated and being smart?
2. According to Asimov, society measures intelligence as a function of academic talent. There are, of course, many kinds of talent, some of which you undoubtedly possess. If you could be very talented in just one area, however, what area would you choose: academics? athletics? art? finance? Explain your choice. How would you use your talent?

ANGELS ON A PIN

Alexander Calandra

Alexander Calandra wrote "Angels on a Pin" for the Saturday Review *in 1968. In it he reveals how a student challenged educational conventions—and won—in a physics course Calandra was teaching at Washington University in St. Louis.*

Preparing to Read

Why do you go to school, to get an education or to learn? In a perfect world, it would mean the same thing no matter how you answered that question. As it is, however, getting an education in our current system can involve more memorization, grade grabbing, and "getting by" than actual inquiry and learning. Tests, the most common measure of performance, usually do little to measure creativity, curiosity, and other indicators of an active, inquiring mind. "Angels on a Pin" tells a story that highlights the difference between education and learning. A teacher, possessing a rigid view of education, asks a question that has many correct and valid answers, yet he insists that only the answer he wants is the correct one. The student, obviously creative and intelligent, has learned his subject well enough that he feels stifled by the boundaries the teacher has imposed on his thinking. He challenges the boundaries, and it takes Calandra's help to resolve their dispute—one in which the student emerges as an able thinker.

S ome time ago, I received a call from a colleague who   1
asked if I would be the referee on the grading of an examination question. He was about to give a student a zero for his answer to a physics question, while the student claimed he should receive a perfect score and would if the system were not set up against the student. The instructor and the student agreed to submit this to an impartial arbiter, and I was selected.

2   I went to my colleague's office and read the examination question: "Show how it is possible to determine the height of a tall building with the aid of a barometer."

3   The student had answered: "Take the barometer to the top of the building, attach a long rope to it, lower the barometer to the street, and then bring it up, measuring the length of the rope. The length of the rope is the height of the building."

4   I pointed out that the student really had a strong case for full credit, since he had answered the question completely and correctly. On the other hand, if full credit were given, it could well contribute to a high grade for the student in his physics course. A high grade is supposed to certify competence in physics, but the answer did not confirm this. I suggested that the student have another try at answering the question. I was not surprised that my colleague agreed, but I was surprised that the student did.

5   I gave the student six minutes to answer the question, with the warning that his answer should show some knowledge of physics. At the end of five minutes, he had not written anything. I asked if he wished to give up, but he said no. He had many answers to this problem; he was just thinking of the best one. I excused myself for interrupting him, and asked him to please go on. In the next minute, he dashed off his answer which read:

6   "Take the barometer to the top of the building and lean over the edge of the roof. Drop the barometer, timing its fall with a stopwatch. Then, using the formula $S = 1/2at^2$, calculate the height of the building."

7   At this point, I asked my colleague if *he* would give up. He conceded, and I gave the student almost full credit.

8   In leaving my colleague's office, I recalled that the student had said he had other answers to the problem, so I asked him what they were. "Oh, yes," said the student. "There are many ways of getting the height of a tall building with the aid of a barometer. For example, you could take the barometer out on a sunny day and measure the height of the barometer, the length of its shadow, and the length of the shadow of the building, and by the use of a simple proportion, determine the height of the building."

9   "Fine," I said. "And the others?"

10   "Yes," said the student. "There is a very basic measurement method that you will like. In this method, you take the barome-

ter and begin to walk up the stairs. As you climb the stairs, you mark off the length of the barometer along the wall. You then count the number of marks, and this will give you the height of the building in barometer units. A very direct method.

"Of course, if you want a more sophisticated method, you 11 can tie the barometer to the end of a string, swing it as a pendulum, and determine the value of 'g' at the street level and at the top of the building. From the difference between the two values of 'g,' the height of the building can, in principle, be calculated."

Finally he concluded, there are many other ways of solving 12 the problem. "Probably the best," he said, "is to take the barometer to the basement and knock on the superintendent's door. When the superintendent answers, you speak to him as follows: 'Mr. Superintendent, here I have a fine barometer. If you will tell me the height of this building, I will give you this barometer.' "

At this point, I asked the student if he really did not know the 13 conventional answer to this question. He admitted that he did, but said that he was fed up with high school and college instructors trying to teach him how to think, to use the "scientific method," and to explore the deep inner logic of the subject in a pedantic way, as is often done in the new mathematics, rather than teaching him the structure of the subject. With this in mind, he decided to revive scholasticism as an academic lark to challenge the Sputnik-panicked classrooms of America.

Vocabulary

To get the most out of reading this essay, you should have a working understanding of the words listed below. Following each word is a parenthetical reference, indicating the paragraph in which the word is used, as well as a definition for the word. Go back and look at the sentence in which the word appears, and see how the definition applies. To help you make this word a part of your active vocabulary, write a sentence of your own using the word in the space provided.

colleague (1): co-worker

arbiter (1): judge, decision maker

_____

_____

barometer (2): device for measuring air pressure

_____

_____

competence (4): ability

_____

_____

proportion (8): ratio

_____

_____

pedantic (13): rigidly academic, pretentious

_____

_____

scholasticism (13): philosophy of education

_____

_____

lark (13): frolic, lighthearted pursuit

_____

_____

Understanding the Essay

1. How is the student's answer correct to the teacher's question, "Show how it is possible to determine the height of a tall building with the aid of a barometer"? How is it incorrect? How does Calandra suggest solving the conflict?

2. Why doesn't the student answer the question quickly when given a second chance? Why do you think Calandra still doesn't give him full credit for his answer?

3. What is one correct answer that the student didn't use on the exam? Try to come up with at least one more answer to the question that is not used as an example in the essay.

4. Does the student know the answer the teacher was looking for? Why didn't he give the teacher the answer that was expected of him?

5. What is Calandra saying about education in this essay? How does the conflict he writes about serve to illustrate his point?

Exploring the Theme: Discussion and Writing

1. If you were the teacher and found yourself in a situation like the one Calandra describes, how would you react? Would you give the student a zero or another chance? Why?

2. Describe either a class that inspired you to explore the subject further or a class in which you learned—and still remember—a lot. Did the teacher encourage you to look at the subject in different ways, or did you do it on your own? What about the class made it a good learning experience?

ANOTHER KIND OF SEX ED

Sharon A. Sheehan

Sharon A. Sheehan is a writer living in Atherton, California. After college, she went to work as a public health officer for the state of California, providing sex education for teenagers. Sheehan draws heavily from her experiences with teenagers and their struggles with sex, birth control, and pregnancy in writing the following selection, which first appeared in the July 13, 1992, issue of Newsweek.

Preparing to Read

The issue of sex education is frequently in the news. Some people would like to see more of it in the schools. Some are very much against it, preferring that social responsibility to be met elsewhere. Over the past twenty years sex education has become a regular part of the curriculum in many of our public schools. Sheehan's title leads readers to think about the kind of sex education they were exposed to in school. What was sex education like in your hometown? Would you have favored a different approach than the one you experienced? What are your expectations of Sheehan's essay, based on her title?

1   Our local newspaper ran an essay recently by the president of the Youth Council. It explained its vote favoring condom machines in high schools. He said that students should be able to get the prophylactics in the school bathroom because they fear personal embarrassment at the checkout counter of the local drugstore.

2   Could it be that many teenagers would rather take their chances with AIDS than run the risk of embarrassment? And what about the risk of pregnancy?

3   Family-planning workers have observed that many teenage

girls cannot bring themselves to march into a clinic and declare that they are planning to lose their virginity. It's too embarrassing. Running the risk of pregnancy is preferable.

After earning a graduate degree in public health, I was employed by the State of California to help solve the problem of teenage pregnancy by educating teenagers about birth control. The fundamental origin of the problem—the premarital sexual activity of teenagers—was accepted as a given. The Planned Parenthood professional assigned to train me pointed out that the real solution to this problem was to eradicate the sense of shame associated with premarital sex.   4

I was stunned. But the logic was obvious: teenage pregnancy is a problem. Birth control is the solution. Shame is the barrier to applying the solution. Therefore eliminate shame in order to solve the problem. But taking a young person's sense of modesty and giving back a pill or a condom wasn't what anyone would call a fair trade.   5

Nonetheless, for the next several months I proceeded to talk to hundreds of teenagers about various methods of birth control. But I was never convinced that I was genuinely helping them.   6

Professionally, I succumbed to the obligatory gag rule: don't say anything that could arouse the sense of shame. In practice, then, I was compelled to imply that all sexual choices were morally neutral. Thus everything that I had learned from my parents' marriage and my own marriage was off-limits. Everything I believed about how human beings form meaningful and lasting relationships was not only irrelevant but counterproductive.   7

The new sexual ideology protected teenagers from shame by saying, "If you feel like you are ready, then it's OK." Ready for what? Ready to build a life together? Ready for conquest? Ready to feel like a slut? Ready to bring a new life into the world? Shame is a powerful word that explodes in many directions. There is a cruel, destructive side to shame. Controlling people by shaming them into self-loathing or compliance, for example. But shame also protects us. It prevents us from treating others in a despicable fashion. And it protects "the sanctity of our unfinished or unready selves."   8

In his book, "The Meaning of Persons," Paul Tournier reflects on a young person's innate sense of modesty: "The appearance of this sense of shame is, in fact, the sign of the birth of a person. And later the supreme affirmation of the person, the great en-   9 gagement of life, will be marked by the handing over of the secret, the gift of the self, the disappearance of shame."

10   Recently, I returned to the high-school campus to talk with students about how they see themselves and what they hope for. Many were offended by the adult assumption that most teens are sexually active. One girl was so uncomfortable that she went to her teacher in Living Skills class to explain that she was not sleeping with her boyfriend. "It's like the adult world invading our world," another girl commented.

11   Yet they are embarrassed to ask the questions they care about most. "What should I look for in a guy?" "How do I know if it's morally right?" "How will I feel afterward?"

12   Behind their "correct," value-free façade lurks a deep sense of loss. They lament the lack of guidelines and moral structure. One girl described it this way: "It used to be that people got married and then they had sex. Then when the baby came there was a place all prepared for it. Now technology has taken away the worry of having children. That leaves sex to float around in everyone's life when there's no guy who's going to stick around."

13   "It used to be that kids wouldn't want to disappoint themselves or each other," a boy remarked. "I think it's really lonely," said another. "It's sad."

14   It's as if the gap between sex and marriage had opened up a huge empty hole in which there were "no real sure thing." A loving relationship that lasts. Hasn't that always been the goal and bottom line? Isn't the real C word for sex education commitment, not condoms?

15   It's time to give the thousands of couples in this country who have been happily married 20, 30, 40, 50 years equal access to sex-education classrooms. One boy told me, "I'd like to hear more stories . . . how they met . . . how they kept the love alive." If you have built a marriage and family the "old-fashioned" way, go to a classroom and tell your story. Share the wisdom gained by keeping the promises of your youth. Let them ask the questions they care about the most.

16   In coming face to face with other human beings, how much do we value the self that we glimpse through their eyes, that flutters past in a gesture or a smile? Sex education is about nothing less than how and when we hand over this astonishing gift of the self. The goal is that we can love and trust and believe enough to commit our whole self and our whole future.

Vocabulary

To get the most out of reading this essay, you should have a working understanding of the words listed below. Following each word is a parenthetical reference, indicating the paragraph in which the word is used, as well as a definition for the word. Go back and look at the sentence in which the word appears, and see how the definition applies. To help you make this word a part of your active vocabulary, write a sentence of your own using the word in the space provided.

prophylactics (1): condoms or rubbers to prevent pregnancy, sexually transmitted diseases, or AIDS

---

embarrassment (1): self-conscious or awkward feeling

---

eradicate (4): get rid of

---

modesty (5): freedom from deceit or vanity

---

succumbed (7): gave in to

---

irrelevant (7): not meaningful

---

counterproductive (7): working against a desired goal

_____

_____

ideology (8): belief system

_____

_____

slut (8): pejorative term for a sexually active woman

_____

_____

despicable (8): contemptible

_____

_____

innate (9): existing from birth

_____

_____

affirmation (9): assertion of something as valid

_____

_____

assumption (10): belief that something is true

_____

_____

lament (12): regret

_____

_____

glimpse (16): to give a brief, fleeting view or look

_____

_____

Understanding the Essay

1. The president of the Youth Council said that he favored placing condom machines in high school bathrooms so students could avoid the embarrassment of purchasing them at the local drugstore. What does Sheehan find wrong with this thinking? Where has she heard a similar argument?

2. What, according to Sheehan, is the meaning of shame? How is shame related to modesty? In what ways can shame be said to "protect" us?

3. Why is Sheehan stunned when the professional from Planned Parenthood tells her that the real solution to teenage pregnancy is "to eradicate the sense of shame associated with premarital sex"?

4. If birth control pills and condoms are not the answer to teenage pregnancy, what, according to Sheehan, is?

5. In paragraph 5 Sheehan summarizes the logic of the family-planning workers. In your opinion, is she fair with the opposition's argument, or does she oversimplify it? What do you think she finds wrong with their logic?

6. What did Sheehan learn during a recent talk with high schoolers? What does she gain by quoting students in paragraphs 10–13?

7. This essay appeared as a "My Turn" column in *Newsweek* in 1992. How would you characterize the readers of *Newsweek?* For what particular segment of that readership has Sheehan written her article? What in her essay led you to this conclusion?

Exploring the Theme: Discussion and Writing

1. For Sheehan, "the real C word for sex education [is] commitment, not condoms." What does commitment mean to you? Is commitment a scary thing for you? For your friends? Explain why or why not.

2. What does Sheehan mean by the statement, "Sex education is nothing less than how and when we hand over this
   astonishing gift of the self"? What does the phrase "gift of
   the self" mean to you?

3. Sheehan admits that she felt personally compromised
   when as a family-planning professional she had to imply
   that "all sexual choices were morally neutral." What do
   you see as the relationship between sex and morals? What
   role, if any, does a healthy sense of shame play in this relationship? Explain your feelings on this important and sensitive issue.

THE WASHED WINDOW

Dorothy Canfield Fisher

Dorothy Canfield Fisher (1879–1958) was born in Kansas but spent most of her adult life in Vermont. She was a renowned writer and educator whose wide experience and diverse interests are reflected in her writing. Fisher wrote many novels, stories, and nonfiction works, such as The Montessori Mother, Home Fires in France, *and* Vermont Tradition. *"The Washed Window" reveals both her writing skill and her interest in education.*

Preparing to Read

We all have certain standards of behavior that we take for granted. We all know what it means to clean up after ourselves, how to speak on the telephone, and how to be courteous to other people. Such lessons are part of being raised in the United States in the twentieth century. But what if we hadn't been taught these basic skills and had to pursue this knowledge on our own? In "The Washed Window," Fisher tells one man's story of the plight of the slaves just before and after the Civil War. Their lot didn't improve with freedom, for the most part, because they hadn't learned how to do anything independently—they'd always been told exactly what to do. The story of how one man learned to think for himself and take responsibility for doing a job correctly shows how important education is. Imagine yourself in this man's shoes. Do you think you would have been able to persevere in your quest for knowledge as he did?

Older people in Arlington have a special interest in the last house you pass as you leave our village to drive to Cambridge. It was built and lived in for many years by our first local skilled cabinetmaker. In the early days nearly every house had one good piece of professionally made furniture, 1 brought up from Connecticut on horseback or in an oxcart. These were highly treasured. But the furniture made here was, for the first generation after 1764, put together by men who just wanted chairs, bed, and a table for the family meals—and those as fast as they could be slammed into shape.

2   For many years Silas Knapp lived in that last house practicing his remarkable skill. Nearly every house of our town acquired in those years one or two pieces of his workmanship. They are now highly prized as "early nineteenth-century, locally-made antiques."

3   He not only made many a fine chest of drawers and bedside stand there: he also brought up a fine family of children. You may never have noticed this house as you drove by, but once, some twenty or thirty years ago, a great American leader, who chanced to pass through Vermont, asked to be shown the old Knapp home. He had been delivering an important address to a large audience in Rutland. When he stood in front of the small low old house he took off his hat and bowed his gray head in silence. Then he explained to the person who had driven him down to Arlington, "For me it is a shrine."

4   This is the story back of his visit to the plain little early nineteenth century artisan's house which to him was a shrine. Viola Knapp was one of the Vermont girls who "went South to teach," taking along with her the attitude towards life she had been brought up to respect. She married there—as the saying goes, "married well"—an army officer of good family. It was a happy, lifelong mating. Viola Knapp Ruffner and her husband, General Ruffner, lived here and there in various cities and towns and brought up a family of five children. It was while the Ruffners were living in West Virginia that—but I'll set the story down as I heard it in my youth, about sixty years ago, from the lips of the distinguished American educator who, as a boy, had been a student of Viola Knapp Ruffner. In his later years, he became one of my father's valued friends.

5   This is about as he used to tell it to us with many more details than I ever saw told in print. "I never knew exactly how old I was when I first saw Mrs. Ruffner, for in the days of slavery, family records—that is, black-family records—were seldom kept. But from what I have been able to learn, I was born, a slave, on a Virginia plantation, about 1858. In my youth, my home was a log cabin about fourteen by sixteen feet square. We

slept on frowsy piles of filthy rags, laid on the dirt floor. Until I was quite a big youth I wore only one garment, a shirt made out of agonizingly rough refuse-flax. We slaves ate corn bread and pork, because those foods could be grown on the plantation without cash expense. I had never seen anything except the slave quarters on the plantation where I was born, with a few glimpses of the 'big house' where our white owners lived. I cannot remember ever, during my childhood and youth, not one single time, when our family sat down together at a table to eat a meal as human families do. We ate as animals do, whenever and wherever an edible morsel was found. We usually took our food up in our fingers, sometimes from the skillet, sometimes from a tin plate held on our knees, and as we chewed on it, we held it as best we could in our hands.

"Life outside our cabin was as slovenly and disordered as inside. The white owners made no effort to keep things up. They really could not. Slaves worked; hence any form of work was too low for white people to do. Since white folks did no work, they did not know how work should be done. The untaught slaves, wholly ignorant of better standards, seldom got around to mending the fences, or putting back a lost hinge on a sagging gate or door. Weeds grew wild everywhere, even in the yard. Inside the big house, when a piece of plastering fell from a wall or ceiling, it was a long time before anybody could stir himself to get it replastered. 6

"After the end of the Civil War, when we were no longer slaves, my family moved to a settlement near a salt mine, where, although I was still only a child, I was employed—often beginning my day's work at four in the morning. There, we lived in even more dreadful squalor, for our poor rickety cabin was in a crowded slum, foul with unspeakable dirt—literal and moral. As soon as I grew a little older and stronger, I was shifted from working in the salt mine to a coal mine. Both mines were then owned by General Lewis Ruffner. 7

"By that time I had learned my letters and could, after a fashion, read. Mostly I taught myself, but with some irregular hours spent in a Negro night school, after an exhausting day's work in the mines. There were no public schools for ex-slaves; the poor, totally unequipped, bare room where colored people, young and old, crowded in to learn their letters was paid for by tiny contributions from the Negroes themselves. 8

9   "About that time I heard two pieces of news, which were like very distant, very faint glimmers in the blackness of the coal mine in which nearly all my waking hours were spent. One was about a school for colored students—Hampton Institute it was—where they could learn more than their letters. The other was that the wife of General Ruffner was from Vermont and that she took an interest in the education of the colored people who worked for her. I also heard that she was so 'strict' that nobody could suit her, and that the colored boys who entered her service were so afraid of her, and found her so impossible to please, that they never stayed long. But the pay was five dollars a month, and keep. That was better than the coal mine—and there was also the chance that she might be willing to have me go on learning. I got up my courage to try. What could be worse than the way I was living and the hopelessness of anything better in the future?

10   "But I can just tell you that, great, lumbering, muscle-bound coal-mining boy that I was, I was trembling when I went to ask for that work. The Ruffners had just moved into an old house that had been empty for some time, and they were not yet established, their furniture not unpacked, the outbuildings not repaired. When I first saw her, Mrs. Ruffner was writing on an improvised desk which was a plank laid across two kegs.

11   "I falteringly told her that I had come to ask for work. She turned in her chair and looked at me silently. Nobody had ever looked at me like that, not at my rags and dirt but as if she wanted to see what kind of person I was. She had clear, steady gray eyes, I remember. Then she said, 'You can try.' After reflection, she went on, 'You might as well start in by cleaning the woodshed. It looks as though it hadn't been touched for years.'

12   "She laid down her pen and took me through a narrow side-passage into the woodshed. It was dark and cluttered with all kinds of dirty, dusty things. A sour, moldy smell came up from them. Great cobwebs hung down from the rough rafters of the low, sloping roof. Stepping back for a moment, she brought out a dustpan and a broom. A shovel leaned against the woodshed wall. She put that in my hand and said, 'Now go ahead. Put the trash you clean out, on that pile in the yard and we'll burn it up later. Anything that won't burn, like broken glass, put into that barrel.' Then she turned away and left me.

13   "You must remember that I never had done any work except

rough, unskilled heavy labor. I had never cleaned a room in my life, I had never seen a clean room in my life. But I was used to doing as I was told, and I was dead set on managing to go ahead with learning more than I would in that poor beginner's school-room. So I began taking out things which anybody could see were trash, like mildewed rags, which fell apart into damp shreds the minute I touched them. There were also, I remember, some moldy heaps of I don't know what, garbage maybe, that had dried into shapeless chunks of bad-smelling filth. In one corner was the carcass of a long-dead dog, which I carried out to the pile of trash in the side yard. Glass was everywhere, broken and unbroken empty whiskey bottles, bits of crockery ware. These I swept with the broom and picking up my sweepings in my hands (I had no idea what a dustpan was for) carried them outside.

"The shed looked to me so much better that I went in to find   14
Mrs. Ruffner. She was still writing. I told her, 'I cleaned it.'
Pushing back her chair she went out to the woodshed with me.

"She made no comment when she first opened the door and   15
looked around her with clear gray eyes. Then she remarked quietly, "There's still some things to attend to. Those pieces of wood
over there you might pile up against the wall in the corner. They
would do to burn. Be sure to clean the floor well before you start
piling the wood on it. And here's another pile of rotten rags, you
see. And that tangle behind the door. You'd better pull it all
apart and see what's there. Throw away the trash that's mixed
with it.' She turned to go back, saying, 'Just keep on till you've
got it finished and then come and tell me.'

"She didn't speak kindly. She didn't speak unkindly. I looked   16
at the woodshed with new eyes and saw that, sure enough, I'd
only made a beginning. I began to pull at the odds and ends in
that dusty mess behind the door. And to my astonishment I felt I
was perspiring. The work wasn't hard for me, you understand. It
was like little boy's play compared to the back-breaking labor I
had always done. And it wasn't that I minded carrying around in
my bare hands things slimy with rot or having liquid filth drip
on my ragged pants. I was used to dirt, and my hands were as
calloused as my feet. What made me sweat was the work I had to
do with my mind. Always before, when somebody had given me
a piece of work to do, he had stood right there to do all the
thinking. Here his orders would have been, 'Pull that piece of

sacking out. That stick, put it on top of the woodpile. Those dried-up chicken bones, scrape them up from the dirt and throw them in the trash pile.' All I would have had to do was to plod along, doing what I was ordered. Now I was the one to give the orders.

17   "Now that I was really thinking about what I was doing, I was amazed to see how little I had done, how much more there was to do than I had seen.

18   "I stooped to pull apart the grimy, mud-colored tangle heaped up back of the door. As I stirred it, a snake crawled out from under it and wriggled towards the door. A big fellow. I wasn't surprised. I was used to snakes. I dropped a stone on his head and carried his long, black body out to the trash pile in the yard.

19   "Now I had come to a corner where chickens evidently roosted every night. Everything was covered with their droppings, like smearings of white paint. I thought nothing of handling them, and taking up the body of one I found lying still and dead in the midst of the rubbish. More rotted rags, a stained, torn pair of pants, too far gone even for me to wear, still smelling foul. Some pieces of wood, not rotten, fit for fuel. Everything I came to had first to be pulled loose from the things it was mixed up with, and enough of the dirt shaken off to let me make out what it was. And then I had to think what to do with it. No wonder that the sweat ran down my face. To see, I had to wipe my eyes with the back of my hands.

20   "Finally, the last of the refuse was taken apart and cleared away and the litter and filth which had dropped from it to the floor was swept together and carried out to the trash pile. I kept looking over my shoulder for somebody to make the decisions, to tell me what to do. 'Throw that away. Save that. Put it with the firewood. Toss that into the barrel with the broken glass.' But there was nobody there to give me orders. I went in to get Mrs. Ruffner. 'I got it done,' I told her.

21   "Laying down her pen, she came again to see. I felt nervous as, silent and attentive, she ran those clear eyes of hers over what I had been doing. But I wasn't at all prepared to have her say again, 'That's better, but there's a great deal still to do. You haven't touched the cobwebs, I see.' I looked up at them, my lower jaw dropped in astonishment. Sure enough, there they

hung in long, black festoons. I had not once lifted my head to see them. 'And how about washing the window? Here, step in here and get a pail of water for that. Here are some clean rags. You'll have to go over it several times to get it clean.'

"She went back into the house and I stood shaken by more new ideas than I could tell you. I hadn't even noticed there was a window, it was so thick with dust and cobwebs. I had never had anything to do with a glass window. In the dark cabins I had lived in, the windows were just holes cut in the walls.   22

"I set to work once more, the sweat running down my face. Suppose she wouldn't even let me try to do her work. I never could get into Hampton! What if I just never could get the hang of her ways? Stricken, scared, I began again to clean that wood-shed! I went over and over every corner of it. Once in a while I stopped stock-still to *look* at it, as I had never looked at anything before, trying really to see it. I don't know that ever in my life afterwards did I care about doing anything right, as much as getting that little old woodshed clean.   23

"When I came to what I thought was the end, I stopped to get my breath. I looked up at the slanting roof. The rafters were not only cleared of cobwebs but bare of dust; the floor was swept clean, not a chip, not a thread, not a glint of broken glass on it. Piles of firewood against the walls. And the window! *I* had washed that window! Five times I had washed it. How it sparkled! How the strong sunshine poured through it! Now the wood-shed was no rubbish pile. It was a room. To me it looked like a parlor. I was proud of it. Till then I had never been proud of anything I had done.   24

"Then for the third time I went to call Mrs. Ruffner to inspect. Big boy as I was, twice her size, my hands were shaking, my lips twitching. I felt sick. Had I done it right this time? Could I ever do anything right?   25

"I watched her face as she passed my work in review, looking carefully up, down, and around. Then she turned to me and, looking straight into my eyes, she nodded and said, 'Now it's clean. Nobody could have done it any better.'   26

"She had opened the door through which I took my first step towards civilized standards of living."   27

He drew a long breath and went on, "For a year and a half I lived with those standards around me, working for Mrs. Ruffner.   28

What I learned from her! It was like breathing new air. I could never say in words what she taught me, for it was not taught in words but in life. She never pronounced such abstract expressions as 'frankness' and 'honesty'—they radiated from her, like sunlight streaming silently through a clean window, as she spoke of the tasks she set me. They were so simple she took them for granted, but they were revelations to me. I have repeated ever so many times the story of what Mrs. Ruffner taught me by the way she lived in her home—lessons of as great a value to me as any education I ever had in all my life. To anybody seeing me from the outside, I would, I suppose, have seemed to be learning only how to clean a filthy yard, how to keep a fence in repair, how to hang a gate straight, how to paint a weather-beaten barn.

29   "And then how to study—how to learn from the books she helped me secure, the books she took for granted and which, for me, were revelations. She took my breath away by suggesting, casually, that I begin to have a library of my own. Me!

30   "It was an old dry-goods box. I knocked the boards out of one side, used them for shelves, and with Mrs. Ruffner's backing to steady me, began with incredulous pride to set up, side by side, one and another of the battered, priceless printed volumes which, under Mrs. Ruffner's roof, I had come to own. I owning books!

31   "And yet, after all, later on when the way ahead was darkly blocked, it was that woodshed which pushed open the door.

32   "It would take too long to tell you all the piled-up difficulties I had to climb over to reach my goal of a real school with real, full-time classroom study. All sorts of things happened as I made my way over the long distance which separated me from Hampton. And when I actually stood before that three-story, brick school building, it looked as though I would not be allowed to enter it as a student. My trip had been longer, harder, had cost more than I had dreamed it could. I was nearly penniless, footsore, dusty, gaunt, unwashed.

33   "The teacher who was in charge of admitting or turning away students gave me a long, doubtful look and told me to wait. Well, I waited. I saw her interviewing other students, better dressed, cleaner, ever so much more promising-looking than I, without a look at me. But I didn't go away. That solid, three-story brick building—all just to provide a chance to study for

people who had never had a chance to study—how could I go away, even if I were not welcome? I waited. After several hours of watching that teacher admit other students, she finally had an idea about me and told me briefly, dubiously, 'The classroom next to this one needs to be cleaned before the Institute opens tomorrow. Do you suppose you could sweep it out? There's a broom over there in the corner.'

"In all my life I never had an order which so uplifted my heart. Could I sweep it out? Oh, Mrs. Ruffner!   34

"I swept that classroom three times. I moved every piece of furniture and swept under each one. There was a closet. I swept that. Joyfully I swept every corner clean. I found a dust cloth. I dusted everything in the room, I turned the cloth and dusted everything again, and again. I was in the middle of my fourth dusting when the teacher opened the door and stepped in. She was a Yankee. She knew what to look for. She took a clean handkerchief from her pocket, shook it out, and passed it over the top of a desk. After one startled look at me, she rubbed the seat of a chair with it.   35

"I stood at ease, my head high, fearing nothing. I did not need anybody's permission to feel sure of myself. I had been asked to perform a task. I had done it.   36

"She passed her testing handkerchief over a window sill, and turned to face me. She was a Yankee and wasted no words. She put the handkerchief back in her pocket, and in a matter-of-fact voice said, 'You're admitted to Hampton.'   37

"I had been set an entrance examination. And thanks to Mrs. Ruffner I had passed it."   38

His name was Booker T. Washington.   39

Vocabulary

To get the most out of reading this essay, you should have a working understanding of the words listed on the next page. Following each word is a parenthetical reference, indicating the paragraph in which the word is used, as well as a definition for the word. Go back and look at the sentence in which the word appears, and see how the definition applies. To help you make

this word a part of your active vocabulary, write a sentence of your own using the word in the space provided.

frowsy (5): musty or stale

_____

_____

refuse-flax (5): rough waste cloth

_____

_____

slovenly (6): dirty, unkempt

_____

_____

squalor (7): filth, poverty

_____

_____

festoons (21): decorative strips hung between two points

_____

_____

abstract (28): theoretical, obscure

_____

_____

incredulous (30): astounded, shocked

_____

_____

gaunt (32): very thin

_____

_____

Understanding the Essay

1. What great American leader visited the small Knapp house? Why is it a shrine to him?

2. Why did the slaves let everything fall into disrepair? Why didn't the white people keep the slave quarters in better repair?

3. Why did the narrator apply to work at Mrs. Ruffner's house, even though he'd heard she was so strict that nobody could suit her?

4. What lesson did the narrator learn simply by cleaning the woodshed? How did Mrs. Ruffner help him go through the door "towards civilized standards of living"?

5. What else did Mrs. Ruffner give the narrator to start his education?

6. How did the narrator gain admission to Hampton?

Exploring the Theme: Discussion and Writing

1. It's clear from the narrator's story that a profound learning experience can occur just as easily outside of a classroom as in it. In this case, the narrator needed to learn how to approach work and life in general before he could succeed in the classroom. Describe the most important lesson you've learned outside the classroom. Who helped to teach you the lesson? Why is it important to you now?

2. What do you think is the most important attribute for succeeding in school? Explain your answer.

WRITING SUGGESTIONS
FOR "EDUCATION"

1. From your own experience, how true is it that success in school comes from "telling testers what they want to hear"? What else does education depend on? How often have your teachers asked you to open a book and let your curiosity take hold of you? Write an essay on what you feel constitutes success in school.

2. Write an essay in which you reflect on your educational experiences—on what has worked well and what hasn't. What one feature of your education has helped you the most? Why was it so valuable? Has anything in your education held you back?

3. We are sometimes taught life's important lessons at strange times and in unexpected places. These lessons become all the more memorable because of the circumstances in which they came about. Has a lesson ever been taught to you when you least expected it? Write an essay explaining what you learned and how the lesson came about.

4. Write a reasoned and well-supported essay in which you present your views of whether or not sex education should be taught in our schools. If you are in favor, give your philosophy about how it should be done. If you are opposed, explain how you think young people should best be informed about sexuality.

5. Write an essay in which your thesis is the following quotation from the noted psychologist B. F. Skinner: "Education is what survives when what has been learnt is forgotten."

6. If tests fail to measure intellectual development and growth, how can they be measured? Would it help to have a conference with each of your teachers for you to be evaluated more personally and pleasantly? Should take-home exams be encouraged and given more support? Write an essay explaining your proposals for improving upon the present testing system.

7. Mrs. Ruffner's standards forced Booker T. Washington to go back over his work and reach a higher level of efficiency and performance. Yet it was Washington himself who sought out that challenge. Where does the aspiration to learn, to do more and better work, come from? Is it innate? Is it unevenly distributed in us, simply waiting to be sparked in some people and not at all present in others? Do most of us have to wait for someone to demand more of us? Write an essay that discusses how our educational system can awaken aspirations that may be dormant in us.

7

WORK

When we consider the notion of work, we are usually overcome by a flood of contradictory thoughts and mixed emotions. Most of us need our jobs but sometimes come to hate them, as we do anything that makes extraordinary demands on us. But think of those who are about to enter the work force, perhaps yourself, who can't find work or those who have been laid off or whose jobs have been curtailed. For them, finding a job would be a cause for celebration and happiness. On the practical level, we must work to earn income. We give of our time and effort, mental and/or physical, in exchange for money and benefits. Some of us think that if we had enough money, we wouldn't need to work, but therein lies another dilemma because work fulfills a larger need for most of us than mere compensation. Perhaps the Spanish philosopher José Ortega y Gasset put it best:

> An *unemployed* existence is a worse negation of life than death itself. Because to live means to have something definite to do— a mission to fulfill—and in the measure in which we avoid setting our life to something, we make it empty . . . Human life, by its very nature, has to be dedicated to something.

If we are fortunate, we will work at jobs that will fulfill our missions and give purpose to our larger lives.

In the first essay in this section, Daniel Meier discusses what it was like to follow his dream in getting a job teaching children, only to find himself in the awkward position of doing what others call "women's work." In recounting her mother's difficult life, Bonnie Smith-Yackel puts the lie to a homemaker as someone who is unemployed. Rose Del Castillo Guilbault then takes us to her summer job on a conveyor belt, a job she thought she would not like but found surprisingly enjoyable for its social component. Lastly, Ellen Goodman draws our attention to the problem of workaholism, to the work ethic within a corporate culture that is always grinding and occasionally deadly.

ONE MAN'S KIDS

Daniel Meier

*Daniel Meier began teaching first grade in 1985, a year
after he earned a master's degree from the Harvard
Graduate School of Education. He wrote the following
essay for the "About Men" column of the New York
Times Magazine (November, 1987).*

Preparing to Read

If you met a young man with a master's degree in education
from Harvard, it's very unlikely that you would guess he now
teaches first grade. We assume things about people based on
their education, sex, and age, including what job they're "suitable" for. Teaching first graders is, in our society, a "woman's
job," just as construction work is a "man's job." Such stereotypes are changing, but "One Man's Kids" not only describes
what Meier likes about teaching young children; it also reveals
that he had to be careful how he answered certain gender-
related questions to succeed in an elementary school job interview. Did you have any male teachers in elementary school?
How would you react if one of your peers pursued a career in a
field dominated by the opposite sex?

I teach first graders. I live in a world of skinned knees, double-
knotted shoelaces, riddles that I've heard a dozen times,
stale birthday cakes, hurt feelings, wandering stories, and
one lost shoe ("and if you don't find it my mother'll kill me"). My
work is dominated by 6-year-olds.

It's 10:45, the middle of snack, and I'm helping Emily open
her milk carton. She has already tried the other end without
success, and now there's so much paint and ink on the carton
from her fingers that I'm not sure she should drink it at all. But I

open it. Then I turn to help Scott clean up some milk he has just spilled onto Rebecca's whale crossword puzzle.

3   While I wipe my milk- and paint-covered hands, Jenny wants to know if I've seen that funny book about penguins that I read in class. As I hunt for it in a messy pile of books, Jason wants to know if there is a new seating arrangement for lunch tables. I find the book, turn to answer Jason, then face Maya, who is fast approaching with a new knock-knock joke. After what seems like the 10th "Who's there?" I laugh and Maya is pleased.

4   Then Andrew wants to know how to spell "flukes" for his crossword. As I get to "u," I give a hand signal for Sarah to take away the snack. But just as Sarah is almost out the door, two children complain that "we haven't even had ours yet." I stop the snack mid-flight, complying with their request for graham crackers. I then return to Andrew, noticing that he has put "flu" for 9 Down, rather than 9 Across. It's now 10:50.

5   My work is not traditional male work. It's not a singular pursuit. There is not a large pile of paper to get through or one deal to transact. I don't have one area of expertise or knowledge. I don't have the singular power over language of a lawyer, the physical force of a construction worker, the command over fellow workers of a surgeon, the wheeling and dealing transactions of a businessman. My energy is not spent in pursuing, climbing, achieving, conquering, or cornering some goal or object.

6   My energy is spent in encouraging, supporting, consoling, and praising my children. In teaching, the inner rewards come from without. On any given day, quite apart from teaching reading and spelling, I bandage a cut, dry a tear, erase a frown, tape a torn doll, and locate a long-lost boot. The day is really won through matters of the heart. As my students groan, laugh, shudder, cry, exult, and wonder, I do too. I have to be soft around the edges.

7   A few years ago, when I was interviewing for an elementary-school teaching position, every principal told me with confidence that, as a male, I had an advantage over female applicants because of the lack of male teachers. But in the next breath, they asked with a hint of suspicion why I chose to work with young children. I told them that I wanted to observe and contribute to the intellectual growth of a maturing mind. What I really felt like saying, but didn't, was that I loved helping a child learn to

write his name for the first time, finding someone a new friend, or sharing in the hilarity of reading about Winnie the Pooh getting so stuck in a hole that only his head and rear show.

I gave that answer to those principals, who were mostly male,   8
because I thought they wanted a "male" response. This meant talking about intellectual matters. If I had taken a different course and talked about my interest in helping children in their emotional development, it would have been seen as closer to a "female" answer. I even altered my language, not once mentioning the word "love" to describe what I do indeed love about teaching. My answer worked; every principal nodded approvingly.

Some of the principals also asked what I saw myself doing   9
later in my career. They wanted to know if I eventually wanted to go into educational administration. Becoming a dean of students or a principal has never been one of my goals, but they seemed to expect me, as a male, to want to climb higher on the career stepladder. So I mentioned that, at some point, I would be interested in working with teachers as a curriculum coordinator. Again, they nodded approvingly.

If those principals had been female instead of male, I wonder   10
whether their questions, and my answers, would have been different. My guess is that they would have been.

At other times, when I'm at a party or a dinner and tell   11
someone that I teach young children, I've found that men and women respond differently. Most men ask about the subjects I teach and the courses I took in my training. Then, unless they bring up an issue such as merit pay, the conversation stops. Most women, on the other hand, begin the conversation on a more immediate and personal level. They say things like "those kids must love having a male teacher" or "that age is just wonderful, you must love it." Then, more often than not, they'll talk about their own kids or ask me specific questions about what I do. We're then off and talking shop.

Possibly, men would have more to say to me, and I to them, if   12
my job had more of the trappings and benefits of more traditional male jobs. But my job has no bonuses or promotions. No complimentary box seats at the ball park. No cab fare home. No drinking buddies after work. No briefcase. No suit. (Ties get stuck in paint jars.) No power lunches. (I eat peanut butter and jelly, chips, milk, and cookies with the kids.) No taking clients out for cocktails. The only place I take my kids is to the playground.

13   Although I could have pursued a career in law or business, as several of my friends did, I chose teaching instead. My job has benefits all its own. I'm able to bake cookies without getting them stuck together as they cool, buy cheap sewing materials, take out splinters, and search just the right trash cans for useful odds and ends. I'm sometimes called "Daddy" and even "Mommy" by my students, and if there's ever a lull in the conversation at a dinner party, I can always ask those assembled if they've heard the latest riddle about why the turkey crossed the road. (He thought he was a chicken.)

Vocabulary

To get the most out of reading this essay, you should have a working understanding of the words listed below. Following each word is a parenthetical reference, indicating the paragraph in which the word is used, as well as a definition for the word. Go back and look at the sentence in which the word appears, and see how the definition applies. To help you make this word a part of your active vocabulary, write a sentence of your own using the word in the space provided.

singular (5): one-track

---

exult (6): rejoice

---

intellectual (8): mental, academic

---

curriculum (9): topics for study

Understanding the Essay

1. How long does the series of events Meier describes in paragraphs 2–4 take? What point does he make with this description?
2. In what ways is teaching first grade not traditional male work?
3. How does Meier define success in his job?
4. Why must Meier carefully phrase his answers to certain questions when he interviews with a male principal?
5. How do most men react when Meier describes his work in casual conversation? How do women usually react?
6. What are Meier's job "benefits?"

Exploring the Theme: Discussion and Writing

1. Discuss the differences between the reactions of men and women to Meier's job. Why were the male principals suspicious of his motivation to teach young children? Why can Meier afford to describe his job in emotional terms to women but not to men? Why don't men generally like to discuss Meier's line of work?
2. Would you consider a career in a field traditionally dominated by the opposite sex (a male nurse, a female welder, and so on)? Why or why not? What difficulties would you expect along the way?

MY MOTHER NEVER WORKED

Bonnie Smith-Yackel

Bonnie Smith-Yackel grew up on a midwestern farm. Her family overcame their almost constant financial and environmental hardships through her parents' hard work. In the following essay, Smith-Yackel contrasts her view of the work her mother did with society's point of view.

Preparing to Read

Think about the job you want after you finish school. It probably offers some combination of salary, benefits, creative expression, and recognition from others. Yet one important and influential job offers little or none of the above: homemaker. Smith-Yackel's essay describes why the very words *homemaker* and *housewife* (or *househusband*) have become almost derogatory in modern society. No matter how diligent, successful, and admired a homemaker is within the home, there is almost no recognition from outside. The irony of Smith-Yackel's story is a poignant reminder about why men and women today are forced to choose between spending time with their children and being viewed in some ways as a failure by society, or forging success in society outside the home and leaving most of the child rearing to others.

1   "Social Security Office." (The voice answering the telephone sounds very self-assured.)

2   "I'm calling about . . . I . . . my mother just died . . . I was told to call you and see about a . . . death-benefit check, I think they call it. . . ."

3   "I see. Was your mother on Social Security? How old was she?"

"Yes . . . she was seventy-eight. . . ." 4

"Do you know her number?" 5

"No . . . I, ah . . . don't you have a record?" 6

"Certainly. I'll look it up. Her name?" 7

"Smith. Martha Smith. Or maybe she used Martha Ruth 8
Smith. . . . Sometimes she used her maiden name . . . Martha
Jerabek Smith."

"If you'd care to hold on, I'll check our records—it'll be a few 9
minutes."

"Yes. . . ." 10

Her love letters—to and from Daddy—were in an old box, 11
tied with ribbons and stiff, rigid-with-age leather thongs: 1918
through 1920; hers written on stationery from the general store
she had worked in full-time and managed, single-handed, after
her graduation from high school in 1913; and his, at first, on
YMCA or Soldiers and Sailors Club stationery dispensed to the
fighting men of World War I. He wooed her thoroughly and persistently by mail, and though she reciprocated all his feelings for
her, she dreaded marriage. . . .

"It's so hard for me to decide when to have my wedding 12
day—that's all I've thought about these last two days. I have
told you dozens of times that I won't be afraid of married life,
but when it comes down to setting the date and then picturing
myself a married woman with half a dozen or more kids to look
after, it just makes me sick. . . . I am weeping right now—I hope
that some day I can look back and say how foolish I was to dread
it all."

They married in February, 1921, and began farming. Their 13
first baby, a daughter, was born in January, 1922, when my
mother was 26 years old. The second baby, a son, was born in
March, 1923. They were renting farms; my father, besides working his own fields, also was a hired man for two other farmers.
They had no capital initially, and had to gain it slowly, working
from dawn until midnight every day. My town-bred mother
learned to set hens and raise chickens, feed pigs, milk cows,
plant and harvest a garden, and can every fruit and vegetable
she could scrounge. She carried water nearly a quarter of a mile
from the well to fill her wash boilers in order to do her laundry
on a scrub board. She learned to shuck grain, feed threshers,
shock and husk corn, feed corn pickers. In September, 1925, the
third baby came, and in June, 1927, the fourth child—both

daughters. In 1930, my parents had enough money to buy their own farm, and that March they moved all their livestock and belongings themselves, 55 miles over rutted, muddy roads.

14　　In the summer of 1930 my mother and her two eldest children reclaimed a 40-acre field from Canadian thistles, by chopping them all out with a hoe. In the other fields, when the oats and flax began to head out, the green and blue of the crops were hidden by the bright yellow of wild mustard. My mother walked the fields day after day, pulling each mustard plant. She raised a new flock of baby chicks—500—and she spaded up, planted, hoed, and harvested a half-acre garden.

15　　During the next spring their hogs caught cholera and died. No cash that fall.

16　　And in the next year the drought hit. My mother and father trudged from the well to the chickens, the well to the calf pasture, the well to the barn, and from the well to the garden. The sun came out hot and bright, endlessly, day after day. The crops shriveled and died. They harvested half the corn, and ground the other half, stalks and all, and fed it to the cattle as fodder. With the price at four cents a bushel for the harvested crop, they couldn't afford to haul it into town. They burned it in the furnace for fuel that winter.

17　　In 1934, in February, when the dust was still so thick in the Minnesota air that my parents couldn't always see from the house to the barn, their fifth child—a fourth daughter—was born. My father hunted rabbits daily, and my mother stewed them, fried them, canned them, and wished out loud that she could taste hamburger once more. In the fall the shotgun brought prairie chickens, ducks, pheasant, and grouse. My mother plucked each bird, carefully reserving the breast feathers for pillows.

18　　In the winter she sewed night after night, endlessly, begging cast-off clothing from relatives, ripping apart coats, dresses, blouses, and trousers to remake them to fit her four daughters and son. Every morning and every evening she milked cows, fed pigs and calves, cared for chickens, picked eggs, cooked meals, washed dishes, scrubbed floors, and tended and loved her children. In the spring she planted a garden once more, dragging pails of water to nourish and sustain the vegetables for the family. In 1936 she lost a baby in her sixth month.

19　　In 1937 her fifth daughter was born. She was 42 years old. In 1939 a second son, and in 1941 her eighth child—and third son.

But the war had come, and prosperity of a sort. The herd of 20
cattle had grown to 30 head; she still milked morning and evening. Her garden was more than a half acre—the rains had
come, and by now the Rural Electricity Administration and indoor plumbing. Still she sewed—dresses and jackets for the children, housedresses and aprons for herself, weekly patching of
jeans, overalls, and denim shirts. Still she made pillows, using
the feathers she had plucked, and quilts every year—intricate
patterns as well as patchwork, stitched as well as tied—all necessary bedding for her family. Every scrap of cloth too small to be
used in quilts was carefully saved and painstakingly sewed together in strips to make rugs. She still went out in the fields to
help with the haying whenever there was a threat of rain.

In 1959 my mother's last child graduated from high school. 21
A year later the cows were sold. She still raised chickens and
ducks, plucked feathers, made pillows, baked her own bread,
and every year made a new quilt—now for a married child or for
a grandchild. And her garden, that huge, undying symbol of
sustenance, was as large and cared for as in all the years before.
The canning, and now freezing, continued.

In 1969, on a June afternoon, mother and father started out 22
for town so that she could buy sugar to make rhubarb jam for a
daughter who lived in Texas. The car crashed into a ditch. She
was paralyzed from the waist down.

In 1970 her husband, my father, died. My mother struggled 23
to regain some competence and dignity and order in her life. At
the rehabilitation institute, where they gave her physical therapy and trained her to live usefully in a wheelchair, the therapist
told me: "She did fifteen pushups today—fifteen! She's almost
seventy-five years old! I've never known a woman so strong!"

From her wheelchair she canned pickles, baked bread, 24
ironed clothes, wrote dozens of letters weekly to her friends and
her "half dozen or more kids," and made three patchwork house-
coats and one quilt. She made balls and balls of carpet rags—
enough for five rugs. And kept all her love letters.

"I think I've found your mother's records—Martha Ruth 25
Smith; married to Ben F. Smith?"

"Yes, that's right." 26

"Well, I see that she was getting a widow's pension. . . ." 27

"Yes, that's right." 28

"Well, your mother isn't entitled to our $255 death benefit." 29

30   "Not entitled! But why?"
31   The voice on the telephone explains patiently:
32   "Well, you see—your mother never worked."

Vocabulary

To get the most out of reading this essay, you should have a working understanding of the words listed below. Following each word is a parenthetical reference, indicating the paragraph in which the word is used, as well as a definition for the word. Go back and look at the sentence in which the word appears, and see how the definition applies. To help you make this word a part of your active vocabulary, write a sentence of your own using the word in the space provided.

thongs (11): strips, ties

---

reciprocated (11): returned

---

capital (13): money

---

cholera (15): a serious, sometimes fatal disease marked by severe gastrointestinal symptoms

---

---

sustenance (21): nourishment

Understanding the Essay

1. What was Martha's objection to marriage? Do you think her attitude changed over the years?
2. What three events made it even more difficult than usual for the Smith family to survive on the farm?
3. After the family installed electricity and indoor plumbing, what kept Martha busy?
4. Why did Martha keep working so hard, even after she was confined to a wheelchair and could have enjoyed a more leisurely life?
5. Martha worked hard for her entire married life. Why won't the government give her daughter a death benefit?

Exploring the Theme: Discussion and Writing

1. If you have children, will you be willing to be a househusband or a housewife if your spouse earns enough to support the family? Why or why not?
2. Child care is becoming a large problem in our society. It is not valued highly, yet the penalties for poor child care are high, because poorly raised or ignored children today become dysfunctional adults tomorrow. What changes could make child care more appreciated? How might society reward child care workers and parents instead of ignoring them?

HISPANIC, USA: THE CONVEYOR-BELT LADIES

Rose Del Castillo Guilbault

Rose Del Castillo Guilbault wrote about her experiences working with migrant workers for the San Francisco Chronicle *(April 15, 1990).*

Preparing to Read

Summer jobs are a part of most students' lives. For many, such jobs are a cross to bear to earn spending money, tuition, and/or book money for the academic year. Del Castillo Guilbault faced a job that didn't challenge her—picking blemished tomatoes off a conveyor belt—and co-workers whom she didn't want to know. "Hispanic, USA: The Conveyor-Belt Ladies" describes how she was able to move beyond her own youthful arrogance after she came to know and admire the "conveyor-belt ladies," Mexican migrant workers who faced poverty and prejudice and still dealt with their lot with humor and grace. Have you worked the same summer job for a few years? Have you ever gained something beyond your wages from working at a job or with people that you might otherwise have avoided?

1   The conveyor-belt ladies were the migrant women, mostly from Texas, I worked with during the summers of my teenage years. I call them conveyor-belt ladies because our entire relationship took place while sorting tomatoes on a conveyor belt.

2   We were like a cast in a play where all the action occurs on one set. We'd return day after day to perform the same roles, only this stage was a vegetable-packing shed, and at the end of the season there was no applause. The players could look forward only to the same uninspiring parts on a string of grim real-life stages.

The women and their families arrived in May for the carrot   3
season, spent the summer in the tomato sheds and stayed
through October for the bean harvest. After that, they emptied
the town, some returning to their homes in Texas (cities like
McAllen, Douglas, Brownsville), while others continued on the
migrant trail, picking cotton in the San Joaquin Valley or grape-
fruits and oranges in the Imperial Valley.

Most of these women had started in the fields. The vegetable   4
packing sheds were a step up, easier than the back-breaking,
grueling work the field demanded. The work was more tedious
than strenuous, paid better, provided fairly steady hours and
clean bathrooms. Best of all, you weren't subjected to the
elements.

The summer I was 16, my mother got jobs for both of us as   5
tomato sorters. That's how I came to be included in the seasonal
sorority of the conveyor belt.

The work consisted of standing and picking flawed tomatoes   6
off the conveyor belt before they rolled off into the shipping
boxes at the end of the line. These boxes were immediately
loaded onto waiting delivery trucks, so it was crucial not to let
imperfect tomatoes through.

The work could be slow or intense, depending on the quality   7
of the tomatoes and how many there were. Work increased when
the company's deliveries got backlogged or after rainy weather
had delayed picking.

During those times, it was not unusual to work from 7 A.M. to   8
midnight, playing catch-up. I never heard anyone complain
about the overtime. Overtime meant desperately needed extra
money.

I was not happy to be part of the agricultural work force. I   9
would have preferred working in a dress shop or baby-sitting,
like my friends. But I had a dream that would cost a lot of
money—college. And the fact was, this was the highest-paying
work I could do.

But it wasn't so much the work that bothered me. I was   10
embarrassed because only Mexicans worked at packing sheds. I
had heard my schoolmates joke about the "ugly, fat Mexican
women" at the sheds. They ridiculed the way they dressed and
laughed at the "funny way" they talked. I feared working with
them would irrevocably stigmatize me, setting me further apart
from my Anglo classmates.

11   At 16 I was more American than Mexican and, with adolescent arrogance, felt superior to these "uneducated" women. I might be one of them, I reasoned, but I was not like them.

12   But it was difficult not to like the women. They were a gregarious, entertaining group, easing the long, monotonous hours with bawdy humor, spicy gossip and inventive laments. They poked fun at all the male workers and did hysterical impersonations of a dyspeptic Anglo supervisor. Although he didn't speak Spanish (other than *"Mujeres, trabajo, trabajo!"* Women, work, work!), he seemed to sense he was being laughed at. That would account for the sudden rages when he would stamp his foot and forbid us to talk until break time.

13   "I bet he understands Spanish and just pretends so he can hear what we say," I whispered to Rosa.

14   *"Ay, no, hija,* it's all the buzzing in his ears that alerts him that these *viejas* (old women) are bad-mouthing him!" Rosa giggled.

15   But it would have been easier to tie the women's tongues in a knot than to keep them quiet. Eventually the ladies had their way and their fun, and the men learned to ignore them.

16   We were often shifted around, another strategy to keep us quiet. This gave me ample opportunity to get to know everyone, listen to their life stories and absorb the gossip.

17   Pretty Rosa described her romances and her impending wedding to a handsome field worker. Bertha, a heavy-set, dark-skinned woman, told me that Rosa's marriage would cause nothing but headaches because the man was younger and too handsome. Maria, large, moon-faced and placid, described the births of each of her nine children, warning me about the horrors of childbirth. Pragmatic Minnie, a tiny woman who always wore printed cotton dresses, scoffed at Maria's stupidity, telling me she wouldn't have so many kids if she had ignored that good-for-nothing priest and gotten her tubes tied!

18   In unexpected moments, they could turn melancholic: recounting the babies who died because their mothers couldn't afford medical care; the alcoholic, abusive husbands who were their "cross to bear"; the racism they experienced in Texas, where they were branded "dirty Mexicans" or "Mexican dogs" and not allowed in certain restaurants.

19   They spoke with the detached fatalism of people with lim-

ited choices and alternatives. Their lives were as raw and brutal as ghetto streets—something they accepted with an odd grace and resignation.

I was appalled and deeply affected by these confidences. The injustices they endured enraged me; their personal struggles overwhelmed me. I knew I could do little but sympathize.   20

My mother, no stranger to suffering, suggested I was too impressionable when I emotionally told her the women's stories. "That's nothing," she'd say lightly. "If they were in Mexico, life would be even harder. At least there's opportunities here, you can work."   21

My icy arrogance quickly thawed, that first summer, as my respect for the conveyor-belt ladies grew.   22

I worked in the packing sheds for several summers. The last season also turned out to be the last time I lived at home. It was the end of a chapter in my life, but I didn't know it then. I had just finished junior college and was transferring to the university. I was already over-educated for seasonal work, but if you counted the overtime, no other jobs came close to paying so well, so I went back one last time.   23

The ladies treated me with warmth and respect. I was a college student, deserving of special treatment.   24

Aguedita, the crew chief, moved me to softer and better-paying jobs within the plant. I went from the conveyor belt to shoving boxes down a chute and finally to weighing boxes of tomatoes on a scale—the highest-paying position for a woman.   25

When the union's dues collector showed up, the women hid me in the bathroom. They had decided it was unfair for me to have to join the union and pay dues, since I worked only during the summer.   26

"Where's the student?" the union rep would ask, opening the door to a barrage of complaints about the union's unfairness.   27

Maria (of the nine children) tried to feed me all summer, bringing extra tortillas, which were delicious. I accepted them guiltily, always wondering if I was taking food away from her children. Others would bring rental contracts or other documents for me to explain and translate.   28

The last day of work was splendidly beautiful, warm and sunny. If this had been a movie, these last scenes would have been shot in soft focus, with a crescendo of music in the background.   29

30   But real life is anti-climactic. As it was, nothing unusual happened. The conveyor belt's loud humming was turned off, silenced for the season. The women sighed as they removed their aprons. Some of them just walked off, calling *"Hasta la próxima!"* Until next time!

31   But most of the conveyor-belt ladies shook my hand, gave me a blessing or a big hug.

32   "Make us proud!" they said.

33   I hope I have.

Vocabulary

To get the most out of reading this essay, you should have a working understanding of the words listed below. Following each word is a parenthetical reference, indicating the paragraph in which the word is used, as well as a definition for the word. Go back and look at the sentence in which the word appears, and see how the definition applies. To help you make this word a part of your active vocabulary, write a sentence of your own using the word in the space provided.

migrant (3): moving, one who doesn't remain in one place

_____

_____

sorority (5): all-female group, sisterhood

_____

_____

irrevocably (10): finally, irreversibly

_____

_____

stigmatize (10): brand, attach a negative label

_____

_____

gregarious (12): sociable, friendly

_____

_____

bawdy (12): lewd, risqué

_____

_____

dyspeptic (12): surly, unfriendly

_____

_____

pragmatic (17): practical

_____

_____

fatalism (19): acceptance of fate

_____

_____

crescendo (29): peak volume, climax of a musical piece

_____

_____

Understanding the Essay

1. Why was a job in the vegetable packing sheds a step up for many of the women who worked there?
2. Why did Del Castillo Guilbault work in the sheds, even though she was unhappy about her job?
3. How did the women resolve their conflict with their male supervisors? What technique did the men use to try to stop the women from conversing while they worked?
4. What were the women usually like as co-workers? Why did they have unexpected melancholic moments?

5. Why did Del Castillo Guilbault receive special treatment from the women during her last summer at the shed? Why was she promoted?

6. What was anticlimactic about Del Castillo Guilbault's last day in the shed?

Exploring the Theme:
Discussion and Writing

1. What was your best summer job? What made it appealing? What was your worst summer job? What made it bad?

2. Del Castillo Guilbault says, "We were like a cast in a play" but "The players could look forward only to the same uninspiring parts on a string of grim real-life stages." Add abusive husbands, racism, and poverty, and hardship hardly described the lot of the women Del Castillo Guilbault worked with. Imagine being transported into such a life. How would you keep up your spirits? How would you need to change your outlook on life? How would your interactions with other people change?

THE COMPANY MAN

Ellen Goodman

Ellen Goodman graduated from Radcliffe College in 1963. She is a columnist for the Boston Globe, *and her column is now carried by newspapers throughout the country. The following article is from her book* Close to Home, *a collection of her columns published in 1979.*

Preparing to Read

Every school has its "grinds"—the students who excel through sheer endurance and discipline. After graduation, the competition for jobs can seem even more cutthroat, creating an atmosphere in which overambitious workers can thrive. Whether they were grinds in school or not, they work incredible hours and put their jobs before everything else. They are workaholics. In the United States, where some would argue opportunity is there for those who are willing to work hard, it seems strange that a person can work *too* hard. "The Company Man" is a profile of a man who literally worked himself to death. It's also a scathing look at the corporate mentality that encouraged his one-track way of life—and hastened his death. Do you have some "workaholism" in you? Is it possible to effectively balance work, personal interests, and family?

H e worked himself to death, finally and precisely, at 3:00   1
A.M. Sunday morning.
The obituary didn't say that, of course. It said that he   2
died of a coronary thrombosis—I think that was it—but everyone among his friends and acquaintances knew it instantly. He was a perfect Type A, a workaholic, a classic, they said to each other and shook their heads—and thought for five or ten minutes about the way they lived.

This man who worked himself to death finally and precisely   3 at 3:00 A.M. Sunday morning—on his day off—was fifty-one years old and a vice-president. He was, however, one of six vice-presidents, and one of three who might conceivably—if the president died or retired soon enough—have moved to the top spot. Phil knew that.

4   He worked six days a week, five of them until eight or nine at night, during a time when his own company had begun the four-day week for everyone but the executives. He worked like the Important People. He had no outside "extracurricular interests," unless, of course, you think about a monthly golf game that way. To Phil, it was work. He always ate egg salad sandwiches at his desk. He was, of course, overweight, by 20 or 25 pounds. He thought it was okay, though, because he didn't smoke.

5   On Saturdays, Phil wore a sports jacket to the office instead of a suit, because it was the weekend.

6   He had a lot of people working for him, maybe sixty, and most of them liked him most of the time. Three of them will be seriously considered for his job. The obituary didn't mention that.

7   But it did list his "survivors" quite accurately. He is survived by his wife, Helen, forty-eight years old, a good woman of no particular marketable skills, who worked in an office before marrying and mothering. She had, according to her daughter, given up trying to compete with his work years ago, when the children were small. A company friend said, "I know how much you will miss him." And she answered, "I already have."

8   "Missing him all these years," she must have given up part of herself which had cared too much for the man. She would be "well taken care of."

9   His "dearly beloved" eldest of the "dearly beloved" children is a hard-working executive in a manufacturing firm down South. In the day and a half before the funeral, he went around the neighborhood researching his father, asking the neighbors what he was like. They were embarrassed.

10   His second child is a girl, who is twenty-four and newly married. She lives near her mother and they are close, but whenever she was alone with her father, in a car driving somewhere, they had nothing to say to each other.

11   The youngest is twenty, a boy, a high-school graduate who

has spent the last couple of years, like a lot of his friends, doing enough odd jobs to stay in grass and food. He was the one who tried to grab at his father, and tried to mean enough to him to keep the man at home. He was his father's favorite. Over the last two years, Phil stayed up nights worrying about the boy.

The boy once said, "My father and I only board here." 12

At the funeral, the sixty-year-old company president told the 13
forty-eight-year-old widow that the fifty-one-year-old deceased had meant much to the company and would be missed and would be hard to replace. The widow didn't look him in the eye. She was afraid he would read her bitterness and, after all, she would need him to straighten out the finances—the stock options and all that.

Phil was overweight and nervous and worked too hard. If he 14
wasn't at the office, he was worried about it. Phil was a Type A, a heart-attack natural. You could have picked him out in a minute from a lineup.

So when he finally worked himself to death, at precisely 3:00 15
A.M. Sunday morning, no one was really surprised.

By 5:00 P.M. the afternoon of the funeral, the company presi- 16
dent had begun, discreetly of course, with care and taste, to make inquiries about his replacement. One of three men. He asked around: "Who's been working the hardest?"

Vocabulary

To get the most out of reading this essay, you should have a working understanding of the words listed below. Following each word is a parenthetical reference, indicating the paragraph in which the word is used, as well as a definition for the word. Go back and look at the sentence in which the word appears, and see how the definition applies. To help you make this word a part of your active vocabulary, write a sentence of your own using the word in the space provided.

obituary (2): death notice

Type A (2): personality type, intense competitive person

_____

_____

conceivably (3): possibly

_____

_____

extracurricular (4): referring to things or activities outside of school or work

_____

_____

marketable (7): salable, valuable

_____

_____

deceased (13): a person who has died

_____

_____

Understanding the Essay

1. Why is the time of Phil's death important? What does it say about Phil before you know anything else about him?
2. Approximately how many hours a week did Phil work? Why does Goodman say that he was "of course" overweight?
3. Who survived Phil? Describe his family.
4. Why were the neighbors "embarrassed" when Phil's oldest son asked them about his father before the funeral?
5. Why didn't Phil's widow let the company president know how she really felt at the funeral?
6. Reread the final paragraph. According to this paragraph, what was the "moral" of the essay?

Exploring the Theme:
Discussion and Writing

1. What makes a workaholic work so much? Passion for the job? Greed? A competitive personality? Explain what causes workaholism. Can it be a positive trait in certain situations?

2. Predict the type of worker you'll be after you enter the work force. A workaholic? A steady worker? A procrastinator? Explain your answer based on past experience in work or school.

WRITING SUGGESTIONS
FOR "WORK"

1.   Michael Harrington has written, "More and more university students are convinced that work in American society is morally empty, aesthetically ugly, and, under conditions of automation, economically unnecessary." Write an essay in which you argue for or against Harrington's assertion.

2.   What kind of work would you like after you finish college? What would satisfy you about that job? Have you already had any experience in that area? What will you do if you acquire the position and it does not turn out to be all you had hoped? Write an essay about your future work plans.

3.   What is a workaholic? Do some reading on this recently much-examined hazard of the workplace. Are you a workaholic? Do you think you might be prone to turning into one? In light of increased competition in the marketplace, especially from abroad, are we as a society making too much of the negative aspects of working hard? Write an essay on workaholism in which you examine one or more of these questions or other questions that arise out of your reading.

4.   Like Daniel Meier, do you desire to work in a profession or at a job traditionally held by members of the opposite sex? What special problems do you expect to encounter in doing so? Have you thought about how you will respond to comments and actions that reflect stereotypic attitudes toward "men's work" and "women's work"? Write an essay explaining what you want to do and what you think you'll encounter in pursuing your objectives.

5.   Did only one of your parents work or both? Write an essay in which you discuss your parent or parents' jobs. What special conditions, benefits, or deprivations arose out of their employment situation? What kind of work did they do while you were a youngster? Did that kind of work influence you and the kind of work you yourself want to pursue? Did their work make you any more or less attracted to a college education than might have been the case?

6. What special problems do women face in the workplace? What provisions have been made, or should be made, to lessen or eliminate those problems? What is the so-called "glass-ceiling"? Have you or anyone you know had any personal experiences with it? What is sexual harrassment? What about maternity leave and day care? Write an essay on some aspect of the challenges facing women in the workforce.

8

A MULTICULTURAL SOCIETY

In "Eggs, Twinkies and Ethnic Stereotypes," one of the essays in this section, Jeanne Park writes, "We all hold misleading stereotypes of people that limit us as individuals in that we cheat ourselves out of the benefits different cultures can contribute. We can grow and learn from each culture whether it be Chinese, Korean or African-American." Park really captures the problem facing America. We let our racial and ethnic prejudices get in the way of our benefiting from perhaps the most multiethnic society on earth.

In recent years there has been a wave of interest in promoting multiculturalism, or the principle of ethnic and cultural inclusiveness. As a result, we are now starting to see history, and the great variety of peoples that made it, from new and exciting perspectives. Americans no longer view the world from the narrow confines of a Euro- or Anglocentric stance. But we walk a tightrope here also, trying to balance our identity as Americans with our allegiance to our diverse ethnic heritages. Perhaps Bette Bao Lord, a Chinese immigrant, said it best in an essay in *Newsweek* in 1992: "I do not believe that the loss of one's native culture is the price that one must pay for becoming an American." Nor is the answer, it would seem, to isolate ourselves in the smaller circle of our ethnicity, for this would fracture our national identity as Americans. As Arthur Schlesinger, Jr., writes, "The growing diversity of the American population makes the quest for unifying ideals and a common culture all the more urgent. In a world savagely rent by ethnic and racial antagonisms, the United States must continue as an example of how a highly differentiated society holds itself together." As Americans, we all benefit when we can maintain the diversity and unity that have come to be our defining strength as a nation.

THE CULT OF ETHNICITY, GOOD AND BAD

Arthur Schlesinger, Jr.

Arthur Schlesinger, Jr., came into prominence in 1961 when President John F. Kennedy appointed him as special assistant for Latin American Affairs. A Thousand Days, Schlesinger's book on the Kennedy presidency, won a Pulitzer prize for biography. A professor at the City University of New York, Schlesinger is widely recognized for his more than a dozen books on American history.

Preparing to Read

A motto long associated with the United States and that has appeared on our coins is the Latin phrase *e pluribus unum,* "from many one." The phrase implies that though we are a nation of immigrants, we have joined together to forge a new country with its own identity. Although we have come together to become Americans, we also have a strong desire to maintain our ethnic identities. Arthur Schlesinger worries that the recent "eruption in ethnicity" may. threaten the very ideals that have made America strong.

T he history of the world has been in great part the history of the mixing of peoples. Modern communication and transport accelerate mass migrations from one continent to another. Ethnic and racial diversity is more than ever a salient fact of the age. 1

But what happens when people of different origins, speaking different languages and professing different religions, inhabit the same locality and live under the same political sovereignty? Ethnic and racial conflict—far more than ideological conflict— is the explosive problem of our times. 2

3   On every side today ethnicity is breaking up nations. The Soviet Union, India, Yugoslavia, Ethiopia, are all in crisis. Ethnic tensions disturb and divide Sri Lanka, Burma, Indonesia, Iraq, Cyprus, Nigeria, Angola, Lebanon, Guyana, Trinidad—you name it. Even nations as stable and civilized as Britain and France, Belgium and Spain, face growing ethnic troubles. Is there any large multiethnic state that can be made to work?

4   The answer to that question has been, until recently, the United States. "No other nation," Margaret Thatcher has said, "has so successfully combined people of different races and nations within a single culture." How have Americans succeeded in pulling off this almost unprecedented trick?

5   We have always been a multiethnic country. Hector St. John de Crèvecoeur, who came from France in the 18th century, marveled at the astonishing diversity of the settlers—"a mixture of English, Scotch, Irish, French, Dutch, Germans and Swedes . . . this promiscuous breed." He propounded a famous question: "What then is the American, this new man?" And he gave a famous answer: "Here individuals of all nations are melted into a new race of men." *E pluribus unum.*

6   The U.S. escaped the divisiveness of a multiethnic society by a brilliant solution: the creation of a brand-new national identity. The point of America was not to preserve old cultures but to forge a new, *American* culture. "By an intermixture with our people," President George Washington told Vice President John Adams, immigrants will "get assimilated to our customs, measures and laws: in a word, soon become one people." This was the ideal that a century later Israel Zangwill crystalized in the title of his popular 1908 play *The Melting Pot.* And no institution was more potent in molding Crèvecoeur's "promiscuous breed" into Washington's "one people" than the American public school.

7   The new American nationality was inescapably English in language, ideas and institutions. The pot did not melt everybody, not even all the white immigrants; deeply bred racism put black Americans, yellow Americans, red Americans and brown Americans well outside the pale. Still, the infusion of other stocks, even of nonwhite stocks, and the experience of the New World reconfigured the British legacy and made the U.S., as we all know, a very different country from Britain.

8   In the 20th century, new immigration laws altered the composition of the American people, and a cult of ethnicity erupted

both among non-Anglo whites and among nonwhite minorities. This had many healthy consequences. The American culture at last began to give shamefully overdue recognition to the achievements of groups subordinated and spurned during the high noon of Anglo dominance, and it began to acknowledge the great swirling world beyond Europe. Americans acquired a more complex and invigorating sense of their world—and of themselves.

But, pressed too far, the cult of ethnicity has unhealthy conse-   9 quences. It gives rise, for example, to the conception of the U.S. as a nation composed not of individuals making their own choices but of inviolable ethnic and racial groups. It rejects the historic American goals of assimilation and integration. And, in an excess of zeal, well-intentioned people seek to transform our system of education from a means of creating "one people" into a means of promoting, celebrating and perpetuating separate ethnic origins and identities. The balance is shifting from *unum* to *pluribus*.

That is the issue that lies behind the hullabaloo over "multi-   10 culturalism" and "political correctness," the attack on "Eurocentric" curriculum and the rise of the notion that history and literature should be taught not as disciplines but as therapies whose function is to raise minority self-esteem. Group separatism crystalizes the differences, magnifies tensions, intensifies hostilities. Europe—the unique source of the liberating ideas of democracy, civil liberties and human rights—is portrayed as the root of all evil, and non-European cultures, their own many crimes deleted, are presented as the means of redemption.

I don't want to sound apocalyptic about these developments.   11 Education is always in ferment, and a good thing too. The situation in our universities, I am confident, will soon right itself. But the impact of separatist pressures on our public schools is more troubling. If a Kleagle of the Ku Klux Klan wanted to use the schools to disable and handicap black Americans, he could hardly come up with anything more effective than the "Afrocentric" curriculum. And if separatist tendencies go unchecked, the result can only be the fragmentation, resegregation and tribalization of American life.

I remain optimistic. My impression is that the historic forces   12 driving toward "one people" have not lost their power. The eruption of ethnicity is, I believe, a rather superficial enthusiasm stirred by romantic ideologues on the one hand and by unscrupulous con men on the other: self-appointed spokesmen whose claim to represent their minority groups is carelessly accepted by the media. Most American-born members of minority groups, white or nonwhite, see themselves primarily as Americans rather than primarily as members of one or another ethnic group. A notable indicator today is the rate of intermarriage across ethnic lines, across religious lines, even (increasingly) across racial lines. "We Americans," said Theodore Roosevelt, "are children of the crucible."

13   The growing diversity of the American population makes the quest for unifying ideals and a common culture all the more urgent. In a world savagely rent by ethnic and racial antagonisms, the U.S. must continue as an example of how a highly differentiated society holds itself together.

Vocabulary

To get the most out of reading this essay, you should have a working understanding of the words listed below. Following each word is a parenthetical reference, indicating the paragraph in which the word is used, as well as a definition for the word. Go back and look at the sentence in which the word appears, and see how the definition applies. To help you make this word a part of your active vocabulary, write a sentence of your own using the word in the space provided.

salient (1):   prominent, striking

_____

_____

ideological (2):   having assertions, theories, aims that constitute a political, social, and economic program

_____

_____

assimilated (6):   absorbed into a cultural tradition

_____

_____

infusion (7):   introduction, instillation

---

reconfigured (7):   reshaped

---

spurned (8):   rejected with disdain

---

inviolable (9):   unassailable

---

ferment (11):   state of agitation or tumult

---

unscrupulous (12):   unprincipled

---

quest (13):   search

Understanding the Essay

1. What is Schlesinger's thesis, and where is it stated?
2. According to Schlesinger, upon what principle was America founded? How does ethnicity threaten this principle?

3. What examples does Schlesinger use to support his claim that "Ethnic and racial conflict—far more than ideological conflict—is the explosive problem of our times"?

4. How has the United States managed to avoid the conflicts of ethnicity? Is the situation changing today? Explain.

5. What forces, according to Schlesinger, have precipitated the eruption of ethnicity? Does Schlesinger take these forces seriously? Why, or why not?

6. What have been the positive consequences of the new cult of ethnicity? The negative ones? How does one go about encouraging and building upon the beneficial aspects of diversity?

Exploring the Theme:
Discussion and Writing

1. Schlesinger claims that "no institution was more potent in molding Crèvecoeur's 'promiscuous breed' into Washington's 'one people' than the American public school." Do you agree with his assessment? How have our public schools helped foster an American identity and mold the American people?

2. In the end Schlesinger is essentially optimistic. He believes that America can and "must continue as an example of how a highly differentiated society holds itself together." Do you share Schlesinger's optimism or do you fear that "if separatist tendencies go unchecked, the result can only be the fragmentation, resegregation and tribalization of American life"? Why, or why not?

EGGS, TWINKIES AND ETHNIC STEREOTYPES

Jeanne Park

In reflecting on her early education and upbringing, Jeanne Park discovered that she was exposed to ethnic stereotypes at a very young age. In "Eggs, Twinkies and Ethnic Stereotypes," Park explains how such stereotyping—which is based on ignorance and forms the basis for bigotry—is damaging to all races. As she puts it, "We all hold misleading stereotypes of people that limit us as individuals in that we cheat ourselves out of the benefits different cultures can contribute." Her essay first appeared in the New York Times *on April 20, 1990.*

Preparing to Read

When you look around the library or a classroom at your school, how many races do you see? As America's population becomes more and more diverse, everyone will eventually rub elbows with people from a wide variety of cultures and races. Yet even living side by side with people from different ethnic backgrounds, many students get to know only individuals from their own race—all others are categorized, labeled, and avoided. Labels such as "egg" and "Twinkie" demonstrate the stigma sometimes faced by those who interact with other races. What labels and stereotypes are you aware of in your school and community?

W ho am I?   1
For Asian-American students, the answer is a diligent,   2
hardworking and intelligent young person. But living
up to this reputation has secretly haunted me.

The labeling starts in elementary school. It's not uncommon   3
for a teacher to remark, "You're Asian, you're supposed to do

well in math." The underlying message is, "You're Asian and you're supposed to be smarter."

4   Not to say being labeled intelligent isn't flattering, because it is, or not to deny that basking in the limelight of being top of my class isn't ego-boosting, because frankly it is. But at a certain point, the pressure became crushing. I felt as if doing poorly on my next spelling quiz would stain the exalted reputation of all Asian students forever.

5   So I continued to be an academic overachiever, as were my friends. By junior high school I started to believe I was indeed smarter. I became condescending toward non-Asians. I was a bigot; all my friends were Asians. The thought of intermingling occurred rarely if ever.

6   My elitist opinion of Asian students changed, however, in high school. As a student at what is considered one of the nation's most competitive science and math schools, I found that being on top is no longer an easy feat.

7   I quickly learned that Asian students were not smarter. How could I ever have believed such a thing? All around me are intelligent ambitious people who are not only Asian but white, black and Hispanic.

8   Superiority complexes aside, the problem of social segregation still exists in the schools. With few exceptions, each race socializes only with its "own kind." Students see one another in the classroom, but outside the classroom there remains distinct segregation.

9   Racist lingo abounds. An Asian student who socializes only with other Asians is believed to be an Asian Supremacist or, at the very least, arrogant and closed off. Yet an Asian student who socializes only with whites is called a "twinkie," one who is yellow on the outside but white on the inside.

10   A white teen-ager who socializes only with whites is thought of as prejudiced, yet one who socializes with Asians is considered an "egg," white on the outside and yellow on the inside.

11   These culinary classifications go on endlessly, needless to say, leaving many confused, and leaving many more fearful than ever of social experimentation. Because the stereotypes are accepted almost unanimously, they are rarely challenged. Many develop harmful stereotypes of entire races. We label people before we even know them.

Labels learned at a young age later metamorphose into more   12
visible acts of racism. For example, my parents once accused
and ultimately fired a Puerto Rican cashier, believing she had
stolen $200 from the register at their grocery store. They later
learned it was a mistake. An Asian shopkeeper nearby once beat
a young Hispanic youth who worked there with a baseball bat
because he believed the boy to be lazy and dishonest.

We all hold misleading stereotypes of people that limit us as   13
individuals in that we cheat ourselves out of the benefits different cultures can contribute. We can grow and learn from each
culture whether it be Chinese, Korean or African-American.

Just recently some Asian boys in my neighborhood were at-   14
tacked by a group of young white boys who have christened
themselves the Master Race. Rather than being angered by this
act, I feel pity for this generation that lives in a state of bigotry.

It may be too late for our parents' generation to accept that   15
each person can only be judged for the characteristics that set
him or her apart as an individual. We, however, can do better.

Vocabulary

To get the most out of reading this essay, you should have a
working understanding of the words listed below. Following
each word is a parenthetical reference, indicating the paragraph
in which the word is used, as well as a definition for the word.
Go back and look at the sentence in which the word appears, and
see how the definition applies. To help you make this word a
part of your active vocabulary, write a sentence of your own
using the word in the space provided.

diligent (2):   studious, hardworking

---

condescending (5):   arrogant, superior-acting

---

elitist (6):   snobbish or superior

_____

_____

segregation (8):   separation by category or group

_____

_____

metamorphose (12):   change, become altered

_____

_____

bigotry (14):   intolerance of other beliefs or races

_____

_____

Understanding the Essay

1. Why did the stereotype of the hardworking and intelligent Asian student both flatter and haunt Park?
2. What made Park realize that she and her Asian peers were not smarter than students of other races?
3. What is an egg? What is a Twinkie?
4. What effect do labels like egg and Twinkie have on students? How do they promote harmful stereotypes?
5. According to the stories that Park tells, what stereotypes do Asians believe about Hispanics?
6. Why do stereotypes limit our growth as individuals?

Exploring the Theme: Discussion and Writing

1. Describe the five or six students you spend the most time with in school. Is your group racially integrated? How did

you meet them? How does your group interact with groups that contain races other than your own?

2. What are some racial slurs you know? How do racial slurs promote bigotry?

SUBTLE LESSONS IN RACISM

Kirsten Mullen

Kirsten Mullen is a writer who lives in North Carolina. She has carefully observed the schooling of her eleven-year-old son and will soon go through the same process with her three-year-old son. She wrote the following piece for the November 6–8, 1992 USA Weekend.

Preparing to Read

Racism can take many forms. Some are obvious and quickly confronted, but others are easily overlooked because they're so subtle. Think back to your elementary school days, for example—how many different ethnic groups were used in examples or were represented in the curriculum? Chances are there weren't many, and, from Mullen's point of view, many practices that are discriminatory toward blacks and other minorities are still quite common. In the following reading Mullen describes a school where the teachers were dedicated and bright, the principal was open-minded, but, to her mind, racist behavior occurred frequently.

1   If you had told me that this would happen, I wouldn't have believed you. I mean, these are the '90s; ours is an integrated world.

2   Besides, it isn't politically correct.

3   During my child's six years attending an inner-city public elementary school, the racial makeup flipped from 60 percent black pupils and 40 percent white to the reverse. The teachers were well-educated, thoughtful, enlightened. School was the last place where I expected to encounter racism.

4   I spent a fair amount of time volunteering at my son's school. I enjoyed collaborating with his teachers, and I remain in awe of the incredible job that they do despite their charges'

myriad abilities and the parents' varying levels of support. But the racial problems were there from the beginning.

During the first week of kindergarten, I observed five wiggle worms working at the blackboard in my son's class. Two were black. While the group's creative hum was louder than their teacher wished to condone (my presence may have had something to do with her low tolerance level), it seemed acceptable 5-year-old behavior. Still, I wasn't surprised when she shot them the eye. What floored me, though, was her calling only the two black pupils by name, insisting that they sit down. And this was a black teacher!

A month later, another parent and I observed the principal, a progressive white woman, in a nearly identical situation. Three boys were skipping brightly, if noisily, down a hall. "I'll bet she reprimands the [lone] black [child]," I said. She did. When I asked the principal why, she replied, "I know his mother, and she would not have approved of his behavior." I suppose the other boys' parents would have been oblivious?

Then there were the Christmas angels. The third-graders were busily making angels for their bulletin board. But there was only one small problem: Their teacher had provided only pink and white construction paper. My then-8-year-old came home disgruntled and not just a little confused. "I didn't think I could ask for brown," he said. "I didn't want her to get mad at me."

When I approached his teacher, she began somewhat defensively, saying: "I'm really surprised to hear this. [He's] a real leader in the class, and the children look up to him. If he had asked for brown paper, his classmates would have saluted his choice and probably followed." But the burden of race should not have fallen on the shoulders of an 8-year-old, I argued.

"There is so much everyone is asking of us," his teacher continued wearily. "We feed the children breakfast; some of them are here when we arrive and here when we leave [in before- and after-school care programs]; we teach sex education; we try not to favor boys over girls—and now this. But you're right. We need to be more sensitive to the matter of race."

Another teacher found herself in deep water when, in an attempt to teach the kids not to judge a book by its cover, she posted the words "Read an Ugly Book" on the wall in various colors, selecting brown and black for "Ugly." When I pointed it out, she said she had not been conscious of the implications of her choice.

11   Along that same line, my husband and I asked the school librarian to remember the global community when she produced bulletin-board designs featuring seasonal greetings or announcing coming events that included images of people. What was she thinking, we wondered, when she concocted a winter wonderland peopled with three blonds?

12   These encounters were far from painless for me. I was terrified the first time I brought up the subject of race at school. My palms were clammy, my heart was racing, and I could not have done it without rehearsing in the bathroom mirror. But all of the discussions since then have been easier. I also remember the day when our principal shared a teacher's (and perhaps her own) opinion about us: "[Those] two are never satisfied." We gave the question back to her and asked, "Are you?" This discussion became the first of many on the subject of race that the three of us came to appreciate.

13   Sometimes opportunities to spark such discussion come from unexpected quarters. This past spring, the delightful 6-year-old daughter of a friend decided to create a special card for her teacher, who was black and had just delivered her first child. But none of the periodicals in her family's collection featured brown babies. "Um . . . I hope you aren't offended by this request," my friend began nervously. "But do you have any magazine pictures of brown babies?"

14   I was touched by her request and encouraged by our conversation, because a similar situation seven years ago had led me to collect images of people of color. Take as many as you need, I told her.

15   One thing's certain: If you keep your eyes open and are willing to bring up this subject, you will find ample opportunities to make a difference in your children's lives. And as more of us embrace the subject, it ceases to be taboo.

Vocabulary

To get the most out of reading this essay, you should have a working understanding of the words listed on the next page. Following each word is a parenthetical reference, indicating the paragraph in which the word is used, as well as a definition for the word. Go back and look at the sentence in which the word appears, and see how the definition applies. To help you make

this word a part of your active vocabulary, write a sentence of your own using the word in the space provided.

integrated (1):   combined

_____

_____

enlightened (3):   educated, informed

_____

_____

collaborating (4):   working together

_____

_____

myriad (4):   countless

_____

_____

reprimands (6):   scolds

_____

_____

disgruntled (7):   upset

_____

_____

taboo (15):   forbidden, shunned by society

_____

_____

Understanding the Essay

1. What is Mullen's opinion of the teachers at her son's school?

2. Why do you think the teachers singled out the black students to scold when they were in a multiracial group? Why does Mullen think they did?

3. What do the teachers have to do besides teach in the school?

4. How did Mullen feel when she first brought up the subject of race at her son's school? Why did its difficulty change for her?

5. According to Mullen, how will the discussion of racial issues cease to be taboo?

Exploring the Theme: Discussion and Writing

1. Describe several examples of behavior or symbolism that Mullen might consider racist, based on what she considers to be racist in her article. Do you think they are racist? Why or why not?

2. As one of the teachers hinted to Mullen, sometimes it feels as if it's very difficult to do or say *anything* these days without someone taking offense. Those previously ignored or slighted—women, nonwhites, people with alternative life-styles—are on the lookout for negative images and portrayals of themselves. At the same time, a large segment of our society hangs on to traditional, Eurocentric ways of viewing the world. What do you think about this issue?

THE MIDDLE-CLASS
BLACK'S BURDEN

Leanita McClain

Free-lance writer Leanita McClain was a voice for middle-class African-Americans and a champion of civil rights in this country. For McClain, who committed suicide in 1984, racial equality was never more than a "hollow victory." First published in Newsweek *in 1980, McClain's essay is a powerful appeal to whites and African-Americans alike to strive for true racial equality.*

Preparing to Read

Perhaps you have seen the provocative bumper sticker that proclaims: "As long as one of us is oppressed, we are all oppressed." What does this mean for Americans? How does oppression manage to affect all our lives wherever it exits? Leanita McClain, a succesful middle-class African-American, knew all too well that "As long as we are denigrated as a group, no one of us has made it."

I am a member of the black middle-class who has had it with being patted on the head by white hands and slapped in the face by black hands for my success.   1

Here's a discovery that too many people still find startling: when given equal opportunities at white-collar pencil pushing, blacks want the same things from life that everyone else wants. These include the proverbial dream house, two cars, an above-average school and a vacation for the kids at Disneyland. We may, in fact, want these things more than other Americans because most of us have been denied them so long.   2

Meanwhile, a considerable number of the folks we left behind in the "old country," commonly called the ghetto, and the   3 militants we left behind in their antiquated ideology can't be-rate middle-class blacks enough for "forgetting where we came from." We have forsaken the revolution, we are told, we have sold out. We are Oreos, they say, black on the outside, white within.

4   The truth is, we have not forgotten; we would not dare. We are simply fighting on different fronts and are no less war weary, and possibly more heartbroken, for we know the black and white worlds can meld, that there can be a better world.

5   It is impossible for me to forget where I came from as long as I am prey to the jive hustler who does not hesitate to exploit my childhood friendship. I am reminded, too, when I go back to the old neighborhood in fear—and have my purse snatched—and when I sit down to a business lunch and have an old classmate wait on my table. I recall the girl I played dolls with who now rears five children on welfare, the boy from church who is in prison for murder, the pal found dead of a drug overdose in the alley where we once played tag.

6   My life abounds in incongruities. Fresh from a vacation in Paris, I may, a week later, be on the milk-run Trailways bus to Deep South backcountry attending the funeral of an ancient uncle whose world stretched only 50 miles and who never learned to read. Sometimes when I wait at the bus stop with my attaché case, I meet my aunt getting off the bus with other clean-ing ladies on their way to do my neighbors' floors.

7   But I am not ashamed. Black progress has surpassed our greatest expectations; we never saw much hope for it, and the achievement has taken us by surprise.

8   In my heart, however, there is no safe distance from the wretched past of my ancestors or the purposeless present of some of my contemporaries; I fear such a fate can reclaim me. I am not comfortably middle class; I am uncomfortably middle class.

9   I have made it, but where? Racism still dogs my people. There are still communities in which crosses are burned on the lawns of black families who have the money and grit to move in.

10   What a hollow victory we have won when my sister, dressed in her designer everything, is driven to the rear door of the luxury high rise in which she lives because the cab driver, noting only her skin color, assumes she is the maid, or the nanny, or the cook, but certainly not the lady of any house at this address.

11   I have heard the immigrants' bootstrap tales, the simplistic

reproach of "why can't you people be like us." I have fulfilled the entry requirements of the American middle class, yet I am left, at times, feeling unwelcome and stereotyped. I have overcome the problems of food, clothing and shelter, but I have not overcome my old nemesis, prejudice. Life is easier, being black is not.

I am burdened daily with showing whites that blacks are 12 people. I am, in the old vernacular, a credit to my race. I am my brothers' keeper, and my sisters', though many of them have abandoned me because they think that I have abandoned them.

I run a gauntlet between two worlds, and I am cursed and so 13 blessed by both. I travel, observe and take part in both; I can also be used by both. I am a rope in a tug of war. If I am a token in my downtown office, so am I at my cousin's church tea. I assuage white guilt. I disprove black inadequacy and prove to my parents' generation that their patience was indeed a virtue.

I have a foot in each world, but I cannot fool myself about 14 either. I can see the transparent deceptions of some whites and the bitter hopelessness of some blacks. I know how tenuous my grip on one way of life is, and how strangling the grip of the other way of life can be.

Many whites have lulled themselves into thinking that race 15 relations are just grand because they were the first on their block to discuss crab grass with the new black family. Yet too few blacks and whites in this country send their children to school together, entertain each other or call each other friend. Blacks and whites dining out together draw stares. Many of my co-workers see no black faces from the time the train pulls out Friday evening until they meet me at the coffee machine Monday morning. I remain a novelty.

Some of my "liberal" white acquaintances pat me on the 16 head, hinting that I am a freak, that my success is less a matter of talent than of luck and affirmative action. I may live among them, but it is difficult to live with them. How can they be sincere about respecting me, yet hold my fellows in contempt? And if I am silent when they attempt to sever me from my own, how can I live with myself?

Whites won't believe I remain culturally different; blacks 17 won't believe I remain culturally the same.

I need only look in a mirror to know my true allegiance, and 18 I am painfully aware that, even with my off-white trappings, I am prejudged by my color.

19 As for envy of my own people, am I to give up my career, my standard of living, to pacify them and set my conscience at ease? No. I have worked for these amenities and deserve them, though I can never enjoy them without feeling guilty.

20 These comforts do not make me less black, nor oblivious to the woe in which many of my people are drowning. As long as we are denigrated as a group, no one of us has made it. Inasmuch as we all suffer for every one left behind, we all gain for every one who conquers the hurdle.

Vocabulary

To get the most out of reading this essay, you should have a working understanding of the words listed below. Following each word is a parenthetical reference, indicating the paragraph in which the word is used, as well as a definition for the word. Go back and look at the sentence in which the word appears, and see how the definition applies. To help you make this word a part of your active vocabulary, write a sentence of your own using the word in the space provided.

proverbial (2): that which has become an object of common reference, as in a proverb

_____

_____

militants (3): people who are ready and willing to fight, warlike

_____

_____

antiquated (3): old, obsolete, old-fashioned

_____

_____

meld (4): blend, merge, unite

_____

_____

incongruities (6): inconsistencies, disagreements

_____

_____

nemesis (11): unbeatable rival

_____

_____

vernacular (12): native language or dialect of a country or place

_____

_____

gauntlet (13): severe trial, ordeal of being caught in a crossfire

_____

_____

assuage (13): pacify, calm

_____

_____

denigrated (20): defamed, belittled

_____

_____

Understanding the Essay

1. What is McClain's thesis, and where does she state it?

2. In paragraph 1, McClain says she "has had it with being patted on the head by white hands and slapped in the face by black hands for my success." Why do white people pat her head, and why do black people slap her face? Why do these actions anger McClain?

3. McClain believes that some African-Americans think she has sold them out. Why do they think that way about her?

4. What exactly is McClain's "burden"? Where does she best explain it? Do you agree with her assessment of the middle-class black's plight? Explain.

5. How does McClain see herself as a middle-class African-American? What does she mean when she says, "I am uncomfortably middle class"?

6. What is McClain's assessment of race relations in America in 1980? Has much changed since she wrote this essay? Explain.

Exploring the Theme: Discussion and Writing

1. What are the "immigrants' bootstrap tales" to which McClain refers in paragraph 11? If your parents or grandparents are immigrants, what stories have they shared with you? Why has the experience of African-Americans differed from that of other immigrant groups?

2. Speaking for middle-class African-Americans, McClain says, "we know the black and white worlds can meld, that there can be a better world." Do you agree? In your opinion, what is needed to fight racism and promote cultural diversity in America?

WRITING SUGGESTIONS FOR "A MULTICULTURAL SOCIETY"

1.   Elementary and high school is where many of us learned society's basic values. Describe your years in school. Can you think of anything—no matter how subtle—your teachers did that might have been discriminatory toward nonwhite students? Did you think your school was racist while you were there? Looking back, is your assessment still the same? In what ways did your teachers influence your views—either positively or negatively—of the different races? Write an essay in which you recount one or more experiences that helped shape your attitudes toward racial differences.

2.   Arthur Schlesinger, Jr., believes there have been many "healthy consequences" of the new interest in ethnicity, not the least of which is that "Americans [have] acquired a more complex and invigorating sense of their world—and of themselves." Have the recent calls for multiculturalism on college campuses across the country affected your school and its admissions policy or curriculum? Write an essay in which you explore both the benefits and the drawbacks of multiculturalism on your campus.

3.   Schlesinger refers to the "hullabaloo over 'multiculturalism' and 'political correctness.' " What exactly is "political correctness," and how does it affect students and faculty at your institution? Write an essay in which you define "political correctness," using examples from your own experiences, observations, or reading.

4.   A Chinese immigrant once wrote, "I do not believe that the loss of one's native culture is the price one must pay for becoming an American." Do you believe it is possible for a person to become an American and still maintain his or her native culture? Using several of the articles in this section, write an essay in which you present your position on this issue.

5.   What stereotypes do you have of other ethnic groups? How much actual contact do you have with these groups? Where did you learn these stereotypes? Do you believe, as Jeanne Park does, that "labels learned at a young age later metamorphose

into more visible acts of racism"? What would you need to know to change your opinion of these groups? Write an essay in which you discuss some of the stereotypes you hold and how they limit you as an individual.

6.   Jeanne Park believes that you can tell a lot about yourself by taking into account the people with whom you socialize. Who is in your social group, and why do they fit in? Write an essay in which you analyze your social group and draw some conclusions about its reasons for being.

7.   Using several articles from this section, write an essay in which you explore the relationship between stereotypes and prejudice.

9

LANGUAGE AND DIVERSITY

As a nation of diverse peoples, we can use our language to bring us together as well as separate us. When the language we use serves us well, it reveals itself to be at the very heart of what makes us civilized. We use speech and writing to communicate with one another, as well as to carry out our daily affairs. Inasmuch as we use language to define ourselves, we also reveal no less than the common bond of our humanity through our speech and writing. We recognize one another as people sharing the same space and moment in time, hoping to learn from the past and looking toward the future.

Sometimes language fails to serve us well. When our language consciously or inadvertently confines or diminishes others, when it puts them down or abuses them in some way—whether because of race, ethnic origin, gender, sexual orientation, religion, age, or physical or mental impairment—it also confines and diminishes the users of such language. To recognize the power of language both to liberate and to imprison is to come to some sense of our responsibility to use language thoughtfully and carefully.

Malcolm X was a Black Muslim leader and powerful speaker who discovered the limitations of his street language while in prison. In our opening selection, he tells of the liberation he felt when he took control of English. Specifically, he recounts how he discovered the dictionary, confronted his illiteracy, and taught himself to read and write. His newfound command over the English language allowed him to take control of his life, elevating him from the streets of Harlem to an even greater prominence. In the next selection, Mauricio Molina jumps into the debate on bilingualism in the United States. He argues that whereas it is nice that Spanish translations are available for just

252 *Language and Diversity*

about all aspects of American life, there are no incentives for Hispanics to learn English as other immigrant groups do. Finally, we present two articles that take opposing viewpoints on the issue of offensive language. Diane Cole believes that we should speak up when another's language diminishes us but cautions us not to be offensive in doing so. Eve Drobot, on the other hand, believes that some people have taken the sensitivity issue much too far and, in effect, stifle expression.

COMING TO AN AWARENESS
OF LANGUAGE

Malcolm X

On February 21, 1965, Malcolm X, the Black Muslim leader, was shot to death as he addressed a rally in Harlem. He was thirty-nine years old. The year before, with the assistance of the late Alex Haley, the author of Roots, *Malcolm X told his story in* The Autobiography of Malcolm X *(1964), a moving account of his search for fulfillment. In 1992 Spike Lee's movie* Malcolm X *examined the life of one of the most articulate and powerful African-Americans in the United States during the early 1960s.*

Preparing to Read

Most of us think of language as we think of the air we breathe: We cannot survive without it, but we take it for granted nearly all the time. Seldom are we conscious of language's real power to lead—or mislead—us. In the following selection from the *Autobiography*, Malcolm X tells how his inability to express himself made him feel like a prisoner of language and how he ultimately discovered and mastered the power of language. Think about your own language for a few minutes. Have you ever felt somehow handicapped by it? How has your language affected those around you? Explain how language influences or shapes your perceptions of the world.

I 've never been one for inaction. Everything I've ever felt strongly about, I've done something about. I guess that's why, unable to do anything else, I soon began writing to people I had known in the hustling world, such as Sammy the Pimp, John Hughes, the gambling house owner, the thief Jump-steady, and several dope peddlers. I wrote them all about Allah and Islam and Mr. Elijah Muhammad. I had no idea where most of them lived. I addressed their letters in care of the Harlem or Roxbury bars and clubs where I'd known them.

2   I never got a single reply. The average hustler and criminal was too uneducated to write a letter. I have known many slick sharp-looking hustlers, who would have you think they had an interest in Wall Street; privately, they would get someone to read a letter if they received one. Besides, neither would I have replied to anyone writing me something as wild as "the white man is the devil."

3   What certainly went on the Harlem and Roxbury wires was that Detroit Red was going crazy in stir, or else he was trying some hype to shake up the warden's office.

4   During the years that I stayed in the Norfolk Prison Colony, never did any official directly say anything to me about those letters, although, of course, they all passed through the prison censorship. I'm sure, however, they monitored what I wrote to add to the files which every state and federal prison keeps on the conversion of Negro inmates by the teachings of Mr. Elijah Muhammad.

5   But at that time, I felt that the real reason was that the white man knew that he was the devil.

6   Later on, I even wrote to the Mayor of Boston, to the Governor of Massachusetts, and to Harry S. Truman. They never answered; they probably never even saw my letters. I hand-scratched to them how the white man's society was responsible for the black man's condition in this wilderness of North America.

7   It was because of my letters that I happened to stumble upon starting to acquire some kind of a homemade education.

8   I became increasingly frustrated at not being able to express what I wanted to convey in letters that I wrote, especially those to Mr. Elijah Muhammad. In the street, I had been the most articulate hustler out there—I had commanded attention when I said something. But now, trying to write simple English, I not only wasn't articulate, I wasn't even functional. How would I sound writing in slang, the way I would *say* it, something such as, "Look, daddy, let me pull your coat about a cat. Elijah Muhammad—"

Many who today hear me somewhere in person, or on television, or those who read something I've said, will think I went to school far beyond the eighth grade. This impression is due entirely to my prison studies.

It had really begun back in the Charlestown Prison, when Bimbi first made me feel envy for his stock of knowledge. Bimbi had always taken charge of any conversation he was in, and I had tried to emulate him. But every book I picked up had few sentences which didn't contain anywhere from one to nearly all of the words that might as well have been in Chinese. When I just skipped those words, of course, I really ended up with little idea of what the book said. So I had come to the Norfolk Prison Colony still going through only book-reading motions. Pretty soon, I would have quit even these motions, unless I had received the motivation that I did.

I saw that the best thing I could do was get hold of a dictionary—to study, to learn some words. I was lucky enough to reason also that I should try to improve my penmanship. It was sad. I couldn't even write in a straight line. It was both ideas together that moved me to request a dictionary along with some tablets and pencils from the Norfolk Prison Colony school.

I spent two days just riffling uncertainly through the dictionary's pages. I'd never realized so many words existed! I didn't know *which* words I needed to learn. Finally, just to start some kind of action, I began copying.

In my slow, painstaking, ragged handwriting, I copied into my tablet everything printed on that first page, down to the punctuation marks.

I believe it took me a day. Then, aloud, I read back, to myself, everything I'd written on the tablet. Over and over, aloud, to myself, I read my own handwriting.

I woke up the next morning, thinking about those words—immensely proud to realize that not only had I written so much at one time, but I'd written words that I never knew were in the world. Moreover, with a little effort, I also could remember what many of these words meant. I reviewed the words whose meanings I didn't remember. Funny thing, from the dictionary's first page right now, that "aardvark" springs to mind. The dictionary had a picture of it, a long-tailed, long-eared, burrowing African mammal, which lives off termites caught by sticking out its tongue as an anteater does for ants.

16   I was so fascinated that I went on—I copied the dictionary's next page. And the same experience came when I studied that. With every succeeding page, I also learned of people and places and events from history. Actually the dictionary is like a miniature encyclopedia. Finally the dictionary's A section had filled a whole tablet—and I went on into the B's. That was the way I started copying what eventually became the entire dictionary. It went a lot faster after so much practice helped me pick up handwriting speed. Between what I wrote in my tablet, and writing letters, during the rest of my time in prison I would guess I wrote a million words.

17   I suppose it was inevitable that as my word-base broadened, I could for the first time pick up a book and read and now begin to understand what the book was saying. Anyone who has read a great deal can imagine the new world that opened. Let me tell you something: from then until I left that prison, in every free moment I had, if I was not reading in the library, I was reading on my bunk. You couldn't have gotten me out of books with a wedge. Between Mr. Muhammad's teachings, my correspondence, my visitors . . . and my reading of books, months passed without my even thinking about being imprisoned. In fact, up to then, I never had been so truly free in my life.

Vocabulary

To get the most out of reading this essay, you should have a working understanding of the words listed on the next page. Following each word is a parenthetical reference, indicating the paragraph in which the word is used as well as a definition for the word. Go back and look at the sentence in which the word appears, and see how the definition applies. To help you make this word a part of your active vocabulary, write a sentence of your own using the word in the space provided.

inaction (1):   lack or absence of action

frustrated (8): prevented from accomplishing a purpose or fulfilling a desire

---

articulate (8): speaking in or characterized by clear, expressive language

---

functional (8): capable of performing

---

emulate (10): to strive to equal or excel, especially through imitation

---

tablets (11): pads of writing paper glued together along one edge

---

inevitable (17): incapable of being avoided or prevented

Understanding the Essay

1. Malcolm X narrates his story in the first person. Why is the first person particularly appropriate?

2. What motivated Malcolm X to undertake his "prison studies"?

3. What does Malcolm X mean when he says he was "going through only book-reading motions"? How did he solve this problem?

4. What important distinction does Malcolm X make between being "articulate" and being "functional" in his speaking and writing?

5. In what ways is a dictionary like a "miniature encyclopedia"? From your own experience, how do dictionaries and encyclopedias differ from each other?

6. How has Malcolm X organized his essay?

Exploring the Theme: Discussion and Writing

1. In his final sentence, Malcolm X confesses that "I never had been so truly free in my life," even though he was in prison. What is the nature of this freedom that he feels? What does freedom mean to you? Are there, for example, different kinds of freedom?

2. Malcolm X solved the problem of his own illiteracy by carefully studying the dictionary. Would this be a practical solution to the national problem of illiteracy? Suggest alternatives to Malcolm X's approach.

WHY SPANISH TRANSLATIONS?

Mauricio Molina

In 1960 Mauricio Molina moved to the United States from Central America. He was forewarned by his parents that if he wanted to "thrive" he would have to learn English. Much to his surprise, however, he found Spanish translations available wherever he turned, which caused him to wonder why speakers of Spanish are so privileged in our society. His essay was first published in the March 12, 1980 issue of the New York Times.

Preparing to Read

As people from all over the world immigrate to the United States, they bring their native language with them. Yet, to function well here, it is assumed they need to learn English. As Molina points out, however, this is true only if they're not Hispanic. So even though a test for a driver's license in Chinese would be very difficult to come by, Hispanics have the luxury of having the tests translated into Spanish for them. Spanish translations are available for just about everything that one needs to get by, to the extent that Hispanics don't even have to learn English. Molina argues that this is wrong—Hispanics have the opportunity to learn English along with everyone else. What do you think? How exclusively English should the United States be?

I was naive 20 years ago. I say this because I came here from 1
Central America and readily accepted what my parents told
me. What they told me was that if I wanted to thrive here I
had better learn English. English, it seems, was the language
that people spoke in this country. In my innocence and naïveté,
however, it never occurred to me that I really didn't have to. I
can see now that I could have refused.

2   Yes, English is the language of the United States. But if it is, why can I take the written part of my driver's license test in Spanish? If it is, why are businesses forced to provide Spanish translations of practically every blank credit application or contract agreement? And not just businesses—government offices must also have quite a number of Spanish translations for those who want them.

3   Clearly, my old language did not get left behind. Don't misunderstand; this is real nice. It allows me to luxuriate in the knowledge, sweet indeed, that I am privileged. Without a doubt this is the land of opportunity. And I know it. But for those of us whom people call "Hispanics," it's a little bit more. It's the land where opportunity itself is served and seasoned as if this were the old country.

4   How stupid you must think me for complaining! Should we not simply take the opportunity and run? Why complain? Complaining may only spoil the fun for those among us who don't want to learn English.

5   But I choose to complain. I do it because questions nag at me. For instance, just who are those people for whom the Spanish translations are provided? It's a good guess that they're not Chinese, or French, or Serbo-Croatian. Of course, we know them already as "Hispanics." But what in the world does this mean?

6   A Hispanic is someone who came, or whose ancestors came, from a region where Spanish is the only language spoken. Nothing more. Racially, a Hispanic may be anything. It's a mistake to say "Hispanic" and mean by the term a black Cuban just as much as it would puzzle a Chilean named O'Hara.

7   As to who precisely among Hispanics has a need for the Spanish translations, I can't tell yet for sure. If you'll follow me a bit, though, we may together unravel this puzzle and learn something.

8   I would divide Hispanics living in the United States into two groups: those who were born in this country and those who came from elsewhere. It is easy to see that a number of individuals in the latter group, people who perhaps knew no English when they arrived, may have linguistic problems here. Logically, some among them may have need of Spanish translations.

9   The first group I mentioned, made up of people born and reared here, should have no need of any translations, right? Well, not exactly. I'm told that many among them know English

very poorly, if at all. So of course they need the help. But here I hope you'll forgive me if I pause to say that I think this is a very strange thing. I mean, isn't it odd in this day and age that people born right here in the United States may not somehow have mastered English?

Who, then, are the translations meant for? Ah, you probably 10 guessed it by now. They're meant for a goodly cross section of Hispanics—average, reasonably healthy and intelligent children and adults.

I regard these translations as a waste of effort and money. To 11 me they constitute a largesse of opportunity totally lacking a logical foundation. And what is the "logic" behind them? The answer I get is that these people are favored so that they may not suffer, because of their handicap, a diminution of their constitutional rights. The thing isn't done out of kindness, but simply out of a sense of fair play.

Fair play? I think not. Unfairness would be to deny these 12 people the opportunity to learn English. But the question is, are they being denied? From where I live I couldn't throw a rock out the window without risking severe injury to a number of English teachers. And at various places nearby—YMCAs, colleges, high schools, grammar schools, convention halls—English courses are available for the foreign-born or anyone else who needs them. That, ladies and gentlemen, is opportunity. It's there, but it won't pull you by the nose.

This country has been, is and, I pray, will continue to be, the 13 land of opportunity. It has never been a place where the lazy came to be coddled. It has never been a haven for those who would not look out for their needs.

What do I think should be done? I think that no Spanish 14 translations should be made of anything. Except for one. Spanish translations should be made, and distributed widely, detailing the availability of English courses throughout Hispanic communities.

What if people don't bother to attend? Well, it's a free country. 15

Vocabulary

To get the most out of reading this essay, you should have a working understanding of the words listed below. Following each word is a parenthetical reference, indicating the paragraph in which the word is used, as well as a definition for the word. Go back and look at the sentence in which the word appears, and see how the definition applies. To help you make this word a part of your active vocabulary, write a sentence of your own using the word in the space provided.

thrive (1):   prosper

_____

_____

naïveté (1):   innocence, lack of experience

_____

_____

luxuriate (3):   enjoy, revel

_____

_____

linguistic (8):   referring to language

_____

_____

largesse (11):   generous giving

_____

_____

diminution (11):   lessening, decrease

_____

_____

coddled (13):   pampered

_____

_____

Understanding the Essay

1. Why didn't Molina have to learn English? Why did he learn it anyway?
2. Why is America the land of opportunity, and a little bit more, for Hispanics?
3. How does Molina define "Hispanic"?
4. Who "needs" Spanish translations, according to Molina?
5. Why doesn't Molina think that Spanish translations should be so readily available? What is the one Spanish-language document that he would like to see distributed?

Exploring the Theme: Discussion and Writing

1. In May 1993, Dade County in Florida repealed a directive that made it illegal to conduct county business in any language other than English. Its repeal was mostly on behalf of the Spanish-speaking community in the area. Molina, according to this article, would have argued to keep the English-only directive in place. Should the United States be English-only, or should we accommodate the use of other languages for official business? How should we decide which other languages to accommodate?
2. If you lived in another country, it's likely that you could "get by" with only English, and that you would find an English-speaking community. Would you want to hang on to English as your primary language? Do you think you would seek out instruction in the native language? Why, or why not?

DON'T JUST STAND THERE

Diane Cole

Diane Cole lives and writes in New York City. She has written many articles about psychological and career issues for the Washington Post, *the* Wall Street Journal, Newsweek, *and other national publications. She wrote the following article in April 1989 for "A World of Difference," a special insert in the* New York Times *sponsored by the Anti-Defamation League of the Jewish organization B'nai B'rith.*

Preparing to Read

How do you react when someone says something that offends you personally or that you consider to be a slur against a group of people who aren't present to defend themselves? The most common reactions are to fume in silence or to verbally attack the offending party. Cole faced this situation and was unable to come up with a response, so she consulted experts to find out two things. First, is a response important? Second, if it is, what is the best way to respond? She found out that the common reactions are both counterproductive—confronting the offending party is important, but there are right and wrong ways to do it.

1 It was my office farewell party, and colleagues at the job I was about to leave were wishing me well. My mood was one of ebullience tinged with regret, and it was in this spirit that I spoke to the office neighbor to whom I had waved hello every morning for the past two years. He smiled broadly as he launched into a long, rambling story, pausing only after he delivered the punch line. It was a very long pause because, although he laughed, I did not: This joke was unmistakably anti-Semitic.

2 I froze. Everyone in the office knew I was Jewish; what could

he have possibly meant? Shaken and hurt, not knowing what else to do, I turned in stunned silence to the next well-wisher. Later, still angry, I wondered, what else should I—could I—have done?

Prejudice can make its presence felt in any setting, but hearing its nasty voice in this way can be particularly unnerving. We do not know what to do and often we feel another form of paralysis as well: We think, "Nothing I say or do will change this person's attitude, so why bother?"   3

But left unchecked, racial slurs and offensive ethnic jokes "can poison the atmosphere," says Michael McQuillan, adviser for racial/ethnic affairs for the Brooklyn borough president's office. "Hearing these remarks conditions us to accept them; and if we accept these, we can become accepting of other acts."   4

Speaking up may not magically change a biased attitude, but it can change a person's behavior by putting a strong message across. And the more messages there are, the more likely a person is to change that behavior, says Arnold Kahn, professor of psychology at James Madison University, Harrisonburg, Va., who makes this analogy: "You can't keep people from smoking in *their* house, but you can ask them not to smoke in *your* house."   5

At the same time, "Even if the other party ignores or discounts what you say, people always reflect on how others perceive them. Speaking up always counts," says LeNorman Strong, director of campus life at George Washington University, Washington, D.C.   6

Finally, learning to respond effectively also helps people feel better about themselves, asserts Cherie Brown, executive director of the National Coalition Building Institute, a Boston-based training organization. "We've found that, when people felt they could at least in this small way make a difference, that made them more eager to take on other activities on a larger scale," she says. Although there is no "cookbook approach" to confronting such remarks—every situation is different, experts stress—these are some effective strategies.   7

When the "joke" turns on who you are—as a member of an ethnic or religious group, a person of color, a woman, a gay or lesbian, an elderly person, or someone with a physical handicap—shocked paralysis is often the first response. Then, wounded and vulnerable, on some level you want to strike back.   8

9   Lashing out or responding in kind is seldom the most effective response, however. "That can give you momentary satisfaction, but you also feel as if you've lowered yourself to that other person's level," Mr. McQuillan explains. Such a response may further label you in the speaker's mind as thin-skinned, someone not to be taken seriously. Or it may up the ante, making the speaker, and then you, reach for new insults—or physical blows.

10   "If you don't laugh at the joke, or fight, or respond in kind to the slur," says Mr. McQuillan, "that will take the person by surprise, and that can give you more control over the situation." Therefore, in situations like the one in which I found myself—a private conversation in which I knew the person making the remark—he suggests voicing your anger calmly but pointedly: "I don't know if you realize what that sounded like to me. If that's what you meant, it really hurt me."

11   State how *you* feel, rather than making an abstract statement like, "Not everyone who hears that joke might find it funny." Counsels Mr. Strong: "Personalize the sense of 'this is how I feel when you say this.' That makes it very concrete"—and harder to dismiss.

12   Make sure you heard the words and their intent correctly by repeating or rephrasing the statement: "This is what I heard you say. Is that what you meant?" It's important to give the other person the benefit of the doubt because, in fact, he may *not* have realized that the comment was offensive and, if you had not spoken up, would have had no idea of its impact on you.

13   For instance, Professor Kahn relates that he used to include in his exams multiple-choice questions that occasionally contained "incorrect funny answers." After one exam, a student came up to him in private and said, "I don't think you intended this, but I found a number of those jokes offensive to me as a woman." She explained why. "What she said made immediate sense to me," he says. "I apologized at the next class, and I never did it again."

14   But what if the speaker dismisses your objection, saying, "Oh, you're just being sensitive. Can't you take a joke?" In that case, you might say, "I'm not so sure about that, let's talk about that a little more." The key, Mr. Strong says, is to continue the dialogue, hear the other person's concerns, and point out your own. "There are times when you're just going to have to admit defeat and end it," he adds, "but I have to feel that I did the best I could."

When the offending remark is made in the presence of 15 others—at a staff meeting, for example—it can be even more distressing than an insult made privately.

"You have two options," says William Newlin, director of 16 field services for the Community Relations division of the New York City Commission on Human Rights. "You can respond immediately at the meeting, or you can delay your response until afterward in private. But a response has to come."

Some remarks or actions may be so outrageous that they 17 cannot go unnoted at the moment, regardless of the speaker or the setting. But in general, psychologists say, shaming a person in public may have the opposite effect of the one you want: The speaker will deny his offense all the more strongly in order to save face. Further, few people enjoy being put on the spot, and if the remark really was not intended to be offensive, publicly embarrassing the person who made it may cause an unnecessary rift or further misunderstanding. Finally, most people just don't react as well or thoughtfully under a public spotlight as they would in private.

Keeping that in mind, an excellent alternative is to take the 18 offender aside afterward: "Could we talk for a minute in private?" Then use the strategies suggested above for calmly stating how you feel, giving the speaker the benefit of the doubt, and proceeding from there.

At a large meeting or public talk, you might consider passing 19 the speaker a note, says David Wertheimer, executive director of the New York City Gay and Lesbian Anti-Violence Project: You could write, "You may not realize it, but your remarks were offensive because. . . ."

"Think of your role as that of an educator," suggests James M. 20 Jones, Ph.D., executive director for public interest at the American Psychological Association. "You have to be controlled."

Regardless of the setting or situation, speaking up always 21 raises the risk of rocking the boat. If the person who made the offending remark is your boss, there may be an even bigger risk to consider: How will this affect my job? Several things can help minimize the risk, however. First, know what other resources you may have at work, suggests Caryl Stern, director of the A World of Difference–New York City campaign: Does your personnel office handle discrimination complaints? Are other grievance procedures in place?

22   You won't necessarily need to use any of these procedures, Ms. Stern stresses. In fact, she advises, "It's usually better to try a one-on-one approach first." But simply knowing a formal system exists can make you feel secure enough to set up that meeting.

23   You can also raise the issue with other colleagues who heard the remark: Did they feel the same way you did? The more support you have, the less alone you will feel. Your point will also carry more validity and be more difficult to shrug off. Finally, give your boss credit—and the benefit of the doubt: "I know you've worked hard for the company's affirmative action programs, so I'm sure you didn't realize what those remarks sounded like to me as well as the others at the meeting last week. . . ."

24   If, even after this discussion, the problem persists, go back for another meeting, Ms. Stern advises. And if that, too, fails, you'll know what other options are available to you.

25   It's a spirited dinner party, and everyone's having a good time, until one guest starts reciting a racist joke. Everyone at the table is white, including you. The others are still laughing, as you wonder what to say or do.

26   No one likes being seen as a party-pooper, but before deciding that you'd prefer not to take on this role, you might remember that the person who told the offensive joke has already ruined your good time.

27   If it's a group that you feel comfortable in—a family gathering, for instance—you will feel freer to speak up. Still, shaming the person by shouting "You're wrong!" or "That's not funny!" probably won't get your point across as effectively as other strategies. "If you interrupt people to condemn them, it just makes it harder," says Cherie Brown. She suggests trying instead to get at the resentments that lie beneath the joke by asking open-ended questions: "Grandpa, I know you always treat everyone with such respect. Why do people in our family talk that way about black people?" The key, Ms. Brown says, "is to listen to them first, so they will be more likely to listen to you."

28   If you don't know your fellow guests well, before speaking up you could turn discreetly to your neighbors (or excuse yourself to help the host or hostess in the kitchen) to get a reading of how they felt, and whether or not you'll find support for speaking up. The less alone you feel, the more comfortable you'll be speaking

up: "I know you probably didn't mean anything by that joke, Jim, but it really offended me. . . ." It's important to say that *you* were offended—not state how the group that is the butt of the joke would feel. "Otherwise," LeNorman Strong says, "you risk coming off as a goody two-shoes."

If you yourself are the host, you can exercise more control;   29
you are, after all, the one who sets the rules and the tone of behavior in your home. Once, when Professor Kahn's party guests began singing offensive, racist songs, for instance, he kicked them all out, saying, "You don't sing songs like that in my house!" And, he adds, "they never did again."

> At school one day, a friend comes over and says, "Who do you   30
> think you are, hanging out with Joe? If you can be friends with
> those people, I'm through with you!"

Peer pressure can weigh heavily on kids. They feel vulnera-   31
ble and, because they are kids, they aren't as able to control the urge to fight. "But if you learn to handle these situations as kids, you'll be better able to handle them as an adult," William Newlin points out.

Begin by redefining to yourself what a friend is and examin-   32
ing what friendship means, advises Amy Lee, a human relations specialist at Panel of Americans, an intergroup-relations training and educational organization. If that person from a different group fits your requirement for a friend, ask, "Why shouldn't I be friends with Joe? We have a lot in common." Try to get more information about whatever stereotypes or resentments lie beneath your friend's statement. Ms. Lee suggests: "What makes you think they're so different from us? Where did you get that information?" She explains: "People are learning these stereotypes from somewhere, and they cannot be blamed for that. So examine where these ideas came from." Then talk about how your own experience rebuts them.

Kids, like adults, should also be aware of other resources to   33
back them up: Does the school offer special programs for fighting prejudice? How supportive will the principal, the teachers, or other students be? If the school atmosphere is volatile, experts warn, make sure that taking a stand at that moment won't put you in physical danger. If that is the case, it's better to look for other alternatives.

These can include programs or organizations that bring kids   34 from different backgrounds together. "When kids work together across race lines, that is how you break down the barriers and see that the stereotypes are not true," says Laurie Meadoff, president of CityKids Foundation, a nonprofit group whose programs attempt to do just that. Such programs can also provide what Cherie Brown calls a "safe place" to express the anger and pain that slurs and other offenses cause, whether the bigotry is directed against you or others.

35   In learning to speak up, everyone will develop a different style and a slightly different message to get across, experts agree. But it would be hard to do better than these two messages suggested by teenagers at CityKids: "Everyone on the face of the earth has the same intestines," said one. Another added, "Cross over the bridge. There's a lot of love on the streets."

Vocabulary

To get the most out of reading this essay, you should have a working understanding of the words listed below. Following each word is a parenthetical reference, indicating the paragraph in which the word is used, as well as a definition for the word. Go back and look at the sentence in which the word appears, and see how the definition applies. To help you make this word a part of your active vocabulary, write a sentence of your own using the word in the space provided.

ebullience (1):   exuberance, zest

---

anti-Semitic (1):   prejudiced against Jews

---

coalition (7):   alliance

---

abstract (11):   indirect, theoretical

_____

_____

rift (17):   break, fracture

_____

_____

rebuts (32):   counters, discredits

_____

_____

volatile (33):   unstable, explosive

_____

_____

Understanding the Essay

1. How did Cole react to her colleague's anti-Semitic joke? Was hers the correct response, according to the experts?
2. What is the potential consequence of tolerating offensive statements and jokes?
3. According to the article, what is the best strategy for confronting someone who has offended you in a private conversation? What should you do if someone has made an inappropriate remark in a public setting, such as a meeting?
4. Why is it rarely a good idea to confront someone in a public setting?
5. What options does a person have if the boss is making offensive remarks?
6. Why are uncomfortable situations for adults, like being the butt of a racist joke, even worse for kids?
7. What is a good way to promote understanding and acceptance among kids?

272 Language and Diversity

Exploring the Theme:
Discussion and Writing

1. For what audience is Cole writing her essay? Could the essay influence others, including those who might disagree with some of her assumptions? Explain your answers.

2. Everyone has heard blatantly offensive comments of discriminatory jokes intended to wound a certain group of people. But what is the definition of offensive? Cole, as a Jewish woman, has every reason to be angered by sexist or anti-Semitic jokes or stories. But the next essay in this section, "Come, Let Me Offend You" by Eve Drobot, argues that people are too easily offended these days. If taken to extremes, Cole's methods of dealing with slurs would lead to innumerable hushed conversations such as "I'm not sure you realized what you were saying, but your insensitive comments about [computer scientists, bird watchers, Frosted Flakes lovers, or whatever] really offended me," and, as Drobot argues, it would become risky to say anything about anybody. Where do *you* think the line between the offensive and the acceptable should be drawn?

COME, LET ME OFFEND YOU

Eve Drobot

Eve Drobot is a free-lance writer, book reviewer, and tele-
vision interviewer. She graduated from Tufts University
in 1973 with a degree in history and has worked for the
Toronto Globe and Mail *newspaper as a columnist. The*
author of five books, she wrote the following piece for the
September 28, 1992 issue of Newsweek.

Preparing to Read

Have you ever told what you thought was a good joke or
story, only to have upset someone by your "insensitive" comments? Maybe you *were* insensitive; maybe your joke *was* offensive to a certain group. Or maybe you ran into what Drobot
terms another person's "special interest." A little sensitivity is
fine—and has helped decrease the number of blatantly racist
and sexist jokes told—but Drobot argues that such sensitivity
has gone too far. It is hard to say much of anything these days
without offending someone. As a result, communication is cut
off, because to say something to someone else is to invite indigna-
tion. Drobot, as her title implies, favors free expression over
sensitivity. Do you agree?

C an we talk? It is becoming increasingly difficult, because I   1
never know when I'm inadvertently going to offend you.
Here I go, raving about the divine veal piccata I had at
that hot new trattoria, and you're gritting your teeth and about
to pop a blood vessel because you haven't had a chance to inform
me that you're a raging vegetarian who spends his weekends
stuffing envelopes for People for Ethical Treatment of Animals.

I mean, how can we ever talk if you've always got an agenda   2
I have no way of knowing about? There we are at a party discuss-

ing censorship—at least, I think we're discussing censorship—
when you bring everything to a grinding halt by announcing
you're a Muslim who believes the *fatwa* against Salman Rushdie
is entirely justified. Or, God forbid, I tell a good, old-fashioned
heterosexual joke and you stare at me straight-faced and explain
you are a lesbian female separatist.

3   Everywhere I turn, it seems that certain things are no longer
deemed appropriate conversation. We are awash in earnestness,
afraid to open our mouths because we never know when our
words are going to hurt somebody's feelings.

4   I can understand—even applaud—the taboos on racist and
sexist jokes (unless we've established a priori that we're both
feminists, in which case, have you heard the one about the man
who was so dumb that . . .). But is there anything left to have an
opinion on these days besides the weather? Oh, but now you tell
me you're an environmentalist, and I have no right to complain
about the rain because the atmosphere has been raped by pollu-
tion, and if I've used so much as one squirt of hair spray in my
life it's probably all my fault anyway. Pardon me.

5   You see, it has become simply impossible for us to speak to
one another as long as you insist on wearing your special interests and sensitivities on your sleeve.

6   Now, wait a minute. *There's* a concept. Why don't you wear
your agenda on your sleeve, literally? We could develop an entire iconography of sensibilities. Pins, badges, what have you—
I'm open to suggestions. Devout Christians wear crosses around
their necks; some Jews display a Star of David or Hebrew letters
on a chain. We could carry this idea further.

7   Let's start with a classic and work from there. Take a pink
triangle (for gay) and add sequins if you're a drag queen. If
you're a male bisexual, how about a pink triangle bisected by
the biological symbol for female? Or, if you're a female bisexual,
a pink triangle bisected by the biological symbol for male?

8   Are you sensitive about being a single mother? Let the world
know by displaying Dan Quayle's face with a red slash through
it.

9   We could issue broccoli stickpins to vegetarians, bunny
heads in profile to animal-rights activists. A pentacle for practicing witches, a golden calf for ardent pagans. A baby basket in
front of a door if you were adopted. A child with a suitcase if
your parents were immigrants. An ear if someone in your family

is deaf, an ear and a musical note if someone in your family is tone-deaf. The possibilities are endless: define your sore point and design an insignia. Wear it proudly, if not defiantly.

Stamps and Stickers

And let's not stop with badges. How about making little stamps   10 or stickers to affix to anything you write? Let's say you write a letter to the editor protesting the fatuousness of this article. Append your offended affiliation visually to the letter, thereby ensuring that your opinion will be judged not on the merit of your argument but on the merit of your minority-group adherence.

This sort of symbolic shorthand would certainly have helped   11 get a fellow I know out of a fix he recently found himself in. A major publishing house asked him to select some poems to include in an anthology. Silly liberal-minded fool that he is, he simply chose poems he thought were good. His selections were returned to him for further clarification. Could he please let the publisher know which poems were written by gays, third-generation Americans, Native Americans, refugees, Young Republicans and those who use wheelchairs? When he had supplied the appropriate designation for each entry, then—and only then—could the publisher know that the editor had made the demographically representative choices.

Now, I realize I am probably dating myself, or setting myself   12 up as a total Pollyanna, but wasn't there a time when the goal was *not* to notice the things that set us apart? Weren't we once working toward a perfect world, where we would see past color, race, creed, gender, ethnic background and physical limitations, straight through to talent and ability? What ever happened to that idea?

I can't pinpoint exactly where it went off the rails, but there   13 must definitely have been a moment in time when somebody figured out there was more to be gained by being indignant than by being right.

You see, we can't talk, we can't think, we can't presume to   14 judge unless we have all the pertinent information. And the most pertinent information these days is: whom does this offend?

Labeling yourself by your narrowest interests has become   15 quite the rage during the past few years. I'm just surprised that no one has thought of taking this trend one logical step further and making these labels outwardly visible. Who knows? There might even be money to be made.

16   I wish I could take credit for this clever badge idea, but unfortunately, I can't. Some insane fellow with a ridiculous mustache came up with it more than 50 years ago. He wanted homosexuals to wear those pink triangles, Jews to wear yellow Stars of David, and so on. His motives weren't as pure as mine, I grant you. He wanted to kill people. I merely want to avoid hurting their feelings.

Vocabulary

To get the most out of reading this essay, you should have a working understanding of the words listed below. Following each word is a parenthetical reference, indicating the paragraph in which the word is used, as well as a definition for the word. Go back and look at the sentence in which the word appears, and see how the definition applies. To help you make this word a part of your active vocabulary, write a sentence of your own using the word in the space provided.

inadvertently (1):   unintentionally, accidentally

_____

_____

trattoria (1):   Italian restaurant

_____

_____

separatist (2):   person who withdraws from a larger group, dissenter

_____

_____

taboos (4):   forbidden topics or behavior

_____

_____

pentacle (9):   five-pointed star of symbolic significance in paganism

_____

_____

pagans (9):   people with beliefs that predate monotheism or that are outside of a dominant tradition.

_____

_____

insignia (9):   badge, emblem

_____

_____

fatuousness (10):   foolishness

_____

_____

demographically (11):   in terms of population statistics

_____

_____

Pollyanna (12):   persistently optimistic person

_____

_____

Understanding the Essay

1. What topic is unwise to discuss with a "raging vegetarian"? How about a "lesbian female separatist"?
2. Drobot says that certain previously safe topics are no longer considered appropriate conversation. What does she say is the result of never knowing when you're going to hurt someone's feelings?

3. What is one advantage of literally wearing your agenda on your sleeve, for example, a pink triangle for a gay person? What is one disadvantage?

4. What information does the editor want from Drobot's "silly liberal-minded" friend? Why does he want this information?

5. What does Drobot think the goal of society should be? What does she say happened to that goal?

6. Who first came up with the idea of labeling people with badges? Why do you think Drobot compares his motives with her own?

Exploring the Theme:
Discussion and Writing

1. Much of this selection is written tongue in cheek, but the basic message is clear: people are too close-minded and too ready to take offense at what others have to say. This goes against the current thinking that language is an effective weapon against discrimination, and that by heightening awareness of what we say, we start down the road to ending discrimination. Do you agree with Drobot that effective communication is stifled these days because "somebody figured out there was more to be gained by being indignant than by being right"? Or do you think it is important and valuable for people to watch their words so as not to discriminate against or offend a certain group?

2. What do you think of the badge idea? What dangers are involved in allowing yourself to be labeled by a certain narrow interest?

WRITING SUGGESTIONS FOR "LANGUAGE AND DIVERSITY"

1. Diane Cole begins her essay by recalling a party at which someone told an anti-Semitic joke that was offensive to her. Have you ever had a similar experience that offended your racial or ethnic background? How did you feel about it? How did you respond, if at all? Write an essay in which you recount the experience and discuss its impact on you.

2. Eve Drobot writes that "labeling yourself by your narrowest interests has become quite the rage during the last few years." What are your narrowest interests? Are you a vegetarian, animal rights activist, or musician, for example? Write an essay on four such labels that define or tell who you are.

3. Do you think that everyone who comes to America to live should learn English in addition to her or his native language? Why or why not? Write an essay in which you defend your position. If you have had personal experiences or have observed people struggling with a language problem, try to use these examples in your essay.

4. We have all been in situations where our language ability has placed us at a disadvantage, whether engaging in a heated argument, taking an exam, being interviewed for a job, or expressing anger or grief. At times like these, we feel as Malcolm X did, helpless and prisoners of our own language. Write a brief essay in which you recount one such frustrating incident in your life.

5. Where do you stand on the issue of offensive or derogatory language? Are you like Eve Drobot in believing that people are overly sensitive? Are you like Diane Cole in believing that one should stand up to language that belittles or demeans? Or do you have trouble knowing where to draw the line because you tolerate some slurs and jokes but not others? Write an essay that explains your position on this issue.

10

ADDICTIONS

When we think about addictions or substance abuse, we immediately think of stories in the news that are related to our country's so-called war on drugs. There's no denying the fact that America does have a problem with the trafficking and use of illegal drugs. We cannot pick up a current magazine or listen to the evening news without hearing stories of illegal drugs and the problems they create—newborn babies addicted to crack, the efforts of federal agencies to break the Colombian drug connection.

These stories of illegal drugs overshadow Americans' struggles with alcohol, tobacco, food, and nonprescription drugs—our so-called legal addictions. The problem of substance abuse is far more complex and far more pervasive than any of us really knows or is willing to admit. In 1990, for example, 14,000 deaths were attributed to cocaine and heroin. In that same year, 390,000 deaths were attributed to tobacco and 90,000 to alcohol. It's not surprising then that many sociologists believe we are a nation of substance abusers—drinkers, smokers, eaters, and pill poppers. Although the statistics are alarming, they do not begin to suggest the heavy toll of substance abuse on Americans and their families. Loved ones die, relationships are fractured, children are abandoned, job productivity falters, and the dreams of young people are extinguished.

Each of the articles in this section addresses one of America's addictions and helps us to better understand the kinds of problems these addictions cause. Ex-smoker Franklin E. Zimring takes a close look at the growing number of people who have decided to join the ranks of "reformed" smokers. Gail Regier explores the world of habitual drug users—people for whom drug use is their whole life—and Ethan A. Nadelmann champions the idea that to win the war on drugs might just mean to legalize them. Finally, Helen A. Guthrie provides a straightforward look at anorexia nervosa and bulimia, two eating disorders that high school and college-age women are especially prone to.

CONFESSIONS OF AN
EX-SMOKER

Franklin E. Zimring

Franklin E. Zimring is a professor of law at the University of Chicago. He has written many books on the legal profession, and he has written articles for both scholarly and popular magazines. The following article appeared in Newsweek *on April 20, 1987.*

Preparing to Read

Do you smoke? If not, are you bothered when other people do? If so, are you bothered by people who don't and tell you that you shouldn't? With many states placing even tighter restrictions on smoking in public places, arguments concerning personal freedom, public health, and the rights of the individual rage on as a result. Some of the most vocal arguers are the topic of Zimring's essay—the ex-smokers. Ex-smokers can identify with smokers much better than can people who have never smoked, but they are also sometimes judgmental. To encourage a better understanding of ex-smokers—whose numbers are growing, with society's encouragement, every day—Zimring divides them into four groups, according to how they view their peers who still smoke.

1   Americans can be divided into three groups—smokers, non-smokers and that expanding pack of us who have quit. Those who have never smoked don't know what they're missing, but former smokers, ex-smokers, reformed smokers can never forget. We are veterans of a personal war, linked by that watershed experience of ceasing to smoke and by the temptation to have just one more cigarette. For almost all of us ex-smokers, smoking continues to play an important part in our lives. And now that it is being restricted in restaurants around the country

and will be banned in almost all indoor public places in New York State starting next month, it is vital that everyone understand the different emotional states cessation of smoking can cause. I have observed four of them; and in the interest of science I have classified them as those of the zealot, the evangelist, the elect and the serene. Each day, each category gains new recruits.

Not all antitobacco zealots are former smokers, but a substantial number of fire-and-brimstone opponents do come from the ranks of the reformed. Zealots believe that those who continue to smoke are degenerates who deserve scorn not pity and the penalties that will deter offensive behavior in public as well. Relations between these people and those who continue to smoke are strained. 2

One explanation for the zealot's fervor in seeking to outlaw tobacco consumption is his own tenuous hold on abstaining from smoking. But I think part of the emotional force arises from sheer envy as he watches and identifies with each lung-filling puff. By making smoking in public a crime, the zealot seeks reassurance that he will not revert to bad habits; give him strong social penalties and he won't become a recidivist. 3

No systematic survey has been done yet, but anecdotal evidence suggests that a disproportionate number of doctors who have quit smoking can be found among the fanatics. Just as the most enthusiastic revolutionary tends to make the most enthusiastic counterrevolutionary, many of today's vitriolic zealots include those who had been deeply committed to tobacco habits. 4

By contrast, the antismoking evangelist does not condemn smokers. Unlike the zealot, he regards smoking as an easily curable condition, as a social disease, and not a sin. The evangelist spends an enormous amount of time seeking and preaching to the unconverted. He argues that kicking the habit is not *that* difficult. After all, *he* did it; moreover, as he describes it, the benefits of quitting are beyond measure and the disadvantages are nil. 5

The hallmark of the evangelist is his insistence that he never misses tobacco. Though he is less hostile to smokers than the zealot, he is resented more. Friends and loved ones who have been the targets of his preachments frequently greet the resumption of smoking by the evangelist as an occasion for unmitigated glee. 6

7   Among former smokers, the distinctions between the evangelist and the elect are much the same as the differences between
proselytizing and nonproselytizing religious sects. While the
evangelists preach the ease and desirability of abstinence, the
elect do not attempt to convert their friends. They think that
virtue is its own reward and subscribe to the Puritan theory
of predestination. Since they have proved themselves capable
of abstaining from tobacco, they are therefore different from
friends and relatives who continue to smoke. They feel superior,
secure that their salvation was foreordained. These ex-smokers
rarely give personal testimony on their conversion. They rarely
speak about their tobacco habits, while evangelists talk about
little else. Of course, active smokers find such blue-nosed behavior far less offensive than that of the evangelist or the zealot, yet
they resent the elect simply because they are smug. Their air of
self-satisfaction rarely escapes the notice of those lighting up.
For active smokers, life with a member of the ex-smoking elect is
less stormy than with a zealot or evangelist, but it is subtly
oppressive nonetheless.

8   I have labeled my final category of former smokers the serene.
This classification is meant to encourage those who find the other
psychic styles of ex-smokers disagreeable. Serenity is quieter
than zealotry and evangelism, and those who qualify are not as
self-righteous as the elect. The serene ex-smoker accepts himself
and also accepts those around him who continue to smoke. This
kind of serenity does not come easily nor does it seem to be an
immediate option for those who have stopped. Rather it is a goal,
an end stage in a process of development during which some
former smokers progress through one or more of the less-than-
positive psychological points en route. For former smokers, serenity is thus a positive possibility that exists at the end of the rain-
bow. But all former smokers cannot reach that promised land.

9   What is it that permits some former smokers to become serene? I think the key is self-acceptance and gratitude. The fully
mature former smoker knows he has the soul of an addict and is
grateful for the knowledge. He may sit up front in an airplane,
but he knows he belongs in the smoking section in back. He
doesn't regret that he quit smoking, nor any of his previous
adventures with tobacco. As a former smoker, he is grateful for
the experience and memory of craving a cigarette.

10   Serenity comes from accepting the lessons of one's life. And

ex-smokers who have reached this point in their world view have much to be grateful for. They have learned about the potential and limits of change. In becoming the right kind of former smoker, they developed a healthy sense of self. This former smoker, for one, believes that it is better to crave (one hopes only occasionally) and not to smoke than never to have craved at all. And by accepting that fact, the reformed smoker does not need to excoriate, envy or disassociate himself from those who continue to smoke.

Vocabulary

To get the most out of reading this essay, you should have a working understanding of the words listed below. Following each word is a parenthetical reference, indicating the paragraph in which the word is used, as well as a definition for the word. Go back and look at the sentence in which the word appears, and see how the definition applies. To help you make this word a part of your active vocabulary, write a sentence of your own using the word in the space provided.

watershed (1):   landmark, momentous event

_____

_____

fire-and-brimstone (2):   fiery, referring to Hell

_____

_____

degenerates (2):   those who deviate from the normal moral standards

_____

_____

tenuous (3):   flimsy, weak

_____

_____

recidivist (3):   habitual offender, criminal who can't be rehabilitated

_____

anecdotal (4):   based on stories, not hard evidence

_____

vitriolic (4):   angry, outspoken

_____

proselytizing (7):   preaching, persuading

_____

excoriate (10):   scold severely, condemn

_____

Understanding the Essay

1. Why is it more important than ever to understand what Zimring calls "the different emotional states [that] cessation of smoking can cause"?
2. What are Zimring's four groups of ex-smokers? Describe each group in one or two sentences.
3. How do the zealots and the evangelists differ? Who is likely to be a zealot? Why?
4. Why are the elect likely to annoy smokers who are close to them?
5. Why does Zimring label his final group the serene? Why do you think that not all ex-smokers could join this group?

6. What does Zimring say is the key to becoming serene? How might being a part of this elite group of ex-smokers help in other areas of a person's life?

7. What do you think Zimring himself feels about people who still smoke? Do you think he agrees with the restrictions that states are putting on smoking in public places?

Exploring the Theme: Discussion and Writing

1. Are you a nonsmoker, an ex-smoker, or a smoker? How do you feel about smoking? Where do you stand on the right to smoke versus the right to clean air? Do you think the new antismoking laws are good or bad? Defend your answers.

2. Zimring says that the serene "believes that it is better to crave . . . and not to smoke than never to have craved at all." He implies that the serene—the "fully mature former smoker"—is superior to a person who still smokes, someone who has never smoked, and all of the other kinds of ex-smokers. Do you agree with his viewpoint? Explain your answer and discuss how your smoking experiences (or lack of them) might influence your opinion.

LEGALIZE DRUGS

Ethan A. Nadelmann

Ethan A. Nadelmann has postgraduate degrees in international relations and law. He has written extensively on international crime, law enforcement, and U.S. drug policy. The following essay first appeared in the June 13, 1988, New Republic.

Preparing to Read

Few people alive today remember the years of Prohibition, but most of the stories written or told about that era indicate that outlawing alcohol didn't work very well. Imagine a bottle of Bud being the legal equivalent of a line of cocaine, a wine glass carrying the same implications as a crack pipe. Yet today most segments of our society embrace the moderate consumption of alcohol despite all its potential negative impact. Nadelmann argues that the problems of Prohibition parallel the current problems we have with illegal drugs. Many of our drug-related problems are not caused by drug consumption itself but by its illegality. Drugs and crime, he argues, are linked in four ways because drugs are illegal, but those links would be weakened considerably, to the benefit of society, if drugs were legalized. What impact would legalizing drugs have on our society?

1   Hamburgers and ketchup. Movies and popcorn. Drugs and crime.

2   Drugs and crime are so thoroughly intertwined in the public mind that to most people a large crime problem seems an inevitable consequence of widespread drug use. But the historical link between the two is more a product of drug laws than of drugs. There are four clear connections between drugs and crime, and three of them would be much diminished if drugs were legalized. This fact doesn't by itself make the case for legal-

ization persuasive, of course, but it deserves careful attention in the emerging debate over whether the prohibition of drugs is worth the trouble.

The first connection between drugs and crime—and the only   3 one that would remain strong after legalization—is the commission of violent and other crimes by people under the influence of illicit drugs. It is this connection that most infects the popular imagination. Obviously some drugs do "cause" people to commit crimes by reducing normal inhibitions, lessening the sense of responsibility, and unleashing aggressive and other antisocial tendencies. Cocaine, particularly in the form of "crack," has earned such a reputation in recent years, just as heroin did in the 1960s and 1970s and marijuana did in the years before that.

Crack's reputation may or may not be more deserved than   4 those of marijuana and heroin. Reliable evidence isn't yet available. But no illicit drug is as widely associated with violent behavior as alcohol. According to Justice Department statistics, 54 percent of all jail inmates convicted of violent crimes in 1983 reported having used alcohol just prior to committing the offense. The impact of drug legalization on this drug-crime connection is hard to predict. Much would depend on overall rates of drug abuse and changes in the nature of consumption, both imponderables. It's worth noting, though, that any shift in consumption from alcohol to marijuana would almost certainly reduce violent behavior.

This connection between drugs and antisocial behavior—   5 which is inherent and may or may not be substantial—is often confused with a second link between the two that is definitely substantial and not inherent: many illicit drug users commit crimes such as robbery, burglary, prostitution, and numbers-running to earn enough money to buy drugs. Unlike the millions of alcoholics who support their habits for modest amounts, many cocaine and heroin addicts spend hundreds, maybe even thousands, of dollars a week. If these drugs were significantly cheaper—if either they were legalized or drug laws were not enforced—the number of crimes committed by drug addicts to pay for their habits would drop dramatically. Even if the drugs were taxed heavily to discourage consumption, prices probably would be much lower than they are today.

The third drug-crime link—also a byproduct of drug laws—   6 is the violent, intimidating, and corrupting behavior of the drug

traffickers. Illegal markets tend to breed violence, not just because they attract criminally minded people but also because
there are no legal institutions for resolving disputes. During Prohibition violent struggles between bootlegging gangs and hijack-
ings of booze-laden trucks were frequent and notorious. Today's
equivalents are the booby traps that surround marijuana fields;
the pirates of the Caribbean, who rip off drug-laden vessels en
route to the United States; and the machine-gun battles and
executions of the more sordid drug mafias—all of which occasionally kill innocent people. Most authorities agree that the
dramatic increase in urban murder rates over the past few years
is almost entirely due to the rise in drug-dealer killings, mostly
of one another.

7   Perhaps the most unfortunate victims of drug prohibition
laws have been the residents of America's ghettos. These laws
have proved largely futile in deterring ghetto-dwellers from becoming drug abusers, but they do account for much of what
ghetto residents identify as the drug problem. Aggressive, gun-
toting drug dealers often upset law-abiding residents far more
than do addicts nodding out in doorways. Meanwhile other residents perceive the drug dealers as heroes and successful role
models. They're symbols of success to children who see no other
options. At the same time the increasingly harsh criminal penalties imposed on adult drug dealers have led drug traffickers to
recruit juveniles. Where once children started dealing drugs
only after they had been using them for a few years, today the
sequence is often reversed. Many children start using drugs only
after working for older drug dealers for while.

8   The conspicuous failure of law enforcement agencies to deal
with the disruptive effect of drug traffickers has demoralized
inner-city neighborhoods and police departments alike. Intensive crackdowns in urban neighborhoods, like intensive anti-
cockroach efforts in urban dwellings, do little more than chase
the menace a short distance away to infect new areas. By contrast, legalization of drugs, like legalization of alcohol in the
early 1930s, would drive the drug-dealing business off the
streets and out of apartment buildings and into government-
regulated, tax-paying stores. It also would force many of the
gun-toting dealers out of the business and convert others into
legitimate businessmen. Some, of course, would turn to other

types of criminal activities, just as some of the bootleggers did after Prohibition's repeal. Gone, though, would be the unparalleled financial gains that tempt people from all sectors of society into the drug-dealing business.

Gone, too, would be the money that draws police into the   9
world of crime. Today police corruption appears to be more pervasive than at any time since Prohibition. In Miami dozens of law enforcement officials have been charged with accepting bribes, ripping off drug dealers, and even dealing drugs themselves. In small towns and rural communities in Georgia, where drug smugglers from the Caribbean and Latin America pass through, dozens of sheriffs have been implicated in corruption. In one New York police precinct, drug-related corruption has generated the city's most far-reaching police scandal since the late 1960s. Nationwide, over 100 cases of drug-related corruption are now prosecuted each year. Every one of the federal law enforcement agencies with significant drug enforcement responsibilities has seen an agent implicated.

It isn't hard to explain the growth of this corruption. The   10
financial temptations are enormous relative to other opportunities, legitimate or illegitimate. Little effort is required. Many police officers are demoralized by the scope of drug traffic, the indifference of many citizens, a frequent lack of appreciation for their efforts, and the seeming futility of it all; even with the regular jailing of drug dealers, there always seem to be more to fill their shoes. Some police also recognize that their real function is not so much to protect victims from predators as to regulate an illicit market that can't be suppressed but that much of society prefers to keep underground. In every respect, the analogy to Prohibition is apt. Repealing drug prohibition laws would dramatically reduce police corruption. By contrast, the measures currently being proposed to deal with the growing problem, including more frequent and aggressive internal inspection, offer little promise and cost money.

The final link between drugs and crime is the tautological   11
connection: producing, selling, buying, and consuming drugs is a crime in and of itself that occurs billions of times each year nationwide. Last year alone, about 30 million Americans violated a drug law, and about 750,000 were arrested, mostly for mere possession, not dealing. In New York City almost half of

the felony indictments were on drug charges, and in Washington, D.C., the figure was more than half. Close to 40 percent of inmates in federal prisons are there on drug-dealing charges, and that population is expected to more than double within 15 years.

12   Clearly, if drugs were legalized, this drug-crime connection—which annually accounts for around $10 billion in criminal justice costs—would be severed. (Selling drugs to children would, of course, continue to be prosecuted.) And the benefits would run deeper than that. We would no longer be labeling as criminals the tens of millions of people who use drugs illicitly, subjecting them to the risk of arrest, and inviting them to associate with drug dealers (who may be criminals in many more senses of the word). The attendant cynicism toward the law in general would diminish, along with the sense of hostility and suspicion that otherwise law-abiding citizens feel toward police. It was costs such as these that strongly influenced many of Prohibition's more conservative opponents. As John D. Rockefeller wrote in explaining why he was withdrawing his support of Prohibition:

> That a vast array of lawbreakers has been recruited and financed on a colossal scale; that many of our best citizens, piqued at what they regarded as an infringement of their private rights, have openly and unabashedly disregarded the 18th Amendment; that as an inevitable result respect for all law has been greatly lessened; that crime has increased to an unprecedented degree—I have slowly and reluctantly come to believe.

Vocabulary

To get the most out of reading this essay, you should have a working understanding of the words listed on the next page. Following each word is a parenthetical reference, indicating the paragraph in which the word is used, as well as a definition for the word. Go back and look at the sentence in which the word appears, and see how the definition applies. To help you make this word a part of your active vocabulary, write a sentence of your own using the word in the space provided.

illicit (3):   illegal, forbidden

___

___

inhibitions (3):   constraints

___

___

imponderables (4):   subjects one is unable to consider

___

___

inherent (5):   inborn, natural

___

___

notorious (6):   infamous

___

___

sordid (6):   dirty, corrupt

___

___

conspicuous (8):   obvious, easily seen

___

___

tautological (11):   something that seems true by virtue of its own logic

___

___

cynicism (12):   disbelief, distrust

___

___

Understanding the Essay

1. Why are drugs and crime intertwined in the public mind? How would the association be lessened, according to Nadelmann, if drugs were legalized?

2. What drug contributes the most to the frequency of violent crimes? How would the legalization of drugs impact the current rate of crimes committed under the influence of drugs?

3. What would happen to the price of drugs if they were legalized? Why would this reduce drug-related crime?

4. What kind of people are attracted to drug trafficking? How would legalizing drugs change the methods of drug dealers?

5. What is the allure of the drug trade these days? Why are so many enforcement officers tempted to accept bribes? What do many police officers see as their real function concerning the drug trade?

6. How does Rockefeller's quote at the end of the essay relate to our current situation regarding illegal drugs? Why did Nadelmann place it at the very end of his essay?

Exploring the Theme: Discussion and Writing

1. Where do you stand in the "debate over whether the prohibition of drugs is worth the trouble"? Do you agree with Nadelmann's argument that legalizing drugs makes sense in the way that repealing Prohibition did, or do you support the continued, and perhaps increased, efforts to stop their use entirely? Explain your opinions.

2. Compare one or two well-known illegal drugs—marijuana, cocaine, or LSD—with alcohol and tobacco. In what way does each harm individuals or society in general? What are the "advantages" of each, if any? According to the advantages and disadvantages of each, which one(s) should be legal? Which should be illegal? Defend your reasoning.

USERS, LIKE ME: MEMBERSHIP IN THE CHURCH OF DRUGS

Gail Regier

Gail Regier has written short stories and essays for several publications. The following article appeared in the May 1989 issue of Harper's. *Regier now teachs English at Auburn University.*

Preparing to Read

It seems that drugs are everywhere these days. TV news reports the latest crack house raid or drug money murder. The newspaper will inform you that 3.4 percent more ten-year-olds tried cocaine last year than two years ago. Perhaps you have experimented with drugs yourself, despite the risks and the efforts of the people who equate frying an egg with frying your brain on drugs. No matter how much you know about drugs and the drug culture, however, Regier's "Users, Like Me: Membership in the Church of Drugs" still may shock you. Regier explores the world of what he calls the Church of Drugs, the world of the habitual users for whom drug use represents recreation, freedom, creativity, social interaction, and excitement, all at the same time. His description of one New Year's Eve is a straightforward look at the lives of the "martyred elite"—the term he uses to describe himself and his fellow drug users—and the fellowship that bonded them.

Profiles of typical drug users, in the newspapers and on TV, obscure the fact that many users aren't typical. I used to do coke with a violinist who was the most sheltered woman I've ever known. My mushroom connection was a fifty-year-old school-bus driver. And one of my high-school buddies, who moved $1,000 worth of drugs a day in and out of his girlfriend's tattoo shop, would always extend credit to transients and welfare moms—debts he'd let slide after a while when they weren't paid.

2   It's easy to start thinking all users are media stereotypes: ghetto trash, neurotic child stars, mutinous suburban adolescents. Users, the media imagine, can't hold jobs or take care of their kids. Users rob liquor stores.

3   Real users, for all their chilly scorn of the straight world, buy into the same myths, but turn them inside out. The condescension becomes a kind of snobbery: we are different from the straight people, we are special, we are more free. We are spiritual adventurers. When I was twenty-four, which was not that long ago, my friends and I thought nothing was more hip than drugs, nothing more depraved, nothing more elemental. When we were messed up, we seemed to become exactly who we were, and what could be more dangerous and splendid? Other vices made our lives more complicated. Drugs made everything simple and pure.

4   Anyone who hangs around drugs learns not to think too much about all this, learns to watch the bent spoon in the water glass.

5   Some of the users I knew were people with nothing left to lose. The rest of us were in it only a little for the money, more than a lot for the nights we would drive to one place after another, in and out of people's parties, looking for a connection. It was a kind of social life, and we weren't in any hurry.

6   What we had in common was drugs. Getting high bound us together against outsiders, gathered us into a common purpose. No one else understood us and we understood each other so well.

7   New Year's Eve 1979: We're riding around trying to cop some speed. My poet friend Brian is driving and in the backseat is Guy, who is on probation and very uptight because we keep telling him the car is stolen. "You mothers are rounding me," he keeps saying. He doesn't believe us, but the game makes him real paranoid. We make some parties but the speed is always gone before we arrive, so we head for the truck stop where I used to work. The high-school kids who work there always have grass and pills. Their stuff is not so hot, but it's real cheap. Restaurant people have a high rate of casual use; the work's so menial you can't stand it without getting high.

8   The place is full of tired truck drivers and travelers with

whiny kids. The hookers wear miniskirts and army jackets and all have colds. Our favorite waitress, Sherry, combines two parties to get us a booth. She's telling some truckers at the counter about her sexual problems with her husband. They tell her to wear leather panties and she sighs and says that doesn't work.

Fleetwood Mac songs shake the jukebox. Sherry slings us coffee and asks, what's the scam? Brian puts thumb and forefinger to his lips and mimes a toke from a joint. She goes back to the kitchen, and when she comes back tells us that Larry is holding. We take our coffee with us through the door marked AUTHORIZED PERSONNEL. Everybody in the kitchen is drunk. Two of the girls are playing the desert-island game: If you could have only two drugs for the rest of your life, what would they be? Sherry pours some cold duck from a bottle that was in the walk-in cooler. 9

There was a time when the rap here was all baseball and dates, but not anymore. Tonight the drizzle of abstractions is as vacuous as any graduate seminar. The kids say the owner gives them shit for coming to work stoned. They need their jobs but they know how they want to live. I tell them that the Church of Drugs has its own rituals and rules, and its members are a martyred elite. Brian tells Sherry about acid and stained glass. Guy tells the dishwasher how to tell if it's his starter or his alternator that's bad. The kids listen. They are impressed by us. They want to be like us. 10

Drug dealers on TV are vampires: oily, smooth, psychotic, sexy, human paradigms of the narcotics they sell. Larry is a skinny punk who is studying auto body at the vo-tech high school. Wearing a GMC cap and a long, stained apron, he stands behind a grease-blackened grill covered with steaks and bacon and skillets asizzle with eggs. 11

"Watch this shit," he tells another aproned kid, and motions to us to follow him. The kid protests that he'll get behind. Larry leads us back to the storeroom, past shelves of #10 cans and signs that read ALL DELIVERIES C.O.D. and ABSOLUTELY NO FIREARMS ALLOWED ON THESE PREMISES. He takes a baggie from his gym bag and shows us some speeders he says are pharmaceutical. The black capsules have the right markings on them, but they unscrew too easily and the bone-white powder inside isn't bitter enough. We tell him no thanks, but buy a joint from him for a dollar. 12

13   When I was selling drugs I made a lot of money, but I usually got stoned on the profits. It was black money and it seemed the highs I bought with it were free and therefore sweeter. I was a college dropout with a kid and a nervous wife. I worked as a cook in a Mexican café fifty hours a week and brought home $200. For that $200 I could buy half a kilo of sinsemilla, break it down into finger bags, and double my money. Selling meant I always had drugs—though we didn't that New Year's eve. Dealing, with its arcana of mirrors and scales, was a guild mystery, a secret, forbidden craft. It was a ticket to places I couldn't get to any other way. I got to know guys who drove Cadillacs and carried forged passports, guys who cooked acid and smack in basement labs, women who wore lots of rings and called every man Jones.

14   Brian and I smoke the joint on the back porch of the truck stop. The rain, we decide, is very righteous. Eighteen-wheelers grind and hiss their gaudy lights onto the interstate. Diane, a sloe-eyed, peach-skinned fifteen-year-old, comes out and vamps us for a couple of hits. I tell her about those cocaine nights when the room fills with snowflakes sifting down slow as if they were under water. She's kissing Brian and I've got my hand up her short skirt, but she refuses to get in the car with us.

15   Downtown by the hospital, we get in a confusion with some ambulance guys with their cherry top on. Bald tires skid on the wet pavement. Brian decides to let me drive. We stop at my house, where my wife is watching *Dick Clark's New Year's Rockin' Eve*. Her eyes are red from crying, but she tries to smile.

16   "Dan and Jan were here," she says. "Don't you remember we invited them?"

17   I look in the refrigerator for wine. There isn't any.

18   "Brian and Guy are in the car," I say. "I've got to run them home."

19   "Then will you come back?"

20   "Come with us if you want." I know she won't. Our son's asleep upstairs.

21   "Don't get speed," she says.

22   "We're not."

23   "You get mean when you do speed."

24   I want to get wired. I head for the door.

25   We make the Steak N'Ale. In a real city there would be black guys pushing stuff on the sidewalk out front, but this is Spring-

field, Missouri, and we can't score. The manager, our connection, isn't around. At the bar we order shots of whiskey. The place is full of pretty girls, and even the ones who don't drink are drunk, but we're not looking for girls.

Guy says, "We should go see Casey." Casey is an old guy who   26
sold black-market penicillin in post-war Europe. Brian doesn't
know Casey but he knows he's expensive, and he fusses about
that. But Guy and I are studying on how good Casey's crystal
meth is and how Casey could get us a set of points so we could
hit it.

On our way we boost three wine glasses and a bottle of   27
Korbel from somebody's table. Sitting in the car, we drink to
ourselves and the dying year. Brian wets his fingertip in the
champagne and strokes it gently round and round the rim of his
glass, making space noises rise from the crystal. We all do it, but
then the noises turn spooky and we get paranoid. We drop the
glasses out the window and drive.

Prudence is sitting on the front porch watching the rain. She   28
kisses me and I taste her tongue. I introduce my friends and she
kisses them.

"Casey's inside."   29

"Has he got meth?"   30

She shrugs. The business is Casey's gig. Prudence is twenty   31
and has a cat named Lenin and a one-year-old baby. She's kept
the job she had before she moved in with Casey: evening attendant at a laundry near the college. Her place is the cleanest in
town. My buddies and I would drop in to wash some jeans and
score a little pot, and end up hanging around all evening eating
candy bars and flirting with Prudence.

On the weekends Prudence ran a perpetual carport sale,   32
things she made and stuff taken in barter from customers with
cash-flow problems. Clothes and belt buckles, pipes and bottles,
bootleg eight-tracks and cassettes with typed labels, old skin
mags, car stereos and CB radios trailing cut wires.

The living room is brightly lit as always; Prudence leaves   33
her pole lamps on twenty-four hours a day. Casey is sprawled
among pillows on an old couch ripe with cigarette scars, culling
sticks and seeds from some dope on the glass-topped coffee table. Framed beneath the glass are large-denomination bills from
several South American countries. Casey's favorite objects litter
the shelf below: brass pipes with small screw fittings, ceramic

ashtrays from the commune at Ava, a rifle scope he uses to case visitors coming up the rutted driveway.

34   A candy dish holds pills—speckled birds and bootleg ludes coloring a base of Tylenol with codeine, bought over-the-counter in Canada. Casey offers us some, and I sift thumb and forefinger carefully through the pile and pick out two black beauties for tomorrow. Brian starts to take a handful and I sign him not to. Casey scarfs codeine the whole time we talk.

35   Prudence and I go to the kitchen to mix a fruit jar of gin and orange juice, stay there a little while to touch and neck. She has painted everything in the kitchen white, walls and floors and cabinets and fixtures, and in the glare of many bare bulbs the room is stark as a laboratory. White-painted plaster peels off the walls in loops and splinters. There are no dishes or pans; Prudence buys only things she can cook in her toaster oven.

36   Last time I was over, Casey went after Prudence with a ratchet wrench and I had to talk him down. As we mix the drinks she tells me how she and Casey dropped acid together and now things are better. He's even starting to like the boy. I tell her how my four-year-old thinks acid is the best trick going, because when I'm tripping I play with him so much. We take baths together, drenching the floor with our bathtub games, while my wife sits on the toilet lid, watching us with her bright blue eyes.

37   On the floor, Lenin and the baby take turns peekabooing and pouncing. I'm surprised the baby isn't scared. I've changed my mind and dropped one of the beauties and I'm feeling edgy and fast and tricky. Lenin rubs himself against my ankles and I grow paranoid.

38   "You want to help me water the plants?" Prudence asks.

39   We climb the rungs nailed to the closet wall, push up the trapdoor, and crawl into the attic. Gro-lights illuminate twenty marijuana plants set in plastic tubs. Casey has run a hose up through the wall. I turn the water on and off for her as she crawls back and forth across the rafters on her hands and knees.

40   Downstairs, I can hear Brian on a rap. "Radiation will be the next great vice. They already use it with chemo to kill cancer. Soon they'll discover wavelengths that reproduce the effects of every known drug. The cops will be able to spot users easily 'cause we'll all be bald."

41   Prudence digs out a Mamas and Papas tape and plays "Straight Shooter." Casey tells us how some junkies will put off

shooting-up until the craving starts, like getting real hungry before a steak dinner. I listen, but to me the addict world is as mythical as Oz. I've met junkies, but they were in town only accidentally and soon moved on to Kansas City or New Orleans. Like a symphony orchestra or a pro sports team, a junkie population needs a large urban center to support it.

Casey says that the word "heroin" is a corruption of the German word *heroisch*, meaning "powerful, even in small amounts." I cruise the bookshelf. A rogues' gallery: Henry Miller, Cocteau, Genet, de Sade's *Justine* in scarlet leather, *Story of O*. Casey explains a William Burroughs story he's just read, about a secret society dedicated to discovering the Flesh Tree described in an ancient Mayan codex. This is the rare and sacred plant from which human life originally derived. According to Burroughs, flesh is really a vegetable, and the human system of reproduction is a perversion of its true nature. 42

Casey talks very seriously about acquiring his own Tree of Flesh on his next trip to Mazatlán. He regards the story as journalism rather than parable—or seems to. We spend some time discussing how to care for the Tree of Flesh once Casey obtains it. 43

Guy asks Casey about the crystal meth. 44

"You don't want speed," I say. I'm feeling very articulate now. "What you want is a hit of junk." Guy shakes his head, but Brian looks thoughtful. "For ten minutes," I say, "you'll be as high as you ever thought you wanted to be. Then in half an hour you'll be as high as you *really* ever wanted to be." 45

"And then?" Guy says. 46

"You'll want *more*." 47

Inside the Church of Drugs, heroin users are an elite within the elite, saints of Instant Karma and Instant Death. Their stark games raise them to a place beyond the hype and chatter. 48

"When you shoot up," I tell them, "you're alone before the abyss. That's what shooting up is for." 49

The first time I shot up was the most frightened I've ever been. For me the fear was part of the high. 50

Guy and Brian have never done needles, but Brian is hard for it and helps me work Guy around. "We won't hit you in the vein," I assure him. "Just in muscle tissue, like a vaccination." We each give Casey a twenty. He drags an army-surplus ammo box from under the couch and rummages through it. Prudence puts the baby on the rug and goes to hunt up a needle. 51

52   When she returns with one, Casey measures out the heroin and I cook it in a teaspoon dark with the flames of many lighters. When it's like molten silver, Casey loads, taps bubbles out of the rig, and hits Guy in the shoulder before he can change his mind. Brian thrusts his arm forward eagerly, his eyes ashimmer with the romance of drugs, and I put the needle in him. They both vomit, the way almost everybody does when they get their wings, then go serenely on the nod. The baby is startled and then amused by their upheavals. We get them settled and empty the bucket we had handy for them, then Casey and Prudence hit each other. She has a glass of gin in one hand and breaks it on the coffee table when the spasms hit her.

53   Last to do up, I take my time, pricking the point of the needle into the vein of my inside forearm easing back a little before I push the trigger. Wisps of blood claw up in the glass wand and a white light like a fist of thorns shoves everything away.

54   Later we're stirring around again and starting to talk. The baby has been crying for a while. Brian wipes the shards of broken glass off the coffee table onto the rug in front of the baby, who quiets and reaches for these shiny new toys.

55   After a few cuts the baby learns that broken glass can hurt him. He's crying again. He tries to push the pieces away, but the splinters stick to his hands. He rubs his small fists together and we all start laughing, we can't help it, he's so cute. Prudence claps her hands and cheers on his efforts. He rubs his hands against his face and the blood spots it like clown makeup. The baby cries so hard he starts choking. It seems very funny. Then he starts gnawing at the slivers between his fingers, and that is very funny too.

56   Casey gets straight first and washes the dried blood from the baby's face. Guy can't walk and I help him outside into the cold air. Brian and Prudence are messing around out by the car.

57   Casey comes out on the porch. His fingers are streaked with iodine. He says, "Hey man."

58   I say Yeah.

59   Casey looks at Brian. "Don't bring him back here."

60   These days I'm a guy who goes six months or a year without smoking a joint. I got out of drugs the way a lot of people do. One day I looked around and saw that I was missing a lot of work, my nerves were bad, parties bored me, all my friends were on drugs. I quit selling and then I quit using. You know the story.

Prudence still lives in Springfield, in the same house north of 61
the railroad yards. Casey is gone but the carport sale continues.
Her boy is ten, and maybe there are some fine white scars at the
corners of his mouth. Maybe they're just my imagination.

When I quit drugs I thought the fighting in my marriage 62
would stop. It didn't. It wasn't the drugs my wife had always
hated, it was the fellowship the Church of Drugs provided. She
still wants me home. I'm still not there.

One night last year when I didn't want to go home, I took a 63
manic-depressive writer on a 'shroom run to a stucco structure
known as the House With No Brains. Everyone there was younger than me. Some folks had heroin and tried to missionary us
into doing up. I just said no, but for weeks after that—listen, this
is important—for a long time after that, I thought about junk,
talked about it to people, started once to drive to the House but
turned back. Every time I picked up a spoon or struck a match, I
thought about needle drugs, about how clean and fine things
could be.

Vocabulary

To get the most out of reading this essay, you should have a
working understanding of the words listed below. Following
each word is a parenthetical reference, indicating the paragraph
in which the word is used, as well as a definition for the word.
Go back and look at the sentence in which the word appears, and
see how the definition applies. To help you make this word a
part of your active vocabulary, write a sentence of your own
using the word in the space provided.

neurotic (2):   emotionally or mentally unstable

_____

_____

mutinous (2):   rebellious

_____

_____

condescension (3):   disdain, sense of superiority

---

depraved (3):   wicked, corrupt

---

paranoid (7):   overly suspicious, fearful

---

menial (7):   monotonous, lacking dignity

---

vacuous (10):   empty, shallow

---

martyred (10):   persecuted, harassed

---

paradigms (11):   examples, models

---

arcana (13):   objects cloaked in mystery

---

parable (43):   story, fable

Understanding the Essay

1. What is the media profile of the typical drug user? How do drug users turn the stereotypes inside out?

2. What does Regier mean when he says, "Anyone who hangs around drugs learns not to think too much about all this, learns to watch the bent spoon in the water glass"?

3. Why is casual drug use in restaurants so prevalent? Why do the kids at the truck stop look up to Regier and his friends?

4. Describe Regier's relationship with his wife and compare it with his relationship with his drug buddies. What keeps Regier and his wife together?

5. How has Prudence and Casey's relationship changed since Regier's last visit? What helped to change it?

6. How do Regier and Brian persuade Guy to try heroin? What does the scene with the baby tell you about heroin's effect on people?

7. Why did Regier quit drugs? Has he made a clean break from them?

Exploring the Theme: Discussion and Writing

1. Regier's tone throughout the essay is never negative toward drug use. Even after he describes the baby chewing on broken glass, he says, "Every time I picked up a spoon or struck a match, I thought about needle drugs, about how clean and fine things could be." What is your view of drugs? How is it influenced by personal experience? Has reading Regier's essay changed your opinion of drugs and drug use?

2. Do you think certain drugs should be legalized? Write an essay supporting or opposing the legalization of one or two presently illegal drugs.

EATING DISORDERS—AN ADOLESCENT PROBLEM

Helen A. Guthrie

Helen A. Guthrie is an emeritus professor and former chair of the department of nutrition at the Pennsylvania State University. Born in Canada, Professor Guthrie earned her advanced degrees at Michigan State University and the University of Hawaii. Her special interests are in applied nutrition, nutrition education, and infant nutrition. The following selection is from her widely used text, Introductory Nutrition, *published in 1989.*

Preparing to Read

If you could weigh whatever you wanted, would you want to gain weight or lose it? Chances are, if your entire class pooled its answers to that question and analyzed the results, there would be a big difference between the men's and the women's answers. Society frowns on the male ninety-pound weakling—he's told to bulk up like Charles Atlas to avoid having sand kicked in his face. Yet at the same time, the standard of beauty for women established by female models and movie stars revolves around thinness. The pursuit of thinness has spawned a whole industry of diet plans and exercise gadgets, as well as some serious problems. "Eating Disorders—An Adolescent Problem" is a straightforward look at two disorders—anorexia nervosa and bulimia—that affect young women almost exclusively. Under pressure to be thin, some women start planning their lives around losing weight and either avoiding food or bingeing and purging it. How big a role does food or dieting play in your life?

1   Over the past 10 to 15 years it has become apparent that eating disorders have reached epidemic proportions among adolescents. There are two distinct disor-

ders, *anorexia nervosa* and *bulimia,* which affect adolescents and college-age women more frequently than any other group. Surprisingly, they involve people with a wide range of body weights, from the emaciated to the obese, and usually result from a complex interaction of biochemical, psychological, and social factors.

"Cure" rates for persons with eating disorders are discouraging. Only 50% of recovered clients remain symptom free, 25% live with reduced symptoms, and 25% experience no meaningful remission following therapy. Thus early intervention and prevention of these insidious disorders is the only feasible approach to dealing with the problem. 2

The term *anorexia nervosa* was first used in 1873 by English physician William Gull to describe severely emaciated young women who refused to eat. Anorexia, meaning loss of appetite, is, in a sense, a misnomer, since only about 50% of those afflicted have loss of appetite, and then only in the latter stages. The term, however, remains in clinical and popular use. 3

Anorexia nervosa is found predominantly among adolescent females, affecting one in 250 girls between 12 and 18 years of age. These young women most often come from middle- to upper-class families and are described as intelligent, obedient, even "model" children until the eating disorder emerges. At that point, the constant battle over eating disrupts almost every aspect of life for the girl and her family. 4

The disorder is characterized by a relentless pursuit of thinness, coupled with an intense preoccupation with food, eating, and body weight. Anorexics are expert calorie counters; they eventually eliminate all "fattening" foods (most carbohydrates and all fats) and are frequently vegetarians. They often spend considerable time and effort preparing food for others and insist that others eat while they refrain from eating. Anorexics also display peculiar food-handling behaviors, such as food hoarding, cutting food into minute pieces, toying with food, and dawdling for hours over a very small meal. Transient food fads and rituals are also common. 5

Symptoms of anorexia nervosa include a weight loss of 20% to 25%, amenorrhea for at least 3 months, and distorted body image, with no evidence of organic disease. The disturbance of body image is so extreme that many anorexics continue to view their skeleton-like figures as grossly overweight and complain 6 that they are "too fat" even though significant weight loss is obvious.

7   Other symptoms of anorexia include a sense of ineffectiveness and depression, discomfort after eating, constipation, bingeing, self-induced vomiting, laxative abuse, and hyperactivity. Despite their emaciated state, anorexics will exercise for hours, denying fatigue as they use exercise as yet another strategy to burn calories and further decrease weight.

8   Finally, the classic symptoms of starvation appear, including anemia, electrolyte imbalances, and endocrine and immune dysfunction. If left untreated, the deterioration of brain tissue results in apathy, coma, and death in about 1 in 20 anorexics.

9   The only effective treatment is hospitalization, with treatment by an interdisciplinary team giving the best results. Weight gain and restoration of adequate nutritional status are imperative. Because of the elaborate measures taken by some anorexics to refuse food, refeeding must often be by a nasogastric tube or intravenous feeding (TPN or total parenteral nutrition). Drug therapy is used to reduce hyperactivity and anxiety during mealtime, as well as to stimulate appetite. Psychotherapy, however, remains the cornerstone of treatment. Programs that incorporate behavior modification, family therapy, and nutritional counseling are most successful in the long-term rehabilitation of persons with anorexia nervosa.

10   Bulimia is an even more recent eating disorder, having been first publicized in 1980. The word *bulimia* means "ox hunger," an appropriate description of the voracious appetite displayed by bulimics, who constantly engage in food binges.

11   Bulimia usually begins as an effort to control weight. It involves alternating patterns of bingeing on large quantities of food (from 3000 to 20,000 calories is common), and then 'purging' by self-induced vomiting or by taking laxatives. Fasting and continuous strict dieting may be used separately or in conjunction with purging.

12   Although bulimia may be a complication of anorexia nervosa, it also affects women of normal weight. They tend to be white women of the upper and middle classes and somewhat older than those with anorexia, with 17 years being the average age of onset. Alcoholism, obesity, and depression are found among the family members of bulimics. Bulimics themselves have a tendency toward abuse of alcohol and drugs, shoplifting,

and sexual promiscuity, suggesting problems in controlling their impulsive behaviors. Bulimia is further associated with feelings of low self-esteem, guilt, helplessness, and some distortion of body image.

Bulimics have recurrent episodes of binge eating, consum-   13
ing high-calorie, easily ingested foods such as candy, cookies, cake, and ice cream during a binge. They tend to terminate a binge with sleep or self-induced vomiting, eat surreptitiously during a binge, make repeated attempts to lose weight, experience frequent weight fluctuations, and have fear of not being able to stop eating voluntarily. They are frequently depressed after bingeing.

The complex nature of the bulimic syndrome has critical   14
effects on physical and emotional health. Bingeing and purging begin in an effort to control weight but gradually become a method for dealing with stress and frustration; the pattern is covert and may go on undetected for surprisingly long periods, until it eventually becomes a chronic problem. In addition to the very detrimental effects of rapid weight fluctuation, prolonged bouts of bulimia may result in electrolyte imbalances, ulceration of the gastrointestinal tract, erosion of dental enamel, loss of hair, and irregularities in the menstrual cycle; encephalograms may reveal irregular patterns.

Bulimics may go as long as 6 to 7 years before seeking help.   15
While many bulimics respond favorably to antidepressant drug therapy, this treatment is most effective when combined with psychotherapy and behavior therapy. Nutritional counseling, aimed at regulating eating behavior and weight, further improves the treatment outcomes of bulimic clients but in itself is inadequate.

Vocabulary

To get the most out of reading this essay, you should have a working understanding of the words listed on the next page. Following each word is a parenthetical reference, indicating the paragraph in which the word is used, as well as a definition for the word. Go back and look at the sentence in which the word appears, and see how the definition applies. To help you make this word a part of your active vocabulary, write a sentence of your own using the word in the space provided.

epidemic (1): widespread, spreading quickly, as in a disease

emaciated (1): extremely thin

biochemical (1): the chemistry of living things

remission (2): suppression of a disease in an individual

insidious (2): dangerously difficult to detect

feasible (2): practical

misnomer (3): misleading name

clinical (3): medical

imperative (9): necessary

voracious (10):   having a huge appetite, insatiable

_____

_____

promiscuity (12):   having casual sexual relationships with multiple partners

_____

_____

surreptitiously (13):   secretly, privately

_____

_____

Understanding the Essay

1. What is the cure rate for eating disorders?
2. How do people with anorexia nervosa behave? Describe the type of person who is most likely to have this disorder.
3. What is the end result of untreated anorexia nervosa? What is the best form of treatment for the disorder?
4. What is bulimia? How long has it been a common disorder?
5. What kind of person is most likely to have bulimia? How does this profile differ from that of anorexia?
6. Why is bulimia difficult to diagnose? What health problems can it cause?

Exploring the Theme: Discussion and Writing

1. Guthrie states that eating disorders result from "a complex interaction of biochemical, psychological, and social factors." Describe what you think the psychological and social factors are. Why do you think that the "cure" rates for people with eating disorders are so discouraging?

2. Describe your perception of your own weight and your relationship with food. Do you want to weigh less? More? Have you ever gone on a diet? Do you exercise? How important is your weight to your sense of well-being?

WRITING SUGGESTIONS
FOR "ADDICTIONS"

1. What is your attitude toward smoking and smokers? Have you ever smoked? How do you feel when you are forced to breathe in someone else's smoke? Write an essay in which you present your views on smoking. Be careful to formulate a specific thesis statement before starting to write.

2. For almost thirty years health warnings have appeared on tobacco products and in advertising for these products. Antismoking advocates claim that these warnings have significantly helped their cause. Some people have proposed similar warnings for alcohol products and alcohol advertising. Write an essay in which you argue for or against the use of warning labels for alcoholic beverages.

3. What is your college's or university's policy regarding alcohol consumption on campus? Do college officials strictly enforce the policy? What are the penalties for being caught drinking on campus? Write a letter to the editor of your campus newspaper arguing for changes in the current alcohol policy and its enforcement.

4. Americans are a very weight-conscious people. Most of us at one time or another have felt—or some day will feel—the need "to lose ten pounds." In the extreme, the pursuit of thinness and a beautiful body causes a growing number of people, especially women, to develop eating disorders. How big a role does dieting and food play in your life? Write an essay in which you recount an experience with losing—or gaining—weight. What did you learn about yourself as a result of this experience?

5. Ethan A. Nadelmann is not the first person to propose the legalization of drugs. How seriously do you take his proposal? Is the connection he draws between drugs and crime important? Write an essay in which you agree or disagree with Nadelmann's position that our country's prohibition of drugs is not worth the trouble.

6. Smoking, drinking, eating, and drugs are only four of America's more widely publicized addictions. It's no secret that

Americans are prone to addictive/compulsive behavior. But why?
Are the various addictions to which some of us succumb a way of
dealing with pain—physical, psychological, or spiritual? Are our
addictions merely symptoms for some underlying problem(s)?
Write an essay in which you attempt to answer these important
questions.

7.   Study the following advertisement that appeared in the
December 1992 issue of *Reader's Digest*. What is the ad's basic
message? What does Allstate want you to do after reading this
ad? What is the purpose of the bold message "Tie one on"? Why
has Allstate, an insurance company, produced such an ad in the
first place? Using Kip Turner's student essay in the Introduction
as a model (pp. 24–28), write an essay in which you analyze and
interpret this ad (or one of your own choosing) in the context of
the theme "addictions."

This holiday season, some 150 million people will tie a simple red ribbon on their car antennas, to express their commitment to safe, sober driving. It's part of the "Tie One On For Safety™" campaign sponsored by Mothers Against Drunk Driving (MADD) and The Good Hands People of Allstate.

See your Allstate agent now for your complimentary red ribbon. Together we can help ensure a safe and jolly holiday. And many more happy new years.

Allstate
You're in good hands.

For more tips on being a responsible, safe driver, write to: Allstate, Dept. DD,
P.O. Box 7660, Mt. Prospect, IL 60056-9961. © 1992 Allstate Insurance Company, Northbrook, IL.

Courtesy Allstate Insurance Company

11

THE NATURAL WORLD

Although we are all a part of the natural environment, how many of us stop to think about what that means? Too often we tend to divorce ourselves from the natural order—from its complexities, processes, and interrelationships. We fail to see ourselves as an integral part of a vast environmental network. And by separating ourselves from the environment, we fail to appreciate the intricacies and beauty of the life around us. When was the last time you took an afternoon off from your daily routine to get back to nature and look at it up close?

As children, we were all curious about our world. We wanted to know the names of things, why turtles had shells, how ants carried heavy loads, and how bees made honey or leaves turned colors in the fall. Our senses were alive to the sights, smells, sounds, textures, and tastes that nature offered us. As we grew older we gradually developed worldy interests that directed our attention away from nature. We seemed to lose the curiosity we had as children. That curiosity is not gone, however; it's lying dormant, ready to be awakened in us. The intention, then, in the four essays that follow is to stimulate our curiosity again, to open our senses to the diversity, richness, and surprises of nature.

We begin with an essay on the so-called "baby bird crisis" that occurs when baby birds fall from their nests. In warning us of our awesome responsibility in adopting one of these baby birds, Gale Lawrence gives us insight into the functions performed by adult birds and raises the question of human intervention in the web of nature. The next two essays examine death's role in the natural order. Robert Finch describes the killing of a hornet by a spider, and Annie Dillard captures her terror as she watches a giant water bug suck the insides out of a frog. Finally, Jean George gives an amazing catalog of the wonderful adaptations of nature's creatures to their environments.

BABY BIRDS

Gale Lawrence

Gale Lawrence was born in Springfield, Vermont. A free-lance writer, teacher, and naturalist, Lawrence began her career by writing a weekly column on nature for local newspapers. She is now at work on her fourth book; her first three are The Beginning Naturalist, Field Guide to the Familiar, *and* The Backyard Naturalist.

Preparing to Read

What would you do if you came across a baby bird that had fallen from its nest or a baby raccoon or skunk that was all alone? What's involved in caring for a wild creature? Too often humans think that their intervention will ensure the creature's survival. Not so, says Lawrence. In spite of good intentions, most adoptions of baby animals end in failure. In the following essay, taken from *The Beginning Naturalist,* Lawrence turns her attention to the "baby bird crisis" that occurs every spring. She offers sound advice for those who don't know how to deal with a baby bird that has fallen to the ground.

1   Every spring the "baby bird crisis" occurs. By May many birds have hatched their first broods and are feeding them in the nest while they grow their feathers and learn to fly. Baby birds have a way of tumbling out of their nests, and children have a way of finding them and bringing them home. What should a family do if faced with this "crisis"?

2   First, take the baby bird back to the exact spot where it was found. Look carefully for a nest nearby. If you find the nest and it is accessible, put the bird gently back into the nest. Contrary to popular belief, the mother bird will not reject a baby that has been handled by human beings. A deer, which has a keen sense of smell and fears the human scent, will reject a fawn that has been

handled, but birds are different. If you find the nest and return the baby, you have done the best you can do.

As a next-best measure, tie a small box onto a branch of a tree or shrub near where the bird was found, and put the baby bird in the box. The bird will thus be off the ground and out of the reach of neighborhood cats and dogs. 3

The third best thing you can do is simply to leave the bird in the exact spot where it was found. Parent birds are accustomed to having their young fall out of the nest, and they will feed them on the ground. Of course, the baby bird is more vulnerable on the ground than it is in the nest or in a box, but it still stands a better chance of surviving under its own parents' care than under human care. If the baby bird is found near a house, it is better to keep pet dogs and cats indoors than to bring the baby bird indoors in an attempt to protect it. 4

If the baby is truly abandoned or orphaned—something you can learn only by watching it from a distance for an hour or more—you have a decision to make. You can leave it there to die a natural death—which might in fact be the most humane thing to do. Or you can take it indoors. If you decide to care for it yourself, you are making a substantial commitment. And, even if you live up to your commitment, there is no guarantee that the bird will survive. 5

Two major problems are involved in trying to parent a baby bird. One is feeding it, and the other is preparing it for life in the wild. Parent birds do it all as a matter of course, but a human parent will have to drop other activities for a period of weeks and perhaps install a screened porch or aviary to do the job right. 6

Before you can even address yourself to the problem of feeding, however, you have the more immediate problem of the bird's shock and fright to contend with. Perhaps this is the time to send one member of the family for a book on the care of wild animal young, while another rigs up a heating pad or hot water bottle to warm the baby bird. One good book is *Care of the Wild Feathered and Furred: A Guide to Wildlife Handling and Care* (Santa Cruz: Unity Press, 1973) by Mae Hickman and Maxine Guy. Another is Ronald Rood's *The Care and Feeding of Wild Pets* (New York: Pocket Books, 1976). A third book that is specifically about birds is *Bird Ambulance* (New York: Charles Scribner's Sons, 1971) by Arline Thomas. 7

8   Now comes the problem of feeding. The warm milk in an eye dropper that seems to be everyone's immediate impulse when it comes to feeding animal young may be appropriate for baby mammals, but it will come as a complete surprise to the baby bird. Its parents were probably feeding it mashed worms, caterpillars, insects, and other delicious odds and ends. Therefore, you'll need to do the same. At first you should supply the baby bird with protein-rich foods. Eventually you're going to have to identify the species and learn something about its food habits in the wild if you want the bird to grow up properly. Whether the bird is a seed eater, an insect eater, or a predator will make a difference.

9   Parent birds feed their babies about every ten or fifteen minutes from sunrise to sunset. They also feed them exactly what they need to keep their bowels regulated and their bodies growing properly. They also keep the nest clean by removing the babies' excrement, which usually appears shortly after each feeding. In brief, between finding and preparing appropriate food, feeding, and cleaning up after meals you're not going to have much time for anything else for a while if you decide to parent a baby bird.

10   If you do manage to keep the young bird fed properly and growing, your next problem is providing it with enough space for it to practice flying. You cannot expect a bird to go from your kitchen to the wild with one swoop of its wings. You will need to continue feeding and protecting the bird while it is adjusting to the outdoors. If it had stayed with its parents, it would have had adult birds to follow and imitate, but, with nothing but human beings to encourage it, it will have to make sense out of its environment alone. The young bird that has been raised by humans is at a disadvantage when it comes to competing for food and avoiding the attacks of predators. So even if you do manage to raise a fledgling to adulthood, you have not guaranteed its survival in the wild.

11   If you think I'm trying to sound discouraging, I am. The adoption of a baby bird will probably result in failure. You might even cause a death that would not have occurred had you left the baby bird where it was. Your intentions might be good; the ethical impulse that motivates your actions might be of the best kind. But you should know that even experienced veterinarians have a low success rate in caring for wild animals.

Perhaps the most important thing a child or adult can   12
learn from an encounter with a baby bird is the difference
between wild animals and domestic pets. Whereas puppies and
kittens warm to human attention and become very much a
part of the family, a wild bird never will. Attempting to make
a pet out of a wild animal is a serious disservice to that
animal—so serious, in fact, that there are laws against it. Life
in the wild does not consist of friendly humans, readily available meals, and a protected environment. Wild animals must
remain wild to survive.

Rather than adopt a baby bird, why not "adopt" a whole   13
bird family—from a distance? Chances are there is a bird's nest
somewhere near your home. Or you can build birdhouses to
attract birds to your yard. Learn to watch the bird family from a
distance. If human beings get too close, the parent birds won't
come to the nest. So practice sitting quietly, perhaps with a pair
of binoculars, far enough away from the nest that the adult birds
won't feel threatened.

Watching birds in the wild is a much healthier and more   14
realistic activity than fantasizing that a bird will become your
special friend because you raised it. Unfortunately, movies, television, and children's books have created a "Bambi syndrome"
in us. The young of most species are precious and adorable, but
the desire to fondle and caress and make pets out of wildlings is
dangerously romantic. It should not be encouraged. We'd be
much wiser if we were content to be observers of wildlife. If we
truly care about wild animals, we should be protectors of their
wildness, which enables the best of them to survive.

Vocabulary

To get the most out of reading this essay, you should have a
working understanding of the words listed on the next page.
Following each word is a parenthetical reference, indicating the
paragraph in which the word is used, as well as a definition for
the word. Go back and look at the sentence in which the word
appears, and see how the definition applies. To help you make
this word a part of your active vocabulary, write a sentence of
your own using the word in the space provided.

keen (2):   acutely sensitive

_____

_____

vulnerable (4):   susceptible to attack or injury

_____

_____

aviary (6):   enclosure for confining birds

_____

_____

predator (8):   animal that lives by eating other animals

_____

_____

fledgling (10):   young, inexperienced bird

_____   _____

_____

ethical (11):   in accordance with the accepted principles of right and wrong

_____

_____

romantic (14):   imaginative but impractical

_____

_____

Understanding the Essay

1. Lawrence ends her first paragraph with a question. As a reader, what do you expect Lawrence to do next?

2. According to Lawrence, what three things should a family do when they find a baby bird?

3. Once people bring a baby bird inside, what major problems do they face?

4. What steps are involved in feeding a baby bird?

5. What alternatives to caring for wild animals does Lawrence suggest to her readers?

6. What is the "Bambi syndrome," mentioned in paragraph 14? On what false notions is it based?

Exploring the Theme: Discussion and Writing

1. What experiences have you had caring for abandoned wild animals? Did you encounter the problems that Lawrence discusses? What unexpected things happened? Have you read or heard about people who have successfully raised animals and later returned them to the wild? What seemed to be the secrets of their success?

2. Lawrence says, "Perhaps the most important thing a child or adult can learn from an encounter with a baby bird is the difference between wild animals and domestic pets." What exactly are the differences between them? What is the fascination that people have with wild animals, and why do they continually try to make pets out of them?

3. If you were faced with the decision of leaving an abandoned baby bird outdoors to die a natural death or bringing it indoors, what would you do? Why?

DEATH OF A HORNET

Robert Finch

Born in New Jersey in 1943, Robert Finch received his B.A. at Harvard (1967) and his M.A. in English at Indiana University, Bloomington (1969). He is the author of four books about Cape Cod, where he has lived since 1972, and is coeditor with John Elder of the The Norton Book of Nature Writing. *His first book,* Common Ground: A Naturalist's Cape Cod *(1981), was nominated for the Pulitzer prize. Finch continues to write full-time about the Cape and southern New England. "Insects are so present and so alien to our lives," says Finch, that they provide "a good sounding board" for us as humans.*

Preparing to Read

When they hear the word *naturalist,* many people have a "wild kingdom" image in their minds. Naturalists are seen as travelers to exotic places who wrestle giant anteaters or attach radio collars to polar bears before the tranquilizer dart wears off the animal. Yet the best naturalists can write about a backyard to make it sound as fascinating as anywhere on earth. The process of a spider killing and wrapping its prey is a common occurrence, but in "Death of a Hornet," Finch turns it into a dramatic event. Finch writes about the encounter with such detail that the reader seems to enter the world of the spider's web.

1 For the past half hour I have been watching a remarkable encounter between a spider and a yellow hornet, in which I was an unwitting catalyst. I have found several of these hornets in my study recently, buzzing and beating themselves

against the glass doors and windows, having crawled out, I presume, from the cracks between the still-unplastered sheets of rock lath on the ceiling. Usually I have managed to coax them out the door with a piece of paper or a book, but this morning my mind was abstracted with innumerable small tasks, so when another one of these large insects appeared, buzzing violently like a yellow and black column of electricity slowly sizzling up the window pane above my desk, I rather absentmindedly whacked it with a rolled-up bus schedule until it fell, maimed but still alive, onto the window sill.

My sill is cluttered with natural objects and apparatus used 2
for studying and keeping insects and other forms of local wildlife—various small jars, a microscope box, a dissecting kit, an ancient phoebe's nest that was once built on our front-door light, an aquarium pump, pieces of coral and seaweed, etc.—none of which has been used for several months. They now serve largely as an eclectic substrate for several large, messy spider webs.

In one corner is a rather large, irregular, three-dimensional 3
web occupying a good quarter-cubic-foot of space. It was into this web that the stricken hornet fell, catching about halfway down into the loose mesh and drawing out from her reclusiveness in the corner a nondescript brownish house spider with a body about three-eighths of an inch long. The hornet hung, tail down, twirling tenuously from a single web-thread, while its barred yellow abdomen throbbed and jabbed repeatedly in instinctive attack. The motion could not really be called defensive, as the hornet was surely too far gone to recover, but it was as if it was determined to inflict whatever injury it could on whatever might approach it in its dying. Defense, in insects as in us, it seems, is not founded on the ability to survive but on the resolution to keep from forgiving as long as possible.

The spider rushed out along her strands to investigate the 4
commotion and stopped about an inch short of this enormous creature, three or four times her own size, with what seemed a kind of "Oh, Lord, why me?" attitude, the stance of a fisherman who suddenly realizes he has hooked a wounded shark on his flounder line.

Whether or not her momentary hesitation reflected any such 5
human emotion, the spider immediately set out to secure her oversized prey. After making a few tentative feints toward the

hornet and apparently seeing that it could do no more than ineffectually thrust its stinger back and forth, she approached more deliberately, made a complete circuit around the hanging beast, and suddenly latched onto it at its "neck."

6   At this point I went and got a magnifying glass and stationed myself to observe more closely. The spider did indeed seem to be fastening repeatedly onto the thin connection between the hornet's head and thorax—a spot, I theorized, that might be more easily injected with the spider's paralyzing venom.

7   While she remained attached, all motion in the spider's legs and body ceased, adding to the impression that some intense, concealed activity was taking place at the juncture. If so, it proved effective, for within a very few minutes almost all throbbing in the hornet's abdomen had stopped, and only the flickering of its rear legs indicated that any life remained.

8   During this process, the spider's movements were still very cautious, but also somehow gentle, never violent or awkward as my whacking had been, but almost as solicitous, as if ministering to the stricken hornet, as carefully and as gently as possible ending its struggles and its agony. Her graceful arched legs looked, through the glass, like miniature, transparent, bent soda straws, with dark spots of pigment at the joints.

9   At this point the spider seemed to have made the hornet *hers*—her object, her possession—and her movements became more confident, proprietary, almost perfunctory in contrast. She no longer seemed aware of the hornet as something apart from her, foreign to the web, but rather as a part of it now, ready to be assimilated. She now appeared to begin dancing around the paralyzed insect, her rear legs moving rapidly and rhythmically in a throwing motion towards the object in the center. I did not see any silk coming out of her abdomen, but her legs did not actually appear to touch the spinnerets there, but gradually a light film of webbing, like a thin, foggy sheen, became visible around the hornet's mid-section.

10   She would spin for several seconds, then climb an inch or two and attach a strand to a piece of webbing overhead. I thought at first that she was merely securing the hornet from its rather unstable attachment, but after she had done this a few times, I saw that, with each climb upward, the hornet itself also moved a small fraction of an inch up and to the side.

It was soon clear that the spider was maneuvering this enor- 11
mous insect in a very definite and deliberate manner, using her
spun cables like a system of block and tackle, hoisting and moving her prey through the seemingly random network of spun
silk.

In between these bouts of spinning and hoisting, the spider 12
occasionally stopped and again approached the hornet, now totally motionless and with one of its darkly veined wings bound to
its barred side. She would place herself head down (the usual
position for a spider in a web when not spinning) just above the
hornet's head and, again becoming totally motionless, as if in
some paralysis of ecstacy, seemed to attach her mouth parts to
those of her prey's, as though engaged in some long, drawn-out
death kiss. The two insects would remain attached so for ten to
fifteen seconds at a time, after which the spider would again
resume her hoisting and fastening. Was this some further injec-
tion of venom taking place, or was she beginning to suck the
juices from the wasp's still-living body even as she was moving it
somewhere? I was struck, mesmerized, by this alternation of intimate, motionless contact of prey and predator, and the businesslike, bustling manipulation of an inert object by its possessor.

All in all, the spider has moved the hornet about two inches 13
to the side and one inch upward from the point where it landed,
out of the center portion of the web and nearer the window
frame, where now she crouches motionless behind it, perhaps
using it to conceal herself while waiting for another prey. I
pulled myself away from the corner and put down the magnifying glass, feeling strangely drained from having been drawn in
so strongly to watch such concentrated activity and dispassionate energy. There is something about spiders that no insect pos-
sesses, that makes it seem right that they are not true insects but
belong to a more ancient order of being. I like them in my home,
but they will not bear too close watching.

I look back at the window corner and see that the characters 14
of the drama are still there, once more in miniature tableau. All
is quiet again; the spider remains crouched behind its mummified prey, in that waiting game that spiders have perfected,
where memory and hope play no part. There is only the stillness
of an eternal present and the silent architecture of perfectly
strung possibilities.

Vocabulary

To get the most out of reading this essay, you should have a working understanding of the words listed below. Following each word is a parenthetical reference, indicating the paragraph in which the word is used, as well as a definition for the word. Go back and look at the sentence in which the word appears, and see how the definition applies. To help you make this word a part of your active vocabulary, write a sentence of your own using the word in the space provided.

catalyst (1):   helper, facilitator

_____

_____

lath (1):   building material over which plaster is laid

_____

_____

eclectic (2):   varied, unusual

_____

_____

substrate (2):   base, foundation

_____

_____

feints (5):   movements meant to mislead, fakes

_____

_____

ineffectually (5):   ineffectively, feebly, unproductively

_____

_____

thorax (6):   middle segment of an insect's body

---

solicitous (8):   attentive, concerned

---

assimilated (9):   ingested, absorbed

---

mesmerized (12):   transfixed, fascinated

---

tableau (14):   panorama, scene

Understanding the Essay

1. How did Finch catalyze the encounter between the spider and the hornet?

2. How are humans and insects alike in the way they defend themselves?

3. On several occasions, Finch compares the actions of the spider and the hornet to human actions. What purpose does this serve?

4. How do the spider's movements change once it takes ownership of the hornet?

5. After the hornet is paralyzed and bound, what does the spider do with it? What mesmerizes Finch about this activity?

6. Reread Finch's final two sentences. What do they mean to you? Why does Finch say that spiders have perfected the waiting game?

Exploring the Theme:
Discussion and Writing

1. With a magnifying glass observe an everyday natural scene—a spider's web, an anthill, a bird's nest, or whatever else you come across. Describe in sharp detail some of what you see, making it as easy as possible for the reader to picture what you observe.

2. Finch says of spiders, "I like them in my home, but they will not bear too close watching." Of the animals that you've seen up close, which one can you least bear watching? What do you dislike about it? Try to write about the animal from a scientific, not emotional, point of view.

TERROR AT TINKER CREEK

Annie Dillard

Annie Dillard was born in Pittsburgh and attended Hollins College. She now makes her home in Middletown, Connecticut, where she is writer in residence at Wesleyan University. A poet and journalist, Dillard has written a number of books, her most recent ones being An American Childhood *and* A Writer's Life. *In 1974, she published* Pilgrim at Tinker Creek, *a fascinating collection of observations of the natural world for which she was awarded the Pulitzer prize for nonfiction.*

Preparing to Read

Nature constantly surprises us. The view from a mountaintop takes our breath away. The miracle of new life gives us hope. And tornadoes and other natural disasters remind us that nature can be cruel as well. What are your most memorable experiences with nature? Has an encounter with nature ever terrified you? In the following selection from *Pilgrim at Tinker Creek*, Dillard tells of one such encounter when feelings of amusement quickly turned to terror. As you read her recounting of the experience, notice how the varied structures of Dillard's sentences enhance the emotional impact of her narration.

A couple of summers ago I was walking along the edge of   1
the island to see what I could see in the water, and
mainly to scare frogs. Frogs have an inelegant way of
taking off from invisible positions on the bank just ahead of
your feet, in dire panic, emitting a froggy "Yike!" and splashing
into the water. Incredibly, this amused me, and incredibly, it
amuses me still. As I walked along the grassy edge of the island, I got better and better at seeing frogs both in and out of
the water. I learned to recognize, slowing down, the difference

in texture of the light reflected from mudbank, water, grass, or frog. Frogs were flying all around me. At the end of the island I noticed a small green frog. He was exactly half in and half out of the water, looking like a schematic diagram of an amphibian, and he didn't jump.

2   He didn't jump; I crept closer. At last I knelt on the island's winterkilled grass, lost, dumbstruck, staring at the frog in the creek just four feet away. He was a very small frog with wide, dull eyes. And just as I looked at him, he slowly crumpled and began to sag. The spirit vanished from his eyes as if snuffed. His skin emptied and drooped; his very skull seemed to collapse and settle like a kicked tent. He was shrinking before my eyes like a deflating football. I watched the taut, glistening skin on his shoulders ruck, and rumple, and fall. Soon, part of his skin, formless as a pricked balloon, lay in floating folds like bright scum on top of the water: it was a monstrous and terrifying thing. I gaped bewildered, appalled. An oval shadow hung in the water behind the drained frog; then the shadow glided away. The frog skin bag started to sink.

3   I had read about the giant water bug, but never seen one. "Giant water bug" is really the name of the creature, which is an enormous, heavy-bodied brown beetle. It eats insects, tadpoles, fish, and frogs. Its grasping forelegs are mighty and hooked inward. It seizes a victim with these legs, hugs it tight, and paralyzes it with enzymes injected during a vicious bite. That one bite is the only bite it ever takes. Through the puncture shoot the poisons that dissolve the victim's muscles and bones and organs—all but the skin—and through it the giant water bug sucks out the victim's body, reduced to a juice. This event is quite common in warm fresh water. The frog I saw was being sucked by a giant water bug. I had been kneeling on the island grass; when the unrecognizable flap of frog skin settled on the creek bottom, swaying, I stood up and brushed the knees of my pants. I couldn't catch my breath.

Vocabulary

To get the most out of reading this essay, you should have a working understanding of the words listed on the next page. Following each word is a parenthetical reference, indicating the

paragraph in which the word is used, as well as a definition for the word. Go back and look at the sentence in which the word appears, and see how the definition applies. To help you make this word a part of your active vocabulary, write a sentence of your own using the word in the space provided.

dire (1):   having dreadful or terrible consequences

_____

_____

schematic (1):   pertaining to or in the form of a scheme or outline

_____

_____

dumbstruck (2):   surprised or confused

_____

_____

taut (2):   pulled or drawn tight

_____

_____

appalled (2):   filled or overcome with horror or dismay

_____

_____

enzymes (3):   substances produced by living organisms that function as biochemical catalysts

_____

_____

Understanding the Essay

1. Why does Dillard choose to describe the scene that she does? What is she saying about nature?

2. Why does Dillard wait until nearly the end of the passage to make it clear that a giant water bug was responsible for the frog's death?

3. Why could Dillard not catch her breath after the experiences she describes?

4. Paragraph 1 contains sentences that are varied in both length and structure. Identify two loose sentences and two periodic sentences, and compare the effects of each on the narrative.

5. A simile is a comparison introduced by *like* or *as*. For example, paragraph 2 contains the simile "formless as a pricked balloon." Identify two other similes in this selection and explain what they contribute to the description.

6. Can you characterize Dillard's words to describe the water bug in paragraph 3? What does word choice indicate about her feelings about the bug?

Exploring the Theme:
Discussion and Writing

1. We all know that in the natural world there is a food chain and that some creatures prey on others. Have you ever witnessed such an encounter in nature or on television? Was your reaction similar to that of Dillard's? How do you explain your reaction?

2. After watching the attack on the frog by the water bug, Annie Dillard says, "I couldn't catch my breath." If you have ever had a similar response to an event, not necessarily tied to something in nature, describe it so that readers can understand your fright or dismay.

THAT ASTOUNDING
CREATOR—NATURE

Jean George

Naturalist and nature writer Jean George is the author of many books, including My Side of the Mountain, Julie of the Wolves, *and* The American Walk Book. *She is a roving reporter for* Reader's Digest *and a contributor to such magazines as* National Wildlife, Audubon, *and* National Geographic.

Preparing to Read

Many of nature's creatures seem to have strange habits or appearances. Only when we consider where they live—their habitats—do we begin to understand why they do what they do or look the way they do. This intriguing relationship between creatures and their environments never ceases to fascinate Jean George. As she says, "Give nature an environment or situation and she will evolve a creature, adapting a toe here, an eye there, until the being fits the niche." What animals do you know of that have evolved so as to better survive in their environment? As you read the following essay, notice how all of George's many examples illustrate and support her main point about nature.

A bird that eats feathers, a mammal that never drinks, a fish that grows a fishing line and worm on its head to catch other fish. Creatures in a nightmare? No, they are very much with us as co-inhabitants of this earth.

Nature has fashioned most animals to fit the many faces of the land—moose to marshes, squirrels to trees, camels to deserts, frogs to lily pads. Give nature an environment or situation and she will evolve a creature, adapting a toe here, an eye there, until the being fits the niche. As a result of this hammering and fitting, however, some really unbelievable creatures circle the sun with us.

3   One summer in Maine I saw a sleek mother horned grebe herding her three bobbing young to supper among the green pickerelweed. Suddenly I noticed through my binoculars that she was feeding her babies quantities of feathers from a deserted duck's nest. As she stuffed the dry feathers into the gaping mouths, she made two or three pokes to get each one down. Finally she worked a dozen or so down her own throat; then, sailing low on the water, she vanished contentedly among the plants.

4   I later learned that 60 percent of the grebe's diet is feathers. When I asked why, a biologist from the U.S. Fish and Wildlife Service answered, "Because nature finds a use for everything. Feathers seem to act as a strainer to prevent fishbones from entering and damaging the intestines."

5   Australia has many strange beasts, one of the oddest of which is the koala. Perfectly adapted to one specific tree, the eucalyptus, this living teddy bear does not need anything else, not even a drink! The moisture in the leaves is just right for the koala, making it the only land animal that doesn't need water to supplement its food.

6   The creature with the fishing line on its head was created for the dark canyons of the sea. Here food is so scarce that the deep-sea angler fish, which preys on smaller fish, grew a line and an appendage on the end that wiggles like a worm. This catches the attention of the occasional passerby. A fish approaches the bait, and the toothy angler swirls up and swallows him.

7   The gigantic ocean bottom creates other problems. A male angler fish could swim for years without meeting a female of his own species. Nature's solution to this problem is for the female to carry a dwarfed husband tightly fused to her body. Marine biologists believe that this nuptial begins when the eggs first hatch and there are many fry of both sexes. A male then grabs hold of a female with his mouth and hangs on until he has literally become a part of her. His mouth becomes fused to her stomach, and for the rest of his life the male remains attached to his mate, marking the most amazing union on earth.

8   Sound has shaped the bodies of many beasts. Noise tapped away at the bullfrog until his ears became bigger than his eyes. Now he hears so well that at the slightest sound of danger he

quickly plops to safety under a sunken leaf. The rabbit has long ears to hear the quiet "whoosh" of the owl's wings, while the grasshopper's ears are on the base of his abdomen, the lowest point of his body, where he can detect the tread of a crow's foot or the stealthy approach of a shrew.

Sometimes food will determine an animal's appearance.   9
Earthworms have shaped the woodcock, a snipelike bird of the forest floor. This creature has a long narrow bill that looks like a pencil and fits neatly into the burrows of the worms. But the bill has its disadvantages; with it buried deep in a worm hole the woodcock is vulnerable to attack from above. To counteract this danger the woodcock has eyes near the top of his head. This singular device permits him to scan the trees for danger even when his beak is buried. A successful arrangement for longevity—but it certainly creates an odd-looking creature.

The need to catch elusive prey has evolved some staggering   10
biological tricks. The sea anemone, a flowerlike animal of the tidemark, is usually riveted to one spot; yet it feeds on darting fish. A diabolically clever trap was necessary to catch them, so the anemone developed tentacles with bombs in the end of each. When a fish forages into these tentacles the ends shoot a thin thread into the fish's body. The thread in turn explodes a paralyzing poison. The stunned fish is hauled in by the tentacles and shoved into the anemone's gullet.

Nature seems to have gone all out in creating preposterous   11
gadgets for self-defense. The jacana, a bird of the American tropics, for instance, is endowed with spurs which unfold like a switchblade at the bend of the bird's wings and with which he can slash his enemies to shreds.

Lizards are professionals in the art of warding off attack.   12
The two-headed skink, whose tail is shaped like his head, confuses his enemy. A hawk, upon attacking this fellow, anticipates that he will run in the direction of the lifted head and make allowance for the movement. However, the bird usually strikes nothing, for he is aiming at the tail. The real head took off the other way.

In order to travel in a hostile world, the Portuguese man-of-   13
war first mastered the art of floating. To do this it evolved a purple bag and inflated it with gas from a special gland. As a crowning idea it also grew a sail! Launched, the man-of-war can blow away from enemies or approach food by putting its sail up

and down. When severely threatened, it forces the gas out of the
float and submerges.

14   There is hardly any environment, however hostile, that some
creature has not mastered. Land is, of course, the nemesis of the
fish. If they flop out on it they die. If their ponds dry up, they are
helpless. Given this situation, it was almost certain that some
fish would evolve a way to beat it; and so there is a lungfish. It is
an air breather and must come to the surface every 20 minutes
or so; otherwise it drowns. When the ponds of Africa dry up in
the arid season, the lungfish wrap themselves in mud and wait it
out, sometimes for years. When the rains finally return, they
resume their water life.

15   Just as nature adds things on creatures that need them, so
she occasionally takes things away from those that don't. The
adult Mayfly, for example, has no mouth or stomach. Last year,
by a northern New York lake, I found myself amid hundreds of
thousands of these insects. I told the conservation officer whom I
was with that I was glad they didn't bite. He replied that they
have no mouths to bite with. "An adult Mayfly lives but one day,"
he explained, "and that day is devoted entirely to pleasure. They
do nothing but dance and mate all their short life, and so they do
not need a mouth."

16   With all this elaborate evolution, it is not surprising that
some of nature's inventions got out of hand. Into this category
falls the speedometer of reindeer. A tendon snaps back and forth
over a bone in the reindeer's foot, noisily tapping out the speed of
his gait. Useless. And so is the nose on the stomach of the scorpion
and the featherlike tongue of the toucan, a bird of Africa.

17   But probably the most dumbfounding of nature's extraordinary creations is the horned toad of our Southwest. A herpetologist once invited me to observe one of these lizards right after it
had molted. In a sand-filled glass cage I saw a large male. Beside
him lay his old skin. The herpetologist began to annoy the beast
with mock attacks, and the old man of the desert with his vulnerable new suit became frightened. Suddenly his eyeballs red-
dened. A final fast lunge from my friend at the beast and I froze
in astonishment—a fine spray of blood shot from the lizard's
eye, like fire from a dragon! The beast had struck back with a
weapon so shocking that it terrifies even the fiercest enemy.

18   Later I walked home, pondering the bizarre methods for

survival with which evolution has endowed earth's creatures, sometimes comical, sometimes pathetic. I knew the biologists were right: If any adaptation is possible, nature has tried it.

Vocabulary

To get the most out of reading this essay, you should have a working understanding of the words listed below. Following each word is a parenthetical reference, indicating the paragraph in which the word is used, as well as a definition for the word. Go back and look at the sentence in which the word appears, and see how the definition applies. To help you make this word a part of your active vocabulary, write a sentence of your own using the word in the space provided.

fashioned (2):   shaped or formed

_____

_____

niche (2):   habitat supplying factors necessary for existence

_____

_____

stealthy (8):   marked by slow, deliberate, secret movement

_____

_____

longevity (9):   long life

_____

_____

tentacles (10):   elongated flexible tactile or prehensile process borne by animals chiefly on the head or about the mouth

_____

_____

arid (14):   without moisture, extremely dry

_____

_____

pathetic (18):   evoking pity

_____

_____

Understanding the Essay

1. What is Jean George's thesis, or main point, in this essay? Where does she state it?

2. According to George, what are some of the main environmental factors that have caused creatures to evolve in the ways they have? Which one did you find the most interesting? Why?

3. What is the relationship of paragraphs 3–6 to paragraph 1?

4. How are paragraphs 11–13 related? How has the author unified them?

5. Identify several of the transitional devices that George uses to connect paragraphs 14 through 18.

6. Explain how George's concluding paragraph summarizes her essay. In what ways does this paragraph restate her thesis?

Exploring the Theme: Discussion and Writing

1. Select a creature not mentioned in George's essay and read about it in the library. What methods has it evolved to ensure its survival? Into which of George's survival categories would you place your creature? Make a brief report on your creature to the class.

2. Just as other animals adapt to their environments, humans must adapt to theirs. Sometimes humans have it in

their power to change or leave their environment instead of adapting or making concessions. Discuss any adaptations that you and your friends have made to "survive" in your environment. How have you tried to change your environment?

WRITING SUGGESTIONS FOR
THE "NATURAL WORLD"

1.   When we attempt to rescue animals from danger, are we interfering with nature in an unjustified way? Gale Lawrence claims that most of these efforts, at least as far as animal babies are concerned, are fruitless anyhow. So why do we make the attempt? Do we feel guilty because, as humans, we may be upsetting nature's balance? Write an essay in which you argue for or against human intervention in nature's ways.

2.   Play the role of a naturalist for a few hours. Examine the nature you see in and around your home. Observe spiders, houseflies, ants, birds, dogs, cats, or other creatures to which you have easy access. Take notes on what you observe and try to be as objective or scientific as you can. Try, also, to avoid any preconceived expectations. Describe the creature you choose and its various activities, either in isolation or among others of its kind, or as it interacts with other members of the animal kingdom.

3.   How has nature surprised you? Have you lived through a tornado, a hurricane, a flood? Have you confronted creatures in the wild? Have you seen animals give birth, fight for their survival, or go through the process of dying? Or have you been surprised by the little things in nature, as Annie Dillard was? Review your experiences with nature, especially what surprised you, and write an essay in which you convey your fascination to your readers.

4.   Why should we be concerned about the extinction of a species? After all, many species have already become extinct and many are becoming so at this very moment. Must we save every species, even if the natural environment has changed in ways that make it no longer suitable for the species to survive? Write an essay in which you express your point of view on the question of extinction.

5.   At what point for you does the concern for the environment become excessive, if at all? Have we passed that point already? Should we be giving more or less time to advocates of business and jobs in our environmental policies? Write an essay in which you express your ideas on the question of development versus the environment.

6. What is the value of open spaces? the wilderness? How much wilderness do we need? Can we afford to set aside wilderness areas as the world population expands? Will we be able to preserve our open spaces in the future? Write an essay in which you try to capture the value of wilderness areas and argue for their protection and preservation.

12

LIFE AND DEATH

Though death lies ahead for all of us, historically it has been an "unthinkable" topic, one always shrouded in secrecy and fear. In saying "Nobody knows, in fact, what death is, nor whether it is not perhaps the greatest of all blessings; yet people fear it as if they surely knew it to be the worst of evils," Socrates captures the paradox surrounding death. Death remains unknown, and people fear the unknown. It may be for this reason that Americans generally avoid discussing the topic, preferring to personify it as some dark and evil force, the traditional grim reaper or Emily Dickinson's coachman, who comes to take us away. Consequently, we've all had difficulty in dealing with dying friends and relatives. Recent books and articles on death and dying, the right-to-die movement, and assisted suicide may be changing this, however, by fostering a new openness. People seem to be much more willing to talk about death today than they were as little as twenty-five years ago.

Today we are confronted by death in ways that are bizarre, puzzling, and even contradictory. The old rules don't seem to apply anymore, and there is no guiding principle to help us. Only questions. We know that we must all die, but may we choose the moment and the means of our death? May a person in extreme pain be permitted to put an end to both pain and life, or may a doctor or a friend do so for that individual? Does capital punishment have a place in a civilized world? Does society—invoking the notion that life is not necessarily better than no life—have the right to take the lives of citizens? And when we die, is our consciousness snuffed out or do we live on as disembodied or reincarnated souls? Despite our new openness about death, it continues to be no less mysterious than it has always been.

Death challenges our reason and our faith to the fullest. As you read the essays in this section and discuss them with your classmates, ask yourself what you believe about death. What we believe can make a great difference not only in the way we die but also in the way we live.

A CRIME OF COMPASSION

Barbara Huttmann

Barbara Huttmann is the associate director of nursing services in Children's Hospital of San Francisco. She has written two books, The Patient's Advocate *and* Code Blue: A Nurse's True-Life Story, *that reveal her interest in patients' rights. She wrote the following essay for* Newsweek *in 1983.*

Preparing to Read

One of the arguments against allowing the terminally ill to end their lives—whether through the deliberate withholding of treatment or through active assistance—is that we shouldn't play God; we shouldn't decide *when* death is acceptable. Yet it could be said that we already play God by prolonging lives well beyond the body's natural endurance. The ability to save people who otherwise would have died prematurely is wonderful, but using the same skill and technology to prolong a pain-filled life raises difficult questions. Huttmann, in "A Crime of Compassion," describes the reality of prolonging a life that is filled with nothing but suffering and the longing for death. And yet when she gave the suffering patient what he wanted, by doing nothing, she was blasted as a murderer. What are the dangers in allowing terminally ill patients to decide when they will die?

1   "**M**urderer," a man shouted. "God help patients who get *you* for a nurse."

2   "What gives you the right to play God?" another one asked.

3   It was the Phil Donahue show where the guest is a fatted calf and the audience a 200-strong flock of vultures hungering to pick at the bones. I had told them about Mac, one of my favorite

cancer patients. "We resuscitated him 52 times in just one month. I refused to resuscitate him again. I simply sat there and held his hand while he died."

There wasn't time to explain that Mac was a young, witty, macho cop who walked into the hospital with 32 pounds of attack equipment, looking as if he could single-handedly protect the whole city, if not the entire state. "Can't get rid of this cough," he said. Otherwise, he felt great.

Before the day was over, tests confirmed that he had lung cancer. And before the year was over, I loved him, his wife, Maura, and their three kids as if they were my own. All the nurses loved him. And we all battled his disease for six months without ever giving death a thought. Six months isn't such a long time in the whole scheme of things, but it was long enough to see him lose his youth, his wit, his macho, his hair, his bowel and bladder control, his sense of taste and smell, and his ability to do the slightest thing for himself. It was also long enough to watch Maura's transformation from a young woman into a haggard, beaten old lady.

When Mac had wasted away to a 60-pound skeleton kept alive by liquid food we poured down a tube, i.v. solutions we dripped into his veins, and oxygen we piped to a mask on his face, he begged us: "Mercy . . . for God's sake, please just let me go."

The first time he stopped breathing, the nurse pushed the button that calls a "code blue" throughout the hospital and sends a team rushing to resuscitate the patient. Each time he stopped breathing, sometimes two or three times in one day, the code team came again. The doctors and technicians worked their miracles and walked away. The nurses stayed to wipe the saliva that drooled from his mouth, irrigate the big craters of bedsores that covered his hips, suction the lung fluids that threatened to drown him, clean the feces that burned his skin like lye, pour the liquid food down the tube attached to his stomach, put pillows between his knees to ease the bone-on-bone pain, turn him every hour to keep the bedsores from getting worse, and change his gown and linen every two hours to keep him from being soaked in perspiration.

At night I went home and tried to scrub away the smell of decaying flesh that seemed woven into the fabric of my uniform. It was in my hair, the upholstery of my car—there was no washing it away. And every night I prayed that Mac would die, that his agonized eyes would never again plead with me to let him die.

9   Every morning I asked his doctor for a "no-code" order. Without that order, we had to resuscitate every patient who stopped breathing. His doctor was one of several who believe we must extend life as long as we have the means and knowledge to do it. To not do it is to be liable for negligence, at least in the eyes of many people, including some nurses. I thought about what it would be like to stand before a judge, accused of murder, if Mac stopped breathing and I didn't call a code.

10   And after the fifty-second code, when Mac was still lucid enough to beg for death again, and Maura was crumbled in my arms again, and when no amount of pain medication stilled his moaning and agony, I wondered about a spiritual judge. Was all this misery and suffering supposed to be building character or infusing us all with the sense of humility that comes from impotence?

11   Had we, the whole medical community, become so arrogant that we believed in the illusion of salvation through science? Had we become so self-righteous that we thought meddling in God's work was our duty, our moral imperative and our legal obligation? Did we really believe that we had the right to force "life" on a suffering man who had begged for the right to die?

12   Such questions haunted me more than ever early one morning when Maura went home to change her clothes and I was bathing Mac. He had been still for so long, I thought he at last had the blessed relief of coma. Then he opened his eyes and moaned, "Pain . . . no more . . . Barbara . . . do something . . . God, let me go."

13   The desperation in his eyes and voice riddled me with guilt. "I'll stop," I told him as I injected the pain medication.

14   I sat on the bed and held Mac's hands in mine. He pressed his bony fingers against my hand and muttered, "Thanks." Then there was one soft sigh and I felt his hands go cold in mine. "Mac?" I whispered, as I waited for his chest to rise and fall again.

15   A clutch of panic banded my chest, drew my finger to the code button, urged me to do something, anything . . . but sit there alone with death. I kept one finger on the button, without pressing it, as a waxen pallor slowly transformed his face from person to empty shell. Nothing I've ever done in my 47 years has taken so much effort as it took *not* to press that code button.

Eventually, when I was as sure as I could be that the code   16
team would fail to bring him back, I entered the legal twilight
zone and pushed the button. The team tried. And while they were
trying, Maura walked into the room and shrieked, "No . . . don't
let them do this to him . . . for God's sake . . . please, no more."

Cradling her in my arms was like cradling myself, Mac, and   17
all those patients and nurses who had been in this place before,
who do the best they can in a death-denying society.

So a TV audience accused me of murder. Perhaps I am guilty.   18
If a doctor had written a no-code order, which is the only *legal*
alternative, would he have felt any less guilty? Until there is legislation making it a criminal act to code a patient who has requested the right to die, we will all of us risk the same fate as Mac.
For whatever reason, we developed the means to prolong life, and
now we are forced to use it. We do not have the right to die.

Vocabulary

To get the most out of reading this essay, you should have a
working understanding of the words listed below. Following
each word is a parenthetical reference, indicating the paragraph
in which the word is used, as well as a definition for the word.
Go back and look at the sentence in which the word appears, and
see how the definition applies. To help you make this word a
part of your active vocabulary, write a sentence of your own
using the word in the space provided.

resuscitated (3):   revived

_____

_____

irrigate (7):   wash out, flush

_____

_____

lucid (10):   coherent, aware

_____

_____

imperative (11):   necessity

_____

_____

waxen (15):   like wax

_____

_____

pallor (15):   paleness, lack of color

_____

_____

Understanding the Essay

1. How does Huttmann describe the Phil Donahue show? Do you think the audience's reaction would have been different if she'd had time to tell Mac's story?

2. What happened to Mac in six months? What happened to Maura?

3. Why are nurses more sympathetic to a patient's request for a "no-code" order than doctors? Why do some doctors refuse to issue a "no-code" order?

4. What questions would Huttmann ask a spiritual judge?

5. How does Huttmann "kill" Mac? Why does this act lead her into a legal "twilight zone"?

6. Huttmann's last sentence says, "We do not have the right to die." According to her, how can we gain that right?

Exploring the Theme: Discussion and Writing

1. Do you think Huttmann is guilty of murder? Should there be a law against calling a "code blue" if a person requests to die in peace? Explain your answers.

2. Most people consider the humane killing of pets and other animals to be the kindest thing to do in certain cases. "We couldn't let Fido suffer," they say. Why is the concept of ending a person's painful life a much more volatile issue? What human trait compels us to prolong a human life by whatever means possible, even if it's only so that the patient can die tomorrow instead of today?

WHOSE LIFE IS IT ANYWAY?

Ellen Goodman

Ellen Goodman was born in Boston in 1941. After gradu-
ating from Radcliffe College in 1963, she worked as a
reporter and researcher for Newsweek. *In 1967 she be-*
gan working at the Boston Globe *and, since 1974, Good-*
man has been a full-time columnist. "At Large," her
widely syndicated column, appears in nearly four hun-
dred newspapers across the country. Four collections of
her columns: Close to Home, At Large, Keeping in
Touch, *and* Making Sense, *have been published. Ellen*
Goodman wrote the following commentary about Eliza-
beth Bouvia's right to die in December 1983.

Preparing to Read

Imagine that you've made up your mind to die, even though
your body isn't likely to fail you in the near future. No one can
stop you, but what can you ask of society along the way to
death? If the police stop you about to jump off a bridge, they'll
try to talk you down; if you go into a coma, doctors will hook you
up to a respirator. But if you demand death, should society help
you? Goodman's essay about Elizabeth Bouvia responds with a
strong no. Perhaps an innate optimism makes us feel uncomfortable with ending a life that—perhaps—has better days ahead.
Instead of irreversibly ending a depressed person's life, Goodman argues, society should do what it can to help the person out
of depression and into a better life. What do you think?

1   For a time, life has been imitating art in Riverside, Califor-
       nia. The courtroom case of a twenty-six-year-old quadriple-
       gic, Elizabeth Bouvia, is every bit as dramatic as the script
of the movie, *Whose Life Is It Anyway?*

2   In September 1983, Bouvia admitted herself to the psychiat-

ric ward of Riverside General Hospital with one goal in mind: to starve to death under their roof. She wanted doctors to give her only the medical attention needed to ease pain.

Unlike the character in the movie, Bouvia had been para- 3 lyzed since birth with cerebral palsy. Her grit was well-recorded in daily life and academic degrees. But after a failed marriage, failed attempts at pregnancy, and deepening depression over her future, her only determination was to die: "I choose no longer to be dependent on others."

Hers is a case that pushes just about all the buttons on our 4 finely engineered ethical panel. The right-to-life and the right-to-die buttons. The one that labels suicide as a rational act and the one that labels suicide as a crazy act. The one that opposes medical intervention against a patient's will and the one that supports medical intervention to save lives.

It presents us with the dilemma that we've been edging up to 5 slowly, case after case. Ever since Karen Ann Quinlan, we've debated whether a hospital could, should, keep someone "alive" after brain death. Today we discuss the ethics of "heroic" care for the terminally ill as well.

Slowly, we have also asserted certain rights to medical care. 6 In 1973, in the case of a woman named Roe, the courts determined that a pregnant woman seeking an abortion had the right to privacy. Recently, in the case of a baby named Doe, the courts determined that parents could deny life-prolonging surgery to a severely handicapped infant. On our own we can refuse therapy, even maintenance therapy like dialysis, and willfully shorten our lives.

Meanwhile suicide, at least among the elderly or ill, has 7 gained a certain odd legitimacy. In March 1983, the writer Arthur Koestler, ill with leukemia, committed suicide and his healthy wife, Cynthia, joined him. She was described as "devoted." A Florida couple in their eighties carefully killed themselves as a "solution to the problems of aging." The sheriff commented on how "thoughtful" they were.

In this atmosphere, Elizabeth Bouvia's request to be allowed 8 to starve with painkillers and without force feeding seems almost routine. After all, if the parents of Baby Doe have the right to deny treatment, then doesn't the patient herself have the right to refuse it? If Roe has the right to "control her own body," then doesn't Bouvia? Isn't suicide a civil right?

9   The reality is that the Bouvia case has pushed over the established ethical line. We are now entering into a moral arena
where words like "rights" begin to lose their meaning.

10   "I'm not asking for anybody to kill me," this woman has said.
"I'm asking that the natural process of death take over." But
refusing food is no more a natural process of death than falling is
when you jump off a bridge.

11   What makes this case different from other "right-to-die"
cases is that, however miserable she regards her life, Bouvia is
not suffering a fatal disability. What makes it different is that
she is not just proposing suicide; she is asking for the help of
doctors. Indeed, Bouvia checked into a ward that specializes in
preventing suicide. There are, as Freud said, no accidents.

12   The California Superior Court judge made a proper distinction last week when he ruled that, yes, Bouvia had the right to
kill herself—it is her life, anyway—but not "with the assistance
of society." If she did not continue to accept nourishment, the
judge would allow the hospital to force-feed her. Now, as I write
this in December 1983, the young woman has refused sufficient
liquid protein to sustain her ninety-five-pound body.

13   No matter how uncomfortable the idea, I think it is appropriate, even imperative, for the hospital to forcibly feed its
despairing patient. Psychiatric wards are not suicide centers
where people come for help in terminating their despair.

14   Deep down, I'm afraid it is too easy for society to "understand" the unhappiness of a quadriplegic instead of alleviating
it. It's too easy for us to begin to regard suicides of the sick or the
aged as "thoughtful" solutions.

15   If we support Elizabeth Bouvia's civil-rights stand, then
sooner or later we would passively watch a woman step off a
ledge and a man swallow sleeping pills. As we stood there, by-
standers, would we then remind each other not to interfere? The
"right to die" can easily become an excuse for our own unwilling-
ness to reach out and help.

Vocabulary

To get the most out of reading this essay, you should have a
working understanding of the words listed on the next page.
Following each word is a parenthetical reference, indicating the

paragraph in which the word is used, as well as a definition for the word. Go back and look at the sentence in which the word appears, and see how the definition applies. To help you make this word a part of your active vocabulary, write a sentence of your own using the word in the space provided.

quadriplegic (1):   person paralyzed from the neck down

_____

_____

ethical (4):   moral, relating to what society deems to be correct

_____

_____

dialysis (6):   treatment for kidney failure

_____

_____

legitimacy (7):   validity, correctness

_____

_____

imperative (13):   necessary

_____

_____

Understanding the Essay

1. What does Bouvia want to do? Why?

2. With what dilemma does Bouvia's case present society? What other cases have brought up similar questions?

3. How does Goodman feel about the "legitimacy" of suicide for the ill or elderly?

4. Why does Bouvia's case push over the established ethical line? What makes it different from other right-to-die cases?

5. Does Goodman agree with the judge's decision in the case? Why?

6. What dangers does Goodman cite in supporting Bouvia's desire to die in the manner she chooses?

Exploring the Theme:
Discussion and Writing

1. If you were the judge deciding the Bouvia case, what would you decide? Why? Defend your answer.

2. What is your opinion of assisted suicide in general, including that of the terminally ill? Does it disturb you that it has gained legitimacy, or do you think people should have the ability to choose how they die?

THE DEATH PENALTY
IS A STEP BACK

Coretta Scott King

Coretta Scott King was the spouse of civil rights leader Martin Luther King, Jr., who was assassinated in 1968. In keeping with the philosophy of non-violence that they both promoted during the civil rights struggle, she continues to strongly oppose the execution of violent criminals.

Preparing to Read

Have you or anyone in your family ever been the victim of violence? If so, you may have said or thought, "I'd like to **kill** the person who did this" and meant it at the time. And although few people really want to return to the days of vigilante justice, or an eye-for-an-eye way of thinking, the death penalty for particularly brutal crimes has been used more and more in recent years. Whether proponents of state-sponsored execution argue that it deters violent crime or maintain that it's the only punishment that suits certain crimes, they firmly believe that the death penalty has a place in our society. King strongly disagrees. Aside from opposing it on moral grounds, she argues that our legal system is dangerously imperfect—far too imperfect to have the authority to legally put someone to death.

When Steven Judy was executed in Indiana [in 1981], America took another step backwards towards legitimizing murder as a way of dealing with evil in our society. 1

Although Judy was convicted of four of the most horrible and brutal murders imaginable, and his case is probably the worst in recent memory for opponents of the death penalty, we still have to face the real issue squarely: Can we expect a decent society if the state is allowed to kill its own people? 2

357

3   In recent years, an increase of violence in America, both individual and political, has prompted a backlash of public opinion on capital punishment. But however much we abhor violence, legally sanctioned executions are no deterrent and are, in fact, immoral and unconstitutional.

4   Although I have suffered the loss of two family members by assassination, I remain firmly and unequivocally opposed to the death penalty for those convicted of capital offenses.

5   An evil deed is not redeemed by an evil deed of retaliation. Justice is never advanced in the taking of a human life.

6   Morality is never upheld by legalized murder. Morality apart, there are a number of practical reasons which form a powerful argument against capital punishment.

7   First, capital punishment makes irrevocable any possible miscarriage of justice. Time and again we have witnessed the specter of mistakenly convicted people being put to death in the name of American criminal justice. To those who say that, after all, this doesn't occur too often, I can only reply that if it happens just once, that is too often. And it has occurred many times.

8   Second, the death penalty reflects an unwarranted assumption that the wrongdoer is beyond rehabilitation. Perhaps some individuals cannot be rehabilitated; but who shall make that determination? Is any amount of academic training sufficient to entitle one person to judge another incapable of rehabilitation?

9   Third, the death penalty is inequitable. Approximately half of the 711 persons now on death row are black. From 1930 through 1968, 53.5% of those executed were black Americans, all too many of whom were represented by court-appointed attorneys and convicted after hasty trials.

10   The argument that this may be an accurate reflection of guilt, and homicide trends, instead of a racist application of laws lacks credibility in light of a recent Florida survey which showed that persons convicted of killing whites were four times more likely to receive a death sentence than those convicted of killing blacks.

11   Proponents of capital punishment often cite a "deterrent effect" as the main benefit of the death penalty. Not only is there no hard evidence that murdering murderers will deter other potential killers, but even the "logic" of this argument defies comprehension.

Numerous studies show that the majority of homicides com-   12
mitted in this country are the acts of the victim's relatives,
friends and acquaintances in the "heat of passion."

What this strongly suggests is that rational consideration of   13
future consequences is seldom a part of the killer's attitude at
the time he commits a crime.

The only way to break the chain of violent reaction is to   14
practice nonviolence as individuals and collectively through our
laws and institutions.

Vocabulary

To get the most out of reading this essay, you should have a
working understanding of the words listed below. Following
each word is a parenthetical reference, indicating the paragraph
in which the word is used, as well as a definition for the word.
Go back and look at the sentence in which the word appears, and
see how the definition applies. To help you make this word a
part of your active vocabulary, write a sentence of your own
using the word in the space provided.

legitimizing (1):   making acceptable

_____

_____

capital punishment (3):   death penalty

_____

_____

abhor (3):   hate, despise

_____

_____

sanctioned (3):   approved, authorized

_____

_____

unequivocally (4):   absolutely, without doubt

_____

_____

irrevocable (7):   irreversible

_____

_____

miscarriage (7):   failure, breakdown

_____

_____

specter (7):   vision

_____

_____

inequitable (9):   unequal

_____

_____

deterrent (11):   discouragement, obstacle

_____

_____

Understanding the Essay

1. According to King, what is the real issue concerning the death penalty?
2. Why has the death penalty gained more support from the public in recent years? Why is King a good spokesperson for opponents of the death penalty?
3. What are King's reasons for opposing the death penalty?
4. Why does King believe that capital punishment does not deter violent crime?
5. How does King propose to combat violence in our society?

Exploring the Theme:
Discussion and Writing

1. Do you support or oppose the death penalty? Why? Have King's arguments influenced your opinion? Explain.

2. King says that the increase in support for the death penalty has been caused by the increase in violent crime in our society. What is the cause of this increase in violence? How can it be combated outside of the legal system?

SNOW

Julia Alvarez

Julia Alvarez was born in 1950 in New York City but spent most of her first ten years in the Dominican Republic before her family moved back to the United States. She is a widely published poet and writer of short fiction; her most recent collection is How the Garcia Girls Lost Their Accents. *Alvarez teaches English and creative writing at Middlebury College.*

Preparing to Read

Anyone born after World War II has lived a lifetime of constant awareness—conscious or unconscious—of the possibility of nuclear apocalypse. The comprehension of one's own mortality can be disturbing enough without the added necessity of contemplating the wholesale destruction of entire populations of human beings. Before you read this essay, take a moment to recall your own feelings about the threat of nuclear war, and how those feelings changed as you grew from a child to a teenager to an adult. What role did world politics play in the changes in your attitude toward the threat of nuclear war?

1   In the summer of 1960 my family emigrated to the United States, fleeing the tyrant Trujillo. In New York we found a small apartment with a Catholic school nearby, taught by the Sisters of Charity, hefty women in long black gowns and bonnets that made them look like peculiar dolls in mourning. I liked them a lot, especially my grandmotherly fifth grade teacher, Sister Zoe.

2   As the only immigrant in my class, I was put in a special seat in the first row by the window, apart from the other children, so that Sister Zoe could tutor me without disturbing them. Slowly, she enunciated the new words I was to repeat: *laundromat, corn flakes, subway, snow.*

Soon I picked up enough English to understand holocaust 3
was in the air. Sister Zoe explained to a wide-eyed classroom
what was happening in Cuba. Russian missiles were being assembled, trained supposedly on New York City. Kennedy, looking worried too, was on the television at home, explaining we
might have to go to war.

At school, we had air raid drills. An ominous bell would go 4
off and we'd file out into the hall, fall to the floor, cover our
heads with our coats, and imagine our hair falling out, the bones
in our arms going soft. At home, Mother and I said a rosary every
night for world peace. I heard new vocabulary: nuclear bomb,
radioactive, Third World War. Sister Zoe explained how it would
happen. She drew a picture of a mushroom on the blackboard
and dotted a flurry of chalk marks for the dusty fallout that
would kill us all.

The months grew cold. November, December. It was dark 5
when I got up in the morning, frosty when I stepped outside. One
morning as I sat daydreaming out the window I saw dots in the
air like the ones Sister Zoe had drawn—random at first, and
then lots and lots. I shrieked, "The bomb, the bomb!"

Sister Zoe jerked around, her full black skirt ballooning as 6
she hurried to my side. A few girls began to cry.

But suddenly, Sister's shocked look faded. "Why, dear child, 7
that's snow!" she laughed.

"Snow," I repeated. I looked out the window warily. All my life 8
I had heard about the white crystals that fell out of American
skies in the winter. From my desk I watched the fine powder dust
the sidewalk and parked cars below. Each flake was different,
Sister Zoe had said, like a person, irreplaceable and beautiful.

Vocabulary

To get the most out of reading this essay, you should have a
working understanding of the words listed on the next page.
Following each word is a parenthetical reference, indicating the
paragraph in which the word is used, as well as a definition for
the word. Go back and look at the sentence in which the word
appears, and see how the definition applies. To help you make
this word a part of your active vocabulary, write a sentence of
your own in the space provided.

emigrated (1):   left one country to settle in another

_____

_____

immigrant (2):   person from one country who becomes a permanent resident in another

_____

_____

holocaust (3):   large-scale destruction, especially by fire

_____

_____

trained on (3):   aimed at

_____

_____

ominous (4):   threatening

_____

_____

Understanding the Essay

1. Where is the thesis of this essay located?

2. How has Alvarez organized her essay?

3. Does Alvarez prepare the reader for the ending, or is it a total surprise? List three reasons for your answer.

4. How does the last sentence make you feel? Is the analogy of snowflakes to human individuality effective for you as the reader?

5. What reflections on life and death did this experience provide for the writer? What reflections does it offer you?

Exploring the Theme: Discussion and Writing

1. Alvarez's essay affirms the beauty and irreplaceability of human life at the same time (or perhaps because) it rues the seeming imminence of nuclear war. Write an essay in which some aspect of the idea of death or dying reaffirms something positive about your life.

2. Choose either a contemporary or historical situation as an example and write an essay arguing for or against the use of nuclear weapons. Pretend that Julia Alvarez is going to be the first person to read it.

Writing Activities

1. Write an essay in which you argue either for or against the legalization of euthanasia or "mercy killing." Be sure to review the arguments by Barbara Huttmann and Ellen Goodman before starting to write.

2. When people debate the issue of euthanasia, the concept of "quality of life" inevitably gets introduced. What does "quality of life" mean to you? Write an essay in which you define this concept. Be sure to consider such questions as: At what point does a person's quality of life become so poor that that person should be permitted to end his or her life? Is what's poor for one person, poor for another? And, are humans playing God when they start terminating human life?

3. After reading the article by Ellen Goodman, what are your thoughts on the "right to die"? Should society assist people in committing suicide when they demand to die? Did you find yourself agreeing with Goodman's conclusion that the " 'right to die' can easily become an excuse for our own willingness to reach out and help"? Where do you personally draw the line? Is it okay to assist some people and not others? Write an essay in which you agree or disagree with Goodman's position on the issue.

4. Coretta Scott King strongly opposes the use of capital punishment; in fact, she calls the death penalty "legalized murder." Where do you stand on the issue of the death penalty? Is the death penalty ever appropriate? If a society can decide in favor of the death penalty, how does it then decide which crimes will be so punished? Write an essay in which you clearly present your thinking on the issue of capital punishment.

II

ON BECOMING A BETTER WRITER

13

WRITERS ON
WRITING

Have you ever thought about the way you write? Most writers
follow what is known as the writing process when they write.
Each one of us may go about it in a slightly different or individu-
alized manner, but the stages and overall progression are surprisingly similar from one writer to the next. Most writers prewrite,
write, revise, and edit—in that order. This is probably how you
already write, but chances are you haven't attached these labels
to the various steps of the process.

Prewriting is the stage in which you decide on a topic, gather
your ideas and information, and decide what your approach to
the subject will be. While you are carrying out these activities,
you are refining what you want to say and why you want to say
it. With a thesis and purpose in mind you are ready for the
writing stage. Here your goal is to create a draft as quickly as
possible, not stopping to labor over a particular word or sentence structure. Your main goal is to get your ideas on paper.

With a draft in hand you have something to work with, and
this is where revision comes into play. You might decide that
your thesis needs adjustment so that it better fits the ideas and
examples that you've captured in your rough draft. You might
decide that you need to generate yet more examples or reorder
them. Finally, revision is that stage in which you develop and
clarify what you have written, making it both complete and
accurate.

Once you have revised your essay so that it says what you
want it to say, you are ready for the editing stage. Here you
scrutinize your best draft to eliminate any errors of spelling,
grammar, punctuation, and mechanics. After thoroughly editing, you are ready to prepare your final copy. As you take control
of your own writing process and start to feel comfortable with it,

you'll come to see writing as a series of practical decisions that must be made to turn blank pages into a finished piece of work.

It quickly becomes clear to anyone learning to write that the more familiar one becomes with the writing process and especially one's own writing habits, the faster the writing improves. To help you gain familiarity with the writing process and its various aspects, we begin with an essay that overviews writing as a building process. The other four selections look at the particulars of freewriting, getting ideas, reducing clutter, and analyzing audience. We believe that the more you know about the process and the way you use it, the more control you will have as a writer. The selections in this chapter are, then, a road map for you to follow in turning those blank pages into lively and informative prose compositions.

WRITING IS BUILDING

Roger H. Garrison

Roger Garrison was professor of English at Westbrook College in Portland, Maine, before his untimely death in 1984. He was one of the first instructors to give credence to the process approach in teaching writing, and he pioneered the conference method of responding to individual students' writing.

Preparing to Read

In "Writing Is Building," a chapter from his highly respected book *How a Writer Works*, Garrison gives us one of the clearest and most concise overviews of the steps involved in the writing process. In so doing, he takes the mystery out of moving from the blank page to the completed essay. As you read, think about the steps that you take in writing a composition and how you might improve your work habits, given Garrison's description of the process.

D espite their differences of mind, background, and temperament, most professional writers work through a remarkably similar sequence of *prewriting, writing, revising,* and *editing.* 1

This sequence implies a clear order of priorities in building a piece of writing, whether for a single paragraph or a ten-page article. It can help you identify what to do first, second, third, and so on. 2

1. Idea or subject
2. Information (content)   } Prewriting
3. Your point of view
4. Rough draft (a draft is a first-sketch try)

5. Organization (logical sequence of information) ⎫ Revising
6. Sentences (grammar, rhythm, tone)   ⎬ and
7. Diction (best words, spelling)   ⎭ editing

You will learn to write more effectively, and more quickly, if you follow this sequence, too. But keep in mind that this sequence is only a guide and that each step of the writing process is likely to blend into the other. Sometimes prewriting will go quickly, but revising may be slow and frustrating. Or the reverse may be true. Much depends on your subject, your grasp of it, and perhaps on the pressure of a deadline.

3   Three basic demands control your writing: your purposes, your reader, and your attitude toward your subject.

> PURPOSE: Why are you writing? Is it a description, an analysis, a summary of information, a complaint, an argument to persuade? (Suggestion: It often helps before you try a first draft to state your purpose in *one* sentence.)

> READER: Is your writing a response to a teacher's assignment or an employer's demand? Is it to a general audience? Your reader's needs or expectations in each case will be different. Thus the form and tone of your response is an appropriate response to your specific audience.

> ATTITUDE: Your own feelings or convictions will influence not only the form of presentation but also the shape and rhythm of sentences and, especially, your choices of words.

4   Form follows function. This is true in nature, and it is true for writing. Form—the total architecture of a work, no matter how trivial—is the expression of *your* meaning and the way you want it to be received.

1. Prewriting

5   *Prewriting* is everything you do before you try a first draft. The *idea* comes first. What are you going to write about? Generally, inexperienced writers' ideas are too inclusive, like Capital Punishment, Abortion, Divorce, Energy, the Generation Gap, or Politics. Limit your subject, narrow it, focus it. How? One analogy: Think of your whole subject as a large pie, and cut one narrow

slice of it. Another analogy: A great movie director said, "A movie is simple. It's just long shots, medium shots, and close-ups. But what's the best mix of these to tell your story? Ah, then it's not so simple." Like a movie, writing is a mix of "shots."

For your first attempts at writing, start with small slices, with closeups. Try just one paragraph. A paragraph is a single developed unit of meaning. If you learn to write good paragraphs, you can write longer, more complex statements.   6

Suppose your general subject is energy. One paragraph's thin slice of that large pie could be the British thermal unit (BTU), a standard measurement of heat, or a calorie, a basic "unit" of heat. Plain definition is easy; the dictionary supplies it. But if you want to explain BTU to a reader, you need information.   7

2. Information

Information (content) is the second prewriting step, and the most important. You cannot write anything (even poetry) without information. You need facts, details, examples. What is a BTU? How is it used? What are differing BTU values for various fuels? In what ways is a BTU an energy-measurement tool? And so on. You will probably need sources to find facts. Make a list of the facts you need quickly, in any order. Your information list should have at least twice as much as you eventually use. Two writer's truisms: Write from richness. Write more about less.   8

Make your list substantive (full of facts). A series of vague or general phrases will not help you much. *Making the list is already writing.* Think of it as a bank of raw material on which you will draw.   9

Here are two brief examples to show how two students handled the problem of focus (cutting a narrow slice of the pie) and of making a fact list for a paragraph on a narrowed-down subject.   10

STUDENT A	STUDENT B
GENERAL SUBJECT: Sports	GENERAL SUBJECT: Energy
TITLE: Our Crummy Basket-ball Team	TITLE: A Family Beats Oil Prices
FACT LIST:	FACT LIST:
Disorganized guys	Ours is eight-room house
Don't care	In 1978, burned 1,726 gal-
Break training all the time	lons oil @ 49¢

FACT LIST:
Cut every practice short
Coach hasn't good control
Lots of griping on team
No school spirit
Student fans throw beer
cans and rubbish on court
Half-time show terrible.
Cheerleaders don't work to-
gether
What's my athletic fee buy-
ing?

FACT LIST
In 1979–80, 872 gallons @
98¢
Difference: insulation, walls,
roof cap, two wood stoves
Cost of insulation and stoves:
$1,500
"Payback" period (when
these paid for) estimated
two years. Estimated cost
Five cords hardwood (maple,
oak, birch) from own
woodlot per year
1 cord (4' × 4' × 8') = 200
gallons oil
Family sweats to cut wood.
Callused hands from split-
ting

11 Clearly, student A is going to have a problem developing his paragraph. The only specific statement in his list is "Student fans throw beer cans and rubbish on court." The rest of the list is vague: It needs examples or specific facts. He'll have to make another list, maybe three or four more.

12 Student B, however, obviously speaks from experience, including calluses on the hands. She has facts about the number of gallons of heating oil burned and the rising cost. She knows the equivalent of a cord of hardwood compared to gallons of oil. She is obviously going to do the arithmetic to explain the estimated "payback"—when the investment in insulation and stoves, with the use of wood, is paid off in financial terms.

13 I have deliberately not printed the two resulting paragraphs for a good reason: I want you to examine carefully the nature of the two lists. *Here* is where you learn to be explicit, and you won't get much good from trying to write a paragraph from a vague list. I'll say it again: Making lists *is* writing. *And* thinking. And trying to make something real come off a page of words.

14 ALTERNATIVES Many writers discover that instead of making lists, rearranging them, and listing again, an effective way to begin is free-writing, or "automatic" writing. The idea is simply

to write—anything—for five or ten minutes. Write quickly, without rushing. Don't stop to correct spelling or grammar. Don't stop to look back. If you can't think of a word or phrase, just leave a blank, or write, "I can't think of it," and keep going. Continue writing *something*, even if it is nonsense. If you're stuck, write whatever silly phrases pop into your head—including "Dammit, I'm stuck."

Most of what you produce this way won't make sense; it will   15
be garbage. But more often than not, there will be a jewel in that garbage: a phrase or sentence or even a single word that will begin to express what you are struggling to say. Start again, beginning with the meaningful phrase, and free-write for another five minutes, this time trying to keep as close to the starting idea as you can. Once again, leave blanks where you need more information or can't think of appropriate words.

Remember: The typical hesitations, blocks, frustrations, and   16
irritations are most acute in the getting-started phase of the process. (Is that spelled right? Is this grammatical?) Half-formed ideas and feelings spin in your mind. Words slide off your mental tongue.

Don't hesitate. *Get it down. Fast. In any order.* Whatever it is,   17
no matter how mixed up, *get it down.* You are stockpiling raw material for future construction. *Get it down.* I can't give you a more useful piece of advice.

3. Your Point of View

Once you have your list, you have two key questions to answer: 18
What do I want to say about a BTU and *who* is my audience? (If you have no specific audience, write to yourself.) Here is where point of view overlaps with organization. Write half a dozen lead (opening) sentences. Choose the one that comes closest to your intentions. You will probably rewrite it later, but for now, let it stand. Using the lead as a guide, shuffle the separate elements in your list until the sequence of your information seems logical.

4. Rough Draft

Now write a rough draft of your paragraph—quickly. If you can,   19
put the draft away for a few hours—or longer, if your deadline permits ("let it cool off," writers say). When you pick it up again, put yourself in the place of a reader. Reading aloud often helps.

Listen first for a logical, sensible order of statements or examples. Put question marks in places that don't "feel" right or seem weak or thin. You may need to return to your original information list for more or different material. This is where *revision* (rewriting) begins. This is cut-and-add time, change-around time. You may want to rewrite your lead here. And you will doubtless rewrite it at least once again as you build closer to a final draft. (Revising and editing will be discussed in more detail in the following chapters.)

20   WRITING THIN Inexperienced writers are apt to write "thin" at first. They tend to assume that once stated, something is, in fact, completely said or that a generalized assertion is informative enough for a reader. This is rarely so. Readers crave information packed into small, telling details. For example, "He was fat" is vague. "He was obese" is slightly more explicit because the word suggests gross size. "His belly sagged over his belt and his heavy jowls quivered as he spoke" substitutes visual details for the word *fat* and more accurately reflects the writer's intention.

21   The instinct for detail develops and sharpens with practice.

22   You will usually find that this step-by-step prewriting and rough draft process has to be repeated—more than once—before you feel in clear control of what you want to say. You "recycle" your ideas and information because you discover that you are not as organized as you thought you were. An almost cliché question pinpoints the problem exactly: "How do I know what I think until I say what I mean?" The question is neither flippant nor foolish; indeed, it reflects a potent *process* of learning.

23   For example, here is a first draft of a student's brief paragraph (she had chosen her own subject). Read it carefully. For now, don't try to analyze; simply *respond*. Does it *feel* to you as though she has truly said what she meant to say?

> An event that changed my life was what happened to me a few weeks ago at the hospital. I was there as a nurse's aid. Well, anyway, this man was brought into the emergency room. He was young. About 25 I think. Well, he was in bad shape because he had a heart attack. Everyone rushed around and they brought in all kinds of equipment and they did all kinds of things to him. A couple of the doctors even swore and made jokes. But he died anyway. Right there. It really scared me to realize that someone could be so young and then just die like

that so suddenly. Some people at the hospital don't take their job seriously at all. I think medical people should take their job seriously and realize that what they do is important it can mean the difference between life and death.

For the moment, forget the grammatical errors (there are a few). Has the writer sharply communicated her meaning to you? Or aren't you sure? What, in fact, is the writer's main problem with this paragraph?   24

Let me take you through this one; then I'll give you another sample to work with on your own.   25

Primarily, the writer is not sure *what* she wants to say. There are three, perhaps four, ideas, none of which she has developed. (1) "An event that changed my life": Nothing more is said about such a change. (2) "It really scared me to realize . . .": She says no more about *what* scared her. (3) "Some people . . . don't take their job seriously": She doesn't tell what gave her this idea. (4) "Medical people . . . should realize that what they do . . . can mean the difference between life and death." And then she stops.   26

When the student and I discussed the paragraph, I pointed out her four different statements and asked which one was most vivid or important to her. She said immediately, "I was scared. I'd never seen anybody die before." I said, "That sentence struck me as the most genuine. Tell me—tell a reader—what scared you. What was going on that made it scary?"   27

She said, "Well, they banged his chest with their fists, and one doctor shoved an enormous needle right into his chest. And then they put a couple of electric paddles against his chest and there was a loud bang and his body jumped up a little on the table. Wow. And one of the nurses swore and pointed at the TV monitor, which had a flat white line on it and was making a thin screeching noise—and . . . and . . . the nurses and doctors just stood there and looked at each other and slumped. Then I realized the man was dead."   28

I said, "Why don't you make a list of what you have just told me, plus any other details you remember, and then write a draft showing what scared you?"   29

Her final version, several drafts later, was a vivid narration of a frightening experience. I have deliberately *not* printed it because I wanted you to focus on her first step toward clarifying her real meaning.   30

31   The next brief paragraph was a response to an assignment in a retail merchandising class: Tell a reader briefly what comparison shopping is.

> Comparison shopping is one way to find out quality and prices. For instance, you go to a speciality shop or booteek, a general high quality department store, a discount place, and a general cheap merchandise place, like K-Mart, and you examine a particerler itum. You check prices in each store. Or same type itum. They you try and see whether quality matches price, and you try to note down the differences. Or the same with brand names and non brands. Comparison shopping teaches you what to look for, like design, workmanship, practical use, and things like that. I found a great handbag like this once. All in all, comparison shopping will help you stretch your shopping dollars and you sometimes find real bargins and besides its fun.

32   You're on your own. Rewrite this one, adding any information you wish and making changes wherever you need to. Remember the demand of the assignment.

33   *INSPIRATION* There is, of course, such a thing. It's a quick flash of an idea; a sudden awareness of a relationship not seen before; a strong yen to express a feeling; or a desire to tell another of a special experience. It is, as a writer friend puts it, "an itch you have to scratch."

34   But don't count on it. If you say, "I couldn't write anything because I wasn't inspired," you're kidding yourself. Fortunately, inspiration *can* be bidden, like flame from the stirred embers of a nearly dead fire. The act of writing—anything—almost invariably generates ideas, information, insights. The sculptor August Rodin said, "Make something, and the ideas will come." The "making," no matter how fumbling, even aimless at first, will itself be an inspiration.

35   Remember, don't let lack of inspiration be an excuse; what you are really admitting is lack of will.

36   Some notion of the difficulty and sophistication of the writing act is reflected in an analogy:[1]

> Imagine the Writer perched like Humpty-Dumpty on top of a wall. On one side of the wall, imagine a great heap of all the ma-

---

[1]Adapted from a similar analogy by Elizabeth Bowen.

terial he wants to write about: facts, happenings, feelings, ideas. On the other side of the wall, facing it, is a Reader. He cannot see what the Writer sees; he can see only the wall. (The Writer can see both sides.) The Writer's job is to select from the welter of material on the opposite side of the wall what he wants his Reader to know and understand; to shape this selection into sequence and sense; to translate the sequence into words, sentences, and paragraphs; and finally to post these on the Reader's side of the wall. These written symbols are all that the Reader can use to make contact with the material from the wall's other side.

Vocabulary

To get the most out of reading this essay, you should have a working understanding of the words listed below. Following each word is a parenthetical reference, indicating the paragraph in which the word is used, as well as a definition for the word. Go back and look at the sentence in which the word appears, and see how the definition applies. To help you make this word a part of your active vocabulary, write a sentence of your own using the word in the space provided.

analogy (5):   resemblance in some particulars between things otherwise unlike

_____

_____

truisms (8):   self-evident truths

_____

_____

cord (12):   a measure of wood cut for fuel

_____

_____

explicit (13):   free from all vagueness or ambiguity

_____

_____

acute (16): severe

_____

_____

lead (19): the initial sentence or group of sentences in a prose composition

_____

_____

crave (20): to want greatly

_____

_____

flippant (22): lacking proper respect or seriousness

_____

_____

invariably (34): without change

_____

_____

Understanding the Essay

1. What, according to Garrison, are the main steps in the writing process? What types of activities occur at each stage?

2. In your own words, define *purpose, reader,* and *attitude.*

3. In paragraph 4, Garrison says, "Form follows function." What does he mean by the statement?

4. Why, according to Garrison, will a student have trouble developing an essay on sports?

5. Explain Garrison's analogy in his final paragraph to develop the idea that writing is both difficult and sophisticated. What is the role of inspiration for Garrison in the writing act?

6. Garrison titles his essay "Writing Is Building." In what ways is this true?

Writing Activities

1. Write a one-page description of the way you go about writing a composition. Here are some questions, among others, that you may want to address: What do you do first, what next, and so on? Do you always proceed in the same way? What factors influence the way you write? For example, how do different subjects or audiences influence the way you work? Also, consider how what you have learned from reading Garrison's essay will change your writing habits.

2. Try the assignment that Garrison himself offers in paragraph 32. Rewrite the student paragraph in paragraph 31, adding information where you think necessary and making whatever other changes you think appropriate.

FREEWRITING

Peter Elbow

Peter Elbow is a professor of English at the University of Massachusetts—Amherst. He is widely recognized for his innovative yet sensible and practical ideas about learning to write. His two best-known books, Writing Without Teachers *and* Writing With Power, *have influenced the way writing is taught in our colleges and universities and have helped a whole generation of students to write with confidence and power.*

Preparing to Read

Anyone who wants to learn to write must find his or her voice—that certain quality that puts the stamp of your personality on your writing and makes a reader want to hear what you have to say. One way to find that voice, according to Peter Elbow, is to begin to write without the fear of making mistakes, without the "habit of compulsive, premature editing." This is best done, he believes, through a simple exercise called freewriting—writing, without stopping or correcting, for ten minutes a day, three times a week.

1   The most effective way I know to improve your writing is to do freewriting exercises regularly. At least three times a week. They are sometimes called "automatic writing," "babbling," or "jabbering" exercises. The idea is simply to write for ten minutes (later on, perhaps fifteen or twenty). Don't stop for anything. Go quickly without rushing. Never stop to look back, to cross something out, to wonder how to spell something, to wonder what word or thought to use, or to think about what you are doing. If you can't think of a word or spelling, just use a squiggle or else write, "I can't think of it." Just put down something. The easiest thing is just to put down whatever is in your

mind. If you get stuck it's fine to write "I can't think of what to say, I can't think of what to say" as many times as you want; or repeat the last word you wrote over and over again; or anything else. The only requirement is that you *never* stop.

What happens to a freewriting exercise is important. It must 2 be a piece of writing which, even if someone reads it, doesn't send any ripples back to you. It is like writing something and putting it in a bottle in the sea. The teacherless class helps your writing by providing maximum feedback. Freewritings help you by providing no feedback at all. When I assign one, I invite the writer to let me read it, but also tell him to keep it if he prefers. I read it quickly and make no comments at all and I do not speak with him about it. The main thing is that a freewriting must never be evaluated in any way; in fact there must be no discussion or comment at all.

Here is an example of a fairly coherent exercise (sometimes 3 they are very coherent, which is fine):

> I think I'll write what's on my mind, but the only thing on my mind right now is what to write for ten minutes. I've never done this before and I'm not prepared in any way—the sky is cloudy today, how's that? now I'm afraid I won't be able to think of what to write when I get to the end of the sentence— well, here I am at the end of the sentence—here I am again, again, again, again, at least I'm still writing—Now I ask is there some reason to be happy that I'm still writing—ah yes! Here comes the question again—What am I getting out of this? What point is there in it? It's almost obscene to always ask it but I seem to question everything that way and I was gonna say something else pertaining to that but I got so busy writing down the first part that I forgot what I was leading into. This is kind of fun oh don't stop writing—cars and trucks speeding by somewhere out the window, pens clittering across people's papers. The sky is still cloudy—is it symbolic that I should be mentioning it? Huh? I dunno. Maybe I should try colors, blue, red, dirty words—wait a minute—no can't do that, orange, yellow, arm tired, green pink violet magenta lavender red brown black green—now that I can't think of any more colors—just about done—relief? maybe.

Freewriting may seem crazy but actually it makes simple 4 sense. Think of the difference between speaking and writing. Writing has the advantage of permitting more editing. But that's its downfall too. Almost everybody interposes a massive and complicated series of editings between the time words start to be born into consciousness and when they finally come off the end of the pencil or typewriter onto the page. This is partly because schooling makes us obsessed with the "mistakes" we make in writing. Many people are constantly thinking about spelling and grammar as they try to write. I am always thinking about the awkwardness, wordiness, and general mushiness of my natural verbal product as I try to write down words.

5   But it's not just "mistakes" or "bad writing" we edit as we write. We also edit unacceptable thoughts and feelings, as we do in speaking. In writing there is more time to do it so the editing is heavier: when speaking, there's someone right there waiting for a reply and he'll get bored or think we're crazy if we don't come out with *something.* Most of the time in speaking, we settle for the catch-as-catch-can way in which the words tumble out. In writing, however, there's a chance to try to get them right. But the opportunity to get them right is a terrible burden: you can work for two hours trying to get a paragraph "right" and discover it's not right at all. And then give up.

6   Editing, *in itself,* is not the problem. Editing is usually necessary if we want to end up with something satisfactory. The problem is that editing goes on *at the same time* as producing. The editor is, as it were, constantly looking over the shoulder of the producer and constantly fiddling with what he's doing while he's in the middle of trying to do it. No wonder the producer gets nervous, jumpy, inhibited, and finally can't be coherent. It's an unnecessary burden to try to think of words and also worry at the same time whether they're the right words.

7   The main thing about freewriting is that it is *nonediting.* It is an exercise in bringing together the process of producing words and putting them down the page. Practiced regularly, it undoes the ingrained habit of editing at the same time you are trying to produce. It will make writing less blocked because words will come more easily. You will use up more paper, but chew up fewer pencils.

8   Next time you write, notice how often you stop yourself from writing down something you were going to write down. Or else cross it out after it's written. "Naturally," you say, "it wasn't any good." But think for a moment about the occasions when you

spoke well. Seldom was it because you first got the beginning just right. Usually it was a matter of a halting or even garbled beginning, but you kept going and your speech finally became coherent and even powerful. There is a lesson here for writing: trying to get the beginning just right is a formula for failure— and probably a secret tactic to make yourself give up writing. Make some words, whatever they are, and then grab hold of that line and reel in as hard as you can. Afterwards you can throw away lousy beginnings and make new ones. This is the quickest way to get into good writing.

The habit of compulsive, premature editing doesn't just make writing hard. It also makes writing dead. Your voice is damped out by all the interruptions, changes, and hesitations between the consciousness and the page. In your natural way of producing words there is a sound, a texture, a rhythm—a voice—which is the main source of power in your writing. I don't know how it works, but this voice is the force that will make a reader listen to you, the energy that drives the meanings through his thick skull. Maybe you don't like your voice; maybe people have made fun of it. But it's the only voice you've got. It's your only source of power. You better get back into it, no matter what you think of it. If you keep writing in it, it may change into something you like better. But if you abandon it, you'll likely never have a voice and never be heard.

Vocabulary

To get the most out of reading this essay, you should have a working understanding of the words listed below. Following each word is a parenthetical reference, indicating the paragraph in which the word is used, as well as a definition for the word. Go back and look at the sentence in which the word appears, and see how the definition applies. To help you make this word a part of your active vocabulary, write a sentence of your own using the word in the space provided.

coherent (3):   logically consistent

interposes (4):   puts between

_____

_____

obsessed (4):   preoccupied intensely or abnormally

_____

_____

inhibited (6):   restrained

_____

_____

halting (8):   marked by a lack of sureness or effectiveness

_____

_____

damped (9):   deadened

_____

_____

Understanding the Essay

1. What, according to Elbow, is freewriting? What is the purpose of freewriting?
2. Why is it important that freewriting never be evaluated?
3. What is the difference between writing and speaking, according to Elbow? Why is this difference important to you as you learn to write?
4. What is voice in writing? What happens to your voice, according to Elbow, when it is controlled by "compulsive, premature editing?" Does the example of freewriting he provides in paragraph 3 have voice? Explain.
5. In paragraph 7 Elbow writes, "The main thing about freewriting is that it is *nonediting*." What does he mean by *nonediting?* How will nonediting help you find your voice?

6. In paragraph 9, Elbow refers to "The habit of compulsive, premature editing." What does the phrase mean?

Writing Activities

1. Read over Elbow's directions for freewriting. Also read the example of freewriting he provides in paragraph 3. Try doing ten minutes of freewriting every day for five days, not the three times a week that Elbow suggests. Elbow says it is important that freewriting not be evaluated, but what did you feel about the experience of freewriting itself? Was it as helpful as Elbow said it would be? Did you feel the urge to correct or edit your writing as you wrote? Did you feel your voice begin to emerge? Is freewriting an activity you are likely to continue?

2. If you are already in the habit of doing freewriting, or if you did freewriting for a week as suggested in the previous writing suggestion, review what you have written. Are there any ideas, observations, or thoughts in your freewriting that might be developed into an essay? You might find it helpful to exchange samples of your freewriting with a classmate. Each of you should then underline the part of the freewriting that is the most interesting to you and that you think might be a possible starting point for further writing.

FIVE PRINCIPLES FOR
GETTING GOOD IDEAS

Jack Rawlins

*Jack Rawlins is a professor of composition and literature
at California State University at Chico. He is the author
of* The Writer's Way, *a text that has a strong personal
voice as well as a very loyal following among teachers
and students of composition. In the following essay,
taken from his book, Rawlins presents his five principles
for getting good ideas.*

Preparing to Read

One of the most difficult aspects of learning to write is getting good ideas. Good ideas are not simply picked up and tacked
on to a composition. They are the by-products of an active, indeed interactive, mind that is engaged in the world, continuously connecting and responding to it. Rawlins uses several images to help us understand thinking and ideas: "One popular,
poisonous image for thinking is the light bulb flashing on over
someone's head—the notion that ideas spring from within us,
caused by nothing. To become thinkers, we have to replace that
image with another; think of ideas as billiard balls set in motion
when something collides with them. Ideas are *re*actions—we
have them in response to other things." As you read his suggestions, consider how you get ideas for writing and how you might
use his advice.

1   Brains that get good ideas follow five principles:

Don't begin with a topic.
Think all the time.
To get something out, put something in.

Go from little, concrete things to big, abstract things.
Connect.

We'll talk about each in turn.

Don't Begin with a Topic

Essays rarely begin with subject matter alone. Why would a   2
person say out of the blue, "I think I'll write about linoleum, or
the national debt"? Nor are the kernels of essays always "good
ideas"—they often aren't *ideas* at all, in the sense of whole assertions. Thinking begins in lots of ways:

> WITH A QUESTION: "Is there any real difference be-
> tween the Republicans and the Democrats anymore?"
> "Why is Ralph so mad at me?"
>
> WITH A PROBLEM: "I'm always behind in my work."
> "Violent crimes against women are on the increase."
>
> WITH A PURPOSE: "I want to tell people about what's
> really going on in this class." "I want to let people know
> about alternatives to traditional medicine."
>
> WITH A THESIS: "There are cheaper, healthier alterna-
> tives to regular grocery stores." "Old people are the
> victims of silent injustice in our culture."
>
> WITH A FEELING: anger, frustration, surprise.
>
> WITH A SENSATION OR IMAGE: a smell, a glimpse of a
> bird in flight, an eye-catching TV ad.

What shall we call that thing an essay begins with—the seed,
the spark, the inspiration, the sense of "gotcha"? I'll call it a
prompt.

Think All the Time

If you have a sense of humor, you know that the surest way to   3
prevent yourself from being funny is to have someone (even yourself) demand that you be funny *now*. Comedians have always
bemoaned the fact that people introduce them to friends by
saying, "This is Milton. He's a riot. Be funny, Milton." Thinking's
the same way. Being put on the spot is the surest way of preventing the creative juices from flowing.

4   So don't expect to discover a good prompt by sitting down for a scheduled half-hour of profundity. Minds that think well think all the time. One prolific student wrote that she goes through the world "looking for *writable* things" and is thought weird by her friends because she scribbles notes to herself at parties.

5   Thinking all the time sounds like work, but it isn't. Your mind works all the time whether you want it to or not, the same way your body moves all the time. Any yogi will tell you that it takes years of practice to learn to turn the mind *off*, even for a minute or two. And it's physiologically impossible for your brain to get tired, which is why you can study or write all day, go to bed, and find your mind still racing while your body cries for rest. So I'm really not asking your brain to do anything new; I'm just asking you to *listen* to it.

To Get Something Out, Put Something In

6   One popular, poisonous image for thinking is the light bulb flashing on over someone's head—the notion that ideas spring from within us, caused by nothing. To become good thinkers, we have to replace that image with another; think of ideas as billiard balls set in motion when something collides with them. Ideas are *re*actions—we have them in response to other things.

7   A thinker thinks as life passes through him and does what I call "talking back to the world." Many of us separate our input and output modes; we are either putting information into our brains or asking our brains to produce thoughts, but we don't do both at the same time. I call such people data sponges. But the best time to try to get things out is when things are going in. Let them bounce off you and strike sparks. People do this naturally until they've been taught to be passive; try reading a book to a three-year-old, and listen to her react to everything she hears and sees, or take her to a movie and watch her struggle not to talk back to the screen.

8   Are you a data sponge? To find out, answer the following questions.

Do you find yourself mentally talking back to the newspaper when you read it?

Do you write in the margins of books you read?

Are at least 25 percent of the notes you take during course reading or lectures your own thoughts, questions, doubts, and reactions?

As you meet up with life's outrages, do you find yourself complaining to imaginary audiences?

After a movie, do you feel like you're going to burst until you find someone to talk about it?

When you listen to a speaker or a teacher, do you find yourself itching to get to the question-and-answer period?

If you said yes to these questions, you're not a sponge. If you said no, you're going to have to practice your reacting skills.

Go from Little, Concrete Things to Big, Abstract Things

This principle is a logical consequence of the one before. Since 9 ideas come best in reaction to life's incoming billiard balls, the best thinking follows a predictable course: from little, concrete bits of experience to large abstract implications. You see an ad on TV and start thinking about it, and it leads you to speculations on American consumerism, media manipulation, and the marketing of women's bodies. You overhear a snippet of conversation between a parent and child at the grocery store and start thinking about it, and it leads you to speculations on American child-rearing practices, the powerlessness of children, parental brainwashing, and antiyouth bigotry.

Here's what going from little particulars to big issues is like. 10 I was sitting doing nothing one day when my eyes fell on a box of Girl Scout cookies. The box had on it a picture of a girl and the slogan, "I'm not like anyone else." I reacted. I thought, "Gosh, that sounds lonely." And I valued the reaction enough to notice it and think about it. It led me to a big issue: How does Americans' love of individuality affect their ability to be members of a culture? And I formulated a thesis: Americans love their individuality so much that they'll cut themselves off from everything and everyone to get it. Being unlike everyone else is a curse, because it means you're separated from other human beings by your differentness. I was raised a proud individualist, and I've only recently realized that the reward for being unique is loneliness.

I went from little things to big issues when I drew essays 11 out of Sally's life. When she mentioned that she couldn't drink too heavily in high school because it would affect her shot-putting, I instantly saw the abstract issue illustrated by her experience: People who have things they love dare not practice self-destructive behavior, because they'll destroy what they love in the process. So alcoholism or drug abuse is neither a crime nor a disease nor a moral failure in the individual; it's a symptom of a social failure, the failure of our society to offer the alcoholic or drug addict a life too precious to risk destroying.

12   Beginning writers want to start with large abstractions, in the mistaken belief that the bigger the topic is, the more there is to say about it. It doesn't work out that way. Usually the first sentence of the essay tells whether the writer knows this or not. Essays on friendship that begin "Friendship is one of the most important things in life" are doomed, because the writer doesn't know it. Essays that begin "Mary was my best friend in high school" will thrive, because the writer does know it.

Connect

13   Those who think well make connections between things. An essay begins when two previously unrelated bits in the brain meet and discover a connection. Usually a new stimulus hitches up with an old bit stored long ago in the memory; the incoming billiard ball hits an old one that's just lying there, and they fly off together.

14   It's hard to learn the connecting skill if you don't have it already. Here's what it feels like inside. One day I was sitting in an English Department faculty meeting, and we were discussing an administrative change. A colleague said, "We couldn't do that until we were sure our people would be protected." I thought momentarily, "I wonder how he knows who 'his people' are?" Months later I was vacationing in a small mountain town and picked up the local newspaper. On the front page was an article about the firing of a group of non-union construction workers. The boss had asked the union for workers, but none were available, so he trained out-of-work mill workers. Later the union rep showed up, announced that union workers were now available, and insisted that the others be fired. Something clicked, and I had an essay. My colleague's attitude and the union rep's were the same: I'll watch out for "my people," and everyone else can watch out for himself. I wanted to talk about why people think that way and how they learn to rise above it.

How did I make that connection? Incredible as it sounds, 15
and unbeknownst to me, I must have been checking everything
that came into my brain against the faculty-meeting remark for
a possible connection. Or perhaps I had opened a file in my mind
labeled "people who think in terms of those who belong and
those who don't" and dumped anything related in there as it
came along.

I just read a great essay by Arthur Miller connecting the 16
current prayer-in-school political debate with his memories of
saying the Pledge of Allegiance in elementary school. What
brought the two things together? Miller must have checked
prayer in schools against everything in his memory relating to
state-mandated loyalty and come up with recollections of third
grade. That sounds exhausting, but we all know that when something clicks in memory, we haven't "worked" at all—in fact, the
way to bring the connection that's on the tip of the tongue to the
surface is to forget about it and let the subconscious do its work
unwatched.

The more unlike two things are and the less obvious the con- 17
nection between them is, the fresher and more stimulating the
connection is when you make it. Finding a connection between
mountain climbers and sky-divers is merely okay; finding a
connection between inflation rates and the incidence of breast
cancer will make the world open its eyes. This is the Head
Principle. Mr. Head was an aviation engineer who got interested in downhill skiing. Apparently no one had ever connected
aircraft technology and skiing before; Mr. Head took a few runs
down the hill and realized that he could make a better ski if he
simply made it according to the principles and with the materials used in making airplane wings. He invented the Head ski,
the first metal ski, and made millions of dollars. He then did
the same thing in tennis, by inventing the Prince racket. Apparently aircraft engineers didn't play tennis either.

The Head Principle says you can't predict what will connect 18
with what. So you can't tell yourself what information to seek.
You can only take in experience and information voraciously
and stir it all up together. If I had been formally researching
stupid faculty remarks, I'd never have thought to read up on
northern Californian construction workers. If you're writing
about Charles Dickens and you read only about Charles Dickens,
you're just guaranteeing you won't make any connections except

those other Dickens scholars have already made. Instead, go read *Psychology Today*, read Nixon's memoirs, see a movie, watch a documentary on insect societies, or visit a mortuary. As you talk back to all of it, keep asking yourself, "What is this like? When have I thought things like this before? When was the last time I reacted like this?" When I read about the construction workers, I reacted, and I remembered that I'd had a conversation with myself like that one before sometime. Perhaps that's the key to connecting.

19   It's easy to block ideas from coming by practicing the exact opposite of our idea-getting principles. Just set aside a time for idea-getting, cut yourself off from the outside world by locking yourself in a stimulus-free study room, and muse on a cosmic abstraction. If you're doing any of that, your idea-getting regimen needs overhauling.

Vocabulary

To get the most out of reading this essay, you should have a working understanding of the words listed below. Following each word is a parenthetical reference, indicating the paragraph in which the word is used, as well as a definition for the word. Go back and look at the sentence in which the word appears, and see how the definition applies. To help you make this word a part of your active vocabulary, write a sentence of your own using the word in the space provided.

assertions (2):   declarations

---

profundity (4):   intellectual depth

---

prolific (4):   productive

---

modes (7):   customary or preferred way of doing something

_____

_____

snippet (9):   brief, quotable passage

_____

_____

formulated (10):   stated systematically

_____

_____

stimulus (13):   something that rouses or incites to activity

_____

_____

incidence (17):   occurrence

_____

_____

voraciously (18):   eagerly

_____

_____

regimen (19):   systematic plan

_____

_____

Understanding the Essay

1. What does Rawlins mean by *prompt?*
2. Rawlins advises against beginning your writing by thinking about a topic. What is wrong with thinking about a topic? How does he suggest you begin?

3. What is a "data sponge"? Are you a data sponge? How do you know? What does Rawlins suggest you do if you are a data sponge?

4. What is the point of Rawlins's story about his faculty meeting and the piece in the newspaper "about the firing of a group of non-union construction workers?"

5. What, according to Rawlins, is the Head Principle? Of what is Mr. Head an example for Rawlins?

6. Can you recall any writing experiences when you went from "little particulars to big issues?" Why is it not a good idea to begin with abstractions and move to particulars?

7. What part(s) of the advice Rawlins gives will be most helpful to you in your writing? Explain.

Writing Activities

1. In paragraph 4 Rawlins writes about one of his students who gathers ideas all the time: "One prolific student wrote that she goes through the world 'looking for *writable* things' and is thought weird by her friends because she scribbles notes to herself at parties." Try looking for "writable things" yourself. Take a small notebook along wherever you go to capture those special ideas, snippets of conversation, observations, and surprising facts that may help you in future writing assignments, especially where the topic is left open for you.

2. Rawlins writes, "The more unlike two things are and the less obvious the connection between them is, the fresher and the more stimulating the connection is when you make it." Try using the Head Principle by choosing one of the following pairs of topics and connecting them in an essay:

   a baseball bat and apples

   rollerblading and crossword puzzles

   lipstick and MTV

   termites and surfing

SIMPLICITY

William Zinsser

William Zinsser has had a long career as a journalist, author, and teacher of writing. He is now the executive editor of the Book-of-the-Month Club, but he is perhaps best known for his book On Writing Well. *In it, he imparts much of the practical knowledge about writing that he has gathered over the years. The effectiveness of his own writing is the best example that he knows what he's talking about.*

Preparing to Read

The point that Zinsser makes in this excerpt from *On Writing Well* is that clutter or verbiage, words that do not carry meaning, can get in the way of a writer's message. Such words can also weaken and obscure the words that are doing the work of communicating. As you read, notice how clear and simple the message is that he imparts. And, of course, pay particular attention to how he suggests you reduce the clutter in your writing.

C lutter is the disease of American writing. We are a society strangling in unnecessary words, circular construction, pompous frills and meaningless jargon. 1

Who can understand the viscous language of everyday American commerce and enterprise: the business letter, the interoffice memo, the corporation report, the notice from the bank explaining its latest "simplified" statement? What member of an insurance or medical plan can decipher the brochure that describes what the costs and benefits are? What father or mother can put together a child's toy—on Christmas Eve or any other eve—from the instructions on the box? Our national tendency is to inflate and thereby sound important. The airline pilot who announces that he is presently anticipating experiencing consider- 2 able precipitation wouldn't dream of saying that it may rain. The sentence is too simple—there must be something wrong with it.

3   But the secret of good writing is to strip every sentence to its cleanest components. Every word that serves no function, every long word that could be a short word, every adverb that carries the same meaning that's already in the verb, every passive construction that leaves the reader unsure of who is doing what— these are the thousand and one adulterants that weaken the strength of a sentence. And they usually occur, ironically, in proportion to education and rank.

4   During the late 1960s the president of a major university wrote a letter to mollify the alumni after a spell of campus unrest. "You are probably aware," he began, "that we have been experiencing very considerable potentially explosive expressions of dissatisfaction on issues only partially related." He meant that the students had been hassling them about different things. I was far more upset by the president's English than by the students' potentially explosive expressions of dissatisfaction. I would have preferred the presidential approach taken by Franklin D. Roosevelt when he tried to convert into English his own government's memos, such as this blackout order of 1942:

> Such preparations shall be made as will completely obscure all Federal buildings and non-Federal buildings occupied by the Federal government during an air raid for any period of time from visibility by reason of internal or external illumination.

5   "Tell them," Roosevelt said, "that in buildings where they have to keep the work going to put something across the windows."

6   Simplify, simplify. Thoreau said it, as we are so often reminded, and no American writer more consistently practiced what he preached. Open *Walden* to any page and you will find a man saying in a plain and orderly way what is on his mind:

> I went to the woods because I wished to live deliberately, to front only the essential facts of life, and see if I could not learn what it had to teach, and not, when I came to die, discover that I had not lived. I did not wish to live what was not life, living is so dear; nor did I wish to practice resignation, unless it was quite necessary. I wanted to live deep and suck

out all the marrow of life, to live so sturdily and Spartan-like as to put to rout all that was not life, to cut a broad swath and shave close, to drive life into a corner, and reduce it to its lowest terms, and, if it proved to be mean, why then to get the whole and genuine meanness of it, and publish its meanness to the world; or if it were sublime, to know it by experience, and be able to give a true account of it.

How can the rest of us achieve such enviable freedom from clutter? The answer is to clear our heads of clutter. Clear thinking becomes clear writing; one can't exist without the other. It's impossible for a muddy thinker to write good English. You may get away with it for a paragraph or two, but soon the reader will be lost, and there's no sin so grave, for the reader will not easily be lured back.   7

Who is this elusive creature, the reader? The reader is someone with an attention span of about sixty seconds—a person assailed by forces competing for the minutes that might otherwise be spent on a magazine or a book. At one time these forces weren't so numerous or so possessive: newspapers, radio, spouse, home, children. Today they also include a "home entertainment center" (TV, VCR, video camera, tapes and CDs), pets, a fitness program, a lawn and a garden and all the gadgets that have been bought to keep them spruce, and that most potent of competitors, sleep. The person snoozing in a chair, holding a magazine or a book, is a person who was being given too much unnecessary trouble by the writer.   8

It won't do to say that the reader is too dumb or too lazy to keep pace with the train of thought. If the reader is lost, it's usually because the writer hasn't been careful enough. The carelessness can take any number of forms. Perhaps a sentence is so excessively cluttered that the reader, hacking through the verbiage, simply doesn't know what it means. Perhaps a sentence has been so shoddily constructed that the reader could read it in any of several ways. Perhaps the writer has switched pronouns in midsentence, or has switched tenses, so the reader loses track of who is talking or when the action took place. Perhaps Sentence B is not a logical sequel to Sentence A—the writer, in whose head the connection is clear, hasn't bothered to provide the missing link. Perhaps the writer has used an important word incorrectly by not taking the trouble to look it up. The writer may think that "sanguine" and "sanguinary" mean the same   9 thing, but the difference is a bloody big one. The reader can only infer (speaking of big differences) what the writer is trying to imply.

10   Faced with such obstacles, readers are at first remarkably tenacious. They blame themselves—they obviously missed something, and they go back over the mystifying sentence, or over the whole paragraph, piecing it out like an ancient rune, making guesses and moving on. But they won't do this for long. The writer is making them work too hard, and they will look for one who is better at the craft.

11   Writers must therefore constantly ask: What am I trying to say? Surprisingly often they don't know. Then they must look at what they have written and ask: Have I said it? Is it clear to someone encountering the subject for the first time? If it's not, that's because some fuzz has worked its way into the machinery. The clear writer is someone clearheaded enough to see this stuff for what it is: fuzz.

12   I don't mean that some people are born clearheaded and are therefore natural writers, whereas others are naturally fuzzy and will never write well. Thinking clearly is a conscious act that writers must force upon themselves, just as if they were embarking on any other project that requires logic: adding up a laundry list or doing an algebra problem. Good writing doesn't come naturally, though most people obviously think it does. The professional writer is constantly being bearded by strangers who say they'd like to "try a little writing sometime"—meaning when they retire from their real profession, like insurance or real estate. Or they say, "I could write a book about that." I doubt it.

13   Writing is hard work. A clear sentence is no accident. Very few sentences come out right the first time, or even the third time. Remember this as a consolation in moments of despair. If you find that writing is hard, it's because it *is* hard. It's one of the hardest things that people do.

Vocabulary

To get the most out of reading this essay, you should have a working understanding of the words listed on the next page. Following each word is a parenthetical reference, indicating the

paragraph in which the word is used, as well as a definition for the word. Go back and look at the sentence in which the word appears, and see how the definition applies. To help you make this word a part of your active vocabulary, write a sentence of your own using the word in the space provided.

pompous (1):   excessively ornate

_____

_____

decipher (2):   make out the meaning of something indistinct or obscure

_____

_____

adulterants (3):   elements that debase or corrupt

_____

_____

mollify (4):   soothe or quiet

_____

_____

enviable (7):   highly desirable

_____

_____

assailed (8):   attacked with violence or words

_____

_____

tenacious (10):   holding fast

_____

_____

bearded (12):   boldly confronted

Understanding the Essay

1. What exactly does Zinsser mean by clutter? Why does he call it a disease? Is calling it a disease an exaggeration?

2. How does Zinsser think that we can free our writing of clutter?

3. Zinsser claims that clutter increases with an increase in rank and education. Why is that true?

4. Zinsser asks several questions in paragraph 2. How do these questions further his purpose in this essay?

5. In paragraph 11, Zinsser says that writers must constantly ask themselves some questions. What are these questions and why are they important?

6. What relationship does Zinsser see between clear thinking and clear writing? Most people would agree that you can't write clearly if your thinking is muddy, but can you think clearly and still not be able to write clearly? Explain.

Writing Activities

1. All the following sentences contain clutter. Revise each one to reduce verbiage and still maintain its meaning.

   a. The folk singer who is carrying the guitar usually wears a hat which has a wide brim.

   b. The absolutely incredible play of Monica Seles amazed the very enthusiastic tennis fans.

   c. Children like fishing, but after fishing for more than several hours they get tired of it because it becomes boring to them.

   d. Maggie took her cat to a doctor who treats sick animals.

e. Yesterday Liz called up Phoebe on the telephone to tell her about the meeting.

2. Now that you have practiced eliminating clutter, take a piece of your finished writing and make several passes through it, eliminating clutter without losing meaning. Put the composition aside for a day or so, then return to it with the same idea. Were you able to eliminate yet more clutter? How, finally, do you assess your writing? Is it clutter-free? relatively free? very cluttered? How will your assessment help you improve your writing?

WRITING FOR AN AUDIENCE

Linda Flower

Linda Flower is professor of English at Carnegie-Mellon University. She has been a leading researcher in the composing process for many years, and the results of her investigations have shaped and informed her influential writing text, Problem-Solving Strategies for Writing, *from which this selection is taken.*

Preparing to Read

Linda Flower's interest in this essay is a consideration of audience—the people for whom we write. She believes that any writer must establish a "common ground" between the writer and the reader, one that lessens their differences in knowledge, attitudes, and needs. Although we can never be certain who might read what we write, it is nevertheless important for us to have a target audience in mind. All the decisions that we make as writers are influenced by that real or imagined reader.

1   The goal of the writer is to create a momentary common ground between the reader and the writer. You want the reader to share your knowledge and your attitude toward that knowledge. Even if the reader eventually disagrees, you want him or her to be able for the moment to *see things as you see them.* A good piece of writing closes the gap between you and the reader.

Analyze Your Audience

2   The first step in closing that gap is to gauge the distance between the two of you. Imagine, for example, that you are a student writing your parents, who have always lived in New York City, about a wilderness survival expedition you want to go on over spring break. Sometimes obvious differences such as age or

background will be important, but the critical differences for writers usually fall into three areas: the reader's *knowledge* about the topic, his or her *attitude* toward it, and his or her personal or professional *needs*. Because these differences often exist, good writers do more than simply express their meaning; they pinpoint the critical differences between themselves and their reader and design their writing to reduce those differences. Let us look at these three areas in more detail.

KNOWLEDGE. This is usually the easiest difference to handle.   3
What does your reader need to know? What are the main ideas you hope to teach? Does your reader have enough background knowledge to really understand you? If not, what would he or she have to learn?

ATTITUDES. When we say a person has knowledge, we usually   4
refer to his conscious awareness of explicit facts and clearly defined concepts. This kind of knowledge can be easily written down or told to someone else. However, much of what we "know" is not held in this formal, explicit way. Instead it is held as an attitude or image—as a loose cluster of associations. For instance, my image of lakes includes associations many people would have, including fishing, water skiing, stalled outboards, and lots of kids catching night crawlers with flashlights. However, the most salient or powerful parts of my image, which strongly color my whole attitude toward lakes, are thoughts of cloudy skies, long rainy days, and feeling generally cold and damp. By contrast, one of my best friends has a very different cluster of associations: to him a lake means sun, swimming, sailing, and happily sitting on the end of a dock. Needless to say, our differing images cause us to react quite differently to a proposal that we visit a lake. Likewise, one reason people often find it difficult to discuss religion and politics is that terms such as "capitalism" conjure up radically different images.

As you can see, a reader's image of a subject is often the   5
source of attitudes and feelings that are unexpected and, at times, impervious to mere facts. A simple statement that seems quite persuasive to you, such as "Lake Wampago would be a great place to locate the new music camp," could have little impact on your reader if he or she simply doesn't visualize a lake as a "great place." In fact, many people accept uncritically any

statement that fits in with their own attitudes—and reject, just as uncritically, anything that does not.

6   Whether your purpose is to persuade or simply to present your perspective, it helps to know the image and attitudes that your reader already holds. The more these differ from your own, the more you will have to do to make him or her *see* what you mean.

7   NEEDS. When writers discover a large gap between their own knowledge and attitudes and those of the reader, they usually try to change the reader in some way. Needs, however, are different. When you analyze a reader's needs, it is so that you, the writer, can adapt to him. If you ask a friend majoring in biology how to keep your fish tank from clouding, you don't want to hear a textbook recitation on the life processes of algae. You expect the friend to adapt his or her knowledge and tell you exactly how to solve your problem.

8   The ability to adapt your knowledge to the needs of the reader is often crucial to your success as a writer. This is especially true in writing done on a job. For example, as producer of a public affairs program for a television station, eighty percent of your time may be taken up planning the details of new shows, contacting guests, and scheduling the taping sessions. But when you write a program proposal to the station director, your job is to show how the program will fit into the cost guidelines, the FCC requirements for relevance, and the overall programming plan for the station. When you write that report your role in the organization changes from producer to proposal writer. Why? Because your reader needs that information in order to make a decision. He may be *interested* in your scheduling problems and the specific content of the shows, but he *reads* your report because of his own needs as station director of that organization. He has to act.

9   In college, where the reader is also a teacher, the reader's needs are a little less concrete but just as important. Most papers are assigned as a way to teach something. So the real purpose of a paper may be for you to make connections between two historical periods, to discover for yourself the principle behind a laboratory experiment, or to develop and support your own interpretation of a novel. A good college paper doesn't just rehash

the facts; it demonstrates what your reader, as a teacher, needs to know—that you are learning the thinking skills his or her course is trying to teach.

Effective writers are not simply expressing what they know, like the student madly filling up an examination bluebook. Instead they are *using* their knowledge: reorganizing, maybe even rethinking their ideas to meet the demands of an assignment or the needs of their reader. 10

Sometimes it is also necessary to decide who is your primary audience as opposed to your secondary audience. Both may read your paper, but the primary audience is the reader you most want to teach, influence, or convince. When this is the case, you will want to design the paper so the primary reader can easily find what he or she needs. 11

Vocabulary

To get the most out of reading this essay, you should have a working understanding of the words listed below. Following each word is a parenthetical reference, indicating the paragraph in which the word is used, as well as a definition for the word. Go back and look at the sentence in which the word appears, and see how the definition applies. To help you make this word a part of your active vocabulary, write a sentence of your own using the word in the space provided.

critical (2):   crucial

_____

_____

salient (4):   prominent

_____

_____

impervious (5):   not capable of being affected

_____

_____

recitation (7):   act of enumerating

---

relevance (8):   relation to the matter at hand

Understanding the Essay

1. What for Flower should be the goal of the writer?

2. What does Flower mean by the "distance" between the writer and the reader? How, according to Flower, do writers close the gap between themselves and their readers?

3. Why does Flower spend so little time on "knowledge?" Why is it important to know the difference between knowledge and attitude?

4. What, according to Flower, does a good college paper do? What does she mean when she says that effective writers do not simply express what they know, they *use* their knowledge?

5. Flower wrote this selection for college students. How well did she assess your knowledge, attitude, and needs about the subject of a writer's audience?

Writing Activities

1. Let's assume that you have had an experience while in college that affected you significantly—a bout with the flu that landed you in the campus infirmary, being turned down by the fraternity or sorority of your choice, being elected to a class office. You want to write to a friend at another school as well as to your parents about what has happened. What do you need to consider about these different audiences before you begin writing your two letters?

2. You are planning to write an argument about gun control, animal testing, censorship, or some other controversial issue. You imagine that your audience might be of any one of three attitudes with respect to the position you take: sympathetic, indifferent, or hostile. What decisions might you make in each case about the need for background information, definitions of key terms, extended explanations, and evidence, as well as the appropriateness of analogies and figurative and emotionally charged language? What overall tone might be the most appropriate in each situation?

14

THESIS

The *thesis* of an essay is its main idea, the point it is trying to make. The thesis is often expressed in a one- or two-sentence statement, although sometimes it is implied or suggested rather than stated directly. The thesis statement controls and directs the content of the essay: everything that the writer says must be logically related to the thesis statement.

Usually the thesis is presented early in an essay, sometimes in the first sentence. A thesis statement can be short and pithy, or it can be complex and detailed. Here are some thesis statements that begin essays:

> Friendships, like love affairs, can run out of steam.
>
> —*Stephanie Mansfield*

> Clutter is the disease of American writing.
>
> —*William Zinsser*

> Even if they grow up in the same neighborhood, on the same block, or in the same house, girls and boys grow up in different worlds of words.
>
> —*Deborah Tannen*

> The person who set the course of my life in the new land I entered as a young war refugee—who, in fact, nearly dragged me onto the path that would bring all the blessings I've received in America—was a salty-tongued, no-nonsense schoolteacher named Marjorie Hurd.
>
> —*Nicholas Gage*

Often writers prepare readers for a thesis statement with a couple of sentences or even a paragraph that establishes a context. Notice, in the following two-paragraph sequence, how David L. Evans eases the reader into his thesis about black male college candidates instead of presenting it abruptly in the first sentence.

As a college admissions officer I am alarmed at the dearth of qualified black male candidates. Often in high schools that are 90 percent black, *all* the African-American students who come to my presentation are female! This gender disparity persists to college matriculation, where the black male population almost never equals that of the female.

What is happening to these young men? Who or what is influencing them? I submit that the absence of black role models and slanted television images of black males have something to do with it.

—*David L. Evans*

On occasion a writer may even purposefully delay the presentation of a thesis until the middle or end of an essay. If the thesis is controversial or needs extended discussion and illustration, the writer might present it later to make it easier for the reader to understand and accept it. Appearing near or at the end of an essay, a thesis also gains prominence.

Some kinds of writing do not need thesis statements. These include descriptions, narratives, and personal writing such as letters and diaries. But any essay that seeks to explain or prove a point has a thesis that is usually set forth in a thesis statement.

THE DIFFERENCE BETWEEN A BRAIN AND A COMPUTER

Isaac Asimov

Born in the former Soviet Union, Isaac Asimov emigrated to the United States in 1923. His death in April 1992 ended a long, prolific career as a science fiction and nonfiction writer. Asimov was uniquely talented at making a diverse range of topics—from Shakespeare to atomic physics, histories, theories of time, the Bible, and detective fiction—not only comprehensible but entertaining to the general reader. Asimov earned three degrees at Columbia University and later taught biochemistry at Boston University. At the time of his death, he had published more than five hundred books.

In the following essay, Asimov compares the human brain to a computer, and comes to some exciting and terrifying conclusions.

Preparing to Read

The words "The Difference Between" in Asimov's title indicates that in his essay he will be comparing the human brain to a computer. "The difference between a brain and a computer can be expressed in a single word: complexity," writes Asimov. He uses the idea of what "thinking" is and what "programs"are to draw parallels between the way brains and computers function. In what ways do *you* think brains and computers are similar? Do you agree with Asimov's prediction that someday computers may surpass humans and do a "better job of running the earth" than we do?

1   The difference between a brain and a computer can be expressed in a single word: complexity.

2   The large mammalian brain is the most complicated thing,

for its size, known to us. The human brain weighs three pounds, but in that three pounds are ten billion neurons and a hundred billion smaller cells. These many billions of cells are interconnected in a vastly complicated network that we can't begin to unravel as yet.

Even the most complicated computer man has yet built   3 can't compare in intricacy with the brain. Computer switches and components number in the thousands rather than in the billions. What's more, the computer switch is just an on-off device, whereas the brain cell is itself possessed of a tremendously complex inner structure.

Can a computer think? That depends on what you mean by   4 "think." If solving a mathematical problem is "thinking," then a computer can "think" and do so much faster than a man. Of course, most mathematical problems can be solved quite mechanically by repeating certain straightforward processes over and over again. Even the simple computers of today can be geared for that.

It is frequently said that computers solve problems only be-   5 cause they are "programmed" to do so. They can only do what men have them do. One must remember that human beings also can only do what they are "programmed" to do. Our genes "program" us the instant the fertilized ovum is formed, and our potentialities are limited by that "program."

Our "program" is so much more enormously complex,   6 though, that we might like to define "thinking" in terms of the creativity that goes into writing a great play or composing a great symphony, in conceiving a brilliant scientific theory or a profound ethical judgment. In that sense, computers certainly can't think and neither can most humans.

Surely, though, if a computer can be made complex enough,   7 it can be as creative as we. If it could be made as complex as a human brain, it could be the equivalent of a human brain and do whatever a human brain can do.

To suppose anything else is to suppose that there is more to   8 the human brain than the matter that composes it. The brain is made up of cells in a certain arrangement and the cells are made up of atoms and molecules in certain arrangements. If anything else is there, no signs of it have ever been detected. To duplicate the material complexity of the brain is therefore to duplicate everything about it.

9   But how long will it take to build a computer complex enough to duplicate the human brain? Perhaps not as long as some think. Long before we approach a computer as complex as our brain, we will perhaps build a computer that is at least complex enough to design another computer more complex than itself. This more complex computer could design one still more complex and so on and so on and so on.

10   In other words, once we pass a certain critical point, the computers take over and there is a "complexity explosion." In a very short time thereafter, computers may exist that not only duplicate the human brain—but far surpass it.

11   Then what? Well, mankind is not doing a very good job of running the earth right now. Maybe, when the time comes, we ought to step gracefully aside and hand over the job to someone who can do it better. And if we don't step aside, perhaps Supercomputer will simply move in and push us aside.

Vocabulary

To get the most out of reading this essay, you should have a working understanding of the words listed below. Following each word is a parenthetical reference, indicating the paragraph in which the word is used, as well as a definition for the word. Go back and look at the sentence in which the word appears, and see how the definition applies. To help you make this word a part of your active vocabulary, write a sentence of your own using the word in the space provided.

mammalian (2): belonging or pertaining to the class *Mammalia;* characteristic of mammals

_____

_____

neurons (2): nerve cells

_____

_____

components (3): parts; elements; constituents

_____

_____

programmed (5): prepared with a systematic plan for solving a problem

_____

_____

genes (5): units of heredity

_____

_____

ovum (5): egg

_____

_____

conceiving (6): forming an idea

_____

_____

equivalent (7): equal in value, force, measure, significance

_____

_____

duplicate (8): make a copy exactly like an original

_____

_____

Understanding the Essay

1. Asimov states his thesis in the one-sentence paragraph that opens the essay. What does he accomplish by using this strategy?

2. Does Asimov restate his thesis elsewhere in the essay? If so, why?

3. What is so important about the definition of "thinking"? What is the difference between "thinking" and being "programmed"?

4. Asimov states that if a computer "could be made as complex as a human brain, it could be the equivalent of a human brain and do whatever a human brain can do." Explain what he means when he adds, in paragraph 8, that to "suppose anything else is to suppose that there is more to the human brain than the matter that composes it."

5. What, according to the author, is a "complexity explosion"?

6. How would you describe Asimov's vision of the future in paragraph 11? How does this final paragraph relate to Asimov's thesis?

Writing Activities

1. Whether you agree or disagree with Asimov, develop your own thesis about "The Difference Between a Brain and a Computer." Brainstorm and list the ways in which your information or evidence would have to differ from Asimov's to support the new thesis.

2. Find an essay that you have written previously and underline the thesis statement. Does everything else in the essay relate to this thesis? Why or why not? How might you have to rewrite your thesis or reshape your evidence to better serve your purpose in writing the essay?

THE ISSUE ISN'T SEX, IT'S VIOLENCE

Caryl Rivers

Novelist and professor of journalism, Caryl Rivers was born in 1937. After completing her undergraduate program at Trinity College in Washington, D.C., and earning a master's degree from Columbia University in New York City, she launched her career as a news writer. Her stories have appeared in Saturday Review, New York Times Magazine, McCall's, *and* Boston Magazine. *Since 1966 she has taught journalism at Boston University. Rivers's essay was first published in the* Boston Globe *on September 15, 1985.*

Preparing to Read

From Rivers's title we know that she will be writing about violence. The growing incidence of violence in America, especially against women, disturbs us all, but what are we doing about it? In her thesis Rivers identifies the problem and calls for change: "But violence against women is greeted by silence. It shouldn't be." She then proceeds to develop her thesis by showing how we are bombarded in television, radio, films, magazines, recordings, and videos by images of explicit violence against women coupled with the absence of widespread public outrage. What can be done to address this major social problem of violence against women in this country?

A fter a grisly series of murders in California, possibly inspired by the lyrics of a rock song, we are hearing a familiar chorus: Don't blame rock and roll. Kids will be kids. They love to rebel, and the more shocking the stuff, the better they like it.

1

2   There's some truth in this, of course. I loved to watch Elvis shake his torso when I was a teen-ager, and it was even more fun when Ed Sullivan wouldn't let the cameras show him below the waist. I snickered at the forbidden "Rock with Me, Annie" lyrics by a black Rhythm and Blues group, which were deliciously naughty. But I am sorry, rock fans, that is not the same thing as hearing lyrics about how a man is going to force a woman to perform oral sex on him at gunpoint in a little number called "Eat Me Alive." It is not in the same league with a song about the delights of slipping into a woman's room while she is sleeping and murdering her, the theme of an AC/DC ballad that allegedly inspired the California slayer.

3   Make no mistake, it is not sex we are talking about here, but violence. Violence against women. Most rock songs are not violent—they are funky, sexy, rebellious, and sometimes witty. Please do not mistake me for a Mrs. Grundy. If Prince wants to leap about wearing only a purple jock strap, fine. Let Mick Jagger unzip his fly as he gyrates, if he wants to. But when either one of them starts garroting, beating, or sodomizing a woman in their number, that is another story.

4   I always find myself annoyed when "intellectual" men dismiss violence against women with a yawn, as if it were beneath their dignity to notice. I wonder if the reaction would be the same if the violence were directed against someone other than women. How many people would yawn and say, "Oh, kids will be kids," if a rock group did a nifty little number called "Lynchin," in which stringing up and stomping on black people were set to music? Who would chuckle and say, "Oh, just a little adolescent rebellion" if a group of rockers went on MTV dressed as Nazis, desecrating synagogues and beating up Jews to the beat of twanging guitars?

5   I'll tell you what would happen. Prestigious dailies would thunder on editorial pages; senators would fall over each other to get denunciations into the Congressional Record. The president would appoint a commission to clean up the music business.

6   But violence against women is greeted by silence. It shouldn't be.

7   This does not mean censorship, or book (or record) burning. In a society that protects free expression, we understand a lot

of stuff will float up out of the sewer. Usually, we recognize the ugly stuff that advocates violence against any group as the garbage it is, and we consider its purveyors as moral lepers. We hold our nose and tolerate it, but we speak out against the values it proffers.

But images of violence against women are not staying on the fringes of society. No longer are they found only in tattered, paper-covered books or in movie houses where winos snooze and the scent of urine fills the air. They are entering the mainstream at a rapid rate. This is happening at a time when the media, more and more, set the agenda for the public debate. It is a powerful legitimizing force—especially television. Many people regard what they see on TV as the truth; Walter Cronkite once topped a poll as the most trusted man in America.

Now, with the advent of rock videos and all-music channels, rock music has grabbed a big chunk of legitimacy. American teen-agers have instant access, in their living rooms, to the messages of rock, on the same vehicle that brought them Sesame Street. Who can blame them if they believe that the images they see are accurate reflections of adult reality, approved by adults? After all, Big Bird used to give them lessons on the same little box. Adults, by their silence, sanction the images. Do we really want our kids to think that rape and violence are what sexuality is all about?

This is not a trivial issue. Violence against women is a major social problem, one that's more than a cerebral issue to me. I teach at Boston University, and one of my most promising young journalism students was raped and murdered. Two others told me of being raped. Recently, one female student was assaulted and beaten so badly she had $5,000 worth of medical bills and permanent damage to her back and eyes.

It's nearly impossible, of course, to make a cause-and-effect link between lyrics and images and acts of violence. But images have a tremendous power to create an atmosphere in which violence against certain people is sanctioned. Nazi propagandists knew that full well when they portrayed Jews as ugly, greedy, and powerful.

The outcry over violence against women, particularly in a sexual context, is being legitimized in two ways: by the increasing movement of these images into the mainstream of the media in TV, films, magazines, albums, videos, and by the silence about it.

13   Violence, of course, is rampant in the media. But it is usually set in some kind of moral context. It's usually only the bad guys who commit violent acts against the innocent. When the good guys get violent, it's against those who deserve it. Dirty Harry blows away the scum, he doesn't walk up to a toddler and say, "Make my day." The A Team does not shoot up suburban shopping malls.

14   But in some rock songs, it's the "heroes" who commit the acts. The people we are programmed to identify with are the ones being violent, with women on the receiving end. In a society where rape and assaults on women are endemic, this is no small problem, with millions of young boys watching on their TV screens and listening on their Walkmans.

15   I think something needs to be done. I'd like to see people in the industry respond to the problem. I'd love to see some women rock stars speak out against violence against women. I would like to see disc jockeys refuse air play to records and videos that contain such violence. At the very least, I want to see the end of the silence. I want journalists and parents and critics and performing artists to keep this issue alive in the public forum. I don't want people who are concerned about this issue labeled as bluenoses and bookburners and ignored.

16   And I wish it wasn't always just women who were speaking out. Men have as large a stake in the quality of our civilization as women do in the long run. Violence is a contagion that infects at random. Let's hear something, please, from the men.

Vocabulary

To get the most out of reading this essay, you should have a working understanding of the words listed on the next page. Following each word is a parenthetical reference, indicating the paragraph in which the word is used, as well as a definition for the word. Go back and look at the sentence in which the word appears, and see how the definition applies. To help you make this word a part of your active vocabulary, write a sentence of your own using the word in the space provided.

grisly (1):   gruesome, horrible

_____

_____

allegedly (2):   supposedly

_____

_____

desecrating (4):   abusing or destroying something sacred

_____

_____

prestigious (5):   highly respected

_____

_____

advocates (7):   recommends, supports

_____

_____

sanction (9):   authorize, approve

_____

_____

cerebral (10):   intellectual, theoretical

_____

_____

rampant (13):   widespread

_____

_____

endemic (14):   prevalent, common in society

_____

_____

forum (15):   outlet like a magazine or radio show for discussing questions of public interest

---

Understanding the Essay

1. Rivers's thesis is stated in paragraph 6. What kinds of evidence does she use to support her thesis?

2. What was Rivers's purpose in writing this essay? Explain.

3. Why is Rivers particularly worried about teenagers brought up on "Sesame Street"? Do you find her concern justified or not?

4. Rivers states, "Violence against women is a major social problem, one that's more than a cerebral issue to me." How does she show how violence has touched her own life? What do these personal experiences add to her argument?

5. If Rivers is not for "censorship, or book (or record) burning," what is she arguing for?

6. What specific suggestions for action does Rivers make? Did you find her appeal persuasive? Why or why not?

Writing Activities

1. Rivers admits "it's nearly impossible, of course, to make a cause-and-effect link between lyrics and images and acts of violence." Do you think such a link exists? What kinds of evidence would you need to establish such a link?

2. According to Rivers, "violence against women is greeted by silence." Has the situation changed since she wrote this essay in 1985? What still needs to be done? Compose two or three possible thesis statements for an essay based on your class discussion.

3. For you, what are the limits on free speech, or does anything go? How far are you willing to go to defend your own First Amendment rights? State your position on this issue in a single sentence. What kinds of examples would you need to support your position statement?

DEBATING MORAL QUESTIONS

Vincent Ryan Ruggiero

Born in 1934 in Queens, New York, Vincent Ryan Ruggiero earned his B.A. at Siena College and his master's degree at the College of St. Rose (Albany). He has written more than a dozen books on rhetoric, morality, language, and the arts of thinking and writing. Ruggiero is a professor emeritus of State University of New York at Delhi. He lives in Florida, giving seminars in business and education, and continues to write. Of the following piece he says, "Contrary to a current popular notion, moral judgment is proper, and it's best made by applying creative and critical thinking."

Preparing to Read

"Debating Moral Questions" sounds like a huge topic, but the debate Ruggiero primarily addresses in his essay is "whether it is proper to debate moral issues." Ruggiero argues in his thesis that "it is impossible to avoid making value judgments" based on morality, both within a culture and between different cultures. The author uses numerous historical and contemporary examples to support his argument, including stories of heroism, parental negligence, and human rights abuses against women. Do you think it is "proper to debate moral issues"? What kinds of value judgments do you make in your day-to-day life?

1   Nowhere is modern thinking more muddled than over the question of whether it is proper to debate moral issues. Many argue it is not, saying it is wrong to make "value judgments." This view is shallow. If such judgments were wrong, then ethics, philosophy, and theology would be unacceptable in

a college curriculum—an idea that is obviously silly. As the following cases illustrate, it is impossible to avoid making value judgments.

Raoul Wallenberg was a young Swedish aristocrat. In 1944   2
he left the safety of his country and entered Budapest. Over the next year he outwitted the Nazis and saved as many as 100,000 Jews (he was not himself Jewish) from the death camps. In 1945 he was arrested by the Russians, charged with spying, and imprisoned in a Russian labor camp. He may still be alive there.[1] Now, if we regard him as a hero—as there is excellent reason to do—we are making a value judgment. Yet if we regard him neutrally, as no different from anyone else, we are also making a value judgment. We are judging him to be neither hero nor villain, but average.

Consider another case. In late 1981 a 20-year-old mother left   3
her three infant sons unattended in a garbage-strewn tenement in New York City. Police found them there, starving, the youngest child lodged between a mattress and a wall, covered with flies and cockroaches, the eldest playing on the second-floor window ledge. The police judged the mother negligent, and the court agreed. Was it wrong for them to judge? And if we refuse to judge, won't that refusal itself be a judgment in the mother's favor?

No matter how difficult it may be to judge such moral issues,   4
we *must* judge them. Value judgment is the basis not only of our social code, but of our legal system. The quality of our laws is directly affected by the quality of our moral judgments. A society that judges blacks inferior is not likely to accord blacks equal treatment. A society that believes a woman's place is in the home is not likely to guarantee women equal employment opportunity.

Other people accept value judgments as long as they are   5
made *within* a culture, and not about other cultures. Right and wrong, they believe, vary from one culture to another. It is true that an act frowned upon in one culture may be tolerated in another, but the degree of difference has often been grossly exaggerated. When we first encounter an unfamiliar moral view, we

---

[1]In October 1981, President Reagan and the United States Congress granted Raoul Wallenberg honorary U.S. citizenship.

are inclined to focus on the difference so much that we miss the similarity.

6　For example, in medieval Europe animals were tried for crimes and often formally executed. In fact, cockroaches and other bugs were sometimes excommunicated from the church. Sounds absurd, doesn't it? But when we penetrate beneath the absurdity, we realize that the basic view—that some actions are reprehensible and ought to be punished—is not so strange. The core idea that a person bitten by, say, a dog, has been wronged and requires justice is very much the same. The only difference is our rejection of the idea that animals are responsible for their behavior.

7　Is it legitimate, then, for us to pass judgment on the moral standards of another culture? Yes, if we do so thoughtfully, and not just conclude that whatever differs from our view is necessarily wrong. We can judge, for example, a culture that treats women as property, or places less value on their lives than on the lives of men. Moreover, we can say a society is acting immorally by denying women their human rights. Consider the following cases.

8　In nineteenth-century Rio de Janeiro, Brazil, a theatrical producer shot and killed his wife because she insisted on taking a walk in the botanical gardens against his wishes. He was formally charged with her murder, but the judge dismissed the charge. The producer was carried through the streets in triumph. The moral perspective of his culture condoned the taking of a woman's life if she disobeyed her husband, even in a relatively small matter. A century later that perspective had changed little. In the same city, in 1976, a wealthy playboy, angry at his lover for flirting with others, fired four shots into her face at point-blank range, killing her. He was given a two-year suspended sentence in light of the fact that he had been "defending his honor."

9　Surely it is irresponsible for us to withhold judgment on the morality of these cases merely because they occurred in a different culture. It is obvious that in both cases the men's response, murder, was out of all proportion to the women's "offenses," and therefore demonstrated a wanton disregard for the women's human rights. Their response is thus properly judged immoral. And this judgment implies another—that the culture condoning such behavior is guilty of moral insensitivity.

Vocabulary

To get the most out of reading this essay, you should have a working understanding of the words listed below. Following each word is a parenthetical reference, indicating the paragraph in which the word is used, as well as a definition for the word. Go back and look at the sentence in which the word appears, and see how the definition applies. To help you make this word a part of your active vocabulary, write a sentence of your own in the space provided.

judgments (1):   opinions, estimations, notions, conclusions

_____

_____

ethics (1):   branch of philosophy dealing with values relating to human conduct

_____

_____

theology (1):   study of God, divine things, or religious truth

_____

_____

neutrally (2):   without positive or negative associations or judgments

_____

_____

negligent (3):   guilty of neglecting a duty

_____

_____

tolerated (5):   allowed without prohibition or hindrance; permitted

_____

_____

excommunicated (6): cut off from communion or membership, as of a church

_____

_____

reprehensible (6): deserving of reproof; blameworthy

_____

_____

legitimate (7): in accordance with established rules, principles, or standards

_____

_____

condoned (8): pardoned, forgave, or overlooked (something illegal or objectionable)

_____

_____

wanton (9): malicious and unjustifiable

_____

_____

Understanding the Essay

1. Where in paragraph 1 is Ruggiero's thesis located? Why did he choose to place it there?
2. What examples does Ruggiero use to support his claim that "it is impossible to avoid making value judgments"? Do they effectively illustrate the author's point?
3. Ruggiero states, "No matter how difficult it may be to judge such moral issues, we _must_ judge them." What does he mean?
4. What point does the example of medieval punishment of animals support? How does this relate to Ruggiero's thesis?

5. What moral judgments about Brazilian culture is Ruggiero making by using the examples in paragraph 8? Do you agree?
6. How does paragraph 9 relate to paragraph 1?

Writing Activities

1. Which of the following thesis statements might be an adequate substitute for Ruggiero's: (1) "It is probably not possible to avoid making value judgments," (2) "It is one's right and obligation to make value judgments," or (3) "Even when trying *not* to make a value judgment, we are still judging." How might the less effective statements be changed into better ones?
2. Write the thesis statement for an essay that takes the opposite position about debating moral issues. Is there a difference between value judgments being right or wrong, and being unavoidable? What kinds of evidence would you use to support your thesis? Could you turn any of Ruggiero's examples to your own advantage?

15

ORGANIZATION

In an essay, ideas and information cannot be presented all at once; they have to be arranged in some order. That order is the essay's organization.

The pattern of organization in an essay should be suited to the writer's subject and purpose. For example, if you are writing about your experience working in a fast-food restaurant, and your purpose is to tell about the activities of a typical day, you might present those activities in chronological order. If, on the other hand, you wish to argue that working in a bank is an ideal summer job, you might proceed from the least rewarding to the most rewarding aspect of this job; this is called "climactic" order.

Some often-used patterns of organization are time order, space order, and logical order. Time order, or chronological order, is used to present events as they occurred. A personal narrative, a report of a campus incident, or an account of a historical event can be most naturally and easily related in chronological order. The description of a process, such as the refinishing of a table, the building of a stone wall, or the way to serve a tennis ball, almost always calls for a chronological organization. Of course, the order of events can sometimes be rearranged for special effect. For example, an account of an auto accident may begin with the collision itself and then go back in time to tell about the events leading up to it. Two essays that are models of chronological order are Zora Neale Hurston's "How It Feels to Be Colored Me" (pp. 57–63) and Annie Dillard's "Terror at Tinker Creek" (pp. 331–334).

Space order is used when describing a person, place, or thing. This organizational pattern begins at a particular point and moves in some direction, such as left to right, top to bottom, east to west, outside to inside, front to back, near to far, around, or over. In describing a house, for example, a writer could move from top to bottom, from outside to inside, or in a circle around the outside. Eudora Welty's "Miss Duling" (pp. 112–118) is an essay that uses space as an organizing principle.

Logical order can take many forms depending on the writer's purpose. These include: general to specific, most familiar to least familiar, and smallest to biggest. Perhaps the most common type of logical order is order of importance. Notice how the writer uses this order in the following paragraph:

> The Egyptians have taught us many things. They were excellent farmers. They knew all about irrigation. They built temples which were afterwards copied by the Greeks and which served as the earliest models for the churches in which we worship nowadays. They invented a calendar which proved such a useful instrument for the purpose of measuring time that it has survived with a few changes until today. But most important of all, the Egyptians learned how to preserve speech for the benefit of future generations. They invented the art of writing.

By organizing the material according to the order of increasing importance, the writer places special emphasis on the final sentence. In writing a descriptive essay you can move from the least striking to the most striking detail, so as to keep your reader interested and involved in the description. In an explanatory essay you can start with the point that readers will find least difficult to understand and move on to the most difficult; that's how teachers organize many courses. Or, in writing an argumentative essay, you can move from your least controversial point to the most controversial, preparing your reader gradually to accept your argument. Essays organized according to a principle of logical order include David and Barbara Bjorklund's "The Heroes We Know" (pp. 94–97), Howard Solomon, Jr.'s "Best Friends" (pp. 159–163), and Franklin E. Zimring's "Confessions of an Ex-Smoker" (pp. 282–287).

THE BOX MAN

Barbara Lazear Ascher

Barbara Lazear Ascher, who received her B.A. from Bennington College in 1968 and her law degree from Cardozo School of Law in New York City in 1979, is a freelance essayist, short story writer, and contributor to Ms., Arts Revue, *the* New York Times, *the* Nation, *and the* Village Voice. *Her collected works appear in* Playing after Dark *and* The Habit of Loving. *The following selection is set in Ascher's current home, New York City.*

Preparing to Read

Ascher uses the example of a solitary character—"The Box Man"—and the profiles of two other lonely souls to make a point about how life "is a solo voyage." As you read, notice how Ascher describes the Box Man and his routine, reminisces about her own childhood dreams, introduces two more characters, and then speculates on or struggles with her adult ideas about solitude. How does she move from one segment to the next? What does she seem to want to accomplish by using this format? What is the overall effect she creates?

1   The Box Man was at it again. It was his lucky night.

2   The first stroke of good fortune occurred as darkness fell and the night watchman at 220 East Forty-fifth Street neglected to close the door as he slipped out for a cup of coffee. I saw them before the Box Man did. Just inside the entrance, cardboard cartons, clean and with their top flaps intact. With the silent fervor of a mute at a horse race, I willed him toward them.

3   It was slow going. His collar was pulled so high that he appeared headless as he shuffled across the street like a man who must feel Earth with his toes to know that he walks there.

Standing unself-consciously in the white glare of an over-   4
head light, he began to sort through the boxes, picking them up,
one by one, inspecting tops, insides, flaps. Three were tossed
aside. They looked perfectly good to me, but then, who knows
what the Box Man knows? When he found the one that suited his
purpose, he dragged it up the block and dropped it in a doorway.

Then, as if dogged by luck, he set out again and discovered,   5
behind the sign at the parking garage, a plastic Dellwood box,
strong and clean, once used to deliver milk. Back in the doorway the grand design was revealed as he pushed the Dellwood
box against the door and set its cardboard cousin two feet in
front—the usual distance between coffee table and couch. Six
full shopping bags were distributed evenly on either side.

He eased himself with slow care onto the stronger box,   6
reached into one of the bags, pulled out a *Daily News,* and
snapped it open against his cardboard table. All done with the
ease of IRT Express passengers whose white-tipped, fair-haired
fingers reach into attaché cases as if radar-directed to the *Wall
Street Journal.* They know how to fold it. They know how to stare
at the print, not at the girl who stares at them.

That's just what the Box Man did, except that he touched his   7
tongue to his fingers before turning each page, something grandmothers do.

One could live like this. Gathering boxes to organize a   8
life. Wandering through the night collecting comforts to fill
a doorway.

When I was a child, my favorite book was *The Boxcar Chil-*   9
dren. If I remember correctly, the young protagonists were orphaned, and rather than live with cruel relatives, they ran away
to the woods to live life on their own terms. An abandoned boxcar
was turned into a home, a bubbling brook became an icebox. Wild
berries provided abundant desserts and days were spent in the
happy, adultless pursuit of joy. The children never worried where
the next meal would come from or what February's chill might
bring. They had unquestioning faith that berries would ripen and
streams run cold and clear. And unlike Thoreau, whose deliberate
living was self-conscious and purposeful, theirs had the ease of
children at play.

Even now, when life seems complicated and reason slips, I   10
long to live like a Boxcar Child, to have enough open space and
freedom of movement to arrange my surroundings according to

what I find. To turn streams into iceboxes. To be ingenious with simple things. To let the imagination hold sway.

11   Who is to say that the Box Man does not feel as Thoreau did in his doorway, not " . . . crowded or confined in the least," with "pasture enough for . . . imagination"? Who is to say that his dawns don't bring back heroic ages? That he doesn't imagine a goddess trailing her garments across his blistered legs?

12   His is a life of the mind, such as it is, and voices only he can hear. Although it would appear to be a life of misery, judging from the bandages and chill of night, it is of his choosing. He will ignore you if you offer an alternative. Last winter, Mayor Koch tried, coaxing him with promises and the persuasive tones reserved for rabid dogs. The Box Man backed away, keeping a car and paranoia between them.

13   He is not to be confused with the lonely ones. You'll find them everywhere. The lady who comes into our local coffee shop each evening at five-thirty, orders a bowl of soup and extra Saltines. She drags it out as long as possible, breaking the crackers into smaller and smaller pieces, first in halves and then halves of halves and so on until the last pieces burst into salty splinters and fall from dry fingers onto the soup's shimmering surface. By 6 P.M., it's all over. What will she do with the rest of the night?

14   You can tell by the vacancy of expression that no memories linger there. She does not wear a gold charm bracelet with silhouettes of boys and girls bearing grandchildren's birthdates and a chip of the appropriate birthstone. When she opens her black purse to pay, there is only a crumpled Kleenex and a wallet inside, no photographs spill onto her lap. Her children, if there are any, live far away and prefer not to visit. If she worked as a secretary for forty years in a downtown office, she was given a retirement party, a cake, a reproduction of an antique perfume atomizer and sent on her way. Old colleagues—those who traded knitting patterns and brownie recipes over the water cooler, who discussed the weather, health, and office scandal while applying lipstick and blush before the ladies' room mirror—they are lost to time and the new young employees who take their places in the typing pool.

15   Each year she gets a Christmas card from her ex-boss. The envelope is canceled in the office mailroom and addressed by

memory typewriter. Within is a family in black and white against a wooded Connecticut landscape. The boss, his wife, who wears her hair in a gray page boy, the three blond daughters, two with tall husbands and an occasional additional grandchild. All assembled before a worn stone wall.

Does she watch game shows? Talk to a parakeet, feed him   16
cuttlebone, and call him Pete? When she rides the buses on her Senior Citizen pass, does she go anywhere or wait for something to happen? Does she have a niece like the one in Cynthia Ozick's story "Rosa," who sends enough money to keep her aunt at a distance?

There's a lady across the way whose lights and television stay   17
on all night. A crystal chandelier in the dining room and matching Chinese lamps on Regency end tables in the living room. She has six cats, some Siamese, others Angora and Abyssinian. She pets them and waters her plethora of plants—African violets, a ficus tree, a palm, and geraniums in season. Not necessarily a lonely life except that 3 A.M. lights and television seem to proclaim it so.

The Box Man welcomes the night, opens to it like a lover. He   18
moves in darkness and prefers it that way. He's not waiting for the phone to ring or an engraved invitation to arrive in the mail. Not for him a P.O. number. Not for him the overcrowded jollity of office parties, the hot anticipation of a singles' bar. Not even for him a holiday handout. People have tried and he shuffled away.

The Box Man knows that loneliness chosen loses it sting and   19
claims no victims. He declares what we all know in the secret passages of our own nights, that although we long for perfect harmony, communion, and blending with another soul, that this is a solo voyage.

The first half of our lives is spent stubbornly denying it. As   20
children we acquire language to make ourselves understood and soon learn from the blank stares in response to our babblings that even these, our saviors, our parents, are strangers. In adolescence when we replay earlier dramas with peers in the place of parents, we begin the quest for the best friend, that person who will receive all thoughts as if they were her own. Later we assert that true love will find the way. True love finds many ways, but no escape from exile. The shores are littered

with us, Annas and Ophelias, Emmas and Juliets, all outcasts from the dream of perfect understanding. We might as well draw the night around us and find solace there and a friend in our own voice.

21   One could do worse than be a collector of boxes.

Vocabulary

To get the most out of reading this essay, you should have a working understanding of the words listed below. Following each word is a parenthetical reference, indicating the paragraph in which the word is used, as well as a definition for the word. Go back and look at the sentence in which the word appears, and see how the definition applies. To help you make this word a part of your active vocabulary, write a sentence of your own in the space provided.

fervor (2):   steady intensity of feeling or expression

_____

_____

unself-consciously (4):   without consciousness of one's own acts or state of being

_____

_____

attaché cases (6):   small, thin suitcases for carrying business papers

_____

_____

protagonists (9):   ones who take the leading part in a drama, novel, or story

_____

_____

ingenious (10): marked by originality, resourcefulness, and cleverness in conception or execution

_____

_____

paranoia (12): excessive suspiciousness and distrust of others

_____

_____

cuttlebone (16): shell of cuttlefishes used for supplying cage birds with lime and salts

_____

_____

plethora (17): excess; superfluity

_____

_____

communion (19): sharing

_____

_____

exile (20): expulsion or separation from one's country or home

_____

_____

solace (20): source of relief or consolation

_____

_____

Understanding the Essay

1. Where does Ascher state her thesis? How do the opening paragraphs lead up to the main idea?

2. What point is Ascher making when she mentions *The Box-car Children?* How does it relate to the sections that precede and follow it?

3. When Ascher writes that the Box Man "is not to be confused with the lonely ones," what does she mean? How do you know? Why does she include examples of "the lonely ones"?

4. What does Ascher claim the Box Man "knows"? In what ways has she already communicated this to the reader?

5. According to Ascher, the "first half of our lives is spent stubbornly denying" what? What claims does she make to support her argument in paragraph 20? Do you agree with her?

6. Looking back over the essay, you can see that Ascher's organization is very complex. What kind or kinds of order does she use to make her points? Is this strategy effective? Explain.

7. For whom is Ascher writing this essay? Why? Does the organization of her essay help her accomplish her purpose?

Writing Activities

1. One important organizational skill is identifying and grouping items into categories. Put the following items into four separate lists, titled by category: peach, desk, basketball, eggplant, zucchini, soccer, chess, apple, chair, carrot, orange, cauliflower, sofa, banana, lettuce, table.

2. In the following two paragraphs, the authors are using the strategy of comparison and contrast to organize their points. John Fischer writes:

> The Ukrainians are the Texans of Russia. They believe they can fight, drink, ride, sing, and make love better than anybody else in the world, and if pressed will admit it. Their country, too, was a borderland—that's what "U-kraine" means—and like Texas it was originally settled by outlaws, horse thieves, land-hungry farmers, and people who hadn't made a go of it somewhere else. Some of these hard cases banded together, long ago, to raise hell and livestock. They called themselves Cossacks, and they would

have felt right at home in any Western movie. Even today the Ukrainians cherish a wistful tradition of horsemanship, although most of them would feel as uncomfortable in a saddle as any Dallas banker. They still like to wear knee-high boots and big, furry hats, made of gray or black Persian lamb, which are the local equivalent of the Stetson.

Whereas Otto Friedrich writes:

> There is an essential difference between a news story, as understood by a newspaperman or a wire-service writer, and a newsmagazine story. The chief purpose of the conventional news story is to tell what happened. It starts with the most important information and continues into increasingly inconsequential details, not only because the reader may not read beyond the first paragraph, but because an editor working on galley proofs a few minutes before press time likes to be able to cut freely from the end of the story.
>
> A newsmagazine is very different. It is written to be read consecutively from beginning to end, and each of its stories is designed, following the critical theories of Edgar Allan Poe, to create one emotional effect. The news, what happened that week, may be told in the beginning, the middle, or the end; for the purpose is not to throw information at the reader but to seduce him into reading the whole story, and into accepting the dramatic (and often political) point being made.

What is Fischer comparing? How does he structure his comparison within that one paragraph? (You may want to do a brief outline to help you determine the pattern.) What is Friedrich comparing? How does he structure his comparison using two paragraphs? (Again, try an outline.) In what ways are the Fischer and Friedrich pieces similar? How are they different?

CHINA'S ANTIDRUG TRADITION AND CURRENT STRUGGLE

Ling Qing

This piece first appeared in the journal China Today. *In the essay, Ling Qing recalls China's nineteenth-century antidrug movement, its success during the 1950s, and the recent recurrence of drug use in China. Ling Qing contends that to make progress in the contemporary effort to halt the proliferation of drugs in China, "it is necessary for people all over the world to make a concerted effort."*

Preparing to Read

Do you know the history of China's struggle against drug abuse? Opening with an account of Lin Zexu's patriotic anti-opium demonstration, Ling Qing moves on to argue that "narcotics are still polluting the world," and concludes with the history of China's struggle with—and current role in—controlling the international drug trade. As you read, pay close attention to how Ling Qing shifts from one aspect of his argument to the next. How logical is his line of reasoning?

1   China's 1839 banning of opium smoking and the opium trade, led by the Qing court official Lin Zexu . . . moved her onto the world stage in the struggle against drugs. Today, 150 years later, worldwide efforts have brought home the fact that drug abuse seriously imperils human life. To eradicate its harm, it is necessary for people all over the world to make a concerted effort.

2   Using the opium trade, Britain drained China of her silver. In less than a year—July 1837 to June 1838—Britain dumped opium worth 3.4 million pounds into China, seriously harming

the Chinese people. Lin was keenly aware that opium meant no end of trouble for China. In his youth he had begun to investigate its pernicious influence. Later, as an official in Jiangsu Province, he had been outspoken against opium and had submitted a memorial to the throne on its harm. On March 10, 1839, he was sent as imperial commissioner to Guangzhou, on the southern coast, to deal with the problem. On June 3 he ordered the public burning of opium, and on that day 170 chests were burned. The burning continued for 24 days, ending on May 15 and disposing of a total of 1.18 million kilograms of opium, all that had been confiscated or surrendered so far except for eight chests kept for display. This first mighty act against drugs sparked a great patriotic movement of the Chinese people.

When Britain replied with cannon, Lin mobilized the people   3
to fight back. Because a faction in the Qing Dynasty government blamed him for the trouble and wanted to capitulate, Lin suffered all kinds of slanders and retaliation. Even after he was dismissed from office, he kept pointing out to the court the harm being done. He fully deserves to be honored as a hero in China's antiopium movement and a pioneer in the international antidrug movement.

Today, unfortunately, narcotics are still polluting the world.   4
The situation is grim. First, there has been a sharp growth in drug output in recent years. The 1987 production of cocaine in the region from the Andes Mountains to the Amazon River Valley, one of the three major producing areas, is estimated at 162,000 to 204,000 tons, and this amount increased in 1988 and 1989.

Second, traffic in narcotics spawns illegal international orga-   5
nizations and cliques that will stop at nothing, even murder. More and more innocent people are dying under the guns of drug-traffic cliques.

Third, the number of drug addicts has increased sharply.   6
United Nations data reveal hundreds of millions in the West scrambling for marijuana, morphine, heroin and other drugs. A recent United States Department of Justice investigation found that 72 million people, or 37 percent of people in the US over age 12, had used drugs at least once. Drug addiction is also growing rapidly in some developing countries.

Fourth, the number of drug-related deaths is increasing. In   7
the US it rose from 604 in 1984 to 1,696 in 1988.

8   Opium first came to China from Arabia and Turkey in the late seventh and early eighth centuries, its use confined to medicinal purposes. Starting from the 1620s it was taken orally, by the end of the 18th century, smoking of opium was practiced in all parts of the country. In 1949, on the eve of liberation, 20 million Chinese were opium users and opium poppies grew on a million hectares. In 1949, soon after the founding of the People's Republic, the government embarked on a resolute antidrug compaign, and by the end of 1950 drug abuse was wiped out. In the 30 years that followed, China could proudly claim to be one of the world's few drug-free countries.

9   In recent years, however, along with the open policies, drugs have come back. Some international cliques have colluded with Chinese lawbreakers to transport narcotics across China's borders. At the same time, drug abuse has increased in these provinces and spread farther inland. In 1987 Chinese police and drug details cracked 56 narcotics-traffic cases and seized 137 kg of opium and 43 kg of heroin. In 1989 these numbers rose to 269 kg of opium and 488 kg of heroin. A total of 749 traffickers were arrested, involving 547 cases. These figures show that the menace is growing.

10   In the four months up through last March, in the biggest case of international drug smuggling in the history of new China, 51 persons, 221 kg of heroin and 1.6 million yuan RMB as well as guns and vehicles were seized. Opium was burned at the June 26 meeting held in Yunnan to observe the 130th anniversary of the Opium War and the third annual International Drug Prohibition Day. This was an act of real significance, for China is again faced with an arduous and complicated struggle against drug abuse.

11   China's own history and the present international antidrug struggle show that the spread of drug trafficking for enormous profits is a chronic malady of capitalism. The 19th-century opium trade with China was one of the sources for primitive accumulation of capital in the United Kingdom. Today the US and Western Europe are the main markets for narcotics. With a value of over US $500 billion yearly, narcotics rank second only to the munitions industry in value of traffic, according to a survey issued last February by the UN. In Western Europe drug use and smuggling work hand in hand with prostitution and violence to produce a hotbed of crime. Now this virus has infected many third-world countries.

12   Why doesn't drug prohibition work? I believe the main

reason is collusion between officials and traffickers. Money smoothes the way for the passage of narcotics, whether in the producing, trafficking or consuming countries, thus poisoning the whole world. The next 10 years will see decisive efforts on the part of the United Nations concerning the drug problem. Many countries, including China, have already joined the urgent call for joint efforts to fight and rid the world of this scourge.

Reviewing the past helps one understand the present. Today's struggle can draw inspiration from Lin Zexu's opium ban. For instance, after he reached Guangzhou and saw the extent of the smuggling, his plan quickly turned from prohibiting opium addiction to cutting off opium at the source. Today's narcotics ban is a struggle that brooks no delay. Since 1983 a series of laws have been passed in China that stipulate the standards for conviction and sentencing of drug producers, traffickers and transporters, and also penalties for drug abusers, small producers of the opium poppy and users of narcotics.   13

In March 1983 the Chinese government established a committee, consisting of representatives of the public health, foreign affairs and public security ministries and the customs office, to coordinate drug control. It has been a force in promoting the struggle against narcotics. The government has also set up special antinarcotics units in some key regions.   14

Recognizing the common harm to mankind, China hopes to make a greater contribution to the world struggle against drugs. She is now strengthening cooperation with the responsible organizations of the United Nations and taking the initiative in developing bilateral and multilateral cooperation with countries along her borders.   15

Vocabulary

To get the most out of reading this essay, you should have a working understanding of the words listed on the next page. Following each word is a parenthetical reference, indicating the paragraph in which the word is used, as well as a definition for the word. Go back and look at the sentence in which the word appears, and see how the definition applies. To help you make this word a part of your active vocabulary, write a sentence of your own using the word in the space provided.

imperils (1):   endangers

---

eradicate (1):   erase, put an end to

---

concerted (1):   concentrated, strong

---

pernicious (2):   destructive, malicious, evil

---

capitulate (3):   give in, surrender

---

slanders (3):   false statements that damage a person's reputation

---

retaliation (3):   act of revenge; repayment or counterattack

---

cliques (5):   small, exclusive groups of people

---

malady (11):   sickness, illness

munitions (11):   military weapons, equipment

_____

_____

collusion (12):   secret, deceitful agreement

_____

_____

scourge (12):   cause of wide-spread affliction

_____

_____

brooks no delay (13):   demands immediate action

_____

_____

stipulate (13):   demand or insist upon as part of an agreement

_____

_____

bilateral (15):   two-sided

_____

_____

multilateral (15):   many-sided

_____

_____

Understanding the Essay

1. What is Ling Qing's thesis? For whom is he writing this essay?
2. Why is the story the author tells in the first three paragraphs so important? What does it illustrate?

3. What are the four main parts to Ling Qing's essay? How would you describe the role of each in supporting the author's overall purpose?

4. List the transitions Ling Qing uses to progress from each part to the next. Do his transitions work? Why or why not?

5. Ling Qing writes that "the spread of drug trafficking for enormous profits is a chronic malady of capitalism." What evidence does he employ to support this claim? Is it persuasive? Explain.

6. Why doesn't the essay end with paragraph 13? What is the purpose of the last two paragraphs? How do they relate to Ling Qing's thesis?

Writing Activities

1. Make an outline of the following paragraph:

> There are roughly three New Yorks. There is, first, the New York of the man or woman who was born here, who takes the city for granted and accepts its size and its turbulence as natural and inevitable. Second, there is the New York of the commuter—the city that is devoured by locusts each day and spat out each night. Third, there is the New York of the person who was born somewhere else and came to New York in quest of something. Of these three trembling cities the greatest is the last—the city of final destination, the city that is a goal. It is this third city that accounts for New York's highstrung disposition, its poetical deportment, its dedication to the arts, and its incomparable achievements. Commuters give the city its tidal restlessness; natives give it solidarity and continuity; but the settlers give it passion. And whether it is a farmer arriving from Italy to set up a small grocery store in a slum, or a young girl arriving from a small town in Mississippi to escape the indignity of being observed by her neighbors, or a boy arriving from the Corn Belt with a manuscript in his suitcase and a pain in his heart, it makes no difference; each embraces New York with the intense excitement of first love, each absorbs New York with the fresh eyes of an adventurer, each generates heat and light to dwarf the Consolidated Edison Company.
>
> —*E. B. White*

How would you describe the author's organizational strategy? If you rearranged the main headings of the outline, would the passage still make sense? How would it be different? How would it be the same? Try rewriting the passage to find out.

2. Choose one of the following pairs of items: capitalism and communism, mathematics and art, football and chess, politics and religion, love and war. Make two lists, one of the similarities and one of the differences between the things you choose. Then write the introductory paragraph to an essay based on your lists.

WHY MEN FEAR WOMEN'S TEAMS

Kate Rounds

"Why Men Fear Women's Teams," which first appeared in Ms. *magazine, reports on the failure of women's professional team sport leagues to survive in the United States, owing to a lack of financial support and media coverage. Rounds's argument centers on the idea that men feel threatened by strong, competitive women athletes and that the male-dominated sports market refuses to support the many efforts that have been made to promote women's professional leagues. Kate Rounds lives in Jersey City, New Jersey.*

Preparing to Read

Whether or not you yourself have ever played team sports, Rounds's essay about women's professional sports teams raises important questions about sexism, money in sports, prejudice, and the role of athletics in American society. As you read, try to locate Rounds's main idea and even anticipate where she might go with it. Also, evaluate her method. Is she using the most efficient and effective strategy to communicate her subject?

1   Picture this. You're flipping through the channels one night, and you land on a local network, let's say ABC. And there on the screen is a basketball game. The players are sinking three-pointers, slam-dunking, and doing the usual things basketball players do. They're high-fiving each other, patting one another on the butt, and then sauntering to the locker room to talk about long-term contracts.

2   Now imagine that the players aren't men. They're women, big sweaty ones, wearing uniforms and doing their version of

what guys thrive on—bonding. So far, this scene is a fantasy and will remain so until women's professional team sports get corporate sponsors, television exposure, arenas, fan support, and a critical mass of well-trained players.

While not enough fans are willing to watch women play   3
traditional team sports, they love to watch women slugging it out on roller-derby rinks and in mud-wrestling arenas. Currently popular is a bizarre television spectacle called *American Gladiators*, in which women stand on pastel pedestals, wearing Lycra tights and brandishing weapons that look like huge Q-Tips. The attraction obviously has something to do with the "uniforms." The importance of what women athletes wear can't be underestimated. Beach volleyball, which is played in the sand by bikini-clad women, rates network coverage while traditional court volleyball can't marshal any of the forces that would make a women's pro league succeed.

It took a while, but women were able to break through sexist   4
barriers in golf and tennis. Part of their success stemmed from the sports themselves—high-end individual sports that were born in the British Isles and flourished in country clubs across the U.S. The women wore skirts, makeup, and jewelry along with their wristbands and warm-up jackets. The corporate sponsors were hackers themselves, and the fans—even men—could identify with these women: a guy thought that if he hit the ball enough times against the barn door, he too could play like Martina. And women's purses were equaling men's. In fact, number-one-ranked Steffi Graf's prize money for 1989 was $1,963,905 and number-one-ranked Stefan Edberg's was $1,661,491.

By contrast, women's professional team sports have failed   5
spectacularly. Since the mid-seventies, every professional league—softball, basketball, and volleyball—has gone belly-up. In 1981, after a four-year struggle, the Women's Basketball League (WBL), backed by sports promoter Bill Byrne, folded. The league was drawing fans in a number of cities, but the sponsors weren't there. TV wasn't there, and nobody seemed to miss the spectacle of a few good women fighting for a basketball. Or a volleyball, for that matter. Despite the success of bikini volleyball, an organization called MLV (Major League Volleyball) bit the dust in March of 1989 after nearly three years of struggling for sponsorship, fan support, and television exposure. As with pro basketball, there was a man behind

women's professional volleyball, real estate investor Robert (Bat) Batinovich. Batinovich admits that, unlike court volleyball, beach volleyball has a lot of "visual T&A mixed into it."

6 What court volleyball does have, according to former MLV executive director Lindy Vivas, is strong women athletes. Vivas is assistant volleyball coach at San Jose State University. "The United States in general," she says, "has problems dealing with women athletes and strong, aggressive females. The perception is you have to be more aggressive in team sports than in golf and tennis, which aren't contact sports. Women athletes are looked at as masculine and get the stigma of being gay." One former women's basketball promoter, who insists on remaining anonymous, goes further. "You know what killed women's sports?" he says. "Lesbians. This cost us in women's basketball. But I know there are not as many lesbians now unless I'm really blinded. We discourage it, you know. We put it under wraps."

7 People in women's sports spend a lot of time dancing around the "L" word, and the word "image" pops up in a way it never does in men's sports. Men can spit tobacco juice, smoke, and even scratch their testicles on national television and get away with it. Bill Byrne, former WBL promoter, knows there isn't a whole lot women can get away with while they're beating each other out for a basketball. "In the old league," he says, "my partner, Mike Conners, from *Mannix*—his wife said, 'Let's do makeup on these kids.' And I knew that the uniforms could be more attractive. We could tailor them so the women don't look like they're dragging a pair of boxer shorts down the floor."

8 The response from the athletes to this boy talk is not always outrage. "Girls in women's basketball now are so pretty," says Nancy Lieberman-Cline. "They're image-conscious." The former Old Dominion star, who made headlines as Martina's trainer, played with the men's U.S. Basketball League, the Harlem Globe Trotters Tour (where she met husband Tim Cline), and with the Dallas Diamonds of the old WBL. "Everyone used to have short hair," she says. "Winning and playing was everything. I wouldn't think of using a curling iron. Now there are beautiful girls out there playing basketball." Lieberman-Cline says she doesn't mind making the concession. "It's all part of the process," she says. "You can't be defensive about everything."

9 Bill Byrne is so certain that women's professional basketball can work that he's organized a new league, the Women's Pro

Basketball League, Inc. (WPBL), set to open its first season shortly. Byrne talks fast and tough, and thinks things have changed for the better since 1981 when the old league went under. "Exposure is the bottom word," he says. "If you get plenty of TV exposure, you'll create household names, and you'll fill arenas. It takes the tube. But I'll get the tube this time because the game of TV has changed. You have cable now. You have to televise home games to show people a product."

There's no doubt that many athletes in the women's sports   10
establishment are leery of fast-talking guys who try to make a buck off women's pro sports, especially when the women themselves don't profit from those ventures. In the old league, finances were so shaky that some players claim they were never paid. "We weren't getting the gate receipts," says Lieberman-Cline. "They'd expect 2,000, get only 400, and then they'd have to decide to pay the arena or pay the girls, and the girls were the last choice. There was a lot of mismanagement in the WBL, though the intent was good." She also has her doubts about the new league: "There are not enough things in place to make it happen, not enough owners, arenas, TV coverage, or players. It's going to take more than optimism to make it work."

Given the track record of women's professional team sports   11
in this country, it's not surprising that the national pastime is faring no better. When Little League was opened to girls by court order in 1974, one might have thought that professional women's basketball could not be far behind. Baseball is a natural for women. It's not a contact sport, it doesn't require excessive size or strength—even little guys like Phil Rizzuto and Jose Lind can play it—and it's actually an individual sport masquerading as a team sport. Still, in recent years, no one's taken a serious stab at organizing a women's professional league.

In 1984, there was an attempt to field a women's minor-   12
league team. Though the Sun Sox had the support of baseball great Hank Aaron, it was denied admission to the Class A Florida State League. The team was the brainchild of a former Atlanta Braves vice president of marketing, Bob Hope. "A lot of the general managers and owners of big-league clubs were mortified," Hope says, "and some players said they wouldn't compete against women. It was male ego or something."

Or something, says softball hall-of-famer Donna Lopiano.   13
"When girls suffer harassment in Little League, that's not ex-

actly opening up opportunities for women," she says. "Girls don't have the access to coaching and weight training that boys have. Sports is a place where physiological advantages give men power, and they're afraid of losing it. Sports is the last great bastion of male chauvinism. In the last eight years, we've gone backward, not only on gender equity but on civil rights." Women of color still face barriers that European American women don't, particularly in the areas of coaching and refereeing. But being a woman athlete is sometimes a bond that transcends race. "We're all at a handicap," says Ruth Lawanson, an African American who played volleyball with MLV. "It doesn't matter whether you're Asian, Mexican, black, or white."

14   Historically, baseball and softball diamonds have not been very hospitable to black men and any women. Despite the fact that even men's softball is not a crowd pleaser, back in 1976, Billie Jean King and golfer Jane Blalock teamed up with ace amateur softball pitcher Joan Joyce to form the International Women's Professional Softball Association (IWPSA). Five years later, without sponsorship, money, or television, the league was history. Billie Jean King has her own special attachment to the team concept. As a girl, she wanted to be a baseball player, but her father gave her a tennis racket, knowing that there wasn't much of a future for a girl in baseball. The story is especially touching since Billie Jean's brother, Randy Moffitt, went on to become a pitcher with the San Francisco Giants. But even as a tennis player, Billie Jean clung to the team idea. She was the force behind World Team Tennis, which folded in 1978, and is currently the chief executive officer of Team Tennis, now entering its eleventh season with corporate sponsorship.

15   On the face of it, Team Tennis is a bizarre notion because it takes what is a bred-in-the-bones individual sport and tries to squeeze it into a team concept. It has the further handicap of not really being necessary when strong women's and men's professional tours are already in place. In the Team Tennis format, all players play doubles as well as singles. Billie Jean loves doubles, she says, because she enjoys "sharing the victory." What also distinguishes Team Tennis from the women's and men's pro tours is fan interaction. Fans are encouraged to behave as if watching a baseball or basketball game rather than constantly being told to shut up and sit down as they are at pro tour events like the U.S. Open. The sense of team spirit among the players—the fact that

they get to root for one another—is also attracting some big names. Both Martina Navratilova and Jimmy Connors have signed on to play Team Tennis during its tiny five-week season, which begins after Wimbledon and ends just before the U.S. Open.

But you have to go back almost 50 years to find a women's 16 professional sports team that was somewhat successful—though the conditions for that success were rather unusual. During World War II, when half the population was otherwise engaged, women were making their mark in the formerly male strongholds of welding, riveting—and baseball. The All-American Girls Professional Baseball League (AAGPBL) fielded such teams as the Lassies, the Belles, and the Chicks on the assumption that it was better to have "girls" playing than to let the national pastime languish. The league lasted a whopping 12 years after its inception in 1943.

The success of this sandlot venture, plagued as it was by the 17 simple-hearted sexism of the forties (the women went to charm school at night), must raise nagging doubts in the mind of the woman team player of the nineties. Can she triumph only in the absence of men? It may be true that she can triumph only in the absence of competition from the fiercely popular men's pro leagues, which gobble up sponsorship, U.S. network television, and the hearts and minds of male fanatics. The lack of male competition outside the United States may be partly responsible for the success of women's professional team sports in Europe, Japan, South America, and Australasia. Lieberman-Cline acknowledges that Europe provides a more hospitable climate for women's pro basketball. "Over there, they don't have as many options," she says. "We have Broadway plays, movies, you name it. We're overindulged with options."

Bruce Levy is a 230-pound bespectacled accountant who 18 escaped from the Arthur Andersen accounting firm 11 years ago to market women's basketball. "It's pretty simple," he says. "People overseas are more realistic and enlightened. Women's basketball is not viewed as a weak version of men's. If Americans could appreciate a less powerful, more scientific, team-oriented game, we'd be two thirds of the way toward having a league succeed."

Levy, who represents many women playing pro basketball 19 abroad, says 120 U.S. women are playing overseas and making up to $70,000 in a seven-month season. They include star players like Teresa Edwards, Katrina McClain, and Lynette Woodard. "A player like Teresa Weatherspoon, everybody recognizes her in Italy," he says. "No one in the U.S. knows her. If there were a pro league over here, I wouldn't be spending all day on the phone speaking bad Italian and making sure the women's beds are long enough. I'd just be negotiating contracts."

20   Levy claims that U.S. businesswomen aren't supporting women's team sports. "In Europe," he says, "the best-run and most publicized teams are run by women who own small businesses and put their money where their mouth is." Joy Burns, president of Sportswomen of Colorado, Inc., pleads no contest. "Businesswomen here are too conservative and don't stick their necks out," she says. MLV's Bat Batinovich, who says he's "disappointed" in U.S. businesswomen for not supporting women's team sports, figures an investor in MLV should have been willing to lose $200,000 a year for five years. Would Burns have done it? "If I'm making good financial investments, why should I?"

21   The prospects for women's professional team sports don't look bright. The reasons for the lack of support go beyond simple economics and enter the realm of deep-rooted sexual bias and homophobia. San Jose State's Lindy Vivas says men who feel intimidated by physically strong women have to put the women down. "There's always a guy in the crowd who challenges the women when he wouldn't think of going one-on-one with Magic Johnson or challenging Nolan Ryan to a pitching contest."

22   Softball's Donna Lopiano calls it little-boy stuff: "Men don't want to have a collegial, even-steven relationship with women. It's like dealing with cavemen."

Vocabulary

To get the most out of reading this essay, you should have a working understanding of the words listed on the next page. Following each word is a parenthetical reference, indicating the paragraph in which the word is used, as well as a definition for the word. Go back and look at the sentence in which the word appears, and see how the definition applies. To help you make this word a part of your active vocabulary, write a sentence of your own using the word in the space provided.

sauntering (1):   walking leisurely

_____

_____

Lycra (3):   skin-tight clothing material

_____

_____

marshal (3):   organize; guide

_____

_____

hackers (4):   inexperienced or unskilled participants

_____

_____

masquerading (11):   pretending to be what one is not

_____

_____

harassment (13):   annoyance; torment; repeated attacks

_____

_____

transcends (13):   rises above; goes beyond

_____

_____

languish (16):   to lose or lack vitality

_____

_____

enlightened (18):   without ignorance or prejudice

_____

_____

homophobia (21):   fear of homosexuals

---

collegial (22):   characterized by equal sharing of authority

---

Understanding the Essay

1. How does Rounds begin her essay? Is it an effective beginning? Explain why or why not.
2. What is Rounds's attitude toward women's professional sports teams? How do you know? List at least three examples.
3. How is Rounds's essay organized? What is the logic or line of reasoning for her argument? (It may be helpful to make a quick outline to answer this question.)
4. What are the main points of this essay? What transitions does Rounds use to move from one point to the next? List at least five examples.
5. When Rounds says that people "in women's sports spend a lot of time dancing around the 'L' word," what does she mean? How does her point relate to paragraphs 5 and 6 (which precede it), and to paragraph 8 (which follows it)?
6. In paragraphs 18–20, Rounds discusses women's professional sports teams in Europe. How does this discussion prepare the reader for her conclusion? Is it necessary and/or effective? Explain.
7. What overall effect does Rounds create in "Why Men Fear Women's Teams"? Explain your reaction to it.

Writing Activities

1. A common organizational strategy in writing involves process analysis—describing a process or giving directions. Write a list of instructions for completing one of the follow-

ing tasks: folding a paper airplane, tying a pair of shoelaces, drawing the figure of an imaginary creature. Then read the list to a partner who must follow your directions exactly. Did you discover that you missed a step? Were your descriptions hard for your partner to understand? What parts were hard for you to write? How might you rewrite your instructions so that they will be clearer?

2. Outline an essay you have written for this class or another course, preferably one that needs improvement. What are the major headings? How do they relate to the thesis? What are the major subheadings? Are they in logical order? Does the entire paper need reorganization? What do you need to add or delete to strengthen the essay?

16

PARAGRAPHS

Within an essay, the paragraph is the most important unit of thought. Like the essay, it has its own main idea, often stated directly in a topic sentence. Like a good essay, a good paragraph is unified: it avoids digressions and develops its main idea. Paragraphs use many of the rhetorical techniques that essays use, techniques such as classification, comparison and contrast, and cause and effect. In fact, many writers find it helpful to think of the paragraph as a very small, compact essay.

Here is a paragraph from an essay on nature's adaptations:

> Sound has shaped the bodies of many beasts. Noise tapped away at the bullfrog until his ears became bigger than his eyes. Now he hears so well that at the slightest sound of danger he quickly plops to safety under a sunken leaf. The rabbit has long ears to hear the quiet "whoosh" of the owl's wings, while the grasshoppers' ears are on the base of his abdomen, the lowest point of his body, where he can detect the tread of a crow's foot or the stealthy approach of a shrew.
>
> —*Jean George*

This paragraph, like all well-written paragraphs, has several distinguishing characteristics: it is unified, coherent, and adequately developed. It is unified in that every sentence and every idea relate to the main idea, stated in the topic sentence, "Sound has shaped the bodies of many beasts." It is coherent in that the sentences and ideas are arranged in a logical, straightforward manner and the relationship among them made clear by effective transitions and subordination. Finally, the paragraph is unified and adequately developed in that it presents three short but representative examples supporting the topic sentence.

How much development is "adequate" development? The answer depends on many things: how complicated or controversial the main idea is; what readers already know and believe; how much space the writer is permitted. Everyone, or nearly

458

everyone, agrees that the earth circles around the sun; a single sentence would be enough to make that point. A writer trying to argue that affirmative action has outlived its usefulness, however, would need many sentences, indeed many paragraphs, to develop that idea convincingly.

Here is another model of an effective paragraph. As you read this paragraph about the resourcefulness of pigeons in evading attempts to control them, pay particular attention to its controlling idea, unity, development, and coherence.

> Pigeons [and their human friends] have proved remarkably resourceful in evading nearly all the controls, from birth-control pellets to carbide shells to pigeon apartment complexes, that pigeon-haters have devised. One of New York's leading museums once put large black rubber owls on its wide ledges to discourage the large number of pigeons that roosted there. Within the day the pigeons had gotten over their fear of owls and were back perched on the owls' heads. A few years ago San Francisco put a sticky coating on the ledges of some public buildings, but the pigeons got used to the goop and came back to roost. The city then tried trapping, using electric owls, and periodically exploding carbide shells outside a city building, hoping the noise would scare the pigeons away. It did, but not for long, and the program was abandoned. More frequent explosions probably would have distressed the humans in the area more than the birds. Philadelphia tried a feed that makes pigeons vomit, and then, they hoped, go away. A New York firm claimed it had a feed that made a pigeon's nervous system send "danger signals" to the other members of its flock.

The controlling idea is stated at the beginning in a topic sentence. Other sentences in the paragraph support the controlling idea with examples. Since all the separate examples illustrate how pigeons have evaded attempts to control them, the paragraph is unified. Since there are enough examples to convince the reader of the truth of the topic statement, the paragraph is adequately developed. Finally, the regular use of transitional words and phrases such as *once, within the day, a few years ago*, and *then*, lends the paragraph coherence.

How long should a paragraph be? In modern essays most paragraphs range from 50 to 250 words, but some run a full page or more and others may be only a few words long. The best answer is that a paragraph should be long enough to develop its main idea adequately. Some authors, when they find a paragraph running very long, may break it into two or more paragraphs so that readers can pause and catch their breath. Other writers forge ahead, relying on the unity and coherence of their paragraph to keep their readers from getting lost.

Articles and essays that appear in magazines and newspapers often have relatively short paragraphs, some of only one or two sentences. The reason is that they are printed in very narrow columns, which make paragraphs of average length appear very long. But often you will find that these journalistic "paragraphs" could be joined together into a few longer, more normal paragraphs. Longer, more normal paragraphs are the kind you should use in all but journalistic writing.

THE ICEMAN'S SECRETS

Leon Jaroff

Leon Jaroff is an award-winning journalist who has held writing and editing positions with Life, Time, *and* Discover *since he first became a reporter in 1951. He currently covers science and medicine stories as a contributor to* Time. *In this essay, Jaroff describes how a German tourist found an intact human corpse in September 1991, believed to be about 5,300 years old, frozen in a glacier in the Alps. Jaroff explores the debate over whom the Iceman "belongs" to, how he came to be so well preserved, and the questions that scientists are now asking about our Neolithic ancestors.*

Preparing to Read

What kinds of information do you think the Iceman's body can tell modern scientists about Stone Age life? What would you want to know about him? In this essay, Jaroff delves into four main issues surrounding the questions raised by the Iceman's discovery. Notice the author's journalistic style, and how he uses paragraphs to clearly separate each point.

W omen have inquired about the possibility of having his   1
baby. Scientists the world over plead for a chance to examine him. Museums compete for bits of his clothing and tools. Nations and provinces bicker over who has custody rights, while anthropologists struggle to discern how he lived and what other ancient secrets he is destined to reveal.

Through it all, the object of this desire and celebrity has   2
remained mute, though his very appearance on the scene has spoken volumes. He is known as the Iceman, a Stone Age wanderer found one year ago remarkably preserved in the melting Similaun glacier high in the Alps. His discovery has already

461

upset some long-held notions about the late Stone Age, chilled relations between Austria and Italy—near whose border he was found—and stimulated tourism and commerce. His age, established by radio-carbon dating as approximately 5,300 years, makes him by far the most ancient human being ever found virtually intact. (Some Egyptian mummies are older, but had their brain and vital organs removed before interment.)

3   "He is a remarkable specimen," says Werner Platzer, an anatomist at Austria's University of Innsbruck. "Scientists have never before had an opportunity to examine such an ancient body." But the Iceman has provided posterity with more than just his body; he literally died with his boots on. His glacial grave has yielded pieces of his clothing, weaponry and other equipment. While most remains of ancient humans are found surrounded by funerary objects (if anything at all), the Iceman "was snatched from life completely outfitted with the implements of everyday existence!" exclaims Markus Egg, the German archaeologist who is overseeing the delicate process of restoring the Iceman's belongings. In effect, the find brings the remote Neolithic period vividly to life, says prehistorian Lawrence Barfield of England's University of Birmingham. "It is as though you are walking around a museum looking at pottery and flint, then turn a corner and find a real person."

4   Examining that person and his implements, scientists have gained new insight into late Stone Age society. They've been stunned by the sophisticated design of his arrows, which reflect a basic grasp of ballistics, and by the ingenuity of his clothing. Even more amazing is the evidence that Neolithic people had discovered the antibiotic properties of plants. Among other surprises, the Iceman has shown irrefutably that human haircuts and tattoos have been in vogue a good deal longer than anyone suspected. Researchers have also begun to reconstruct the extraordinary coincidences of weather and geography that led to the Iceman's death, his long interment and his startling re-emergence 53 centuries later.

5   "I thought at first it was a doll's head," says Helmut Simon, the German tourist who spotted the Iceman on Sept. 19, 1991, while on an Alpine walking trip with his wife. On closer inspection, however, they realized that the head and shoulders protruding from the Similaun glacier were human, and seeing a hole in back of the skull, suspected foul play. Hurrying to a hikers' shel-

ter to report their find, they set in motion a series of blunders that nearly deprived the world of a priceless treasure.

Uncertain about who had jurisdiction, Markus Pirpamer, 6 owner of the shelter, called police on both sides of the border. The Italian carabinieri, believing the body was that of an ill-fated climber, showed no interest. Their Austrian counterparts, who had already pulled eight corpses out of glaciers that summer, said they would investigate by the next afternoon. Pirpamer decided the next morning to go see for himself, and was flabbergasted: "I had seen bodies come out of the glacier," he recalls, "but this was nothing like them. Bodies trapped in the glacier are white and waxy and usually chewed up by the ice. This one was brown and dried out. I could tell that it was really old."

Later that day, an Austrian policeman arrived by helicopter 7 and attempted to free the body with a jackhammer. The brute-force tool chewed up the Iceman's garments and ripped through his left hip, exposing the bone. Fortunately, the officer ran out of compressed air to power the jackhammer before he could do further damage. His superiors decided to wait until the following week to resume the recovery; the helicopter, they explained, was needed for more important things.

Word of the find spread, and over the weekend about two 8 dozen curiosity seekers trudged to the site. Some collected fragments of garments and tools as souvenirs, and one used a pickax to free the body from the melting ice. Overnight, however, the temperature dropped. By the time Innsbruck forensics expert Dr. Rainer Henn arrived to investigate the death, on Monday, Sept. 23, the body was again locked in ice. Having neglected to bring tools, Henn and his team resorted to hacking it out with a borrowed ice pickax and ski pole, largely destroying the archaeological value of the site.

The mistreated corpse, clothed from the waste down when 9 discovered, was now stark naked except for remnants of a boot dangling from his right foot, and bore the marks of his crude recovery. He had also been castrated; it turned out that his penis and most of his scrotum were missing, perhaps accidentally broken off during his recovery and taken by a visitor. Flown out by helicopter and transferred to a hearse, the Iceman and his possessions were transported to Innsbruck. There, one final indignity awaited the body. It became the centerpiece of a press conference in the local morgue. While the Iceman and his tattered belongings lay on a dissecting table under blazing klieg lights, reporters and other hangers-on joked, smoked and even touched the body. Not until late afternoon did someone notice a fungus spreading on the Iceman's skin.

10   It was only then, after five days of heavy-handed mistreatment, that the Iceman was given professional succor. Arriving at the morgue, Konrad Spindler, head of Innsbruck's Institute for Prehistory, was stunned, immediately realizing the significance of the shriveled body. "I thought this was perhaps what my colleague Howard Carter experienced when he opened the tomb of Tutankhamen and gazed into the face of the Pharaoh."

11   Spindler could see that the body had been naturally mummified—quickly dehydrated by icy winds or perhaps by the foehn, the warm, dry North African wind that sweeps across the Alps during winter. To prevent further damage, his team bathed the body in fungicide, wrapped it in a sterilized plastic sheet, covered it with chipped ice and moved it to a refrigerated room at the university. There, except for 30-minute intervals when it is removed for CAT scans and other scientific tests, the Iceman has been stored ever since at 98% humidity and −6°C (21.2°F), the glacial temperature he had grown accustomed to over more than 5,000 years.

A Seasoned Outdoorsman

12   A broad portrait of the Iceman and his times is gradually emerging from the tests and observations. He was a fit man, between 25 and 35, about 1.6 m (5 ft. 2 in.) tall—which was short even in his day—and weighed around 50 kg (110 lbs.). Though his nose had been crushed and his upper lip folded by the weight of ice, it is clear that he had well-formed facial features that would not draw stares from contemporary Tyroleans. Says South Tyrolean archaeologist Hans Notdürfter: "He looks like one of our well-tanned ancestors."

13   An examination of his body revealed no sign of disease and no wounds beyond those that were inflicted during his exhumation. But scientists are still pondering the reason for the bluish tinge of his teeth, which were well worn, probably from a diet of milled grain products.

14   Though the mummified body was completely hairless, investigators have plucked about 1,000 curly brownish-black hairs

from the recovered shreds of clothing. Those that came from the Iceman's head were only 9 cm (3½ in.) long—evidence that humans had been cutting their hair far earlier than anthropologists had believed. More mysterious were the well-defined tattoos: groups of blue parallel lines on the Iceman's lower spine, a cross behind the left knee and stripes on the right ankle. "Since all these tattoos were covered by clothing," says Spindler, "they must have had an inner meaning for the man and not have had the function of identification for other tribes." Some scientists suggest that the designs might have been used to mark the passage from youth to manhood. One fact is certain: until this discovery, it was thought that tattooing originated 2,500 years later.

The Iceman was well prepared for the Alpine chill. His basic   15
garment was an unlined fur robe made of patches of deer, chamois and ibex skin. Though badly repaired at many points, the robe had been cleverly whipstitched together with threads of sinew or plant fiber, in what appears to be a mosaic-like pattern, belying the popular image of cavemen in crude skins. "The person who made the clothes initially was obviously skilled. This indicates that the Iceman was in some way integrated into a community," says prehistorian Egg, who is restoring the clothes at the Roman-Germanic Central Museum in Mainz, Germany. As for the repairs, made with grass thread, Egg says, "We assume he did them himself in the wilderness." Shredded during the Iceman's recovery, the garment arrived at Mainz in nearly a hundred pieces and with so many bits missing that Egg has doubts about ever fully determining the fashion of the times.

For further protection, the Iceman wore a woven grass cape   16
over the garment similar to those used by Tyrolean shepherds as late as the early part of this century. His well-worn size-6 shoes were made of leather and stuffed with grass for warmth. Last month an Italian expedition turned up an additional furry piece of the Iceman's wardrobe, probably a cap.

The Iceman's equipment revealed an unexpected degree of   17
sophistication. His copper ax was initially mistaken by Spindler as evidence that the find dated from the Bronze rather than the Neolithic Age. But the blade turned out to be nearly pure copper, not bronze.

To archaeologists, the Iceman's fur quiver is an even rarer   18
prize. "It is the only quiver from the Neolithic period found in the whole world," Egg marvels. Its cargo of feathered arrows

marks another first. Carved from viburnum and dogwood branches, a dozen of them were unfinished. But two were primed for shooting—with flint points and feathers. The feathers had been affixed with a resin-like glue at an angle that would cause spin in flight and help maintain a true course. "It is significant that ballistic principles were known and applied," says Notdürfter. The quiver also held an untreated sinew that could be made into a bowstring; a ball of fibrous cord; the thorn of a deer's antler, which could be used to skin an animal; and four antler tips, tied together with grass.

19   The bow, which had not yet been notched for a bowstring, is made of yew, which Egg explains is "the best wood in Central Europe for bowmaking and the wood the famous English longbows—like Robin Hood's—were made of." Yew is relatively rare in the Alps, but the Iceman had searched out "the best material."

20   The Neolithic climber was also armed with a tiny flint dagger with a wooden handle; a net of grass, which possibly served as a carrying bag; and a pencil-size stone-and-linden tool that was probably used to sharpen arrowheads and blades. Two birchbark canisters may have been used to carry the embers from a fire, Egg speculates. The Iceman apparently toted much of his gear in a primitive rucksack with a U-shaped wooden frame.

21   *Homo tyrolensis*, as some scientists have dubbed him, also had a leather pouch resembling a small version of the "fanny packs" worn by tourists today. Inside he carried a sharpened piece of bone, probably used to make sewing holes in leather, and a flint-stone drill and blade. A sloeberry, probably his snack food, was found at the site, along with two mushrooms strung on a knotted leather cord. The mushrooms have infection-fighting properties and may have been part of the world's oldest-known first-aid kit. The only decorative item, possibly a talisman, was a small, doughnut-shaped stone disk, with a tassel of string.

The Iceman's Final Hours

22   Prepared as he was for an Alpine outing, how did the Iceman perish? And what was he doing so high in the mountains? To Egg, the evidence suggests that the Iceman could have been a shepherd, part of a group tending sheep or cattle. Ekkehard

Dreiseitel, a University of Innsbruck climatologist, agrees. "We know the weather 5,000 years ago was somewhat warmer. The pasturage in the high Alps [above the tree line] would have been tempting in the summer, since it requires no clearing of the forest." Because the ax resembles those found in Stone Age settlements near Brescia, Italy, Egg suggests that the Iceman and fellow shepherds had worked their way through the Alpine foothills from the south, grazing their flocks. It is also possible that he was seeking flint in the highlands.

At some point, Egg says, the Iceman could have left his   23
group to search for yew to replace a broken bow or to hunt for food. His route may have taken him over the Alpine crest and down to the tree line on the other side. There he cut himself a new bow, fetched more arrow wood, and prepared to rejoin his friends.

It was late summer or autumn—evidenced by the sloeberry,   24
which was then in season—and a sudden storm and drop in temperature while the Iceman was crossing the crest may have forced him to take refuge in a basin 3 m to 5 m (10 ft. to 16 ft.) deep, ridged on both sides. There he died. Writing in last week's issue of *Science*, a team of experts suggested that the Iceman "was in a state of exhaustion perhaps as a consequence of adverse weather conditions. He therefore may have lain down . . . fallen asleep and frozen to death."

While the Iceman lay exposed, a bird might have torn the   25
small hole found on the back of his head, but a heavy snowfall soon covered the body, protecting it from further depredation. Soon the glacier moved in, flowing over the basin. "We know that if he had been trapped in the glacier," says glaciologist Gerhard Markl, "the body and the implements would have been ground up beyond recognition. When we recover bodies from a glacier, we often find a leg there, an arm there."

Safely tucked away in a deep "pool" in the glacial stream,   26
protected from currents and preserved by the frigid −6°C temperature, the Iceman lay undisturbed for more than 53 centuries. And centuries more might have passed before he was discovered were it not for a foehn that last year delivered tons of North African desert sand to the Alpine ridges. "This is a common phenomenon," explains climatologist Dreiseitel, "but in 1991 it coincided with a winter that produced little snow, and the coating of sand increased the rate of melt on the high peaks." All over

the Alps that summer, glaciers retreated—including Similaun. Even then, it was only by chance that the world learned of the Iceman. "By the end of September," says Spindler, "he would have been buried under a half-meter of snow. Most probably, he would have remained in his glacial grave for at least another hundred years."

The Custody Conundrum

27   On Oct. 2, 1991, an Austro-Italian surveying team determined that the find was 92.6 m (101 yds.) inside Italian soil, namely the autonomous region of South Tyrol. The result has been a custody battle every bit as absurd as the bungled recovery effort. "Rome was ready to demand the body back immediately," explains a South Tyrolean scientist. "It was then that we in South Tyrol pointed out that this province has authority over its own culture and patrimony." Innsbruck, of course, wanted to keep the celebrated corpse.

28   Last February a deal was struck requiring the University of Innsbruck to return the Iceman to South Tyrol no later than Sept. 19, 1994—three years from the discovery date. In an act of goodwill, the Innsbruck team last month marked the first anniversary of the discovery with a motorcade that carried the first edition of *Der Mann im Eis*, a 464-page scientific tome, to Bolzano, South Tyrol's capital.

29   With less than two years to go, Innsbruck scientists are hoping to conduct as much research as possible, while struggling with the costs of the Iceman's upkeep—$10,000 a month. To help cover these expenses, they are charging high fees for photo opportunities and using profits from book sales and lecture tours. Rome hasn't made the research effort any easier. Authorities there, furious over the Iceman's mismanaged recovery, declared that the mummy is the archaeological equivalent of "a Leonardo" and warned that it should not be damaged "in any way." When Innsbruck sent out the snippets of flesh "no larger than a sweetening tablet" for carbon dating by experts at Oxford and in Zurich, the Italian government threatened legal action.

30   The bickering has seriously delayed examination of the Iceman's internal organs and analysis of his DNA, tests that could shed light on his diet, immune system and cause of death, and even help identify his closest living descendants. Innsbruck Uni-

versity anatomist Werner Platzer feels frustrated and bewildered: "The Italian ministry has told us that we are not allowed to destroy a bit of the body," he complains. On the other hand, "they say that if no research is carried out, the body must go to Rome for research purposes." As head of the anatomical-research project, Platzer has decided to ignore Rome's objection. This month he will begin doling out minuscule bits of the Iceman for analysis by experts in many nations. "This find is for scientists all over the world," he argues. "It is ridiculous to say this is an Italian or an Austrian matter."

The Iceman's appeal is universal. Austrians have fondly nick-   31
named him "Oetzi" (after the Oeztaler Alps). Thousands of people worldwide have written to express their interest or profess kinship. Some claim to have communicated with him, while several women, unaware of the Iceman's castration, have volunteered to be impregnated with his sperm. In South Tyrol, a small tourist industry, replete with T shirts, pamphlets and escorted hikes to the recovery site, is already flourishing. And proud provincial officials are planning to build a museum around the Iceman and display him in some sort of refrigerated showcase.

Scientists are appalled. An Iceman museum in picturesque   32
South Tyrol would doubtless be a hit, but most experts believe it would be a mistake to display anything but a replica of the mummy. Displaying the body, Platzer says, would be undignified, and "we don't think it could tolerate those conditions." In fact, the Iceman's present custodians are worried that even their best efforts cannot indefinitely preserve the world's most extraordinary time traveler. Full-scale research had better proceed apace. What a sad irony it would be if, after waiting more than 53 centuries to come to light, the Iceman and his ancient secrets would be lost to human folly and politics.

Vocabulary

To get the most out of reading this essay, you should have a working understanding of the words listed on the next page. Following each word is a parenthetical reference, indicating the paragraph in which the word is used, as well as a definition for the word. Go back and look at the sentence in which the word appears, and see how the definition applies. To help you make

this word a part of your active vocabulary, write a sentence of your own in the space provided.

interment (2):   burial

_____

_____

anatomist (3):   specialist in the study of the structures of organisms

_____

_____

implements (3):   objects or tools with which to work

_____

_____

sophisticated (4):   advanced, complicated, elaborate

_____

_____

ingenuity (4):   cleverness, originality, resourcefulness

_____

_____

antibiotic (4):   capable of destroying or preventing the growth of bacteria

_____

_____

irrefutably (4):   not arguably, definitely

_____

_____

vogue (4):   fashion

_____

_____

jurisdiction (6): power over a territory

---

forensics (8): study of the legal application of medicine

---

succor (10): help given in time of need

---

dehydrated (11): deprived of water or moisture

---

mosaic (15): surface pattern of many inlaid parts (as of stones)

---

belying (15): proving untrue

---

quiver (18): pouch for arrows

---

talisman (21): good luck charm

---

adverse (24): unfavorable

---

autonomous (27):   independent

_____

_____

patrimony (27):   inherited property

_____

_____

doling (30):   distributing sparingly

_____

_____

minuscule (30):   tiny

_____

_____

replete (31):   complete, full

_____

_____

Understanding the Essay

1. How does Jaroff introduce his essay on the Iceman? Is his approach appropriate? Effective? What is Jaroff's attitude toward the discovery in the introductory paragraphs?

2. What is the topic sentence of paragraph 4? What details support the topic sentence?

3. Outline paragraphs 14–16. What logical progression links the three paragraphs?

4. Locate the transitions between paragraphs 22 through 26, or "The Iceman's Final Hours." How do they separate the paragraphs but maintain the theme running through them?

5. How does paragraph 28 relate to 27 and 29—the paragraphs that precede and follow it?
6. What point is the author making in paragraphs 30–32? How does the topic sentence of paragraph 30 relate to the last sentence of the essay?
7. What is Jaroff's attitude at the end of the essay toward the Iceman's discovery? How do you know? What evidence are his conclusions based on?

Writing Activities

1. Highlight or underline the topic sentences in the first segment of Jaroff's essay, and use them to make up a quick outline. Could Jaroff's information have been presented in a different order? Why or why not? Why do you think he chose to explore the story in the way he did? Look especially closely at the paragraphs in the first section that begin with quotations. How do these work as transitions, evidence, and topic sentences? See what would happen if you tried to rework each quotation into a different part of the paragraph in which it appears.
2. Rewrite the following passage from William Zinsser's "College Pressures," breaking it into paragraphs:

> What I wish for all students is some release from the clammy grip of the future. I wish them a chance to savor each segment of their education as an experience in itself and not as a grim preparation for the next step. I wish them the right to experiment, to trip and fall, to learn that defeat is as instructive as victory and is not the end of the world. My wish, of course, is naive. One of the few rights that America does not proclaim is the right to fail. Achievement is the national god, venerated in our media—the million-dollar athlete, the wealthy executive—and glorified in our praise of possessions. In the presence of such a potent state religion, the young are growing up old. I see four kinds of pressure working on college students today: economic pressure, parental pressure, peer pressure, and self-induced pressure. It is easy to look around for villains—to blame the colleges for charging too much money, the professors for assigning too much work, the parents for pushing their children too

far, the students for driving themselves too hard. But there are no villains; only victims.

Zinsser originally wrote this passage in three paragraphs. How many did you come up with? How did you choose where to stop one paragraph and begin another?

KNOCK WOOD

Paul Chance

Paul Chance was born in 1941 in Glen Burnie, Maryland, and received his B.S. at Towson State University in 1963. He completed his M.A. in counseling at the University of Northern Colorado in 1966 and his Ph.D. in psychology at Utah State in 1973. He is the author of two books, Learning and Behavior *and* Thinking in the Classroom, *and numerous articles for* Psychology Today, Family Circle, Weight Watchers, *the* New York Times, *and others. Chance is a full-time writer and an adjunct faculty member at Salisbury State University, Maryland, and is planning his next book, which will be a primer on the principles of teaching. When asked about "Knock Wood," Chance claims he's "still not superstitious, and lightning hasn't struck yet!"*

Preparing to Read

In "Knock Wood," Paul Chance explores one of the theories about the origin of superstition—coincidental reward. Before you even read the essay, think for a moment about what "coincidental reward" might mean. Chance describes two behavioral experiments—one with birds and one with humans—that deal with this theory, and then he discusses some of his own ideas about how superstitions are formed. As you read the piece, note how clearly Chance marks the progression of his argument with new, well-defined paragraphs. How does his paragraphing affect the pace and flow of the essay? What function do transitions have in creating these effects?

Years ago I had a fountain pen that I always used for important things such as taking tests and filling out job applications. It was my lucky pen. It didn't have all the right answers, but with it I believed I could present my ignorance in the most favorable light. I was superstitious in those days, but I have reformed. I gave up all my superstitions, thanks largely to the work of psychologists, who showed me how foolish I was.

2   B. F. Skinner did what was probably the first superstition experiment. He had shown earlier that with a few grains of seed, you can get a pigeon to do nearly anything you want. You merely wait for the desired response, or a reasonable approximation of it, and then provide some food. Each time you do this, the rewarded response becomes stronger.

3   But Skinner wondered about the effect of offering food regularly regardless of what the bird did. One day he put a pigeon into a cage and provided grain every 15 seconds. The bird didn't have to lift a feather to earn these meals, but after a while it began behaving oddly—it started turning in counterclockwise circles. Most other birds treated in this way also acquired unnecessary habits. One stretched its neck toward a corner; another made brushing movements toward the floor; a third repeatedly bobbed its head up and down, as if dancing to some imaginary drumbeat. Now, none of this activity had any effect; the food arrived every 15 seconds no matter what. Yet the birds behaved as if their actions made the food appear. They had become "superstitious," but why?

4   Skinner's explanation was quite simple. The first time food arrived, the bird had to be doing *something*. If the bird happened to be bobbing its head up and down (something that pigeons are wont to do), then that response was strengthened—that is, became more likely to occur again. This meant that the next time food arrived, the bird was likely to be bobbing its head. The second appearance of food further strengthened head-bobbing, and the cycle continued. Thus, argued Skinner, superstitious behavior is the product of coincidental reward.

5   There is evidence that coincidental reward plays a role in human superstition. In one study, researchers asked high school students to press one or more telegraph keys. If they pressed the third key from the left, a bell would sound, a light would go on and they would earn a nickel. However, the students made money only if they pressed the key a second time after a short interval. If they simply did nothing for a few seconds and then pressed key 3 again, they would be rewarded. But they didn't know that, so they spent the interval pressing keys. Eventually

the delay period would end, the student would again press key 3, the bell would ring and the light would flash. Key presses that occurred during the delay were strengthened through coincidental reward.

The result was that each student worked out a pattern of key 6 presses, such as 1-1-2-2-3-3 or 4-3-2-1-2-3, and stuck with it. None of this behavior, except pressing key 3, had any effect. But the students were convinced they had worked out the essential combination of key strokes.

Although superstition no doubt owes much to coincidental 7 reward, some psychologists insist there is more to the study. If a boy finds a four-leaf clover and shortly afterward trips over a dollar, he may well believe that such clovers are lucky. But it is unlikely that the coincidental appearance of four-leaf clovers and dollars accounts for the popularity of this superstition. However, a boy may hear adults praise the four-leaf clover's power. And if the boy finds a four-leaf clover and something lucky happens to him a week later, the adult will undoubtedly say, "See, that's because of that four-leaf clover you found." If the boy finds another four-leaf clover and nothing good happens to him until puberty, no one points to the clover's failure.

Indeed, society is far more dedicated to noting evidence in 8 favor of superstition than it is to observing contrary evidence. The prejudice goes a long way toward explaining our superstitious nature. When the survivors of a plane crash are interviewed, some of them inevitably insist that they were saved by prayer. The chances are good that some who did not survive also prayed for all they were worth, but they are now unable to testify about the value of the procedure. Arguing that evidence for superstitions is biased is unlikely to impress believers, who will point to someone who should have died six or seven times in a motorcycle accident but was saved by a good-luck charm to endure the ecstasy of life in a coma. Skeptics might reason that if the charm were going to the trouble of making a miracle, it might have done a better job. But that logic won't disturb the faithful.

Of course, some superstitions probably have a measure of 9 practicality. In the days of wooden ships and iron men, sailors believed that having a woman on board was bad luck. It doesn't take much imagination to find some sense in the idea that the combination of one woman and 30 or 40 men, isolated at sea for months on end, could prove volatile. Similarly, in some primitive societies hunters engage in a ritual bath before stalking their prey to make themselves pure in spirit. The bath also may make them harder to detect, thus improving their chances of success.

10   True superstitions are activities that have no effects on events but exist because of coincidental rewards and society's prejudices. Of course, I no longer have any superstitions. After I learned from my fellow psychologists how foolish superstitions are, I shed them all. A black cat means nothing to me now, nor does a broken mirror. There are no little plastic icons on the dashboard of my car, and I carry no rabbit's foot. I am free of all such nonsense, and I am happy to report no ill effects—knock wood.

Vocabulary

To get the most out of reading this essay, you should have a working understanding of the words listed below. Following each word is a parenthetical reference, indicating the paragraph in which the word is used, as well as a definition for the word. Go back and look at the sentence in which the word appears, and see how the definition applies. To help you make this word a part of your active vocabulary, write a sentence of your own using the word in the space provided.

approximation (2):   something very similar to the original

_____

_____

counterclockwise (3):   a leftward circling motion, as opposed to the movement of clock hands

_____

_____

wont (4):   accustomed

_____

_____

coincidental (4):   events happening at the same time by chance

---
---

telegraph (5):   machine for sending messages by wire

---

contrary (8):   opposite in nature or direction

---

prejudice (8):   unreasoning opinion about something

---

testify (8):   bear witness, give evidence

---

ecstasy (8):   feeling of intense delight or pleasure

---

skeptics (8):   doubters, disbelievers

---

volatile (9):   unpredictable, quickly changing

---

icons (10):   sacred images or likenesses

Understanding the Essay

1. Locate Chance's thesis statement. Could Chance have put it any other place in the essay? Why or why not?

2. Take a close look at the structure of paragraphs 5 and 7. How are their topic sentences alike? How are they different? How do the supporting sentences differ?

3. What is the "prejudice" to which Chance refers in paragraph 8? Does sufficient evidence support his claim?

4. What is Chance's attitude toward superstition? How do you know? Does it change throughout the essay? List examples to support your answers.

5. In paragraph 9, Chance writes that "some superstitions probably have a measure of practicality." What does he mean? What function does paragraph 9 serve in his argument? How is it related to paragraph 10, the concluding paragraph?

6. Describe the structure of paragraph 10. Why is it an effective conclusion?

Writing Activities

1. Reorder the three sentences in this paragraph by George Orwell so that it makes sense:

   She added that to dip your mustache into your beer also turns it flat. The other night a barmaid informed me that if you pour beer into a damp glass it goes flat much more quickly. I immediately accepted this without inquiry; in fact, as soon as I got home I clipped my mustache, which I had forgotten to do for some days.

   How could you tell where to put which sentences? What were the clues?

2. Outline paragraph 3 of "Knock Wood." How are the first and last sentences related? Is there anything you would add to or subtract from the paragraph? Explain why or why not.

How to Mark a Book

Mortimer Adler

Writer, editor, philosopher, and educator Mortimer Adler was born in New York City in 1902. A high school dropout, Adler completed the undergraduate program at Columbia University in three years, but he did not graduate because he refused to take the mandatory swimming test. Adler is recognized for his editorial work on the Encyclopaedia Britannica *and for his leadership of the Great Books Program at the University of Chicago, where adults from all walks of life gathered together twice a month to read and discuss the classics. In the following essay, which first appeared in the* Saturday Review of Literature *in July 1940, Adler explains how to take full ownership of a book by marking it up, by making "it a part of yourself."*

Preparing to Read

As you read Adler's essay, pay particular attention to his paragraphing. Notice how Adler has developed each paragraph around a *topic sentence* that introduces the main idea. By making sure that all of the sentences in each paragraph are related to the idea introduced in the topic sentence, he writes unified paragraphs. Adler is also careful to provide verbal cues ("There are two ways," "Let me develop these three points") that help readers see the organizational connections between the parts of a paragraph and, on a larger scale, between paragraphs.

Y ou know you have to read "between the lines" to get the most out of anything. I want to persuade you to do something equally important in the course of your reading. I want to persuade you to "write between the lines." Unless you do, you are not likely to do the most efficient kind of reading. 1

2   I contend, quite bluntly, that marking up a book is not an act of mutilation but of love.

3   You shouldn't mark up a book which isn't yours. Librarians (or your friends) who lend you books expect you to keep them clean, and you should. If you decide that I am right about the usefulness of marking books, you will have to buy them. Most of the world's great books are available today, in reprint editions, at less than a dollar.

4   There are two ways in which one can own a book. The first is the property right you establish by paying for it, just as you pay for clothes and furniture. But this act of purchase is only the prelude to possession. Full ownership comes only when you have made it a part of yourself, and the best way to make yourself a part of it is by writing in it. An illustration may make the point clear. You buy a beefsteak and transfer it from the butcher's icebox to your own. But you do not own the beefsteak in the most important sense until you consume it and get it into your bloodstream. I am arguing that books, too, must be absorbed in your bloodstream to do you any good.

5   Confusion about what it means to *own* a book leads people to a false reverence for paper, binding, and type—a respect for the physical thing—the craft of the printer rather than the genius of the author. They forget that it is possible for a man to acquire the idea, to possess the beauty, which a great book contains, without staking his claim by pasting his bookplate inside the cover. Having a fine library doesn't prove that its owner has a mind enriched by books; it proves nothing more than that he, his father, or his wife, was rich enough to buy them.

6   There are three kinds of book owners. The first has all the standard sets and best-sellers—unread, untouched. (This deluded individual owns woodpulp and ink, not books.) The second has a great many books—a few of them read through, most of them dipped into, but all of them as clean and shiny as the day they were bought. (This person would probably like to make books his own, but is restrained by a false respect for their physical appearance.) The third has a few books or many—every one of them dog-eared and dilapidated, shaken and loosened by continual use, marked and scribbled in from front to back. (This man owns books.)

7   Is it false respect, you may ask, to preserve intact and unblemished a beautifully printed book, an elegantly bound edi-

tion? Of course not. I'd no more scribble all over a first edition of *Paradise Lost* than I'd give my baby a set of crayons and an original Rembrandt! I wouldn't mark up a painting or a statue. Its soul, so to speak, is inseparable from its body. And the beauty of a rare edition or of a richly manufactured volume is like that of a painting or a statue.

But the soul of a book *can* be separated from its body. A   8
book is more like the score of a piece of music than it is like a painting. No great musician confuses a symphony with the printed sheets of music. Arturo Toscanini reveres Brahms, but Toscanini's score of the C-minor Symphony is so thoroughly marked up that no one but the maestro himself can read it. The reason why a great conductor makes notations on his musical scores—marks them up again and again each time he returns to study them—is the reason why you should mark your books. If your respect for magnificent binding or typography gets in the way, buy yourself a cheap edition and pay your respects to the author.

Why is marking up a book indispensable to reading? First, it   9
keeps you awake. (And I don't mean merely conscious; I mean wide awake.) In the second place, reading, if it is active, is thinking, and thinking tends to express itself in words, spoken or written. The marked book is usually the thought-through book. Finally, writing helps you remember the thoughts you had, or the thoughts the author expressed. Let me develop these three points.

If reading is to accomplish anything more than passing time,   10
it must be active. You can't let your eyes glide across the lines of a book and come up with an understanding of what you have read. Now an ordinary piece of light fiction, like say, *Gone with the Wind,* doesn't require the most active kind of reading. The books you read for pleasure can be read in a state of relaxation, and nothing is lost. But a great book, rich in ideas and beauty, a book that raises and tries to answer great fundamental questions, demands the most active reading of which you are capable. You don't absorb the ideas of John Dewey the way you absorb the crooning of Mr. Vallee. You have to reach for them. That you cannot do while you're asleep.

If, when you've finished reading a book, the pages are filled   11
with your notes, you know that you read actively. The most famous active reader of great books I know is President Hutch-

ins, of the University of Chicago. He also has the hardest schedule of business activities of any man I know. He invariably reads with a pencil, and sometimes, when he picks up a book and pencil in the evening, he finds himself, instead of making intelligent notes, drawing what he calls "caviar factories" on the margins. When that happens, he puts the book down. He knows he's too tired to read, and he's just wasting time.

12   But, you may ask, why is writing necessary? Well, the physical act of writing, with your own hand, brings words and sentences more sharply before your mind and preserves them better in your memory. To set down your reaction to important words and sentences you have read, and the questions they have raised in your mind, is to preserve those reactions and sharpen those questions.

13   Even if you wrote on a scratch pad, and threw the paper away when you had finished writing, your grasp of the book would be surer. But you don't have to throw the paper away. The margins (top and bottom, as well as side), the end-papers, the very space between the lines, are all available. They aren't sacred. And, best of all, your marks and notes become an integral part of the book and stay there forever. You can pick up the book the following week or year, and there are all your points of agreement, disagreement, doubt, and inquiry. It's like resuming an interrupted conversation with the advantage of being able to pick up where you left off.

14   And that is exactly what reading a book should be: a conversation between you and the author. Presumably he knows more about the subject than you do; naturally, you'll have the proper humility as you approach him. But don't let anybody tell you that a reader is supposed to be solely on the receiving end. Understanding is a two-way operation; learning doesn't consist in being an empty receptacle. The learner has to question himself and question the teacher. He even has to argue with the teacher, once he understands what the teacher is saying. And marking a book is literally an expression of your differences, or agreements of opinion, with the author.

15   There are all kinds of devices for marking a book intelligently and fruitfully. Here's the way I do it:

1. *Underlining:* of major points, of important or forceful statements.

2. *Vertical lines at the margin:* to emphasize a statement already underlined.

3. *Star, asterisk, or other doo-dad at the margin:* to be used sparingly, to emphasize the ten or twenty most important statements in the book. (You may want to fold the bottom corner of each page on which you use such marks. It won't hurt the sturdy paper on which most modern books are printed, and you will be able to take the book off the shelf at any time and, by opening it at the folded-corner page, refresh your recollection of the book.)

4. *Numbers in the margin:* to indicate the sequence of points the author makes in developing a single argument.

5. *Numbers of other pages in the margin:* to indicate where else in the book the author made points relevant to the point marked; to tie up the ideas in a book, which, though they may be separated by many pages, belong together.

6. *Circling of key words or phrases.*

7. *Writing in the margin, or at the top or bottom of the page, for the sake of:* recording questions (and perhaps answers) which a passage raised in your mind; reducing a complicated discussion to a simple statement; recording the sequence of major points right through the books. I use the end-papers at the back of the book to make a personal index of the author's points in the order of their appearance.

The front end-papers are, to me, the most important. Some people reserve them for a fancy bookplate. I reserve them for fancy thinking. After I have finished reading the book and making my personal index on the back end-papers, I turn to the front and try to outline the book, not page by page, or point by point (I've already done that at the back), but as an integrated structure, with a basic unity and an order of parts. This outline is, to me, the measure of my understanding of the work. 16

If you're a die-hard anti-book-marker, you may object that the margins, the space between the lines, and the end-papers don't give you room enough. All right. How about using a scratch pad slightly smaller than the page-size of the book—so that the edges of the sheets won't protrude? Make your index, outlines, and even your notes on the pad, and then insert these sheets permanently inside the front and back covers of the book. 17

18   Or, you may say that this business of marking books is going to slow up your reading. It probably will. That's one of the reasons for doing it. Most of us have been taken in by the notion that speed of reading is a measure of our intelligence. There is no such thing as the right speed for intelligent reading. Some things should be read quickly and effortlessly, and some should be read slowly and even laboriously. The sign of intelligence in reading is the ability to read different things according to their worth. In the case of good books, the point is not to see how many of them you can get through, but rather how many can get through you—how many you can make your own. A few friends are better than a thousand acquaintances. If this be your aim, as it should be, you will not be impatient if it takes more time and effort to read a great book than it does a newspaper.

19   You may have one final objection to marking books. You can't lend them to your friends because nobody else can read them without being distracted by your notes. Furthermore, you won't want to lend them because a marked copy is a kind of intellectual diary, and lending it is almost like giving your mind away.

20   If your friend wishes to read your *Plutarch's Lives, Shakespeare*, or *The Federalist Papers*, tell him gently but firmly to buy a copy. You will lend him your car or your coat—but your books are as much a part of you as your head or your heart.

Vocabulary

To get the most out of reading this essay, you should have a working understanding of the words listed below. Following each word is a parenthetical reference, indicating the paragraph in which the word is used, as well as a definition for the word. Go back and look at the sentence in which the word appears, and see how the definition applies. To help you make this word a part of your active vocabulary, write a sentence of your own using the word in the space provided.

mutilation (2):   disfigurement

deluded (6):   deceived

dilapidated (6):   in a state of disrepair, well worn

indispensable (9):   essential

fundamental (10):   basic, central, of major significance

integral (13):   essential or necessary for completeness

fruitfully (15):   productively

protrude (17):   stick out

Understanding the Essay

1. What is Adler's thesis, and where is it stated?
2. Identify the topic sentences in paragraphs 3 through 6. Explain how Adler develops each of these topic sentences.

3. Why does Adler believe that it is important to write out, in the book itself, your reactions to what you read?

4. What kinds of devices does Adler himself use to mark a book intelligently? Do you use any of his devices when you read?

5. What is Adler's attitude toward books? Identify some key words that he uses to describe books that led you to your conclusion.

6. How has Adler organized his explanation of how to mark a book? What is the thrust of the first fourteen paragraphs? Explain how these paragraphs are related to the last six.

Writing Activities

1. Do you mark or highlight your texts as you read them? If so, why? How do you know what to underline and what not to? How does marking help you better understand your reading? Explain how marking helps you study for an exam. Reread the Adler essay and highlight (underline) the topic sentence in each paragraph.

2. To tell another person how to do something, you yourself need a thorough understanding of the process. Analyze one of the following activities, listing the materials you would need and the steps you would follow in completing it:

   a. making your favorite sandwich

   b. preparing for a date

   c. finding an after-school or summer job

   d. playing a simple game

   If you were going to write an essay explaining the process, how many paragraphs would you need? What information would be included in each paragraph?

17

EFFECTIVE SENTENCES

Sentence variety, an important aspect of all good writing, should not be used for its own sake, but rather to express ideas precisely and to emphasize the most important ideas within each sentence. Sentence variety includes subordination, the periodic and loose sentence, the dramatically short sentence, the active and passive voice, and coordination.

To see just what sentence variety can add to your writing, consider the following pair of paragraphs, each describing the city of Vancouver, British Columbia. Although the content of both paragraphs is essentially the same, the first paragraph is written in sentences of nearly same length and pattern and the second paragraph in sentences of varying length and pattern.

Water surrounds Vancouver on three sides. The snow-crowned Coast Mountains ring the city on the northeast. Vancouver has a floating quality of natural loveliness. There is a curved beach at English Bay. This beach is in the shape of a half moon. Residential high rises stand behind the beach. They are in pale tones of beige, blue, and ice-cream pink. Turn-of-the-century houses of painted wood frown upward at the glitter of office towers. Any urban glare is softened by folds of green lawns, flowers, fountains, and trees. Such landscaping appears to be unplanned. It links Vancouver to her ultimate treasure of greenness. That treasure is thousand-acre Stanley Park. Surrounding stretches of water dominate. They have image-evoking names like False Creek and Lost Lagoon. Sailboats and pleasure craft skim blithely across Burrard Inlet. Foreign freighters are out in English Bay. They await their turn to take on cargoes of grain.

Surrounded by water on three sides and ringed to the northeast by the snow-crowned Coast Mountains, Vancouver has a floating quality of natural loveliness. At English Bay, the

489

half-moon curve of beach is backed by high rises in pale tones of beige, blue, and ice-cream pink. Turn-of-the-century houses of painted wood frown upward at the glitter of office towers. Yet any urban glare is quickly softened by folds of green lawns, flowers, fountains, and trees that in a seemingly unplanned fashion link Vancouver to her ultimate treasure of greenness—thousand-acre Stanley Park. And always it is the surrounding stretches of water that dominate, with their image-evoking names like False Creek and Lost Lagoon. Sailboats and pleasure craft skim blithely across Burrard Inlet, while out in English Bay foreign freighters await their turn to take on cargoes of grain.

The difference between these two paragraphs is dramatic. The first is monotonous because of the sameness of the sentences and because the ideas are not related to one another in a meaningful way. The second paragraph is much more interesting and readable; its sentences vary in length and are structured to clarify the relationships among the ideas.

Let's take a close look at the techniques and various sentence structures that you can use to achieve more meaningful variety in your sentences.

Subordination, the process of giving one idea less emphasis than another in a sentence, is one of the most important characteristics of an effective sentence and a mature prose style. Writers subordinate ideas by introducing them either with subordinating conjunctions (*because, if, as though, while, when, after, in order that*) or with relative pronouns (*that, which, who, whomever, what*). Subordinaton not only deemphasizes some ideas, but also highlights others that the writer feels are more important.

Of course, there is nothing about an idea—*any* idea—that automatically makes it primary or secondary in importance. The writer decides what to emphasize, and he or she may choose to emphasize the less profound or noteworthy of two ideas. Consider, for example, the following sentence: "Sarah's father remembers being in school the day Martin Luther King, Jr., was assassinated." Everyone, including the author of the sentence, knows that King's assassination is more noteworthy than Sarah's father being in school. But the sentence concerns Sarah's father, not Martin Luther King, Jr., and so his being in school is stated in the main clause, while the assassination is subordinated in a dependent clause.

Generally, writers place the ideas they consider important in main clauses, and other ideas go into dependent clauses. For example:

When Kristin was eighteen years old, she joined the Big Sister program in Los Angeles.

When Kristin joined the Big Sister program in Los Angeles, she was eighteen years old.

The first sentence emphasizes the Big Sister program; in the second, the emphasis is on Kristin's age.

Another way to achieve emphasis is to place the most important words, phrases, and clauses at the beginning or end of a sentence. The ending is the most emphatic part of a sentence; the beginning is less emphatic; and the middle is the least emphatic of all. The two sentences about Kristin put the main clause at the end, achieving special emphasis. The same thing occurs in a much longer kind of sentence, called a *periodic sentence.* Here is an example from John Updike:

> On the afternoon of the first day of spring, when the gutters were still heaped high with Monday's snow but the sky itself had been swept clean, we put on our galoshes and walked up the sunny side of Fifth Avenue to Central Park.

By holding the main clause back, Updike keeps his readers in suspense and so puts the most emphasis possible on his main idea.

A *loose sentence,* on the other hand, states its main idea at the beginning and then adds details in subsequent phrases and clauses. Rewritten as a loose sentence, Updike's sentence might read like this:

> We put on our galoshes and walked up the sunny side of Fifth Avenue to Central Park on the afternoon of the first day of spring, when the gutters were still heaped high with Monday's snow but the sky itself had been swept clean.

The main idea still gets plenty of emphasis, since it is contained in a main clause at the beginning of the sentence. Yet a loose sentence resembles the way people talk: it flows naturally and is easy to understand.

Another way to create emphasis is to use a *dramatically short sentence.* Especially following a long and involved sentence, a

492   *Effective Sentences*

short declarative sentence helps drive a point home. Here are two examples, the first from Leanita McClain and the second from Maxine Hong Kingston.

> I have overcome the problems of food, clothing and shelter, but I have not overcome my old nemesis, prejudice. Life is easier, being black is not.

> At exactly 7:30 the teacher again picked up the brass bell that sat on his desk and swung it over our heads, while we charged down the stairs, our cheering magnified in the stairwell. Nobody had to line up.

Finally, since the subject of a sentence is automatically emphasized, writers may choose to use the *active voice* when they want to emphasize the doer of an action and the *passive voice* when they want to downplay or omit the doer completely. Here are two examples:

Substance abuse has ruined many people's lives.

Many people's lives have been ruined by substance abuse.

The first sentence emphasizes the abuse that ruined the lives, while the second sentence focuses attention on the lives themselves. The passive voice may be useful in placing emphasis, but it has important disadvantages. As the examples show, and as the terms suggest, active-voice verbs are more vigorous and vivid than the same verbs in the passive voice. Then, too, some writers use the passive voice to hide or evade responsibility. "It has been decided" conceals who did the deciding, whereas "I have decided" makes all clear. So the passive voice should be used only when necessary—as it is in this sentence.

Often, a writer wants to place equal emphasis on several facts or ideas. One way to do this is to give each its own sentence. For example:

The workers inspected the tomatoes. They rejected the bad ones. They packed the good ones in boxes for shipping.

But a long series of short, simple sentences quickly becomes tedious. Many writers would combine these three sentences by using *coordination*. The coordinating conjunctions *and, but, or, nor, for, so,* and *yet* connect words, phrases, and clauses of equal importance:

The workers inspected the tomatoes, rejected the bad ones, and packed the good ones in boxes for shipping.

By coordinating three sentences into one, the writer not only makes the same words easier to read, but also shows that the workers' three activities are equally important parts of a single process. To emphasize the final part of the process, the writer could have combined the three sentences as follows:

After inspecting the tomatoes and rejecting the bad ones, the workers packed the good ones in boxes for shipping.

When parts of a sentence are not only coordinated but also grammatically the same, they are *parallel*. Parallelism in a sentence is created by balancing a word with a word, a phrase with a phrase, or a clause with a clause. Parallelism is often used in speeches—for example, in the last sentence of Lincoln's Gettysburg Address ("government of the people, by the people, for the people, shall not perish from the . . ."). Here is another example, from the beginning of Mark Twain's *The Adventures of Huckleberry Finn:*

Persons attempting to find a motive in this narrative will be prosecuted; persons attempting to find a moral in it will be banished; persons attempting to find a plot in it will be shot.

WHY I FEAR OTHER BLACK MALES MORE THAN THE KKK

Essex Hemphill

In this essay, Essex Hemphill describes what it felt like to be a black man mugged at gunpoint by several younger black men for the thirteen dollars he had in his pocket. Hemphill makes a strong point about the violence that American blacks commit against each other; ultimately he asks, "Why do we excuse black misbehavior by hiding behind charges of racism?" Hemphill lives in Philadelphia.

Preparing to Read

From the essay's title we can already infer that the author is a black male; what kind of fear do you think Hemphill is referring to? As you read the story Hemphill tells, notice the different kinds of sentences and sentence structures he uses to hold your attention. Be especially aware of how he varies the length and type of sentences in order to keep the story moving.

1   Last summer, I was robbed six blocks from my home in Washington, D.C. I had $13 in my pocket. As I strolled to the market in the breezy summer evening, I debated buying a pint of vanilla ice cream to accompany a night of television. Near 16th and Irving Streets, a cocked gun was placed to my head. I had enough presence of mind to remain calm and passive. I didn't want to die for $13. The smallest robber kept singing, "Shoot him! Shoot him! Shoot him!"

2   The robbers were in their late teens or early twenties. A difference of at least 10 to 12 years separated us. The one pressing me against a parked van with his arm against my throat

494

cussed in my face and slammed me again and again against the van. When he released me, I slumped to the ground. They did not run from the scene; they casually walked away and never looked back. If a gun at that moment had suddenly materialized in my hand, I would have used it without mercy. I would have put bullets in their backs. Then I would have stood over their bodies and put bullets in each of their heads.

Need I point out that we were all black males? Need I also   3
say that the Ku Klux Klan is less threatening to me than other black males? Apartheid is less threatening to me than other black males. AIDS is less threatening to me than other black males. Why is it so hard for so many black Americans to acknowledge publicly the crimes blacks commit against other blacks? Why do we excuse black misbehavior by hiding behind charges of racism?

Black protestors march around a store in West Philadelphia,   4
where I now live, taunting the shopkeeper, Yong Chang, with racial slurs and verbal intimidation. The protestors are angry because the shopkeeper's son, 27-year-old Yung Su Chang, killed a black male. The black male, Gregory Dorn, also 27, had reached for a knife during a robbery attempt. Police determined that the shooting was a justifiable homicide and charges against Chang were dropped. To the protestors, this was just another example of injustice against a black male. But I, too, would have shot the robber. He was, after all, committing a robbery. And he was going to use a weapon. Tell me why it is racist to defend your property and your life.

The protestors in Philadelphia complain about the shooting   5
of a black male by a white police officer, but I doubt that they would protest the shooting of a black male by another black over drugs, radios, or sneakers. I doubt the protestors dare go to the sites where drug killings occur and demand that the violence stop.

Vocabulary

To get the most out of reading this essay, you should have a working understanding of the words listed on the next page. Following each word is a parenthetical reference, indicating the

paragraph in which the word is used, as well as a definition for the word. Go back and look at the sentence in which the word appears, and see how the definition applies. To help you make this word a part of your active vocabulary, write a sentence of your own using the word in the space provided.

debated (1): considered, gave thought to

_____

_____

cocked (1): readied to fire

_____

_____

cussed (2): swore

_____

_____

materialized (2): appeared

_____

_____

apartheid (3): South African institutionalized racial segregation and discrimination

_____

_____

justifiable (4): able to be shown reasonable

_____

_____

injustice (4): lack of justice, unjust act or treatment

_____

_____

Understanding the Essay

1. Why did Hemphill write this essay, and for whom did he write it?
2. Where is Hemphill's main idea communicated?
3. Examine the sentences in paragraph 1. Are they long or short? How do they vary from one to the next? What is the effect of keeping short the two sentences about the thirteen dollars?
4. What is the structure of paragraph 3? Four out of the six sentences are in the form of questions. What effect does this create?
5. How would you describe the structure of the first sentence in paragraph 4? How might you rewrite it, or would you keep it just the way it is? Explain.

Writing Activities

1. Rewrite the following passage to make it more interesting to read:

   I went to the store. I bought some vegetables. I also bought some milk. I bought cat food for Fluffy. I thought about buying eggs. I didn't buy the eggs. I realized I had a few at home. I paid for my groceries. I went home.

   No doubt you noticed a lot of repetition in the words and in the pattern of the sentences. How did you make the passage less repetitious? How did you link sentences to make them more complicated? What did you add, subtract, or keep the same?

2. Read over an essay that you have written for this class or another, looking for the sentence patterns. Are the sentences varied? Are they repetitious? Are they too short or too long? Rewrite a paragraph according to what you are learning about effective sentences.

MIYŎK, HEALTH FOOD
FROM THE SEA

Kwon Byung-Rin

*Kwon Byung-Rin was born in 1961 and lives in Seoul,
South Korea, where he attended Han Yang University.
He writes for a weekly tennis magazine and for HEK
Communications, in whose journal,* Seoul, *the follow-
ing piece first appeared. In this essay he describes*
miyŏk, *"a kelp-like species of algae."*

Preparing to Read

What is your attitude toward health food in general? Do you
eat "health food"? Why or why not? Think for a moment about
how you would begin to write about the properties and history
of a favorite food of yours. How does Kwon Byung-Rin write
about *miyŏk?* As you read the essay, pay particular attention to
the sentence patterns the author uses in describing the seaweed,
the history of its use, and the harvesting process.

1   Morning begins early in the seaside village of Kijang,
       Kyŏngsangnam-do where the best quality *miyŏk* (sea-
       weed) in the country is being harvested. Across the
golden sea burnished by the rising sun, a fleet of motor boats
from the village glides toward the *miyŏk* field, the part of the
water embroidered with line after line of white buoys. Some of
the villagers have already arrived there and are pulling up seaweed from the water, fresh and glistening in the sun. *Seaweed*
has always been a popular diet for Koreans who trust that it
purifies blood. It is believed to be especially healthful for women
after childbirth and its soup is fed to them religiously at every
meal for weeks following the delivery. Hence the custom of serv-

ing *miyŏk* soup at the birthday table.

Miyŏk is a kelp-like species of brown algae known by its   2
botanical name *Undaria pinnatifida*. An edible annual loaded
with calcium, iodine, and polysaccharose but with no calories,
this breed of seaweed is a valued health food for weight watchers. It is also known to be efficacious in preventing and controlling diabetes, colon cancer, the cholesterol count in blood, and
arterial sclerosis. Its mineral content is especially valuable because it comes in a highly absorptive form.

Miyŏk consists of a rootlike holdfast, a stemlike stalk or   3
stripe and leaflike blades, the latter two being the edible parts.
Its sporangia, which Koreans call the "ears" of *miyŏk*, have long
been used as a medicinal additive. A recent study reports that
the polysaccharide found, the glutinous fluid on the surface of
the sporangia, can control growth of cancerous cells by inducing
a generation of interferon in the body. Although the study on the
efficacy of its sporangia is incomplete, there never has been any
doubt that *miyŏk* is a seafood extremely beneficial to the human
body system.

It is not clear when it became an important foodstuff for   4
Koreans but there is a record of it being exported to China
during the Koryŏ period (918–1392). It is produced on all sides
of the peninsula but the best comes from Kijang, in the
Kyŏngsangnam-do Province. Located at the southernmost tip
of the East coast, its sea is ideal for *miyŏk* cultivation in terms
of ideal depth and water temperature. Conditions such as a
high tidal range and fast currents make the *miyŏk* grown in this
sea markedly good in flavor.

"Everyone knows that the meat of natural, exercised fish is   5
juicier and more flavorful than the cultivated and thus under-
exercised ones. It's the same with the *miyŏk* that grows doing a
lot of waving and moving due to fast currents," explains Kim
Wan-Chan, the leading fisherman in Kongsu Village of Kijang.

Since 1975, *miyŏk* cultivation has grown rapidly. "It grew so   6
fast actually that soon there was too much of the produce, resulting in a lot of dumping. Some people went way down below
their production cost. So we have worked out a system to control the spore planting at intervals of two weeks so that we can
keep harvesting a set amount throughout the season," says Kim,
who himself has become a *miyŏk* expert.

7   The cultivation starts from September when the first batch of *miyŏk* spores are germinated. It takes 50 days for the plant to grow enough for harvest. The harvest thus takes place continuously from November through April of the next year.

8   "The most important factor is the temperature. The ideal water temperature is 17°–20°C for germination and 5°–17°C for growth of the stripes and blades. Everything should be done under 20°C, never higher nor too much lower." And he worries constantly about the rise in plankton count in the sea which causes the red tide, another natural disaster that the seaweed farmers dread most, after temperature changes, for it causes sickened blemishes on the *miyŏk* blades.

9   Kongsu Village was the first to start *miyŏk* cultivation in the province. Over 100 of the village's 250 families are presently engaged in the cultivation business producing no less than 1,300 tons of *miyŏk* a year in their sea farm that sprawls about 200,000 square meters off their coast. Some of the *miyŏk* harvest from the early morning are sold on the spot in a wet state and some are spread on drying racks and dried naturally by the wind and sun. It takes about three sunny days for the *miyŏk* to dry. The rain and strong wind that blows away the drying strands are the most unwelcome elements of nature.

10   Sometimes *miyŏk* is "salt processed," which is to remove the blades from the stripes, and dip them in boiling water and salt. It can be even more healthful than natural *miyŏk* because it is not only more hygienic but also lightens the iodine content which tends to be rather too heavily loaded. There is also the "dried and condiment added" *miyŏk* which is dried by heated air. The entire production is exported to Japan. One process factory called Samgwang exports 100 tons a year, dried.

11   So Chae-Kon, president of Samgwang, rates Wando Island and Kijang as two best *miyŏk* producers. To his opinion, the Kijang weeds are fat and flavorful because of the quick currents, while the Wando ones, grown in warm, tideless water, are soft and easy to process because of wide blades.

12   The original Kijang *miyŏk* was cultivated by transplanting germinated spores on the chipped surface of rocks near the village, but only a few families are still adhering to the stone-growth method, most turning to the more productive buoy method. Nonetheless, the famed flavor and taste are still there,

the water and the natural conditions being the same. Perhaps it might be even more tasteful than the ancient produce because today's farmers are more ambitious and put in much more care and heart in what they are doing than ever before.

Vocabulary

To get the most out of reading this essay, you should have a working understanding of the words listed below. Following each word is a parenthetical reference, indicating the paragraph in which the word is used, as well as a definition for the word. Go back and look at the sentence in which the word appears, and see how the definition applies. To help you make this word a part of your active vocabulary, write a sentence of your own using the word in the space provided.

burnished (1):   polished

annual (2):   plant that lives for one year or season

polysaccharose (2):   substance with many sugars

efficacious (2):   effective

absorptive (2):   able to be absorbed

sporangia (3):   receptacles in which spores are formed in certain plants

_____

_____

glutinous (3):   gluelike, sticky

_____

_____

inducing (3):   causing

_____

_____

interferon (3):   protein that prevents development of a virus in living cells

_____

_____

cultivation (4):   production, growth

_____

_____

germinated (7):   planted and sprouted

_____

_____

plankton (8):   microscopic organisms that live in salt or fresh water

_____

_____

hygienic (10):   clean, pure

_____

_____

transplanting (12): replanting, relocating plants

Understanding the Essay

1. What is *miyŏk?* Why does Kwon Byung-Rin refer to it as a "health food"? Do you agree with this assessment?
2. What is the point of Kwon Byung-Rin's essay? How is the essay organized? What are its four or five main sections?
3. What is the topic sentence of paragraph 1? How does it differ from the topic sentence of paragraph 2?
4. What kind of sentences does Kwon Byung-Rin use to describe *miyŏk?* What kinds of sentences does he use to analyze processes?
5. Outline paragraph 9. How do the first and last sentences relate to each other?
6. What is the meaning of the last sentence of the essay? How does it relate to the main point?

Writing Activities

1. Read the following paragraph, locate any digressing or irrelevant sentences, and eliminate them:

> When I woke up yesterday morning and saw what a beautiful, sunny day it was, I knew I was going to take my dog for a hike. Ralph wagged his tail expectantly as I packed up a knapsack with a first aid kit, a change of clothes, lunch for me, and dog biscuits for him. He knew what was going on. Last week I had given him a bath. He always could tell when we were going to go somewhere together. He's a good dog, and very obedient.

How did you identify the unnecessary sentence(s)? What would you add to this paragraph, if anything?

2. Break up the following run-on sentences into smaller, more cohesive units:

a. I am going to the dentist tomorrow because I have a tooth-ache which hurts and bothers me especially when I brush my teeth at night and also when I eat hard, chewy foods like carrots and apples and nuts.

b. The best way to fillet a fish is to first cut off the head and gills and slide the knife down both sides of the dorsal fin to remove that, followed by slicing off the pectoral fins, then peeling off the fish's skin and finally gently shaving the meat from each side of the spine, taking care to avoid the tiny riblike bones near the belly.

I HAVE A DREAM

Martin Luther King, Jr.

Born in 1929 in Atlanta, Georgia, Martin Luther King, Jr., was the leading spokesman for the rights of African Americans during the 1950s and 1960s, before he was assassinated in 1968. He established the Southern Christian Leadership Conference, organized many civil rights demonstrations, and opposed the Vietnam War and the draft. For all this work King was awarded the Nobel prize for peace in 1964. King delivered his "I Have a Dream" speech in 1963 from the steps of the Lincoln Memorial to more than 200,000 people who had come to Washington, D.C., to demonstrate for civil rights.

Preparing to Read

In this mighty sermon, referring both to the great documents and speeches of our American past and to the Bible, to patriotic song and to Negro spiritual, King presented his indictment of the present and his vision of the future in the United States. Much of the power of King's sermon derives from his effective use of sentence variety. Read portions of the speech aloud and you will hear the rhythm of his sentences, the emphasis gained with parallel constructions and repetition, and his dramatic use of short sentences. While reading his longer sentences, carefully follow his punctuation so you know when to pause and when to come to a complete stop.

Five score years ago, a great American, in whose symbolic shadow we stand, signed the Emancipation Proclamation. This momentous decree came as a great beacon light of hope to millions of Negro slaves who had been seared in the flames of withering injustice. It came as a joyous daybreak to end the long night of captivity.

1

2   But one hundred years later, we must face the tragic fact that the Negro is still not free. One hundred years later, the life of the Negro is still sadly crippled by the manacles of segregation and the chains of discrimination. One hundred years later, the Negro lives on a lonely island of poverty in the midst of a vast ocean of material prosperity. One hundred years later, the Negro is still languishing in the corners of American society and finds himself an exile in his own land. So we have come here today to dramatize an appalling condition.

3   In a sense we have come to our nation's capital to cash a check. When the architects of our republic wrote the magnificent words of the Constitution and the Declaration of Independence, they were signing a promissory note to which every American was to fall heir. This note was a promise that all men would be guaranteed the unalienable rights of life, liberty, and the pursuit of happiness.

4   It is obvious today that America has defaulted on this promissory note insofar as her citizens of color are concerned. Instead of honoring this sacred obligation, America has given the Negro people a bad check; a check which has come back marked "insufficient funds." But we refuse to believe that the bank of justice is bankrupt. We refuse to believe that there are insufficient funds in the great vaults of opportunity of this nation. So we have come to cash this check—a check that will give us upon demand the riches of freedom and the security of justice. We have also come to this hallowed spot to remind America of the fierce urgency of *now*. This is no time to engage in the luxury of cooling off or to take the tranquilizing drugs of gradualism. *Now* is the time to make real the promises of Democracy. *Now* is the time to rise from the dark and desolate valley of segregation to the sunlit path of racial justice. *Now* is the time to open the doors of opportunity to all of God's children. *Now* is the time to lift our nation from the quicksands of racial injustice to the solid rock of brotherhood.

5   It would be fatal for the nation to overlook the urgency of the moment and to underestimate the determination of the Negro. This sweltering summer of the Negro's legitimate discontent will not pass until there is an invigorating autumn of freedom and equality. 1963 is not an end, but a beginning. Those who hope that the Negro needed to blow off steam and will now be

content will have a rude awakening if the nation returns to business as usual. There will be neither rest nor tranquillity in America until the Negro is granted his citizenship rights. The whirlwinds of revolt will continue to shake the foundations of our nation until the bright day of justice emerges.

But there is something that I must say to my people who   6
stand on the warm threshold which leads into the palace of justice. In the process of gaining our rightful place we must not be guilty of wrongful deeds. Let us not seek to satisfy our thirst for freedom by drinking from the cup of bitterness and hatred. We must forever conduct our struggle on the high plane of dignity and discipline. We must not allow our creative protest to degenerate into physical violence. Again and again we must rise to the majestic heights of meeting physical force with soul force. The marvelous new militancy which has engulfed the Negro community must not lead us to a distrust of all white people, for many of our white brothers, as evidenced by their presence here today, have come to realize that their destiny is tied up with our destiny and their freedom is inextricably bound to our freedom. We cannot walk alone.

And as we walk, we must make the pledge that we shall   7
march ahead. We cannot turn back. There are those who are asking the devotees of civil rights, "When will you be satisfied?" We can never be satisfied as long as the Negro is the victim of the unspeakable horrors of police brutality. We can never be satisfied as long as our bodies, heavy with the fatigue of travel, cannot gain lodging in the motels of the highways and the hotels of the cities. We cannot be satisfied as long as the Negro's basic mobility is from a smaller ghetto to a larger one. We can never be satisfied as long as a Negro in Mississippi cannot vote and a Negro in New York believes he has nothing for which to vote. No, no, we are not satisfied, and we will not be satisfied until justice rolls down like waters and righteousness like a mighty stream.

I am not unmindful that some of you have come here out of   8
great trials and tribulations. Some of you have come fresh from narrow jail cells. Some of you have come from areas where your quest for freedom left you battered by the storms of persecution and staggered by the winds of police brutality. You have been the veterans of creative suffering. Continue to work with the faith that unearned suffering is redemptive.

9   Go back to Mississippi, go back to Alabama, go back to South Carolina, go back to Georgia, go back to Louisiana, go back to the slums and ghettos of our northern cities, knowing that somehow this situation can and will be changed. Let us not wallow in the valley of despair.

10   I say to you today, my friends, that in spite of the difficulties and frustrations of the moment I still have a dream. It is a dream deeply rooted in the American dream.

11   I have a dream that one day this nation will rise up and live out the true meaning of its creed: "We hold these truths to be self-evident; that all men are created equal."

12   I have a dream that one day on the red hills of Georgia the sons of former slaves and the sons of former slaveowners will be able to sit down together at the table of brotherhood.

13   I have a dream that one day even the state of Mississippi, a desert state sweltering with the heat of injustice and oppression, will be transformed into an oasis of freedom and justice.

14   I have a dream that my four little children will one day live in a nation where they will not be judged by the color of their skin but by the content of their character.

15   I have a dream today.

16   I have a dream that one day the state of Alabama, whose governor's lips are presently dripping with the words of interposition and nullification, will be transformed into a situation where little black boys and black girls will be able to join hands with little white boys and white girls and walk together as sisters and brothers.

17   I have a dream today.

18   I have a dream that one day every valley shall be exalted, every hill and mountain shall be made low, the rough places will be made plain, and the crooked places will be made straight, and the glory of the Lord shall be revealed, and all flesh shall see it together.

19   This is our hope. This is the faith with which I return to the South. With this faith we will be able to hew out of the mountain of despair a stone of hope. With this faith we will be able to transform the jangling discords of our nation into a beautiful symphony of brotherhood. With this faith we will be able to work together, to pray together, to struggle together, to go to jail together, to stand up for freedom together, knowing that we will be free one day.

This will be the day when all of God's children will be able to 20
sing with new meaning

> My country, 'tis of thee,
> Sweet land of liberty,
>   Of thee I sing:
> Land where my fathers died,
> Land of the pilgrims' pride,
> From every mountainside
>   Let freedom ring.

And if America is to be a great nation this must become 21
true. So let freedom ring from the prodigious hilltops of New
Hampshire. Let freedom ring from the mighty mountains of
New York. Let freedom ring from the heightening Alleghenies
of Pennsylvania!

Let freedom ring from the snowcapped Rockies of Colorado! 22

Let freedom ring from the curvaceous peaks of California! 23

But not only that; let freedom ring from Stone Mountain of 24
Georgia!

Let freedom ring from Lookout Mountain of Tennessee! 25

Let freedom ring from every hill and molehill of Mississippi. 26
From every mountainside, let freedom ring.

When we let freedom ring, when we let it ring from every 27
village and every hamlet, from every state and every city, we will
be able to speed up that day when all of God's children, black
men and white men, Jews and Gentiles, Protestants and Catho-
lics, will be able to join hands and sing in the words of the old
Negro spiritual, "Free at last! free at last! thank God almighty,
we are free at last!"

Vocabulary

To get the most out of reading this essay, you should have a
working understanding of the words listed on the next page.
Following each word is a parenthetical reference, indicating the
paragraph in which the word is used, as well as a definition for
the word. Go back and look at the sentence in which the word
appears, and see how the definition applies. To help you make
this word a part of your active vocabulary, write a sentence of
your own using the word in the space provided.

symbolic (1):   representing something else by association

_____

_____

seared (1):   caused to wither or dry up

_____

_____

promissory (3):   having the nature of a declaration that something will be done

_____

_____

defaulted (4):   failed to do what is required

_____

_____

invigorating (5):   imparting strength or vitality

_____

_____

inextricably (6):   tied or tangled in a manner incapable of being undone

_____

_____

fatigue (7):   physical or mental weariness resulting from exertion

_____

_____

discords (19):   confused or harsh mingling of sound, lack of agreement

_____

_____

prodigious (21):   impressively great in size, enormous, marvelous

---

Understanding the Essay

1. What is King's message to the people who had gathered in front of the Lincoln Memorial in 1963? What is his message for us today?

2. King's speech can be divided into several sections, each serving a specific purpose. Where are those sections, and what is the purpose of each?

3. Identify several paragraphs in which King uses parallel constructions. Explain what parallelism adds to his sermon.

4. Identify several short sentences (fewer than six words). What do these short sentences add to King's speech? What would have been the effect had he used more of these short sentences?

5. In paragraphs 3 and 4 King uses the analogy of a bad check in talking about America's broken promises to African Americans. Did you find this analogy useful in understanding King's point? Why or why not?

6. King's speech, as has Lincoln's Gettysburg Address, has outlived the occasion for which it was written. In your opinion, why is this so? What qualities of language and thought are the source of its power? What sentences do you consider the most memorable? Why?

Writing Activities

1. Sentence variety includes subordination; simple, compound, and complex sentences; the dramatically short sentence; the active and passive voice; coordination; and parallelism. Identify at least one instance of each of the above

in King's speech. Consult the Glossary of Useful Terms at the end of the text if you need assistance in defining/identifying any of the above sentence constructions.

2. Reread the introduction to this chapter. Review several paragraphs in one of the essays that you have written, paying particular attention to sentence structure. Recast or combine sentences as necessary to make your writing more interesting and effective. In reworking these paragraphs, what did you discover about your own sentence patterns? Do you tend to write short, choppy sentences, or long, involved ones?

GLOSSARY OF USEFUL TERMS

Abstract   See *Concrete/Abstract.*

Allusion   An allusion is a passing reference to a familiar person, place, or thing often drawn from history, the Bible, mythology, or literature. An allusion is an economical way for a writer to capture the essence of an idea, atmosphere, emotion, or historical era, as in "The scandal was his Watergate" or "He saw himself as a modern Job" or "The campaign ended not with a bang but a whimper." An allusion should be familiar to the reader; if it is not, it will add nothing to the meaning.

Analogy   Analogy is a special form of comparison in which the writer explains something unfamiliar by comparing it to something familiar: "A transmission line is simply a pipeline for electricity. In the case of a water pipeline, more water will flow through the pipe as water pressure increases. The same is true of electricity in a transmission line."

Anecdote   An anecdote is a short narrative about an amusing or interesting event. Writers often use anecdotes to begin essays as well as to illustrate certain points.

Argumentation   Argumentation is one of the four basic types of prose. (Narration, description, and exposition are the other three.) To argue is to attempt to persuade a reader to agree with a point of view, to make a given decision, or to pursue a particular course of action. There are two basic types of argumentation: logical and persuasive.

Attitude   A writer's attitude reflects his or her opinion of a subject. The writer can think very positively or very negatively about a subject, or somewhere in between. See also *Tone.*

Audience   An audience is the intended readership for a piece of writing. For example, the readers of a national weekly news magazine come from all walks of life and have diverse interests, opinions, and educational backgrounds. In contrast, the readership for an organic chemistry journal is made up of people whose interests and education are quite similar. The essays in *Themes for Writers* are intended for general readers, intelligent people who may lack specific information about the subject being discussed.

Beginnings and Endings   A beginning is that sentence, group of sentences, or section that introduces an essay. Good beginnings usually identify the thesis or controlling idea, attempt to interest readers, and establish a tone.

An ending is that sentence or group of sentences that brings an essay to a close. Good endings are purposeful and well planned. They can be a summary, a concluding example, an anecdote, or a quotation. Endings satisfy readers when they are the natural outgrowths of the essays themselves and give the readers a sense of finality or completion. Good essays do not simply stop; they conclude.

Cause and Effect   Cause and effect analysis is a type of exposition that explains the reasons for an occurrence or the consequences of an action.

Classification   See *Division and Classification.*

Cliché   A cliché is an expression that has become ineffective through overuse. Expressions such as *quick as a flash, jump for joy,* and *slow as molasses* are clichés. Writers normally avoid such trite expressions and seek instead to express themselves in fresh and forceful language. See also *Diction.*

Coherence   Coherence is a quality of good writing that results when all sentences, paragraphs, and longer divisions of an essay are naturally connected. Coherent writing is achieved through (1) a logical sequence of ideas (arranged in chronological order, spatial order, order of importance, or some other appropriate order), (2) the purposeful repetition of key words and ideas, (3) a pace suitable for your topic and your reader, and (4) the use of transitional words and expressions. Coherence should not be confused with unity. (See *Unity.*) See also *Transitions.*

Colloquial Expressions   A colloquial expression is characteristic of or appropriate to spoken language or to writing that seeks its effect. Colloquial expressions are informal, as *chem, gym, come up with, be at loose ends, won't,* and *photo* illustrate. See also *Diction.* Thus, colloquial expressions are acceptable in formal writing only if they are used purposefully.

Comparison and Contrast   Comparison and contrast is a type of exposition in which the writer points out the similarities and differences between two or more subjects in the same class or category. The function of any comparison and contrast is to clarify—to reach some conclusion about the items being compared and contrasted.

Conclusions   See *Beginnings and Endings.*

Concrete/Abstract A concrete word names a specific object, person, place, or action that can be directly perceived by the senses: *car, bread, building, book, John F. Kennedy, Chicago,* or *hiking.* An abstract word, in contrast, refers to general qualities, conditions, ideas, actions, or relationships which cannot be directly perceived by the senses: *bravery, dedication, excellence, anxiety, stress, thinking,* or *hatred.*

Connotation/Denotation Both connotation and denotation refer to the meanings of words. Denotation is the dictionary meaning of a word, the literal meaning. Connotation, on the other hand, is the implied or suggested meaning of a word. For example, the denotation of *lamb* is "a young sheep." The connotations of *lamb* are numerous: *gentle, docile, weak, peaceful, blessed, sacrificial, blood, spring, frisky, pure, innocent,* and so on.

Controlling Idea See *Thesis.*

Coordination Coordination is the joining of grammatical constructions of the same rank (e.g., words, phrases, clauses) to indicate that they are of equal importance. For example, *They ate hotdogs,* and *we ate hamburgers.*

Deduction Deduction is the process of reasoning from stated premises to a conclusion that follows necessarily. This form of reasoning moves from the general to the specific. See also *Syllogism.*

Definition Definition is one of the types of exposition. Definition is a statement of the meaning of a word. A definition may be either brief or extended, part of an essay or an entire essay itself.

Denotation See *Connotation/Denotation.*

Description Description is one of the four basic types of prose. (Narration, exposition, and argumentation are the other three.) Description tells how a person, place, or thing is perceived by the five senses.

Dialogue Conversation of two or more people as represented in writing. Dialogue is what people say directly to one another.

Diction Diction refers to a writers' choice and use of words. Good diction is precise and appropriate—the words mean exactly what the writer intends, and the words are well suited to the writer's subject, intended audience, and purpose in writing. The word-conscious writer knows that there are differences among *aged, old,* and *elderly; blue, navy,* and *azure;* and *disturbed, angry,* and *irritated.* Furthermore, this writer knows in which situation to use each word. See also *Cliché, Colloquial Expressions, Connotation/Denotation, Jargon, Slang.*

Division and Classification.   Division and classification is one of the types of exposition. When dividing and classifying, the writer first establishes categories and then arranges or sorts people, places, or things into these categories according to their different characteristics, thus making them more manageable for the writer and more understandable and meaningful for the reader. See also *Exposition.*

Dominant Impression   A dominant impression is the single mood, atmosphere, or quality a writer emphasizes in a piece of descriptive writing. The dominant impression is created through the careful selection of details and is, of course, influenced by the writer's subject, audience, and purpose.

Emphasis   Emphasis is the placement of important ideas and words within sentences and longer units of writing so that they have the greatest impact. In general, what comes at the end has the most impact, and at the beginning nearly as much; what comes in the middle gets the least emphasis.

Endings   See *Beginnings and Endings.*

Evaluation   An evaluation of a piece of writing is an assessment of its effectiveness or merit. In evaluating a piece of writing, one should ask the following questions: What is the writer's purpose? Is it a worthwhile purpose? Does the writer achieve the purpose? Is the writer's information sufficient and accurate? What are the strengths of the essay? What are its weaknesses? Depending on the type of writing and the purpose, more specific questions can also be asked. For example, with an argument one could ask: Does the writer follow the principles of logical thinking? Is the writer's evidence sufficient and convincing?

Evidence   Evidence is the information on which a judgment or argument is based or by which proof or probability is established. Evidence usually takes the form of statistics, facts, names, examples or illustrations, and opinions of authorities.

Example   An example illustrates a larger idea or represents something of which it is a part. An example is a basic means of developing or clarifying an idea. Furthermore, examples enable writers to show and not simply to tell readers what they mean.

Exposition Exposition is one of the four basic types of prose. (Narration, description, and argumentation are the other three.) The purpose of exposition is to clarify, explain, and inform. The methods of exposition presented in *Themes for Writers* are process analysis, definition, illustration, classification, comparison and contrast, and cause and effect.

Fallacy See *Logical Fallacies.*

Figures of Speech Figures of speech are brief, imaginative comparisons that highlight the similarities between things that are basically dissimilar. They make writing vivid, interesting, and memorable. The most common figures of speech are:

> *Simile:* An explicit comparison introduced by *like* or *as.* "The fighter's hands were like stone."
>
> *Metaphor:* An implied comparison that makes one thing the equivalent of another. "All the world's a stage."
>
> *Personification:* A special kind of simile or metaphor in which human traits are assigned to an inanimate object. "The engine coughed and then stopped."

Focus Focus is the limitation that a writer gives his or her subject. The writer's task is to select a manageable topic given the constraints of time, space, and purpose. For example, within the general subject of sports, a writer could focus on government support of amateur athletes or narrow the focus further to government support of Olympic athletes.

General See *Specific/General.*

Idiom An idiom is a word or phrase that is used habitually with special meaning. The meaning of an idiom is not always readily apparent to nonnative speakers of that language. For example, *catch cold, hold a job, make up your mind,* and *give them a hand* are all idioms in English.

Illustration Illustration is the use of examples to explain, elucidate, or corroborate. Writers rely heavily on illustration to make their ideas both clear and concrete.

Induction Induction is the process of reasoning to a conclusion about all members of a class through an examination of only a few members of the class. This form of reasoning moves from the particular to the general.

Inductive Leap   An inductive leap is the point at which a writer of an argument, having presented sufficient evidence, moves to a generalization or conclusion. See also *Induction.*

Introductions   See *Beginnings and Endings.*

Irony   The use of words to suggest something different from their literal meaning. For example, when Jonathan Swift proposes in *A Modest Proposal* that Ireland's problems could be solved if the people of Ireland fattened their babies and sold them to the English landlords for food, he meant that almost any other solution would be preferable. A writer can use irony to establish a special relationship with the reader and to add an extra dimension or twist to the meaning.

Jargon   Jargon, or technical language, is the special vocabulary of a trade, profession, or group. Doctors, construction workers, lawyers, and teachers, for example, all have a specialized vocabulary that they use "on the job." See also *Diction.*

Logical Fallacies   A logical fallacy is an error in reasoning that renders an argument invalid.

Metaphor   See *Figures of Speech.*

Narration   One of the four basic types of prose. (Description, exposition, and argumentation are the other three.) To narrate is to tell a story, to tell what happened. While narration is most often used in fiction, it is also important in expository writing, either by itself or in conjunction with other types of prose.

Opinion   An opinion is a belief or conclusion, which may or may not be substantiated by positive knowledge or proof. (If not substantiated, an opinion is a prejudice.) Even when based on evidence and sound reasoning, an opinion is personal and can be changed, and is therefore less persuasive than facts and arguments.

Organization   Organization is the pattern of order that the writer imposes on his or her material. Some often used patterns of organization include time order, space order, and order of importance.

Paradox   A paradox is a seemingly contradictory statement that is nonetheless true. For example, "We little know what we have until we lose it" is a paradoxical statement.

Paragraph   The paragraph, the single most important unit of thought in an essay, is a series of closely related sentences. These sentences adequately develop the central or controlling idea of the paragraph. This central or controlling idea, usually stated in a topic sentence, is necessarily related to the purpose of the whole composition. A well-written paragraph has several distinguishing characteristics: a clearly stated or implied topic sentence, adequate development, unity, coherence, and an appropriate organizational strategy.

Parallelism   Parallel structure is the repetition of word order or grammatical form either within a single sentence or in several sentences that develop the same central idea. As a rhetorical device, parallelism can aid coherence and add emphasis. Franklin Roosevelt's statement, "I see one third of the nation ill-housed, ill-clad, and ill-nourished," illustrates effective parallelism.

Personification   See *Figures of Speech.*

Point of View   Point of view refers to the grammatical person in an essay. For example, first-person point of view uses the pronoun *I* and is commonly found in autobiography and the personal essay; third-person point of view uses the pronouns *he, she,* or *it* and is commonly found in objective writing.

Process Analysis   Process analysis is a type of exposition. Process analysis answers the question *how* and explains how something works or gives step-by-step directions for doing something. See also *Exposition.*

Purpose   Purpose is what the writer wants to accomplish in a particular piece of writing. Purposeful writing seeks to *relate* (narration), to *describe* (description), to *explain* (process analysis, definition, classification, comparison and contrast, and cause and effect), or to *convince* (argumentation).

Rhetorical Question   A rhetorical question is asked for its rhetorical effect but requires no answer from the reader. "When will nuclear proliferation end?" is such a question. Writers use rhetorical questions to introduce topics they plan to discuss or to emphasize important points.

Sentence   A sentence is a grammatical unit that expresses a complete thought. It consists of at least a subject (a noun) and a predicate (a verb).

Simile   See *Figures of Speech.*

Slang   Slang is the unconventional, very informal language of particular subgroups in our culture. Slang, such as *bummed, coke, split, rap, dude,* and *stoned,* is acceptable in formal writing only if it is used selectively for specific purposes.

Specific/General   General words name groups or classes of objects, qualities, or actions. Specific words, on the other hand, name individual objects, qualities, or actions within a class or group. To some extent the terms *general* and *specific* are relative. For example, *clothing* is a class of things. *Shirt,* however, is more specific than *clothing* but more general than *T-shirt.* See also *Diction.*

Strategy   A strategy is a means by which a writer achieves his or her purpose. Strategy includes the many rhetorical decisions that the writer makes about organization, paragraph structure, sentence structure, and diction. In terms of the whole essay, strategy refers to the principal rhetorical mode that a writer uses. If, for example, a writer wishes to show how to make chocolate chip cookies, the most effective strategy would be process analysis. If it is the writer's purpose to show why sales of American cars have declined in recent years, the most effective strategy would be cause and effect analysis.

Style   Style is the individual manner in which a writer expresses his or her ideas. Style is created by the author's particular choice of words, construction of sentences, and arrangement of ideas.

Subordination   Subordination is the use of grammatical constructions to make one part in a sentence dependent on rather than equal to another. For example, the italicized clause in the following sentence is subordinate: They all cheered *when I finished the race.* See also *Coordination.*

Supporting Evidence   See *Evidence.*

Syllogism   A syllogism is an argument that utilizes deductive reasoning and consists of a major premise, a minor premise, and a conclusion. For example,

All trees that lose leaves are deciduous. (major premise)
Maple trees lose their leaves. (minor premise)
Therefore, maple trees are deciduous. (conclusion)
See also *Deduction.*

Symbol   A symbol is a person, place, or thing that represents something beyond itself. For example, the eagle is a symbol of the United States, and the maple leaf, a symbol of Canada.

Syntax Syntax refers to the way in which words are arranged to form phrases, clauses, and sentences, as well as to the grammatical relationship among the words themselves.

Technical Language See *Jargon.*

Thesis A thesis is the main idea of an essay, also known as the controlling idea. A thesis may sometimes be implied rather than stated directly in a thesis statement.

Title A title is a word or phrase set off at the beginning of an essay to identify the subject, to state the main idea of the essay, or to attract the reader's attention. A title may be explicit or suggestive. A subtitle, when used, explains or restricts the meaning of the main title.

Tone Tone is the manner in which a writer relates to an audience, the "tone of voice" used to address readers. Tone may be friendly, serious, distant, angry, cheerful, bitter, cynical, enthusiastic, morbid, resentful, warm, playful, and so forth. A particular tone results from a writer's diction, sentence structure, purpose, and attitude toward the subject.

Topic Sentence The topic sentence states the central idea of a paragraph and thus limits the content of the paragraph. Although the topic sentence normally appears at the beginning of the paragraph, it may appear at any other point, particularly if the writer is trying to create a special effect. Not all paragraphs contain topic sentences. See also *Paragraph.*

Transitions Transitions are words or phrases that link sentences, paragraphs, and larger units of a composition in order to achieve coherence. These devices include parallelism, pronoun references, conjunctions, and the repetition of key ideas, as well as the many conventional transitional expressions such as *moreover, on the other hand, in addition, in contrast,* and *therefore.* See also *Coherence.*

Unity Unity is that quality of oneness in an essay that results when all the words, sentences, and paragraphs contribute to the thesis. The elements of a unified essay do not distract the reader. Instead, they all harmoniously support a single idea or purpose.

Verb Verbs can be classified as either strong verbs (*scream, pierce, gush, ravage,* and *amble*) or weak verbs (*be, has, get,* and *do*). Writers often prefer to use strong verbs in order to make writing more specific or more descriptive.

Voice   Verbs can be classified as being in either the active or
the passive voice. In the active voice the doer of the action is
the subject. In the passive voice the receiver of the action is the
grammatical subject:

> *Active:* Glenda questioned all of the children.

> *Passive:* All the children were questioned by Glenda.

INDEX

For a listing of rhetorical terms useful in working with the "Understanding the Essay" questions for each selection in *Themes for Writers*, see the **Glossary of Useful Terms** on pages 513–521.

Acknowledgments (continued from copyright page)

Bjorklund, David and Barbara, "The Heroes We Know." From *Parents Magazine*, September 1989. Reprinted by permission of Child Development Associates, Inc.

Brott, Armin, "Not All Men Are Sly Foxes." From *Newsweek*, June 1, 1992. Reprinted by permission of the author.

Calandra, Alexander, "Angels on a Pin." From *Saturday Review*, December 21, 1968. Reprinted by permission of the author.

Canfield Fisher, Dorothy, "The Washed Window" from *A Harvest of Stories—From a Half Century of Writings*, © 1956 by Dorothy Canfield Fisher and renewed 1984 by Jean S. Franck, Vivian S. Hixson and James David Scott, reprinted by permission of Harcourt Brace & Company.

Chance, Paul, "Knock Wood." From *Psychology Today*, October 1988. Reprinted with permission from *Psychology Today* Magazine. Copyright © 1988 (Sussex Publishers, Inc.).

Cole, Diane, "Don't Just Stand There." From *The New York Times*, April 16, 1989. Reprinted by permission of the author.

Cooley, Jason, "My Generation?" From *The Burlington Free Press*, November 2, 1992. Reprinted by permission.

Crichton, Jennifer, "College Friends." As appeared in *Ms. Magazine*, October 1985. Reprinted by permission of *Ms. Magazine*, © 1985.

Crichton, Jennifer, "Who Shall I Be?" As appeared in *Ms. Magazine*, October 1984. Reprinted by permission of *Ms. Magazine*, © 1984.

Del Castillo Guilbault, Rose, "Hispanic, USA: The Conveyer Belt Ladies." From *The San Francisco Chronicle*, April 15, 1990. Reprinted by permission of the author.

Dillard, Annie, "Terror at Tinker Creek." Excerpt from *Pilgrim at Tinker Creek* by Annie Dillard. Copyright © 1974 by Annie Dillard. Reprinted by permission of HarperCollins Publishers Inc.

Drobot, Eve, "Come, Let Me Offend You." From *Newsweek*, September 28, 1992. Reprinted by permission of the author.

Elbow, Peter, "Freewriting Exercises." From *Writing Without Teachers* by Peter Elbow. Copyright © 1973 by Oxford University Press, Inc. Reprinted by permission.

Evans, David L., "The Wrong Examples." From *Newsweek*, March 1, 1993. Reprinted by permision of the author.

Finch, Robert, "Death of a Hornet." Reprinted by permission of the author.

Flower, Linda, "Writing for an Audience." Excerpt from *Problem-Solving Strategies for Writing* by Linda Flower, copyright © 1981 by Harcourt Brace & Company, reprinted by permission of the publisher.

Franco, Elvira M., "A Magic Circle of Friends." From *The New York Times*, January 28, 1990. Copyright © 1990 by The New York Times Company. Reprinted by permission.

Friday, Nancy, "Mother Love." From *My Mother/My Self* by Nancy Friday. Reprinted by permission of the author.

Gage, Nicholas, "The Teacher Who Changed My Life." As appeared in *Parade*, December 17, 1989. Reprinted with permission from *Parade* and the author, copyright © 1989.

Garrison, Roger H., "Writing Is Building." From *How a Writer Works* Rev. Ed. by Roger H. Garrison. Copyright © 1985 by the Estate of Roger H. Garrison. Reprinted by permission of HarperCollins Publishers Inc.

George, Jean, "That Astounding Creator—Nature." Reprinted with permission from the January 1964 *Reader's Digest.* Copyright © 1964 by The Reader's Digest Assn., Inc.

Goodman, Ellen, "The Company Man." From *At Large* by Ellen Goodman. Copyright © 1981 by The Washington Post Company. Reprinted by permission of Summit Books, a division of Simon & Schuster, Inc.

Goodman, Ellen, "Whose Life Is It Anyway?" From *Keeping In Touch* by Ellen Goodman. Copyright © 1985 by The Washington Post Company. Reprinted by permission of Summit Books, a division of Simon & Schuster, Inc.

Guthrie, Helen A., "Eating Disorders—An Adolescent Problem." From *Introductory Nutrition* by Helen A. Guthrie. Reprinted by permission of Mosby-Year Book, Inc.

Hemphill, Essex, "Why I Fear Other Black Males More than the KKK." As appeared in *Utne Reader,* January/February 1991. Reprinted by permission of Pacific News Service.

Hurston, Zora Neale, "How It Feels to Be Colored Me." Alice Walker, editor, *I Love Myself When I Am Laughing.* New York: The Feminist Press, 1979.

Huttmann, Barbara, "A Crime of Compassion." From *Newsweek,* August 1983. Reprinted by permission of the author.

Jaroff, Leon, "The Iceman's Secrets." From *Time,* October 26, 1992. Copyright © 1992 Time Inc. Reprinted by permission.

King, Coretta Scott, "The Death Penalty Is a Step Back." Copyright © 1981 by Coretta Scott King. Reprinted by arrangement with Coretta Scott King, c/o Jean Daves Agency as agent for the proprietor.

King, Jr., Martin Luther, "I Have a Dream." Copyright © 1963 by Martin Luther King, Jr., copyright renewed 1991 by Coretta Scott King. Reprinted by arrangement with the Heirs of the Estate of Martin Luther King, Jr., c/o Joan Daves Agency as agent for the proprietor.

Kwon, Byung-Rin, "Miyŏk, Health Food from the Sea." From *Seoul,* May 1991. Reprinted by permission of Seoul.

Lawrence, Gale, "Baby Birds." From *The Beginning Naturalist* by Gale Lawrence, 1979. Reprinted by permission of The New England Press, Inc.

Ling, Qing, "China's Antidrug Tradition and Current Struggle." From *China Today,* December 1990. Reprinted by permission.

Malcolm X, "Coming to an Awareness of Language." From *The Autobiography of Malcolm X* by Malcolm X, with Alex Haley. Copyright © 1964 by Alex Haley and Malcolm X. Copyright © 1965 by Alex Haley and Betty Shabazz. Reprinted by permission of Random House, Inc.

Mansfield, Stephanie, "Death of a Friendship." From *Mademoiselle,* April 1989. Copyright © 1989 by Stephanie Mansfield. Reprinted by permission of the author.

McClain, Leanita, "The Middle-Class Black's Burden." From *A Foot in Each World* by Leanita McClain. Copyright © 1986 by Northwestern University Press. Reprinted by permission.

Meier, Daniel, "One Man's Kids." From *The New York Times,* November 1, 1987. Copyright © 1987 by The New York Times Company. Reprinted by permission.

Molina, Mauricio, "Why Spanish Translations?" From *The New York Times,* March 12, 1980. Copyright © 1980 by The New York Times Company. Reprinted by permission.

Mullen, Kirsten, "Subtle Lessons in Racism." Reprinted by permission of the author.

Nadelman, Ethan A., "Legalize Drugs." From *New Republic,* June 13, 1988. Reprinted by permission of The New Republic, Inc.

Noda, Kesaya E., "Growing Up Asian in America." From *Making Waves* by Asian Women United. Copyright © 1989 by Asian Women United. Reprinted by permission of Beacon Press.

O'Brien, Steven, "One Son, Three Fathers." From *The New York Times*, December 28, 1986. Copyright © 1986 by The New York Times Company. Reprinted by permission.

Park, Jeanne, "Eggs, Twinkies and Ethnic Stereotypes." From *The New York Times*, April 20, 1990. Copyright © 1990 by The New York Times Company. Reprinted by permission.

Pattee, Sarah, "How We Named Our Baby." From *Mothers and Other Midwives Magazine*, Spring 1989. Reprinted by permission of M.O.M. Magazine.

Rawlins, Jack P., "Five Principles for Getting Good Ideas." From *The Writer's Way*, Second Edition by Jack P. Rawlins. Copyright © 1992 by Houghton Mifflin Company. Used with permission.

Regier, Gail, "Users, Like Me: Membership in the Church of Drugs." Copyright © 1989 by *Harper's Magazine*. All rights reserved. Reprinted from the May issue by special permission.

Rivers, Caryl, "The Issue Isn't Sex, It's Violence." From *The Boston Globe*, September 15, 1985. Reprinted by permission of the author.

Rounds, Kate, "Why Men Fear Women's Teams." As appeared in *Ms. Magazine*, January/February 1991. Reprinted by permission of Ms. Magazine, © 1991.

Ruggiero, Vincent Ryan, "Debating Moral Questions." Excerpts from *The Art of Thinking* 3rd Edition by Vincent Ryan Ruggiero. Copyright © 1991 by HarperCollins Publishers, Inc. Reprinted by permission of HarperCollins Publishers, Inc.

Schlesinger, Jr., Arthur, "The Cult of Ethnicity, Good and Bad." From *Time*, July 8, 1991. Copyright © 1991 Time Inc. Reprinted by permission.

Sheehan, Sharon, "Another Kind of Sex Ed." From *Newsweek*, July 13, 1992. Reprinted by permission of the author.

Solomon, Jr., Howard, "Best Friends." Reprinted by permission.

Smith-Yackel, Bonnie, "My Mother Never Worked." From *Women: A Journal of Liberation*, Vol. 4, No. 2, 1975.

Tannen, Deborah, "It Begins at the Beginning." Excerpt from pp. 43–8 from *You Just Don't Understand* by Deborah Tannen, Ph.D. Copyright © 1990 by Deborah Tannen, Ph.D. By permission of William Morrow & Company, Inc.

Ullman, Laura, "Will You Go Out with Me?" From *Newsweek*, 1984. Reprinted by permission of the author.

Welty, Eudora, "Miss Duling." Reprinted by permission of the publishers from *One Writer's Beginnings* by Eudora Welty, Cambridge, Mass.: Harvard University Press, Copyright © 1983, 1984 by Eudora Welty.

Williams, Randall, "Daddy Tucked the Blanket." From *The New York Times*, July 10, 1975. Copyright © 1975 by The New York Times Company. Reprinted by permission.

Zimring, Franklin E., "Confessions of an Ex-Smoker." From *Newsweek*, April 20, 1987. Reprinted by permission of the author.

Zinsser, William, "Simplicity." From *On Writing Well*, Fourth Edition by William Zinsser. Copyright © 1976, 1980, 1985, 1988, 1990 by William K. Zinsser. Reprinted by permission of the author.

Instructor's Manual to Accompany

THEMES
FOR WRITERS

PAUL ESCHHOLZ
ALFRED ROSA

Instructor's Manual

to Accompany

THEMES FOR WRITERS

Instructor's Manual

to Accompany

THEMES FOR WRITERS

by

Paul Eschholz and Alfred Rosa

Prepared by

Mark Wanner and Susan Palmer

For information, write:
St. Martin's Press, Inc.
175 Fifth Avenue
New York, NY 10010

ISBN: 0-312-09457-4

Preface

The purpose of this Instructor's Manual is to help you use <u>Themes for Writers</u> with the greatest effectiveness. We therefore provide for each selection a fairly detailed analysis of the essay as a whole. In these sections of the manual, called "Stylistic Highlights," we give an overview of the essays and share our experiences in teaching them--what to stress, what to explain, what to ask about, what to expect generally from discussions.

In addition, we provide in the section called "Understanding the Essay" suggested responses to the questions following each selection. Our intent is to save you time, not to dictate answers. On occasion you may disagree with our interpretation or emphasis, but we trust that the suggested responses will serve at least as starting points. There are no substitutes for your own experience with each essay or for common sense about what will challenge and engage your students.

The essays in <u>Themes for Writers</u> are grouped into two parts. Part 1 has twelve chapters, each containing four essays on a contemporary theme: Sense of Self, Family Ties, Everyday Heroes and Role Models, Relationships, Friends, Education, Work, A Multiculturalist Society, Language and Diversity, Addictions, The Natural World, and Life and Death. Part 2 has five chapters, each devoted to a rhetorical topic: Writers on Writing, Thesis, Organization, Paragraphs, and Effective Sentences.

The arrangement of the chapters suggests a logical teaching sequence. Our experience has been to get students working with the themes from the start, in this way focusing the student writer's attention on content. The thematic chapters progress from an exploration of personal/experiential issues (Sense of Self, Family Ties) to the societal/abstract issues (Education, Life and Death). This arrangement encourages students to begin with experiences they are familiar with. While students are writing about the themes, you may find it helpful for them to refer, either individually or as a class, to the rhetorical chapters in Part 2 if they experience difficulties with the writing task itself. Because each chapter is self-contained, you can design your own teaching sequence, omitting or emphasizing particular chapters according to your special needs and those of your class.

To help you use the book effectively, we call your attention to the following special features.

General Introduction. The introduction provides guidelines for reading and writing short essays and includes three sample student papers with annotations that highlight the elements of an essay emphasized in the text proper. The sample papers and the analyses that accompany them show how three students went about completing typical thematic writing assignments. Moreover, the sample papers give students a good idea of the length and quality of writing they should be striving to produce. We suggest, therefore, that you assign this introduction early in the course and that you spend as much time as possible discussing the student papers and their salient features.

Chapter Introductions. Before reading the essays in a particular chapter, students should read the chapter introduction. For the thematic chapters, they will find a short overview of the subject that provides a context for the four essays that follow. For the rhetorical chapters, they will find an explanation of the rhetorical principle under consideration and a discussion of how to use it. The information in the introductions will also help students to answer the questions and do the writing assignments that accompany each selection.

Preparing to Read. To get students started with each essay, we include a brief statement about the author as well as a brief introduction to the essay itself. Here we locate the reading within the larger thematic context and ask students to reflect on their own thoughts and attitudes toward it.

Vocabulary. We have tried to emphasize each author's choice of words and have included an exercise on vocabulary building for every essay. These words should become part of every student's active vocabulary. The vocabulary words in these exercises are defined in the text itself and students are asked to compose their own sentences using them.

Understanding the Essay. The study questions for each selection focus on its content, its author's purpose, and the rhetorical strategies used to achieve that purpose. Some of the questions require brief answers, and others are intended to stimulate class discussion. Students experiencing difficulty with the questions on matters of rhetoric or with rhetorical terminology should be encouraged to use the Glossary of Useful Terms at the end of the text.

Exploring the Theme: Discussion and Writing. Two questions that reach beyond the content of the essay encourage students to explore--either in class discussion or in writing--the vicissitudes of the theme at hand. Students are encouraged to bring their own personal experiences, observations, or reading to bear in responding to these questions.

Writing Activities. After each of the essays in Part 2, we have provided several brief rhetorical exercises. These exercises give students the opportunity both to identify in their reading and to practice in their writing the essential elements of a sound essay: Thesis, Organization, Paragraphs, and Effective Sentences. You can assign these exercises as homework or use them during class.

Writing Suggestions. At the end of each thematic chapter, a handful of assignments asks students to write about the theme using one or more of the readings in that chapter.

Glossary of Useful Terms. This glossary provides students with concise definitions of terms useful for discussing the readings and their own writing.

Rhetorical Table of Contents. For those who want to stress the rhetorical strategies (e.g., comparison/contrast, definition, and argument), we have provided an alternate table of contents. Located at the end of the text, this contents lists the essays in the text according to dominant rhetorical strategies. Here, again, it is useful to direct students to this table of contents so that they can locate an essay(s) that uses a strategy like the one they are attempting in their own writing.

Finally, we are interested in hearing from anyone who has constructive ideas about the content or use of either <u>Themes for Writers</u> or this manual. We can be reached at the Department of English, 315 Old Mill, University of Vermont, Burlington, Vermont 05405.

Paul Eschholz
Alfred Rosa
Susan Palmer
Mark Wanner

Contents

xi

Instructor's Manual

to Accompany

THEMES FOR WRITERS

PART ONE <u>Themes for Writers</u>

CHAPTER 1: <u>Sense of Self</u>

WHO SHALL I BE? (p. 33)

Jennifer Crichton

<u>Stylistic Highlights</u>
Crichton's essay explores the transition between high school and college, yet her
first paragraph compares the transience of student life and the ideals of our society
in general, emphasizing the greater importance and appeal of her specific subject.
Thereafter she limits herself to the "blank slate" that almost everyone brings to
college, but she contemplates many of the issues raised by that time of transition.
She guides the reader through the complex subjects of self-identity and self-
transformation by combining abstract discussions of the issues with real-life
examples of how those around her have dealt with them. Note how Crichton
intersperses her autobiographical references throughout the text and gives her
rather sprawling essay a structure by framing it in references to her own
experiences.
       The first essay questions explore self-identity and encourage each student to
address the same issues that Crichton discusses. Discuss what students have
done when they faced "blank slate" situations other than entering college. The
second essay addresses the difficulty of making big changes in one's self-identity.
How much change do students think is possible? What's the difference between
real change and playacting?

<u>Understanding the Essay</u>
1. Crichton emphasizes that high school students like to label their peers, and that
label becomes limiting--any change in a person will be scrutinized and perhaps
ridiculed. Not being known is disorienting because self-identity is based partly on
how others perceive you. When you don't know the people around you, being
able to shape their initial perceptions of you is both liberating and disorienting.

2. Crichton wanted to change her high school image, and college represented a
way to have an identity crisis that, in the Chinese sense, offered her an
opportunity to change without being harshly judged by her peers. Trying to
establish Rusty as her nickname is Crichton's most obvious ploy to change her
self-identity.

1

3. Change is difficult because, as Crichton demonstrates in her examples, we all carry a personal history and self-perception that can be limiting, even though those around us are unaware of it. Thus change feels initially like playacting that will be perceived as false or pretentious.

4. Joan hangs out with the rich kids so no one will know of the poverty she faced as a child. She scared Crichton because, to escape her past, she adopted a facade that was alien to her personality, leaving her anxious and unhappy.

5. This is Crichton's way of restating the cliché: "No matter where you go, there you are." Your own tastes, personality, history, and other traits aren't erased by the blank slate of a new setting. Any real changes that occur will still reflect who you are and what you are comfortable with.

6. Crichton comes to terms with the fact that Rusty is not someone she is or wants to be. She obviously incorporated some parts of Rusty's ideal personality, but as the "Rustys" of the world go after jobs at Citibank, Crichton is secure in her much different plans for the future.

MY GENERATION? (p. 41)

Jason Cooley

<u>Stylistic Highlights</u>
The impact of Cooley's essay is heightened by the terse, disturbing statements that come at the reader in rapid succession, then disappear. Cooley's staccato sentences echo the rhythm of MTV, the so-called bible of his generation. Yet his organization is clear--each paragraph begins with a topic sentence that is then elaborated. And although he is not a recognized writer, his essay carries the weight of authority. Cooley offers up statements for his generation in first-person plural as well as first-person singular, and he backs them with experiences and images that readers can readily identify with. His veiled disclaimer about the universality of his statements is saved until near the end, well after he has hooked the reader with his barrage of negative imagery.

The first essay question may provoke challenges to Cooley's ability to define his generation. Comparisons of students' answers may reveal many different points of view. The second question will bring into the open the possibility that most nineteen-year-olds of any generation feel much the way Cooley does. How are his concerns and influences really different from those of preceding generations?

2

1. Violent, cynical, dysfunctional, trend mongering, greedy, murderous, exploitative, fast, shallow, angry, and many more. If an unusual, but not necessarily incorrect, characteristic is proposed, use it to start a discussion.

2. Cable TV has made Cooley immune to violence and provided him with his "bible" (MTV).

3. Cooley asserts that the anger and the feeling that they've been wronged that he shares with his peers make them potential "murderous psychos."

4. Citing Saturday morning cartoons as traumatic childhood experiences is the trend Cooley identifies. Students can propose any other trend(s) that they've identified.

5. A precise definition is not given, but from the content of the essay students should be able to identify a "slacker" as someone who fears work and turning thirty, has a short attention span, can't identify with others, and so on.

6. Cooley's life resembles the REM song "It's the End of the World As We Know It (And I Feel Fine)" as a haze of mostly incoherent images. He sees no future for himself.

GROWING UP ASIAN IN AMERICA (p. 46)

Kesaya Noda

Stylistic Highlights
Unlike Jennifer Crichton's essay about the potential for changing one's self-identity, Noda's essay is about the difficulties in accepting the various parts of one's self-identity. The title of the essay isn't inaccurate, but "Growing Up Asian in America" leads the reader to expect a more superficial autobiography than Noda presents--perhaps your students can come up with better titles. Noda's essay is long and complex, so she divides her identity into three components--race, nationality, and gender--and explains how she came to terms with each one. Note how she uses the last paragraph in each section to bring her observations and experiences into focus and bring the reader back to the establishment of her self-identity.
     The first essay question gets students to use Noda's process in writing the essay. Challenge your students to find factors that define them other than race, nationality, and gender. The second essay provokes discussion of individual heritage and the tolerance (or intolerance) that American society exhibits toward

those of different ethnic backgrounds. Contrast the experiences of students of European and non-European descent.

<u>Understanding the Essay</u>
1. Noda identifies herself as a Japanese American woman. Her identity as a person of Japanese descent is established by the way she looks and is unavoidable.

2. The shrine where Noda's grandmother grew up is where Noda's family's Japanese identity is rooted. The need to protect it is important because it preserves that part of their identity. In Japan, the family comes before the individual, so that any duty related to the family heritage is of primary importance.

3. Noda learns more about the first Japanese American settlements and what conditions were like there before and during the war. She learns that her parents were powerless to resist their incarceration because they weren't considered to be Americans.

4. Noda's mother is her dark self because Noda knows that they are similar, yet she wants to emulate women who are quite different from her mother in both appearance and thinking.

5. The song represents to Noda the Japanese ability to look at what life gives you with clear eyes, even if it is sad. The quoted verse is very cryptic, so discuss what it means to your students.

6. The epilogue indicates there is a common connection between people, even if they hold different beliefs and have different backgrounds. Noda has spent a long time identifying herself very specifically as a Japanese American woman, but her epilogue indicates that her identity doesn't separate her from others--that being a particular individual does not exclude anyone from enjoying and interacting with those around him or her.

HOW IT FEELS TO BE COLORED ME (p. 57)

Zora Neale Hurston

<u>Stylistic Highlights</u>
Zora Neale Hurston had an exuberance and love of life that transcended the weighty issues that sometimes seem inherent in being an African American. By describing her childhood interaction with white tourists, she displays her joie de vivre and her relative impatience with "racial issues." Yet notice how she does not deny her heritage. Her vivid description of the way jazz flows through her as a

4

feeling, not as something to listen to, emphasizes that she <u>has</u> inherited certain views of life that her white friend has not. At the same time, she won't let her heritage deny her anything either. The first sentence of paragraph 6, "But I am not tragically colored," is both a statement and a lament, a protest to the many who expect her to bow down under the tragic history of her people. As she puts it, "I am off to a flying start and I must not halt in the stretch to look behind and weep."

The first essay question addresses Hurston's positive self-image and her lack of patience with those of her heritage who can't escape the past and meet the future with optimism. What can these people do to share Hurston's joy? The second essay question asks students to focus on one way that Hurston turns a potential negative into a positive--she doesn't have much, but she thinks the game of getting is far more fun than the process of keeping. What do your students think about this point of view?

<u>Understanding the Essay</u>
1. The day Hurston left Eastonville, she entered a world in which she was distinguished by her color from the whites around her. In Eastonville, skin color didn't play any role in defining who she was.

2. Hurston is not very aware of racial differences as a child. The whites differ from the blacks only in that they don't live in her town and they give her dimes for performing. She doesn't have enough interaction with whites and blacks in a mixed-race environment to have much awareness of racial differences.

3. The world is Hurston's oyster--she needs a sharp knife to open it and enjoy what it has to offer.

4. The "brown specter" and the "dark ghost" are the threat to whites of the progress of African-Americans in our culture.

5. Hurston embraces the stereotype that blacks "have rhythm" and whites don't. The second part of the question is a matter of opinion.

6. Hurston compares a person to a bag of assorted items, junk mixed with treasure. While the exterior is easy to identify as one color or another, the contents defy differentiation. Your students should find it an effective analogy, or explain very clearly why it wasn't effective for them.

7. Hurston's attitude is exuberant, life-embracing, optimistic, and generous. It is clear from the essay that any who denied themselves the pleasure of her company missed the chance to meet a wonderful person.

CHAPTER 2: Family Ties

ONE SON, THREE FATHERS (p. 67)

Steven O'Brien

Stylistic Highlights

O'Brien uses a very straightforward writing style and a simple, chronological organization in his essay, making it easy to read and understand. Yet "One Son, Three Fathers" touches on a variety of issues and raises many questions about what defines a parent and a family. O'Brien concisely and effectively communicates his affection for Seb, but his whimsical tone in the beginning--"The first time I met him, he fell asleep in his spaghetti"--disappears during the course of the essay as their relationship, and Seb's parental situation, grows more complicated. By ending the essay with such an open-ended question--"What could I say to Seb?"--O'Brien implies that there will be more questions than answers for both him and Seb--and perhaps for many of his readers--for a long time.

The essay questions stimulate thought about marriage as an institution and the possible consequences associated with the current "easily married, easily divorced" way of thinking. You can also look at marriage from another perspective. O'Brien wonders what he should say to Seb about marriage. What advice or information would your students like to hear from their parents about relationships and marriage?

Understanding the Essay

1. O'Brien spent a lot of time with Seb because his schedule fit Seb's schedule.

2. As a teacher, O'Brien thinks he had a strong desire to help Seb handle his complicated parental situation. He felt he and Brian complemented each other well in giving Seb the tools he needed to grow and learn.

3. O'Brien became sort of a favored uncle to Seb--having much of the fun without imposing the discipline. There are many right answers to why O'Brien ignored the counselor's advice. He loved Seb and wanted to maintain their relationship is probably the most straightforward.

4. O'Brien isn't Seb's natural father or current legal father but has filled the role of father for most of the life that Seb can remember.

5. It seems that Seb is handling the situation very well, as his ability to joke about it demonstrates. O'Brien hears about him by living in the same area.

6. The divorces have made Seb believe that marriage is short-lived and, in the end, very painful. He does not want to get married himself.

HOW WE NAMED OUR BABY (p. 73)

Sarah Pattee

Stylistic Highlights

Pattee's essay demonstrates that even within what could be called a typical nuclear family, new tensions and issues can exist because of changes in society. By giving Harley Mack Pattee Henigson's name to the reader right away, Pattee emphasizes the furor within her family that the four short names produced. The listing of the choices of names Pattee and her husband considered lets us glimpse the difficulties feminists face when they try to express themselves within such entrenched societal activities as marriage and childbearing. Pattee is also careful to separate her attitude toward outside society, which can be quite combative, from her firm embrace of the family as an institution that is an important source of love and understanding for children, no matter what their names are.

The first essay question makes students consider the controversial nature of Pattee's opinions. There is the potential for a lot of debate among students, pitting traditionalists against progressives of both sexes. The essay can also tie in with the third question, which raises the same issues. The second question doesn't ask whether a student agrees with Pattee but merely questions whether Lebell's naming method is reasonable. It also questions the importance of names to society--how important do your students think names are in structuring a society?

Understanding the Essay

1. Harley--they liked the name. Mack--honors a deceased uncle, though Pattee never says who's uncle it was. Pattee + Henigson--to include both parental names. Henigson is the "last" name
because Harley is a boy.

2. Harley's name involved society at large because of society's assumptions and traditions regarding names--assumptions and traditions that Pattee chose to ignore.

3. A simple list will suffice: hyphenation, making the surname Henigson, combining Henigson and Pattee, making the surname Pattee, and Lebell's bilineal naming system.

4. Lebell says that if there are all sons or all daughters in a family, they should have the same surname anyway--the daughters should have the mother's surname, the sons the father's. Pattee doesn't elaborate about why this solution makes her

7

uncomfortable. She does say elsewhere that she and her husband want to avoid ending one parent's name.

5. Pattee is a feminist who obviously married a like-minded man. To her, the use of the man's surname by his wife and children is a bad tradition perpetuated by a patriarchal society. Thus, in naming Harley, she needs to find a solution that she can live with and that carries what she thinks should be carried in a name--the parents' names in a framework of gender equality. The adoption of a different naming system complicates the naming process for Pattee, but underscores its importance to her.

6. Naming Harley makes Pattee and her husband reexamine how equal their marriage really is, why they want children, and what they think it means to be a family.

DADDY TUCKED THE BLANKET (p. 79)

Randall Williams

Stylistic Highlights
For much of his essay about growing up poor, Williams concentrates on the material deprivations he and his siblings endured--the ramshackle houses, the constant mess, the copper wire attaching the soles of his daddy's boots. Yet his title emphasizes that the most important aspect of poverty is its strain on the psyche. He crafts his essay carefully for maximum impact, despite his early lament of the weakness of words to convey his message. Note how he draws attention to key points in his essay by inserting a short, attention-grabbing paragraph. For example, after the powerful passage about his father tucking the blanket, he sums up what happened in his family with a devastating three-word, one-sentence paragraph: "Now they're divorced."
        The first essay question may be difficult for some students if they are or were ashamed of something in their childhood home. It is meant to encourage students to think about how settings can affect people's lives. The second essay question is rather specific, but any rational explanation is acceptable. It can also be a launching point for a discussion of how painful experiences in general can aid a person later.

Understanding the Essay
1. Williams never invited anyone to his house.

2. Poverty becomes more difficult as a child becomes more class-conscious. Also, Williams points out the difficulty a poor child can encounter when he or she first begins to date.

3. The Williamses were a large family. Mr. Williams probably worked for a relatively low wage, and Mrs. Williams had to stay home to try to take care of the children and the house.

4. Because they didn't have enough money to complete the job, they were always moving out anyway. Trying to fix the superficial flaws of a house that is crumbling is more frustrating than rewarding.

5. Mr. and Mrs. Williams had only one outlet for their frustration and anger--each other. It eventually led to their divorce.

6. Williams and his siblings were too well loved to be abused by their parents. It was other children who were the cruelest to them.

MOTHER LOVE (p. 85)

Nancy Friday

Stylistic Highlights
As the structure of the family changes, even motherhood is being reevaluated. Friday questions two relationships in "Mother Love"--that of the mother and daughter, and that of the mother's maternal role and her sexual drive. As a psychologist, Friday is able to make statements about the internal and external forces on women in a way that a layperson can't--the essay is not easily read but carries the weight of authority. Friday helps the reader by starting out with the complex, broad issues facing women of current and previous generations, then concluding with specifics about how they affected her and her mother, both in their relationship with each other and in their individual lives.
Friday's view of a woman's sexuality is somewhat unusual.
        The first essay question addresses how she views sexuality--students can also be encouraged to discuss their views of how society deals with sexuality. The second essay can lead to a general exploration of what feminism and women's rights have accomplished, and what they have not accomplished, for women.

Understanding the Essay
1. The fears are of the dangers that she has faced as a woman before becoming a mother. A son, presumably, will not have to face the same dangers.

2. Women adopt the position of mother protector out of fear.

3. Women were happier in past generations because they had fewer options. Even if they were unhappy with their lives, they had no models for anything else to

do, so they had to suppress their discontent. Modern women, Friday argues, don't have enough energy left over to suppress their unhappiness.

4. The three options for women are work, motherhood, and sexuality. Friday argues that sexuality and eroticism are as important as the other two, and should not be ignored.

5. Friday argues that motherhood and female sexuality are not mutually exclusive because a woman's own body differentiates between sexuality and motherhood-- they are opposite drives that can coexist. She argues that the nonsexual mother- protector role that society sets up as the basis of womanhood is a lie, but when women believe it, it can cause the so-called war between the mother and the woman.

6. Friday never trusted the perfect "mother love" that her own mother claimed to feel for her, so it created tension between them and it made Friday suspicious of love in general.

7. The idea that a perfect love exists between Friday and her mother prevents Friday from being the person she wants to be.

CHAPTER 3: Everyday Heroes and Role Models

THE HEROES WE KNOW (p. 94)

David and Barbara Bjorklund

Stylistic Highlights
The first sentence of "The Heroes We Know" sets the tone for the short, informal piece: "We heard a good story recently from Aunt Ellen." The reader doesn't know who Aunt Ellen is but would like to read her good story. The informality fits the Bjorklunds' topic of "everyday heroes," because they wish to point out that such heroes are easy to find and easy to talk to. Their simple message is made immediate by Aunt Ellen's story, so their other examples and arguments can be brief and easily communicated.
    The first essay is an exercise in autobiographical writing that gets students to think about their relatives in the way that the Bjorklunds encourage. The second essay shows students that they should consider issues that are not addressed in the reading but may be worth thinking about. The Bjorklunds ignore black sheep, which can be as visible as--or more visible than--the "heroic" relatives the Bjorklunds refer to. How should their influence on the family be discussed with children?

10

Understanding the Essay

1. Aunt Ellen is a good guest for her granddaughter's class because she is an immigrant and can tell her story of arriving in America. But because she looks very chic and American, she can also destroy some stereotypes about how immigrants look and act.

2. Aunt Ellen's "exciting saga" is the story of leaving her home in Sweden and adjusting to life in America.

3. Our family tree can fill our children's need for heroes.

4. It is good for children to look to their families for heroes, because families give children heroes to admire with whom they can feel connected and identify.

5. There are any number of answers to this question. It can also serve as a starting point for discussion.

THE TEACHER WHO CHANGED MY LIFE (p. 98)

Nicholas Gage

Stylistic Highlights

"The Teacher Who Changed My Life" is a short autobiography that Gage structures around the positive influences that Marjorie Hurd had on his life. Hurd is an unlikely heroine, as Gage describes with flair: "A formidable, solidly built woman with salt-and-pepper hair, a steely eye and a flat Boston accent, Miss Hurd had no patience with layabouts." His descriptions populate the piece with interesting and knowable people--including himself as he grew up--so although the reader probably isn't a Worcester Greek or a former student of Miss Hurd's, he or she becomes wrapped up in the narrative anyway. The skill with which Gage writes his tribute to Miss Hurd is, in effect, a tribute in itself--not even this piece, he implies, would have been written without her help.

Miss Hurd both taught and directed Gage on the way to his chosen career. Most students aren't that lucky, but both the first and second essay questions will make them think about what gifts of knowledge or direction they have received in the past. Some of the answers to the first essay question will probably be vague. It could be complemented by having students question people in the work force about how they chose their careers.

Understanding the Essay

1. Gage resents his father because he didn't get the family out of Greece in time to save Eleni.

2. Gage joins the newspaper club because he followed a pretty girl into the classroom. He stays because he likes Miss Hurd.

3. The stories are about underdogs, not heroic figures, who act heroically when facing crises.

4. The impact on other people of his award-winning essay about the last time he saw his mother lets him begin to understand the power of the written word. Miss Hurd had to assign him the essay because he wanted to forget the events as much as possible.

5. Gage's father is very proud of his son's writing accomplishments. The second part of the question requires a short description of the father's personality.

6. Miss Hurd gave Gage the tools he needed to write comfortably in English, and she gave him the confidence to do it well.

THE WRONG EXAMPLES (p. 106)

David L. Evans

Stylistic Highlights

"The Wrong Examples" is a good example of a well-crafted opinion piece. Evans begins by stating the problem: there are few qualified black male candidates for colleges. He succinctly states his thesis--that black males lack realistic role models--then proceeds to back it up by addressing the causes, consequences, manifestations, and possible solutions to the problem. Although his thesis is difficult to back up with numbers or other hard data, he keeps to his point and cites readily identifiable examples to support one aspect of his argument at a time. Evans adds to his credibility by starting the piece, "As a college admissions officer . . . ," which lets the reader know his qualifications and point of view immediately.

Evans makes two assumptions that are vital to his argument--TV has a large influence on children and role models strongly influence children's behavior. These are reasonable assumptions, but your students might not think about how they are influenced by TV or their role models. It might be interesting to discuss why they try to emulate media images--by wearing fancy sneakers, copying the latest Cosmo hairdo, or whatever--even though they identify with other role models.

1. African-American females usually have a good role model in their mother. Many males don't have a father around to influence their behavior, so they look to unrealistic models outside of the home.

2. The TV image of successful black males is slanted toward the few athletes and entertainers who make it big through incredible talent--and incredible luck. Such success appears to be more attainable than it really is, so young black males emulate the media stars rather than following the more realistic, but less glamorous, academic route to success. The celebrated black athletes and entertainers represent progress for blacks in society, but they serve as unrealistic role models.

3. More people know about Bo Jackson than Mike Espy because Bo is much more visible in the media--and he makes much more money.

4. Others may treat young blacks differently because of the media image. They may encourage behavior that follows the black male stereotype, even though such behavior may limit their education or future prospects outside of entertainment or athletics.

5. Evans argues that whites have a more diverse choice of media role models to emulate.

6. Evans places a lot of responsibility on the media superstars themselves to emphasize how lucky they have been, and to work to tell young people that their success was never assured. These people can also work to promote education and learning as a better route to success in all careers.

MISS DULING (p. 112)

Eudora Welty

Stylistic Highlights
Compare "Miss Duling" with Nicholas Gage's "The Teacher Who Changed My Life." They both celebrate an educator who has had a positive influence on the life of the author, and they both rely on vivid descriptions to help communicate the personality of their subject. Yet Miss Hurd became Gage's friend, whereas Miss Duling commands Welty's respect, not affection. Miss Duling's bell has become Welty's symbol of absolute authority. "That bell belonged to the figure of Miss Duling as though it grew directly out of her right arm, as wings grew out of an angel or a tail out of the devil." Note the ambiguity of that sentence--authority, as

symbolized by the bell, can be both good and bad. Miss Duling is clearly a hero to Welty, but her authority and influence are frightening.

The first essay question addresses Welty's desire to learn and how it was influenced by Miss Duling and the way she interacted with her parents. School can be an awful place if a student has a poor attitude about learning. How did your students become active in their own education? A suggested discussion for the second essay is negative authority figures. How many students have a positive view of their authority figure, now that they can look back on him or her with a little more objectivity?

Understanding the Essay
1. Miss Duling obviously never married or had much of a life outside of school. Miss Duling considered teaching at Jackson to be a challenge.

2. Many things made Miss Duling a figure of authority. She was demanding, strict, tolerated no nonsense, and was clearly an intimidating presence. The bell and the click of her heels on the floor symbolized her authority.

3. Miss Duling obviously had a lot of influence with former students, even decades later. Therefore, she had a lot of clout with any member of the community who had gone to school at Jackson.

4. Welty says that Miss Duling looks like a pilgrim, with a black-and-white checked dress, a red sweater, black stockings, and black hightop shoes with heels. She also had spectacles on a gold chain around her neck and wore a severe hairdo. Her appearance added to her authority by being as severe and no-nonsense as her personality.

5. Miss Duling wanted her students to be hardworking and disciplined. She strove for perfection, like Welty's mother.

6. Good students were given tickets to baseball games.

CHAPTER 4: Relationships

WILL YOU GO OUT WITH ME? (p. 122)

Laura Ullman

Stylistic Highlights
Ullman writes about dating, but her essay also points out that when society changes in general--even for the better--it's not easy to figure out its new "rules"

14

and expectations. Ullman clearly thinks it is good that women can ask men out, and that casual dates are a nice alternative to formal ones. She and her friends are confused at times, however, about what is expected of them. By framing the discussion of the advantages and problems of casual dating within her own struggle to ask a man out, she catches the reader's attention. Everyone knows how nerve-wracking it can be to ask someone out. By revealing her mental battle, Ullman underscores how much more difficult it must be if the ground rules between men and women are shifting.

The two essay questions get students thinking about the dating scene today. Has it changed much since Ullman's day? Do your students still enjoy "traditional formal dates," which put men and women in traditional roles that some might find offensive these days? What do they do once they're in a more lasting relationship?

<u>Understanding the Essay</u>
1. Ullman infers that women think they must take the initiative at times to have more control over their social lives.

2. Ullman is nervous about asking her friend out on a date, even though she thinks he will accept.

3. Casual dating is more relaxed, involves less preparation and anxiety, encourages friendships before romance, and can improve social lives by making dating less traumatic and more spontaneous. A disadvantage is the financial confusion that Ullman discusses. Can your students identify other disadvantages?

4. John is angry at himself because he thought Ullman wanted to go steady, so he didn't ask her to go Dutch--he was wrong, and he embarrassed both himself and her. Larry takes Ullman's offer to pay as a sign of rejection.

5. Any answer is acceptable as long as it is adequately explained.

NOT ALL MEN ARE SLY FOXES (p. 127)

Armin A. Brott

<u>Stylistic Highlights</u>
How much are children really influenced by what they read and see on TV? The current thinking is that they are very much influenced by outside messages (in fact, TV is cited as a negative influence in "The Wrong Examples"), and groups that have been discriminated against in the past--particularly women and minorities--are very conscious of the images that children's media contain. "Not All Men Are Sly Foxes" is, like "The Wrong Examples," an effective argument piece that introduces a group that is a surprising victim of discrimination in children's

literature--fathers. Brott uses the same tactics that feminist and minority groups have used before him in his arguments. First he establishes that the negative stereotype exists, then he links it to a current societal problem in hopes of winning over a potentially skeptical audience.

The first essay question provokes discussion about what the messages of children's literature should be. If they are meant to reflect society, how should they accomplish that? If they are meant to promote a healthier view of society and to encourage tolerance and understanding, who decides what society should be like? Do your students agree that fathers need to be depicted in a more positive light? The second essay alerts students to the stereotypes that do exist in children's "classics." How far should we go to "revise" these classics in this era of political correctness?

Understanding the Essay

1. Richard Scarry reissued some of his children's classics to depict the female characters performing the same tasks as the male characters.

2. A typical father, in both contemporary and classic children's books, is a secondary parental figure to the mother. He either does not interact much with the children or his interaction is negative.

3. Brott's daughter will ask him what happened to Babar's father.

4. Brott thinks that, since he believes that children's literature does influence children, they should depict characters in a balanced, nondiscriminatory manner. This question can be the basis for a discussion on the essay.

5. Brott believes that the negative stereotypes concerning fathers subtly tell men that they only play a secondary role in parenting and that mothers are the "truer" parents.

IT BEGINS AT THE BEGINNING (p. 133)

Deborah Tannen

Stylistic Highlights

"It Begins at the Beginning" is excerpted from Tannen's book You Just Don't Understand, which deals with the difficulty of men and women in communicating with each other and suggests ways to overcome it. This excerpt uses data and examples to establish that men and women do interact with others very differently--a very important argument for Tannen to convey effectively. Note how she summarizes a summary of what must be a large body of research to explain the basic interactions between boys and girls, then uses a specific example to illustrate

16

her earlier points. She then relates the information about children with how it affects relationships between men and women. This draws the reader into her argument that men and women do communicate differently in relationships, but they can learn to communicate more effectively . . . if they read the book.

Tannen, we hope, has done her research, but it's fun for students to investigate how it holds up to their own experiences. Of necessity, Tannen generalizes about how boys and girls behave with each other. Both essay questions encourage students to either support or contradict Tannen's findings. Another discussion could revolve around exactly how students think men and women differ in their communication styles--do your students have trouble communicating with the other gender?

<u>Understanding the Essay</u>
1. A boy wouldn't enjoy playing house because no one wins and no one loses. A girl wouldn't like baseball because it involves a lot of rules and it is competitive.

2. It would be very unusual for a girl to give such a strong, direct order--she'd probably be very angry or upset--whereas it wouldn't be unusual for a boy to say it.

3. Nick set himself up as being inferior to Joe. If Joe can get the pickle, he's tops in the hierarchy.

4. Boys establish a hierarchy according to who gives the orders--an order-giver is on top, and when a boy is ordered around, it means that he is low on the totem pole. Thus a man is inclined to give orders, not follow them. Girls don't usually give or take orders unless they are in roles--like mother/daughter--where they expect to. If they expect to follow orders from the husband, then they will not resent them.

5. Popular girls are popular because many girls want to be their special friend. Intimacy is important in girls' interactions, however, so only one or two other girls are special friends of a popular girl. The rest are rejected and may resent her. A popular boy can order many friends around--he can thus have large groups of friends as long as he's in charge.

6. Style differences lead to problems in communication between men and women. If people can understand what underlies the differences, they can work to improve their communications with the other gender.

THE STORY OF AN HOUR (p. 141)

Kate O' Flaherty Chopin

Stylistic Highlights
This fictional piece offers a stark commentary about marriage in Chopin's day. For current students, the story conveys how stifling marriage--even a good marriage--could be for young women, perhaps even more effectively than an essay would. As we ponder how the modern family seems to fragment more and more (see "One Son, Three Fathers"), it is interesting and educational to read a work that condemns the absolute rigidity of marriage and family life in the first half of the century. "The Story of an Hour" relates the tragedy of marriage for both partners, even for people as seemingly decent as Mr. and Mrs. Mallard. Mrs. Mallard is an obviously tragic figure, but Brently is also tragic--he is made pathetic in the reader's eyes by Mrs. Mallard's joy at his death, then he must bury his beloved wife. Chopin's prose is spare but it chillingly communicates her contempt for the institution of marriage.

In a few crisp paragraphs, Chopin demonstrates to the contemporary reader that she was ahead of her time in her views--but how much better is marriage today? The second essay question addresses this issue and is meant to provoke discussion about the purpose of marriage. Students should have fun with the first essay question--there's no wrong way to answer it--and it can be used to start a discussion about the techniques Chopin used to make this an effective story.

Understanding the Essay
1. Mrs. Mallard reacts to the news of her husband's death by weeping at first, then becoming very joyful at her new freedom.

2. The joy at her freedom was approaching to possess Mrs. Mallard.

3. It can be inferred that Brently and Josephine's marriage was viewed as a good one from the outside. Brently probably loved Josephine, and Josephine loved him sometimes and was good at stifling her true emotions at other times.

4. Love doesn't matter to Mrs. Mallard because the chance to be her own person overwhelms the desire to love or be loved. She probably thought love was important once--she did marry, and she is surprised by the joy she feels.

5. The joy that killed Mrs. Mallard was the joy she felt at Brently's death, a joy that was cut short by his reappearance. Everyone believed that her joy at seeing her husband alive was what killed her.

CHAPTER 5: <u>Friends</u>

COLLEGE FRIENDS (p. 149)

Jennifer Crichton

<u>Stylistic Highlights</u>
In another essay, Crichton discusses the opportunity for new college students to change their identity. In "College Friends," she examines one aspect of the "blank slate" that we start out with when we enter college--we have no friends. The initial desperate search for a friendly face begets mismatches, but lasting college friendships can be among the most valuable we make. The formation and death of friendships is easy to analyze in this setting, especially in hindsight, and Crichton again mixes general observations with personal experience to explore her topic. College for Crichton was a place to form different kinds of friendships, to get to know friends very well, and to identify how to approach friendship in general. Crichton's analysis is lightened by her slightly self-deprecating, informal tone.

   Both essay questions are meant to serve as a starting point for a topic that most students should enjoy discussing. Friendships are often as mysterious as they are valuable to us. Why do we make friends with certain people and not others? How does a particular friendship differ from others that we have?

<u>Understanding the Essay</u>
1. The first semester of college is filled with friendless desperation, so it is a poor time to find new friends. Friendships are rarely good when formed in desperation.

2. Crichton told personal information to someone new because she was desperate to make new friends. Their friendship faded rather quickly.

3. Crichton met Jean in a film class by arguing about Hitchcock with her. If Jean had been dismissive in that first meeting, they probably wouldn't have become friends.

4. Lovers make lousy best friends because of the sexual tensions, desire, and jealousy that can complicate the relationship. Also, though Crichton doesn't say it outright, they tend to come and go rather quickly, especially in college.

5. College friendships differ from other friendships because we have the opportunity to spend a lot of time with friends--we eat together, study together, and talk together. After college, friendships must be fitted around a schedule, so they are more fragmented.

6. Being with college friends lets Crichton remember when the future was a haze of possibilities, and reminds her that the situation is the same today.

DEATH OF A FRIENDSHIP (p. 155)

Stephanie Mansfield

Stylistic Highlights

Mansfield catches the reader's attention right away with her title, "Death of a Friendship." Friendships end all the time, but people seldom think about how or why they end, or about the consequences of such a "death" for them. It is as Mansfield says--a whole industry is built around "relationship" books but very little is said about how to handle a shifting friendship. Mansfield structures her essay in three parts--the pain an ended friendship can cause, the reasons for friendship "deaths," and ways to handle a friendship that seems to be going downhill. She makes the transition from consequences to possibilities in one sentence--"Friend-shedding is a rite of passage and should be seen as a positive sign of growth."--which allows her stories of pain and hope to coexist within a very short essay.

The first essay lets students explore the topic from a personal standpoint--just as it is interesting to discuss how friendships form, it is interesting to discuss why they die. The second essay question is meant to counter the unabashedly female point of view in the piece. Since Mansfield specifies that she's discussing how women feel at the death of their friendships, it is important to discuss how men feel about it.

Understanding the Essay

1. Mansfield parts company with her friend because they had a gradual loss of faith, were busy with their jobs, and were geographically separated.

2. A woman can be brokenhearted about the end of a friendship because she can be as emotionally dependent on a friend as on a lover.

3. Mansfield emphasizes that a friendship is a delicate balance, and both parties have to be able to honestly wish each other well. An exception to this can be a mentor/student relationship.

4. The best way to reevaluate a friendship is to have a frank discussion about it.

5. A friendship can be helped by cooling it off for a while, whereas a love affair needs consistent maintenance.

BEST FRIENDS (p. 159)

Howard Solomon, Jr.

<u>Stylistic Highlights</u>
Solomon was still a college student when he wrote "Best Friends," a piece whose informality makes it fun to read. Although psychologists and counselors could probably discuss the phenomenon of best friends with graphs, charts, and rows of numbers, Solomon's piece suits laypersons better. It is hard to pin down what makes a particular friend your best friend, but Solomon's many interviews give a good look at what his peers think about the subject, and his personal experience lets the reader know his perspective. As he presents the results of the interviews, Solomon acknowledges specific differences in the responses--his piece therefore becomes as much a discussion as an explanation of what makes a best friend. It must be taken into account that all the interviews he did for the essay were with fellow college students, which Solomon doesn't directly acknowledge. Responses from another age group might differ.

The first essay question is meant to reproduce approximately the questions that Solomon probably asked his interviewees. The second essay question picks up on a particular aspect of best friends that Solomon discusses in the essay but doesn't reach a conclusion for. Do your students agree with one another?

<u>Understanding the Essay</u>
1. The three qualities valued most in a best friend are love, honesty, and reciprocity.

2. Love is the most important quality. The affection and enjoyment they feel in the company of their best friend is very much prized.

3. Respondents disagreed about how many best friends a person can have. Some say one, others just a few, and a few people think they can have many.

4. It takes time to develop a best-friend relationship because you have to know the friend very well and get to know his or her bad points as well as the good. Solomon's interviewees believe a best friend is a best friend for life.

5. Men like their best friend(s) to have one outstanding quality. Women like their best friend(s) to be well-rounded.

6. Solomon says that the security of knowing you're never truly alone, that you have a friend you can count on, is a reason to value a best friend highly.

A MAGIC CIRCLE OF FRIENDS (p. 164)

Elvira M. Franco

Stylistic Highlights
Most students still take the traditional route straight from high school to college, but many people are returning to school after years, even decades, of living in the "real world." What such students lack in academic practice they usually more than make up for with their life experience and common sense. Franco was just such a student; she formed a bond of common experience with a group of women at school that gradually turned into a special group friendship. Although "A Magic Circle of Friends" is a personal narrative, Franco speaks less for herself than for all the women her age who return to school. The essay begins "I thought I was a unique item . . ." but the "I" becomes "We" as she meets her friends, so that by the end of the essay: "We know we are still strong, smart, vital, and, most especially, ready to work." By doing this, Franco demonstrates that college was in many ways a group activity for her, a discovery of her strengths and weaknesses through those of her peers.

The essay question points out that Franco's friendships were developed with people in a similar situation, facing similar pressures. Can students think of other situations in which intense friendships form? How do the views of friendship of forty-year-olds like Franco differ from those of twenty-year-old students?

Understanding the Essay
1. There is no one correct answer to this question. From the content of the essay, the fear of failure is probably the best answer, but other plausible fears could be discussed.

2. Franco and her friends lent one another support for completing assignments and sympathetic ears, and they found enjoyment in one anothers' company. They shared a common level of life experience, and they shared the joy of returning to school.

3. Some women returned to college with a carefree attitude, while others rejoiced in their discovery that learning could be fun.

4. The younger woman was too brash and angry and didn't mesh well with Franco's group. She gradually dropped out of the group and was later treated like a daughter by group members.

5. Franco and her friends have learned that there is no sense in being in a hurry to change the world, as the world is in no hurry to be changed. Also, they might not reach their original goals, but the process of trying to reach them can be rewarding in itself, and it can reveal new and better goals.

6. The goals will be reached by pushing, cajoling, smiling, and negotiating, not by fighting and abrading.

CHAPTER 6: Education

INTELLIGENCE (p. 171)

Isaac Asimov

Stylistic Highlights
By any traditional measurement, Asimov is an extremely intelligent man, as well as a famous one. He doesn't boast when he says that he scored 160 on an intelligence test--it's a simple fact that he's good at such tests. But being intelligent, he ponders what his intelligence really represents and what it can accomplish for him. He establishes his "auto-repair man" as his opposite to represent those who are not in the least intellectual but are still expert at a task that is highly valuable to society. The contrast is neatly set up, and it forces the reader to confront the issue on Asimov's mind--if we define intelligence in a very limited way, then only one subset of people will be perceived as intelligent. The academically brilliant absentminded professors may be completely inept outside the classroom or laboratory, but with the current emphasis on intellectual versus practical skills, they are held up as the models of intelligence. But the reader must wonder with Asimov, are they really smart?
      The first essay question is a fun experiment for students to try. It should make them think about the different types of intelligence that their peers possess. The second essay question should remind students that today's society does reward talents other than the intellectual very handsomely--too handsomely, some would argue (see "The Wrong Examples"). How important is the way we test intelligence?

Understanding the Essay
1. Asimov was still a private and still had KP duty.

2. Asimov considers himself far smarter than his mechanic but is utterly dependent on him to take care of his car.

3. Asimov would fail any intelligence test his mechanic devised. Society considers Asimov the more intelligent of the two because those who decide how intelligence should be measured are similar to him in their intellectual and academic background and values.

4. Asimov's mechanic was confident that Asimov would fall for his joke because he saw Asimov as being too highly educated to be very smart. Asimov is uneasy because he thinks his mechanic's conclusions might have some merit.

ANGELS ON A PIN (p. 175)

Alexander Calandra

Stylistic Highlights
Some test questions have many answers, but it is rare that the teacher who wrote the question, particularly a physics teacher, will consider more than one to be correct. The question that provoked the confrontation in "Angels on a Pin" provided students with a choice: should they show the teacher that they knew what he wanted, or should they merely answer the question correctly in any one of several ways? Calandra writes the story in the spirit in which he participated in it-- as an objective observer. He passes judgment, but he is nonjudgmental about the philosophy of either the teacher or the student. But his dispassionate reporting ably demonstrates that doing well on a test and learning a lot in class are not necessarily related. The student, in this case, has not only answered the question correctly twice but he has also taught his teacher something--he'd better word his questions more carefully.
    The first essay question puts students in the teacher's shoes, to help them see that being a teacher is not as cut-and-dried as it might seem at times. The second essay encourages them to think about the difference between academic effort and learning. Most classes, one hopes, force students to work in an academic sense, but what most encourages them to really explore and learn about a topic?

Understanding the Essay
1. The answer is correct in that it does show how to determine the height of a building by using a barometer. It is incorrect because it wasn't the answer the teacher wanted. Calandra suggests giving the student another chance to answer the question by using his knowledge of physics.

2. The student spends a lot of time deciding which of many answers he wants to offer. Calandra probably doesn't give him full credit because the answer still isn't the one the teacher was looking for.

3. It can be any of the pendulum, barometer units, superintendent gift, or shadow ratio answers. See how creative students can be with the second part of the question.

4. The student does know the answer the teacher is looking for. He doesn't give it because he is protesting that the scientific method that he is supposed to use to solve problems is not necessarily the best way to understand a subject.

5. Calandra is saying that providing the correct answer is not necessarily the sign of an intelligent and able student, and that creative thinking can be stifled by demanding conformist thought. The conflict illustrates this--an able student is initially denied credit, not because he provides a wrong answer but because he doesn't provide the answer the teacher is looking for.

ANOTHER KIND OF SEX ED (p. 180)

Sharon A. Sheehan

Stylistic Highlights
Modern sex ed presents many dilemmas for those who teach it, and Sheehan starts her essay with one of the most controversial topics of the day--how accessible should birth control devices be for teenagers? Should we just teach teenagers how to have sex without having babies or catching diseases? Sheehan, on the front lines of sex ed, disliked this option but in her essay needs to establish her alternative as a positive one, not just another negative don't-have-sex message that she knows doesn't work. Notice how she blasts casual sex without mentioning it--instead she mentions the "huge empty hole" it leaves in teenagers' perceptions of the relationship between sex and marriage. She can then propose her remedy to fill this hole--teaching students how to build a whole relationship, rather than just how to have safe sex--as a way to solve both the mechanical and the moral problems of premarital sex. Her conclusion, "Sex education is about nothing less than how and when we hand over this astonishing gift of self," efficiently summarizes her argument while maintaining a positive view of the role sex should play in people's lives.

The first two essay questions emphasize the thrust of Sheehan's argument-- that sex ed should teach about how to build lasting relationships. Students should think about this in the context of their own beliefs and experiences. The third question has them take a look at the broader picture--do they agree with Sheehan's basic premise that sex and morals are closely linked?

Understanding the Essay

1. Sheehan thinks students should have a healthy sense of shame about their sex lives; they should have to think carefully about what they are doing. Planned Parenthood also advocates eradicating shame on the part of single sexually active teenagers.

2. Shame has two sides--it can exert negative control and it can be self-protecting, as is modesty. Shame can protect us by preventing us from treating others badly.

3. Sheehan is stunned by Planned Parenthood's solution to teenage pregnancy because it ignores the moral issue of premarital sex entirely and concentrates totally on the mechanical prevention of pregnancy.

4. Sheehan believes that teaching commitment and how to form a lasting relationship will help end teenage pregnancy. Instill a healthy sense of shame and teach young people how to incorporate sex into a long-term, loving relationship.

5. This question can be used to start a discussion or as a writing topic. Any answer is acceptable for the first part, as long as the student backs it up adequately. The answer to the second part should touch on the way Planned Parenthood ignores the roles of shame and morals in a person's decision whether to have sex.

6. Sheehan learned that students want to learn about forming lasting relationships, that they are confused about the role sex should play in their lives, and that they are not as sexually active as adults tend to assume they are.

THE WASHED WINDOW (p. 187)

Dorothy Canfield Fisher

Stylistic Highlights
"The Washed Window" is probably one of the best rags-to-riches stories in existence, but it also demonstrates Fisher's interest in education. It involves material wealth and fame but only as secondary issues--Booker T. Washington's pursuit of intellectual riches is the centerpiece of the story. Fisher's simple technique of not revealing the narrator's identity until the end makes the story even more remarkable. The reader is forced to consider Washington's enormous strides to progress from simply cleaning a woodshed to becoming one of the educational leaders of his time. Fisher also uses Washington's own descriptions to great effect. Readers share Washington's queasy feelings when Mrs. Ruffner examines the shed for the third time and root for him as he cleans the room at

26

Hampton. Washington becomes much more than a famous name in the story--he becomes a very human, appealing hero of a good story.

The essay questions both touch on the relationship between school and learning. Washington's lessons taught him how to succeed in school, but he learned them outside the classroom. What do students really need to succeed in school? What do they need to learn outside of school?

<u>Understanding the Essay</u>
1. Booker T. Washington visited the Knapp house. It is a shrine to him because it is where his mentor came from.

2. The slaves let their surroundings fall into disrepair because they had no knowledge of better standards of living. The white people felt that any kind of work was beneath them--they had slaves to work for them--so they didn't fix their own belongings.

3. The narrator takes a chance with Mrs. Ruffner because the pay is better than in the coal mines, and he hopes that she will help him get a better education than he could at the night school he attended to learn to read. Finally, he has nothing to lose.

4. The narrator learns that he can think for himself and do a job correctly without being told exactly what to do. He also learns the value of a job well done, and he sees how he himself can achieve a higher standard of living than he had been used to.

5. Mrs. Ruffner gives the narrator books, teaches him how to study, and helps him start his own library. She shows him how to live just by the way she lives in her home.

6. The narrator thoroughly cleans a classroom to gain admission to Hampton.

CHAPTER 7: <u>Work</u>

ONE MAN'S KIDS (p. 201)

Daniel Meier

<u>Stylistic Highlights</u>
In recent years, it has become unwise to discuss men and women in terms of hunter/provider and nurturer/homemaker. Yet Meier, by taking a traditionally "female" job, discovers that these stereotypes are perpetuated both by what

people do and in their expectations of others. Meier describes his day early in "One Man's Kids"; when compared to the "male" jobs and objectives he later identifies, he is indeed in a "female" job, and he writes a concise "female" essay. Even though he says men can't identify with emotional descriptions, he describes success through simple emotion--his goals are, as he might say, of the heart, not of the intellect. He must risk alienating or at least losing the sympathy of his male audience to fully explain his work. Even Meier's job benefits don't involve the merit pay or box seats at the ballpark that are seductive to his male audience. Instead, they are what bring him closer to the success he seeks with his students-- happiness, interest, enjoyment.

The first essay question involves the difference in reactions between men and women that Meier describes. Men, from Meier's point of view, are rather cold and analytical. What do your students think about the different ways that men and women approach work and emotional expression? The second essay puts students in Meier's shoes--how would they deal with his situation?

Understanding the Essay
1. The series of events takes only five minutes. Meier makes the point that his work is a constant ebb and flow of helping kids with practical and nonpractical tasks, listening to them, and ensuring that they get what they need. He demonstrates that his job is not a typically male job.

2. Teaching first grade is not traditional male work because it does not involve a specific expertise nor does it provide clear-cut goals to pursue.

3. Meier defines success in his job through matters of the heart. If he can keep the kids happy and occupied, he is successful.

4. Male principals expect certain answers from Meier. They are suspicious at the outset because he wants to teach first grade, so he must couch his answers in intellectual, goal-oriented terms.

5. Men want to know what he teaches and his qualifications for the job. Women want to know about his job, and they identify with how his class must feel about having a male teacher--their conversation is more immediate and personal.

6. Meier lists being able to bake cookies without having their sticking together as they cool, buy cheap sewing materials, remove splinters, and find useful odds and ends among his benefits. He can also fill lulls in dinner conversations with the latest riddles enjoyed by six-year-olds.

MY MOTHER NEVER WORKED (p. 206)

Bonnie Smith-Yackel

Stylistic Highlights
In many ways, society equates working with earning a paycheck. Smith-Yackel's description of her mother's life in the context of her phone call to Social Security offers a striking contrast between how she perceives what her mother did when alive and how the government perceives it. Although Martha might have dreaded the life she was to lead before her marriage, she certainly buckled down and saw her labors through. Yet, just as the reader is reeling from the detailed descriptions of Martha's diligence and perseverance, Smith-Yackel reveals the official view of this lifetime of labor: "Well, you see--your mother never worked." "My Mother Never Worked" is more descriptive than argumentative, but by describing her mother's work as a prelude to revealing the government's indifference to it, Smith-Yackel raises important questions without asking them directly.

The first essay question addresses the homemaker's place in society. How important a job do your students think it is? The second question acknowledges that many in our society choose to leave child care to others--in this case, what can society do to help ensure that children are adequately cared for?

Understanding the Essay
1. Martha dreaded the thought of being stuck with six children to take care of. It's hard to say if her attitude changed, but the situation that she had dreaded certainly came to pass.

2. A cholera epidemic killed all the pigs, a drought wiped out all their crops, and dust-bowl conditions made their recovery very difficult.

3. Martha canned, sewed--clothes and quilts--gardened, helped with the haying, milked cows, and raised chickens and ducks.

4. The best answer to this question is that hard work is the life Martha knew best, and she would have had difficulty adjusting to an idle life-style.

5. Martha's daughter won't get a death benefit because Martha never received any pay for the work she did. Thus, in the government's eyes, Martha never worked.

HISPANIC, USA: THE CONVEYOR-BELT LADIES (p. 212)

Rose Del Castillo Guilbault

<u>Stylistic Highlights</u>
For most students, it doesn't really matter what kind of work they do during the summer as long as it helps them pay their bills during the school year. The work they get, however, can open their eyes about jobs, and the people who perform them, that they would have otherwise avoided. Del Castillo Guilbault's mind-numbing conveyor belt job didn't add much to her resume, but it did add to her personal growth by letting her get to know the "conveyor-belt ladies." Note how she writes her essay in three stages. She begins from the outside looking in--the work is tedious and exhausting, her colleagues are "old, fat Mexican women," migrant workers who "could look forward only to the same uninspiring parts on a string of grim real-life stages." As she becomes part of the scene, she reveals the individual personalities and the camaraderie that can transcend the bleak life-style. Then she leaves the ladies behind, underscoring the fact that weighing tomatoes is the highest professional goal her ex-colleagues can aspire to.
    The first essay question has students examine how a short-term job might have helped them to grow or see things differently, even though they might not have liked it. Someone who has had only one job can discuss the good and bad points of it. The second essay question gets students to consider the lives of Del Castillo Guilbault's co-workers. How can they persevere under such difficult conditions?

<u>Understanding the Essay</u>
1. The jobs in the vegetable packing sheds were a step up for the women working in them because they paid better than the jobs in the fields and the work was done inside; thus the women were protected from the elements.

2. Del Castillo Guilbault was unhappy about working in the shed because she would be forced to work with the Mexican migrant workers, whom she considered to be uneducated and beneath her. Also, she was worried that her job might stigmatize her in the eyes of her Anglo classmates.

3. The women simply wore down the male supervisors, so that they ended up basically ignoring each other. The men tried to stop the women from talking by rotating them to different positions on the conveyor belt.

4. Del Castillo Guilbault's co-workers were gregarious, entertaining women who could break up the monotony of the work with humor, gossip, and stories. Their melancholic moments came from the difficult lives they led, facing racism, abusive husbands, and poverty.

30

5. Del Castillo Guilbault received special treatment during her last summer because she was moving on to college that fall. She was probably promoted because of her academic achievements.

6. Del Castillo Guilbault's last day was anticlimactic because nothing unusual happened. The day simply ended, although most of her co-workers did wish her luck.

THE COMPANY MAN (p. 219)

Ellen Goodman

Stylistic Highlights
"Workaholic" became a buzzword a few years ago. What used to be admired as ambition is now identified as a kind of disease, particularly if the "workaholism" is extreme. Yet corporations encourage it in their executives, as Goodman's essay points out with chilling effect. Goodman's skill as a newspaper column writer is apparent in the first sentence--the reader is hooked, wanting to know how the man worked himself to death at such an ungodly hour even before seeing how the Bears did. Throughout, Goodman writes with a brevity that will keep her column from getting slashed by an editor's pen, but that does not keep her story and her opinions from coming through. She skillfully uses the time of day to emphasize her message. At precisely 3:00 A.M. on Sunday, nobody should be working themselves to death. At 5:00 P.M. on the afternoon of the funeral, nobody should be starting a search for the deceased's replacement--the next company man.
        The first essay question encourages students to think about workaholism on an intellectual level. Most of them probably haven't yet had a chance to be workaholics, but what do they think creates one? The second essay asks them to look at themselves and see if they fit the workaholic mode. Do some of them think they'll be workaholics, or are they confident they'll just work hard?

Understanding the Essay
1. The time of Phil's death is important because it is a time of the week when no one with an office job should be working. It says right away that he's a workaholic. Even if he died in his sleep, by saying that he worked himself to death at 3:00 A.M. Sunday morning, Goodman establishes his problem.

2. Phil worked about seventy to seventy-five hours a week. He was overweight because he had no time to exercise.

3. Phil is survived by his wife, two sons, and one daughter. His wife is bitter but gave up competing with his work years ago. His oldest son didn't know him, and his daughter couldn't communicate with him. His youngest son wanted to identify with him and keep him home--he's living on the fringes of society when his father dies.

4. The neighbors were probably embarrassed when asked about Phil because they didn't know him. They wouldn't have had much of a chance to interact with him.

5. Phil's widow needs the company's president to help her sort through Phil's financial matters.

6. The moral of the story is that it's an unending cycle: those who succeed in corporate America are those who work the hardest, and they will have one-track lives like Phil's.

CHAPTER 8: A Multiculturalist Society

THE CULT OF ETHNICITY, GOOD AND BAD (p. 227)

Arthur Schlesinger, Jr.

Stylistic Highlights
Multiculturalism is a hot topic these days. Students protest the lack of racial diversity on college campuses, parents protest the lack of minority figures in elementary school texts, and everywhere educators and public figures scramble to present more ethnically "balanced" material than they had previously. Schlesinger is bucking the trend in "The Cult of Ethnicity, Good and Bad," where he argues that multiculturalism may provoke group separation and ethnic fragmentation rather than greater appreciation of other ethnic groups. To do so, he leads gradually into his arguments against multiculturalism by discussing how the United States achieved relative multiethnic harmony, then by explaining how that harmony has changed over the years. He also acknowledges the abuses of the past and the benefits that "the cult of ethnicity," as he calls it, has had, before he launches into his main argument. His conclusion that our citizens must think of themselves culturally as Americans first is strengthened by the implied consequences of ethnic fragmentation, which comes from his earlier discussion of ethnic troubles elsewhere in the world.

The first essay question addresses the forces that have shaped Americans into a common culture. What roles have schools played? What are some of the other forces at work? The second essay question encourages students to put themselves in Schlesinger's shoes. If they agree with his earlier arguments, do they share his optimism? How many of your students agree with his basic argument that multiculturalism encourages ethnic fragmentation in American culture?

Understanding the Essay

1. Schlesinger's thesis that multiculturalism threatens to disrupt the ideal that binds America together as a nation is stated in paragraph 9.

2. America was founded on the principle that it was not meant to preserve old cultures but to forge a new national identity. Ethnicity seeks to preserve the other cultures--to separate rather than assimilate.

3. Schlesinger discusses the effects of ethnic and racial conflict throughout the world, ranging from nations in crisis to those that face growing problems with ethnic cultures. He also discusses its impact on the one nation that has had a relative lack of ethnic conflict, the United States.

4. The United States managed to avoid the conflicts of ethnicity in the past by forging a new national identity and assimilating newcomers into it. It also pushed non-Caucasians and non-English speakers to the periphery of society. The second part of the question will have a variety of answers.

5. New immigration laws have altered the composition of the American population, and the Eurocentric outlook of the United States has been challenged in the names of multiethnicity and political correctness. Schlesinger takes these phenomena seriously, at least because of the consequences he foresees of them.

6. The positive aspects of the new cult of ethnicity have been a new recognition of the achievements of groups that were previously spurned, and a new and invigorating sense of the world. The negative aspects have been the rejection of the American goals of assimilation and integration, group separatism, and the possibility of the resegregation of American life. Answers to the last part of the question will vary.

EGGS, TWINKIES AND ETHNIC STEREOTYPES (p. 233)

Jeanne Park

Stylistic Highlights

Not all ethnic stereotypes are negative. As Park says, she was expected to be intelligent and hardworking because she was Asian. This is an unusual way to begin an essay on the problem of ethnic stereotyping, because most racial slurs are hardly flattering, but it reveals an interesting point of view in a straightforward

33

essay with a simple message. Park argues that any stereotype has a negative effect by discouraging sharing and understanding between ethnic groups--if someone has labeled a group of people, he or she will be unlikely to try to find out anything about the individuals within the group. After Park describes her own experience with a positive ethnic stereotype, she reveals the problems when a stereotype is believed. Asians can feel superior to others and form their own negative stereotypes. Park points this out in stories about how Asians treat their Hispanic employees, bolstering her argument that any ethnic stereotype is negative and limiting.

The first essay question encourages students to look at themselves and how they interact with others. Do they perpetuate stereotypes or are they, as Park urged, doing better? The second essay question addresses one part of the essay-- how is language used to promote bigotry? How large a role does it play?

Understanding the Essay

1. The stereotype of the hardworking, intelligent Asian flattered Park for obvious reasons. It haunted her because of the pressure it put on her to excel all the time.

2. Park attended a prestigious high school where students of all races excelled and Asians weren't automatically considered to be the most academically gifted.

3. An egg is a white who socializes with Asians. A Twinkie is an Asian who socializes with whites.

4. Labels such as "egg" and "Twinkie" make it difficult for students to socialize with other students outside their own ethnic group. Such labels impose an identity on other ethnic groups without encouraging an effort to understand or interact with them.

5. The stereotype is that Asians believe Hispanics are lazy and can't be trusted.

6. Stereotypes limit our growth as individuals because we cheat ourselves out of the benefits different cultures can contribute to our own enrichment.

SUBTLE LESSONS IN RACISM (p. 238)

Kirsten Mullen

Stylistic Highlights
In "Subtle Lessons in Racism," Mullen points out that there are problems with racism on the part of teachers and administrators, even in a good school. She knows that her audience might not be initially receptive to her arguments--she is trying to break a taboo, as she says at the end--so she structures the piece in a

way that keeps the reader from rejecting the points she wishes to make. Mullen begins by emphasizing that <u>she</u> didn't expect to encounter racism in school, and that in general she admires the teachers at her son's school. She establishes her negative comments about the school in only one context--racism--and doesn't come across as simply a disgruntled parent. Then near the end, after she has discussed her negative experiences, she acknowledges that perhaps she is "never satisfied," but implies that the reader shouldn't be satisfied either. She finishes with a positive story to lighten the early negative ones and to emphasize that breaking the taboo of discussing racism does not need to be confrontational.

The first essay question addresses the problem of what defines racism. Many of Mullen's objections concern very indirectly racist actions--what do your students think about them? The second issue involves tolerance in general. Just how far do we have to go to achieve a nondiscriminatory society?

Understanding the Essay

1. Mullen is in awe of how the teachers do their job in her son's school, but she feels they could be more sensitive to racial issues.

2. The first part of the question is a matter of opinion. Mullen thinks they are singled out for racist reasons.

3. Teachers must feed children breakfast, take care of them in before- and after-school programs, teach sex education, be gender-neutral--and take care to be race-neutral--in their teaching.

4. Mullen was terrified when she first brought up a racial issue at her school. She became less frightened because she saw that she could have an impact, and she seemed to be listened to with respect by the teachers and the principal.

5. The discussion of racial issues will cease to be taboo if more people bring them up and embrace the subject.

THE MIDDLE-CLASS BLACK'S BURDEN (p. 243)

Leanita McClain

Stylistic Highlights

It is impossible to summarize McClain's essay more skillfully than she does herself in the first sentence: "I am a member of the black middle-class who has had it with being patted on the head by white hands and slapped in the face by black hands for my success." She eloquently describes the particular difficulties she has faced, but her basic point has been made, and it stays with the reader throughout the essay. McClain has succeeded professionally but has entered a racial twilight zone through her success--no group claims her as their own. The image of white hands patting her on the head establishes her point that she has not escaped racism, that she is still somewhat of a "freak" to whites. As she says, "Life is easier, being black is not." The black hands slapping her communicate the abuse she receives from blacks--and the pain of the guilt she is unable to escape.

The first essay question addresses the basic racial issues that McClain must face. She <u>has</u> raised herself up by her bootstraps but has been denied the admiration that those from other ethnic backgrounds receive. The second essay question encourages students to consider racism and racial harmony. What can be done to improve race relations?

<u>Understanding the Essay</u>
1. McClain's thesis is that, as a middle-class black, she is rejected by both whites and blacks. She communicates this in the first paragraph.

2. White people pat McClain's head because she's a novelty as a successful black woman. Black people slap her face because they claim she has forgotten where she came from. These actions anger McClain because she cannot succeed and be respected for her accomplishments--the issue of race always comes first.

3. In achieving her success, McClain has accumulated many trappings that blacks associate with whites. She lives in a better neighborhood and has a different pattern to her life from that of many of her former friends and acquaintances.

4. McClain's burden is the uncomfortable position her success has put her in. She best explains this when she describes herself as a "rope in a tug of war" in paragraph 13. Answers will vary for the last part of this question.

5. McClain has fulfilled the "entry requirements" of the American middle class in her life-style, but her skin color makes it difficult for her to truly assimilate into that life-style. She is uncomfortably middle class because she fears she might be reclaimed into the "purposeless present of some of [her] contemporaries."

6. McClain has a dim view of race relations in America in 1980. Her stories of the white reaction to her success underscore her attitude. The second part of the question is a matter of opinion.

COMING TO AN AWARENESS OF LANGUAGE (p. 253)

Malcolm X

Stylistic Highlights
This is an excellent essay to read after the resurgence of interest in Malcolm X that occurred in the early 1990s. The leader who inspired a movie, countless baseball caps, and T-shirts, and whose autobiography sales surged, was an illiterate hustler languishing in prison as a young adult. For people who have had an adequate education, it is hard to imagine expanding one's vocabulary one dictionary page at a time, but Malcolm X gives a vivid account of how he discovered the power of the written word. He was in a situation where he could truly distinguish between verbal and written eloquence, between leading others in person and leading others from afar. Once he discovered the doors that written communication opened for him, there was no stopping him. Notice how, toward the end of the story, he equates illiteracy with incarceration. He is speaking of his own experiences, but just as he had "never been so truly free in my life," he sets an example that others can follow.
　　The first essay question addresses the point about freedom. Exactly how did Malcolm X's literacy set him free? The second essay question involves the technique Malcolm X used to learn how to effectively read and write. Can just anyone pick up a dictionary and use it to turn her- or himself into a good reader and writer?

Understanding the Essay
1. The first person is appropriate because Malcolm X is telling a very personal story that is central to his development as a thinker and communicator.

2. Malcolm X wanted to be able to write letters that had a chance of influencing the people who received them, and he was frustrated by his inability to express himself. He also envied his cellmate, Bimbi, for his knowledge.

3. Malcolm X was only going through the motions when he read because he didn't understand most of the words in the books. He solved this problem by learning the words in the dictionary page by page.

4. He was an articulate speaker, using the slang of his day, but he realized he couldn't carry this over to writing. Therefore, he was not able to command attention with his writing the way he could with his speaking.

5. A dictionary is like a miniature encyclopedia in that the information in it adds up to a broad-based wealth of knowledge.

6. The essay is organized chronologically, focusing on the progression of Malcolm X's education. First he discusses the motivations for his self-education. Then he discusses how he educated himself. He concludes by discussing what his learning gave him in life.

WHY SPANISH TRANSLATIONS? (p. 259)

Mauricio Molina

Stylistic Highlights
Molina's essay is simple and straightforward. It states that Hispanics can get by with little or no English in the United States, and it argues that the United States should insist on English as the only language in which official business is conducted. The fact that he is a Hispanic who had to learn English when he first came here lends weight to his argument--if immigrants need to learn English, he proves by his own example that they can. In his essay, however, Molina touches on many interesting points without discussing them further. For instance, what about the Chinese, French, and Serbo-Croations who have no translations available to them? Would eliminating Spanish translations make it fairer for these groups of immigrants? Should the government give Spanish immigrants a push in the right direction by helping to promote English classes? And how does Molina think the government should protect the civil rights of people learning English who aren't yet proficient at it?
　　The first essay addresses the question of whether English should be our only language. Do your students agree with Molina? The second essay question puts students in the opposite situation--if they could get by with English in a foreign country, as Hispanics can get by with Spanish here, would they try to learn the local language?

Understanding the Essay
1. Molina didn't have to learn English because Spanish translations are everywhere, and he could use them to get by in Spanish. He learned English because he was naive--he believed his parents when they told him he had to learn English to thrive in the United States.

2. America is the land of opportunity and a little bit more for Hispanics because opportunity is served up to them with a Spanish flavor, if they choose it that way.

3. A Hispanic is someone who came, or whose ancestors came, from a region where Spanish is the only language spoken.

4. People who need Spanish translations are those who have just emigrated from a Spanish-speaking country. Such translations are meant for a cross-section of Hispanics, most of who, Molina would argue, should have no need of them.

5. Molina thinks that America shouldn't coddle its recent arrivals. The opportunities are available for those willing to work hard for them, and people who speak other languages don't have the advantages of Hispanics. He would like a list to be distributed in Spanish, of all English classes in each area.

DON'T JUST STAND THERE (p. 264)

Diane Cole

Stylistic Highlights
One wonders what would happen if Cole met Eve Drobot ("Come, Let Me Offend You"). In "Don't Just Stand There," Cole explains how to deal with people like Drobot who say things, whether intentionally or unintentionally, that others find offensive. Cole makes her point by beginning with a personal experience of an anti-Semitic joke--and how it hurt her--then backing up her desire to respond to the joke by quoting what experts in the field said she should do. Readers can identify with her predicament when faced with an offensive joke, which makes the solutions and expert opinions more immediate. The rest of the piece is a how-to manual for dealing with various situations that combines Cole's point of view with extensive research. Note how Cole skillfully presents sample situations and their solutions, again making the expert opinions more accessible to the reader.
    The first essay question shows that Cole is writing to an open-minded audience that is sensitive to the potential for damage that language possesses. Were your students influenced by Cole's essay? In what way? The second essay question addresses the difference between the Drobot essay and the Cole essay. Where should the line between rightful offense and righteous indignation be drawn?

Understanding the Essay
1. Cole froze and didn't respond to her colleague's anti-Semitic joke. This was not the right response--she should have informed him of how the joke had offended her.

2. Tolerating offensive statements and jokes can lead to a desensitization that can lead in turn to the toleration of other discriminatory actions.

3. The best way to confront someone who has offended you is to give the benefit of the doubt and acknowledge that the offensive statement might have been unintentional, but to acknowledge that you were offended. If you are in a group, it

is best to confront the individually in private, with the backing of others in the group, if possible.

4. It is rarely a good idea to confront someone in a public setting because it makes that person defensive and less likely to listen to your point of view.

5. If the boss is making offensive remarks, the worker should get the support of colleagues, if possible. He or she should then meet privately with the boss to discuss the problem, using the same techniques of giving the other party the benefit of the doubt, at least initially. If no progress is made, the worker should know how to make an official protest about the boss's behavior.

6. Children have fewer techniques for dealing with uncomfortable situations like being the butt of a joke, so they are more likely to strike back verbally or physically, escalating the conflict.

7. A good way to promote understanding among children is to have them interact with children of other backgrounds and points of view so that they can learn that stereotypes of other groups aren't true.

COME, LET ME OFFEND YOU (p. 274)

Eve Drobot

<u>Stylistic Highlights</u>
In a collection of essays that are mostly earnest, with a narrow agenda, Drobot's piece is an interesting contrast. Her tongue remains firmly in her cheek from the title through to the last sentence--her response to the thin skins of those she writes about is humor. Her humor is particularly effective because her exaggerated examples are close enough to common experience that the reader can identify with them--and, perhaps, laugh. Drobot has a serious argument, that in their pursuit of political correctness and tolerance, people have become intolerant and narrow-minded. Because she is aware that her argument might offend some of her all-too-earnest audience, however, she makes her point with hyperbole and sarcasm. Her statement "there must definitely have been a moment in time when somebody figured out there was more to be gained by being indignant than by being right" best captures her exasperation, her opinion, and her ability to keep her sense of humor.

The first essay question asks students if they agree with Drobot. Do they think too many people have specific agendas and no sense of humor these days? The second essay question focuses on the badge idea. Drobot says it would save hurt feelings, but she's not very serious about it. Still, some groups <u>have</u> adopted the badge motif, such as the pink triangle for gays. What do your students think?

40

1. It is unwise to discuss veal piccata with a "raging vegetarian."

2. Drobot argues that the new sensitivity makes people afraid to open their mouths for fear of hurting someone's feelings.

3. The advantage of labeling oneself is that people will know one's specific agenda and can avoid giving offense in conversation. A disadvantage of such a system is identified when Drobot reveals that Hitler first came up with and implemented the idea.

4. The editor wants to know the gender and ethnic backgrounds of the poets that Drobot's friend used in his anthology so he can produce a demographically representative book.

5. Drobot says society should work toward a world in which people see past race, creed, gender, ethnic background, and physical limitations to talent and ability. That goal has been sidetracked by the current trend that it is better to be indignant than be right.

6. Hitler first thought of identifying people with badges. Drobot makes this association to point out how counterproductive it is to define oneself--and wish to label others--on such narrow terms.

CHAPTER 10: Addictions

CONFESSIONS OF AN EX-SMOKER (p. 282)

Franklin E. Zimring

Stylistic Highlights
Zimring's essay is an amusing exploration of the mind of the ex-smoker. He identifies three mindsets and describes them so clearly that everyone--smoker, ex-smoker, and non-smoker--can identify at least a few people who belong to one or more of the groups. He facetiously established the groupings "in the interest of science," but his point that smokers and ex-smokers are going to have to understand each other is very valid. By organizing the groups of ex-smokers in the order of stridency, Zimring establishes a progression from zealot to serene that might very well have been his own progression as a maturing ex-smoker. And by positioning the zealot and the evangelist at the "immature" end of the spectrum, Zimring subtly conveys his message that ex-smokers should become less

judgmental of smokers, and that smokers should tolerate the emotional upheaval of ex-smoker friends as best they can.

The first essay question asks students what provoked Zimring's essay in the first place--antismoking legislation. What percentage of your students smoke? Do the smokers feel discriminated against? How tolerant are the ex- and nonsmokers? The second essay question addresses Zimring's potentially controversial assertion that the serene are better for having smoked. Can smoking contribute to a person's life experience?

Understanding the Essay

1. It is important to understand the emotional states that quitting smoking can cause, because the pressures on smokers from restrictive legislation are increasing, and more people are likely to quit.

2. Zealots are the fanatic antismokers who consider smokers to be scum for being unable to quit. Evangelists preach the joys of converting to nonsmoking and the so-called ease of quitting. The elect don't verbally assault smokers, but they exude an annoying smugness about having quit. The serene have come to terms with their former habit and their current status as a nonsmoker.

3. Zealots condemn smokers, while evangelists try to save them by getting them to quit. Doctors are likely to be zealots because they are likely to have been deeply addicted to tobacco in the past.

4. The elect annoy smokers because they exude smugness.

5. The serene are at peace with the fact that they once smoked, so they don't judge either themselves or current smokers harshly. Not all ex-smokers are self-confident enough or comfortable enough with their own actions to become what Zimring terms "serene."

6. Self-acceptance and gratitude help an ex-smoker become serene. Self-acceptance can help in other areas of life as well.

7. This question is a matter of opinion, as long as it is adequately answered. One would infer that Zimring identifies with the serene, so he doesn't judge harshly people who still smoke. He would be indifferent to smoking regulations, because he is not bothered by people smoking near him if he is truly serene.

LEGALIZE DRUGS (p. 288)

Ethan A. Nadelmann

Stylistic Highlights

Nadelmann organizes his thoughts very carefully in this essay. Thus, in addressing what is often an emotional subject, his rather inflammatory argument that drugs should be legalized is presented to the reader in a manner that appears level-headed and well thought out. His two opening paragraphs establish the link between drugs and crime. The point is obvious--they are linked in the public's mind. To argue his point, he identifies four connections between drugs and crime, and uses them to argue that drugs and crime are not necessarily related--drug laws and crime are. He sets up his entire essay by the end of the second paragraph--all he needs to do is discuss each link between drugs and crime, and how the legalization of drugs would perhaps break the link. In his discussion, he equates drug laws with Prohibition, and concludes with the thoughts of Rockefeller, who reluctantly withdrew his support of Prohibition. By doing this, Nadelmann establishes a connection for his argument with another, failed, "drug law."

The first essay question requires students to perform the same exercise as Nadelmann. They must express their opinion and support it. How many students agree with Nadelmann? The second essay question encourages students to consider why certain drugs are illegal. What makes them dangerous to society? Should they be legalized? What differentiates them from our two most popular legal drugs?

Understanding the Essay

1. Nadelmann argues that drugs and crime are linked in the public mind because of drug laws, not because of the consequences of widespread drug use. Therefore, the association would be considerably weakened if drugs were legalized.

2. Alcohol contributes to the greatest number of violent crimes. Nadelmann says that the rate of crimes committed under the influence of drugs would have to be studied to determine whether it rose or fell after drugs were legalized, but he argues that a shift from alcohol to marijuana would reduce crime rates.

3. The price of drugs would plummet if they were legalized. Crime would be reduced as a result because the big money attraction that drugs currently hold would diminish, and the stakes for drug sales would be much lower.

4. All types of people are attracted to drug dealing because of the huge amounts of money that can be made from it, but the criminal element is well represented because of the drug laws. If drugs were legalized, dealers would either have to become mainstream business people or they would have to turn to other forms of high-profit crime, depending on their personalities.

5. The allure is obviously the large amounts of money that can be made. Police officers are likely to take bribes because they are offered a lot of money, they are disillusioned about fighting the drug trade, and they don't receive much public support when they do succeed. Their job is not to stop the drug trade but to keep it underground as much as possible so it isn't visible to certain segments of society.

6. Nadelmann strengthens his parallel of Prohibition and the current situation with drug laws by using the Rockefeller quote. Using it at the end leaves the reader with the parallel uppermost in mind.

USERS, LIKE ME: MEMBERSHIP IN THE CHURCH OF DRUGS (p. 295)

Gail Regier

Stylistic Highlights
Regier's descriptions of his drug exploits are detailed but dispassionate--he avoids emotion and makes no judgments. Yet his piece should have a large impact on most readers. His descriptions prove that users "are different from the straight people . . . When we were messed up, we seemed to become exactly who we were, and what could be more dangerous and splendid?" The perceptions he offers, the events he describes in what must have been a slightly, but not very, unusual night in the Springfield, Missouri, drug scene are so skewed and, to a straight mind, horrifying that the reader accepts Regier's assertion that users turn their own stereotypes inside out. He doesn't pass judgment either on users or those involved in the so-called War on Drugs, but his descriptions argue powerfully that "Just Say No" will do little to deter members of the Church of Drugs from getting high and discovering "how clean and fine things could be."
For those who haven't experienced the "Church of Drugs," Regier's essay will be educational. The first essay question asks students their viewpoint on drugs, and how it might have been changed by Regier's essay. The second essay question addresses the current debate about whether certain drugs should be legalized. Has Regier's essay influenced your students' opinions about this issue?

Understanding the Essay
1. According to the media, a typical drug user is ghetto trash, a neurotic child star, or a mutinous adolescent. Drug users turn the stereotypes inside out because they feel superior to straight people.

2. Drug users learn not to think about what drugs do to them. They learn to enjoy them and clear their minds. This is a difficult question, and other interpretations should be considered.

3. Drug use in restaurants is prevalent because the work is so menial. Regier and his friends are members of the Church of Drugs, so to speak. They live a life that looks attractive to the kids at the truck stop.

4. Regier seems much closer to his drug buddies than to his wife--the drugs bond him with his friends, but he doesn't identify anything specific that bonds him with his wife. The second part of the question is open to interpretation.

5. Prudence and Casey are getting along better, presumably because they dropped acid together to help make their peace.

6. Regier describes heroin as something that will make Guy as high as he would ever want to be. It also has the appeal of danger and fear. The scene with the baby points out how heroin changes the perceptions of those who use it--it's hard to imagine laughing at a bleeding baby chewing on broken glass.

7. Regier became tired of the abuse his body was taking and bored with the life-style. He still craves drugs and the simplicity they seemed to give his life.

EATING DISORDERS--AN ADOLESCENT PROBLEM (p. 306)

Helen A. Guthrie

Stylistic Highlights
This selection is excerpted from a textbook, but it is a good example of a research paper. Guthrie presents her facts in a straightforward and accessible manner, and organizes her presentation in a progression that is easy to follow. She begins with the general phenomenon of both eating disorders--anorexia nervosa and bulimia-- and then discusses what they are, who suffers from them, patients' behavior patterns and symptoms, the physical damage they endure, and the current treatment. The writing style is clinical, but the language is easy enough for a layperson to understand. In a society where those with anorexia nervosa and bulimia are often misunderstood and even the target of jokes (as in the movie Heathers: "Oh, Heather, bulimia! That's so '87!"), Guthrie's clear discussion of the problem is a valuable one.

The first essay question addresses the causes of anorexia and bulimia, as Guthrie doesn't discuss the social factors behind eating disorders. The second essay question asks students to take a look at themselves. How important is weight to them? Is there a gender difference in attitudes toward weight?

1. The "cure" rate is only 50 percent symptom-free and 25 percent with reduced symptoms.

2. Anorexics become obsessed with food and eating. They eat very little but interact with food and think of it often. Anorexics are usually well-behaved females between twelve and eighteen years old from good homes.

3. If anorexia goes untreated, it can lead to deterioration of brain tissue. That can lead to apathy, coma, and even death. The best treatment is hospitalization with care from an interdisciplinary team to address the psychological as well as physical problems.

4. Bulimia is characterized by a pattern of binging and purging of food. It has been recognized as a disorder only since 1980.

5. Young white women from the upper and middle classes with an average age of about seventeen are the most likely to have bulimia. They are a little older than typical anorexics, and they may have a history of behavioral problems.

6. Bulimia is difficult to diagnose because bulimics tend to binge and purge surreptitiously, they often have no outward symptoms other than fluctuating weight, and they don't tend to seek help. Bulimia can cause electrolyte imbalances, ulceration of the GI tract, erosion of dental enamel, loss of hair, and irregularities in the menstrual cycle.

CHAPTER 11: The Natural World

BABY BIRDS (p. 318)

Gale Lawrence

Stylistic Highlights
The "baby bird crisis" demonstrates both the best and worst human tendencies--the urge to help and the ignorance that "helping" can be the cruelest thing to do. Lawrence's essay seeks to inform people about what to do when a baby bird is found, and she pulls no punches. "You can leave it there to die a natural death--which might in fact be the most humane thing to do. Or you can take it indoors." She organizes her essay very clearly--she begins by describing the best course of action to take if a baby bird is found, backed by basic information that explains why returning a baby bird to the nest is desirable. She then discusses the problems of raising a bird if that is the chosen course. Again, she is blunt: "If you

think I'm trying to sound discouraging, I am. The adoption of a baby bird will probably result in failure." She concludes by broadening her discussion to promote a hands-off approach as the best way to interact with all wild birds. Thus, she argues her point that adopting a baby bird is a poor idea in three different, but related, ways.

The first essay question is meant to encourage students to consider Lawrence's points from their own viewpoint. How many of your students have had a "baby bird crisis"? The second essay question is meant to pick up on the "Bambi syndrome" that Lawrence describes in the final paragraph. What makes a domestic animal well suited to life as a pet? The third essay question illustrates what makes the "baby bird crisis" such a wrenching one--could your students leave a helpless bird to die?

Understanding the Essay
1. The reader expects Lawrence to answer the question and to provide information that supports her answers.

2. A family should try to put the bird back in the nest. If that's not possible, they should construct a substitute nest to get the bird off the ground. If that's not possible, they should leave the bird on the ground and watch to see if the parents return for it.

3. Inside, the problems include figuring out what to feed it, giving it the dusk-to-dawn feedings that baby birds require, preparing the bird to return to the wild, and keeping its surroundings clean.

4. First, one must determine what to feed it. Protein-rich foods work at first, but what it eats in the wild will determine what it needs later on. Then it must be fed often--every fifteen minutes or so, from dawn to dusk.

5. Lawrence suggests that we enjoy wild animals by observing them in their natural habitat, from a distance.

6. The "Bambi syndrome" describes the way baby animals are portrayed as cute and cuddly in the media, promoting the desire to touch them and make pets of them. It is based on a notion that we can make pets out of wild animals, and that they are cute and pettable.

DEATH OF A HORNET (p. 324)

Robert Finch

<u>Stylistic Highlights</u>
Many naturalists don't need African safaris to find fascinating wildlife and natural events--they find them in seemingly mundane places in their everyday lives. Notice that when Finch begins his essay by describing how he absentmindedly whacked a hornet that fell into what seems like a housekeeper's nightmare of a window sill, his language is very straightforward and practical. When the spider comes out to tie up the hornet, he personifies it comically: "The spider . . . stopped about an inch short of this enormous creature . . . with what seemed a kind of 'Oh, Lord, why me?' attitude." As he studies the interaction of the spider and the hornet more closely, however, his language becomes more lyrical to emphasize that his close examination of the conflict has lifted it out of the mundane. His descriptions would do justice to the most exotic creatures, which, it is pointed out, we deal with every day--if we would just stop, look closely, and think about what these animals do.
     The first essay question puts students in Finch's position. How well do they write about the natural world that is right under their noses? The second essay question encourages students to write about an emotional topic in a nonemotional--perhaps even scientific--manner.

<u>Understanding the Essay</u>
1. Finch whacked the hornet with his rolled-up bus schedule to catalyze the encounter between it and the spider.

2. Humans and insects will both try to inflict the maximum damage on their foe, even when it seems certain that they won't survive themselves.

3. Personification is an effective technique to describe the action of animals because it makes it easier to identify.

4. The spider appears to have made the hornet her own, and her movements become proprietary.

5. The spider alternates between moving the hornet with a sort of silk block-and-tackle and giving the hornet a sort of death kiss, pausing motionless for ten or fifteen seconds at the hornet's head. Finch is mesmerized by the alternation of intimate contact between predator and prey and the busy, businesslike manipulation of an inert object.

6. There can be different answers to this questions as long as students can defend them. Finch is saying that the world of the spider has no past or future-- only the present. Thus spiders have perfected the waiting game, because they have nothing to remember and no future to anticipate, so they are ready to act when they need to in the present.

TERROR AT TINKER CREEK (p. 331)

Annie Dillard

Stylistic Highlights
With a title like "Terror at Tinker Creek," students probably expect Dillard's essay to be about Freddy Krueger and a hapless teenager, not a giant water bug and a frog. Yet the natural world is full of interactions that, if we witness them or think about them for too long, are horrible. Dillard's writing style emphasizes her change in mood when she saw the frog "deflate." At first she is carefree and cheerfully admits that one motivation for her walk was to scare frogs. Then she sees the frog, and her style changes. She writes with a breathless, staccato rhythm: "it was a monstrous and terrifying thing. I gaped bewildered, appalled." The frog's demise is not unusual or unnatural, but it is, upon close examination, an awful way to die. Dillard doesn't dwell on the event for long. Her one sentence, "I couldn't catch my breath," sums up her feelings in a manner that readers can easily understand.
    The first essay question is meant to encourage students to report on an experience they have had that is similar to Dillard's. Were your students as horrified as Dillard? What were some of the different methods of predation, and do students feel that some are worse than others for the prey? The second essay addresses the effect of the frog's death on Dillard. What provoked similar emotions in your students?

Understanding the Essay
1. Answers will vary for this question, but they should indicate that Dillard wanted to maximize her horror when she witnessed the frog's death, and that, when we think about it, nature's predators can be truly horrifying.

2. Dillard could not catch her breath because what she had observed had absorbed her attention completely and had horrified her.

3. Dillard presents the scene as she saw it. She at first sees the frog deflating before her eyes, then she understands the cause of it. It establishes her confusion when she saw the frog deflate for no apparent reason, then revulsion when she saw the water bug.

4. "The spirit vanished from his eyes as if snuffed"; "his very skull seemed to collapse and settle like a kicked tent"; "He was shrinking . . . like a deflating football." The similes allow Dillard to describe an unfamiliar incident by comparing it to things readers are likely to be familiar with.

5. Sentences 1, 2, and 5 are loose. Sentences 3, 4, and 7 are periodic. The loose sentences communicate Dillard's feelings. The periodic sentences convey her reflections.

6. Dillard uses words like creature, enormous, mighty, vicious, and poisons to describe the water bug. She clearly indicates that the water bug is fearsome, almost evil.

THAT ASTOUNDING CREATOR--NATURE (p. 335)

Jean George

Stylistic Highlights
For "That Astounding Creator--Nature" George did not intend to find interest in the seemingly mundane as Finch ("Death of a Hornet") did. Instead, she catches the reader's interest right away with "some really unbelievable creatures" that, the reader hopes, she will discuss in more detail after the first paragraph. Her point that there are some amazing creatures that have adapted in, to our minds, bizarre ways to their environments is established early and memorably. It is a fertile topic, so she is later able to discuss other examples of startling adaptations in the context of how and why the animals were formed into their current shapes and behaviors. Note how she supports each general statement with one or two specific examples--she is able to effectively illustrate each point, but she does it concisely so that she can describe many of the "unbelievable creatures" in a relatively short essay.
 The first essay question encourages students to explore George's topic in much the same way that George did--through research, categorization, and presentation. Do you have any examples of highly adapted creatures in your area that students could see in person? The second essay question points out that humans are part of nature, too. What have we done to adapt to their self-imposed environments?

Understanding the Essay
1. The thesis is that the process of evolution will create a creature suited to any environment or situation--and it will create very bizarre creatures in the process. It is stated in the second paragraph.

2. Some of the main environmental factors that cause creatures to evolve in certain ways are the presence or absence of water, diet, mating habits, sound, and predatory pressures. Students will have a variety of answers to the second part of the question.

3. Paragraphs 3 through 6 specifically discuss the creatures mentioned briefly in paragraph 1.

4. Paragraphs 11 through 13 are all about the ways that animals can defend themselves from predators. They are unified by the first sentence of paragraph 11.

5. The first sentences of each paragraph acknowledge the content of the paragraph before it, then introduce new topics within the context of the old. Students can identify any part of these transitional sentences. The final sentence of paragraph 16 also sets up a series that is picked up again in paragraph 17.

6. By discussing how she pondered how evolution has endowed earth's creatures with strange adaptations, she encourages readers to remember the specific examples she has discussed earlier in the essay. She restates her thesis in a subtly different way in the last sentence.

CHAPTER 12: Life and Death

A CRIME OF COMPASSION (p. 346)

Barbara Huttmann

Stylistic Highlights
In "A Crime of Compassion," Huttmann says that she enters a "legal twilight zone" by not calling a code blue for her favorite cancer patient Mac when he stops breathing. She also enters a moral twilight zone, as she demonstrates by the way she begins her piece. No matter how grim the suffering of the patient or futile the medical treatment, many people revile those in the medical community who don't sustain human life for as long as is technologically possible. Huttmann establishes right away that she is a murderer in some people's eyes, which catches the reader's attention and underscores the pain felt by all parties in her later explanation of Mac's plight. Her point of view is clearly presented through graphic descriptions of Mac's suffering, and she later reverses one of the questions that had been asked of her by saying, "Had we become so self-righteous that we thought meddling in God's work was our duty?" Her critics accused her of playing

God for not saving Mac, but Huttmann's essay convincingly argues that the medical community had played God by saving him . . . fifty-seven times.

The first essay question directly addresses the issues presented by Huttmann. What do your students think of Huttmann's actions and her proposal for preventing Mac's dilemma from being repeated? The second essay question is a more philosophical inquiry into the root causes of Mac's dilemma. Why is letting someone die who wants to die so abhorrent to many people?

Understanding the Essay

1. Huttmann describes the Donahue show as a place where the guest is a fatted calf and the audience is a large flock of vultures. One would hope that the audience's reaction would have at least been less strident if Huttmann had had time to tell Mac's entire story.

2. Mac went from being a young, witty, macho cop to a sixty-pound skeleton who had lost his wit, his hair, his continence, his sense of taste and smell, and any ability to do something for himself. His wife changed from a young person to a beaten old woman.

3. Nurses are more sympathetic to a patient's request for a no-code order than doctors because they must deal more closely with the patient's suffering. Some doctors believe they must sustain life as long as possible, no matter how much suffering the patient must endure.

4. Huttmann would ask a spiritual judge whether the suffering was meant to build character or infuse us with humility from our impotence.

5. Huttmann "kills" Mac by not calling a code blue when he stops breathing. She enters a legal twilight zone because she does nothing to actively kill him, but because a no-code order had not been issued, she is legally responsible to call the code. It would be hard to prove, however, that she purposely called the code too late to save Mac.

6. Huttmann recommends legislation would that make it a criminal offense to code a patient who has requested the right to die.

WHOSE LIFE IS IT ANYWAY? (p. 352)

Ellen Goodman

Stylistic Highlights
Goodman, in order to discuss Elizabeth Bouvia's case and argue her opinion of it, must deal with a number of thorny issues. As she succinctly describes it: "Here is

a case that pushes just about all the buttons on our finely engineered ethical panel." To accomplish this task in a short space, Goodman organizes her essay very strictly. She starts with a narrow focus by describing Bouvia's situation. She then broadens the focus to discuss the ethical "buttons" that come into play in the case, particularly society's attitude toward the rights of those who wish to commit suicide. She concisely cites other cases and some of the ethical dilemmas they have generated. Goodman brings us back to Bouvia by relating these dilemmas to Bouvia's specific situation, and uses these connections to launch her argument that Bouvia shouldn't be allowed to starve to death. Having established the precedents that had been established in similar cases earlier in the essay, Goodman can then conclude that dangerous new ethical "buttons" might be created if society allows Bouvia to die.

The first question asks students whether they agree with Goodman's arguments. If students agree, encourage arguments other than those she has used in her essay. The second essay deals with the broader topic of assisted suicide. With Dr. Jack Kevorkian and others pushing assisted suicide into the national spotlight, how do your students feel about giving people the right to choose when and how they want to die? Should the terminally ill be given special consideration?

<u>Understanding the Essay</u>
1. Bouvia wants to starve herself to death in a hospital, with doctors assisting her by giving her painkillers. She is depressed, paralyzed, and has decided to end her life.

2. Bouvia's specific case presents society with the dilemma of where it should draw the line concerning the right of the individual to commit suicide. The broader issue is whether society should support medical intervention to save a patient who wishes to die or who is brain-dead. Karen Quinlan and Baby Doe are two other cases that have raised similar questions.

3. Goodman fears legalizing suicide for the ill or the elderly. She feels it could lead to a sense that we shouldn't reach out to help such people if they are "thoughtful" enough to want to end their lives.

4. Bouvia's case brings into question the issue of individual rights. Bouvia is not terminally ill, and she is asking doctors to assist her actively in the process of suicide.

5. Goodman agrees with the judge's ruling that Bouvia doesn't have the right to kill herself with the aid of society. Goodman thinks that psychiatric wards must become suicide centers where patients can learn to overcome their despair.

THE DEATH PENALTY IS A STEP BACK (p. 357)

Coretta Scott King

Stylistic Highlights
King's essay would have quite an impact even if it were poorly written--the title and her name alone would catch most people's attention. After all, who could blame her if she advocated violent retaliation for the violence that has been committed against her family? But the essay that follows is very measured and well organized. She begins powerfully by pointing out her belief that an evil deed is not redeemed by retaliation: "America took another step backwards towards legitimizing murder as a way of dealing with evil in our society." Her discussion of the moral issues carries more weight than it would from an unknown author, because she has had to consider them directly and personally. She then progresses to practical reasons for opposing the death penalty. She offers no new arguments against capital punishment but gives a concise rundown of the injustices and problems associated with it. By keeping her presentation simple, she does nothing to detract from the weight that her name and her basic argument will carry.
   The first essay question addresses students' beliefs on this issue and asks whether King's essay has altered their thinking at all. The second essay question asks students to address the roots of violence in our society. What do they think has caused the rise in violent crime? How can we reduce violence as a society?

Understanding the Essay
1. The real issue concerning the death penalty is: "Can we expect a decent society if the state is allowed to kill its own people?"

2. The increase of violence in the country has generated support for the death penalty. King is a good spokesperson for opponents of the death penalty because she has suffered the loss of two family members to assassination and she still opposes capital punishment.

3. King opposes the death penalty on moral grounds because an evil deed is not redeemed by an evil deed of retaliation. On practical grounds, she argues that the death penalty is irreversible, assumes the wrongdoer is beyond rehabilitation, is racially inequitable, and is not a deterrent.

4. King believes that the death penalty is not a deterrent because most murders are committed in the "heat of passion" between family members or acquaintances, and the perpetrators don't think of future consequences.

5. King proposes that we combat violence by practicing nonviolence as individuals and as a society.

54

SNOW (p. 362)

Julia Alvarez

<u>Stylistic Highlights</u>
Discuss with the class how Alvarez uses this one short anecdote about her
childhood to make a much broader and more sweeping comment on growing up in
the nuclear age. Referring to the Understanding the Essay questions, ask students
to compare their own thoughts about the current potential for nuclear war with
Alvarez's experience as a child in 1960. How do different people confront the fact
of their own mortality, and how does it (or does it not) relate to the comprehension
of mass destruction?

     The first writing activity allows an opportunity for positive, creative thinking
about life and the potential for personal fulfillment. The second exercise gives
students a chance to express their opinions and feelings on the subject of nuclear
war, and to practice addressing their comments to a particular audience--a person
whom they don't know but whose point of view they might choose to take into
account.

<u>Understanding the Essay</u>
1. The thesis statement of this essay is the last sentence, which asserts that all
human beings are "irreplaceable and beautiful" (8). There is irony in the young
girl's mistaking snow for nuclear fallout, given that such a lovely analogy is made
between snowflakes and living people, while fallout is obviously associated with
death.

2. This essay is a narrative organized simply around the chronology of events as
the author remembers them.

3. An insightful reader might find that "snow" as a "new word" in the girl's
vocabulary (2), the reference to a "flurry" of "dusty Fallout" in Sister Zoe's
explanations (4), and the changing setting to "November, December" (5) all
foreshadow the climax of the story and the ending.

4. Answers will vary.

5. As a whole, the story suggests that Alvarez's childhood awareness of nuclear
threat was acute and terrifying. The immeasurability of the loss in human life that
nuclear weaponry represents is staggering but made comprehensible somehow by
the snowflake analogy. The rest of the answer will vary.

PART TWO <u>On Becoming a Better Writer</u>

CHAPTER 13: <u>Writers on Writing</u>

WRITING IS BUILDING (p. 371)

Roger Garrison

<u>Understanding the Essay</u>
1. Prewriting, writing, revision, and editing are the main steps in the writing process. Information, ideas, and the writer's point of view make up the prewriting phase. The reworking of the organization, grammar, and diction of a piece are some aspects of revision and editing.

2. The <u>purpose</u> defines why we write: to persuade, to argue, to entertain, and so on.
The <u>reader</u> is whom we write to, our audience: students, parents businesspeople, and so forth.
Our <u>attitude</u> is how we feel about our material and our audience. It determines the style and diction of our writing.

3. The shape of a thing, including writing, is determined by its purpose. Thus we mold our writing according to its intended effect on our readers.

4. Student A has not made a list of the specific elements of his story. "He'll have to make another list, maybe three or four more."

5. Students will have to show they understand that writing is as much a process of discarding as it is an affirmative act. It sifts through massive amounts of material to choose the few selections that will give the reader a glimpse of what was not chosen as well as what remains.
Garrison admits the existence of inspiration, the "quick flash of an idea." However, the lack of it is no excuse to avoid writing, because it can be bidden, "like a flame from the stirred embers of a nearly dead fire." Thus, for Garrison, to claim a lack of inspiration is to admit a "lack of will."

6. Garrison says writing is a process of parts, each piece contains parts of its own assembled in a definite order for the best results, just as a house or a bridge is built.

FREEWRITING (p. 382)

Peter Elbow

Understanding the Essay
1. Freewriting is writing without stopping or evaluating the result. "Never stop to look back, to cross something out, to wonder how to spell something, to wonder what word or thought to use, or to think about what you are doing." Freewriting unblocks the writing process.

2. Freewriting must never be evaluated because it is an exercise in, as Elbow calls it, nonediting. The writing process should be free of self-editing during the exercise and free of outside editing afterward.

3. Writing permits editing, speech does not. Elbow thinks editing is the downfall of writing. Instead of allowing words to drop naturally from the mind to the page, we interpose a "massive and complicated series of editings." We also tend to edit "unacceptable thoughts and feelings" when we write. As a result, our product can become cumbersome. Speech, on the other hand, may have a "halting or even garbled beginning," but left to move ahead, unedited, it will become "coherent and even powerful."

4. By compulsive, premature editing, Elbow means "that editing goes on at the same time as producing."

5. Voice is a sound, a texture, a rhythm that is the main source of power in writing. Premature editing deadens the writer's "voice." The example of freewriting that Elbow gives has voice. It is conversational--the writer carries on an internal conversation. There are plenty of dashes to loosen up the style, and expressions like "ah, yes" and "Huh? I dunno." Nonediting is explained in question 2.

FIVE PRINCIPLES FOR GETTING GOOD IDEAS (p. 388)

Jack Rawlins

Understanding the Essay
1. Rawlins uses prompt to mean "--the seed, the spark, the sense of 'gotcha.'"

2. Rawlins writes, "Essays rarely begin with subject matter alone," and observes that telling yourself to think on demand about a subject is unproductive: "Being put on the spot is the surest way of preventing the creative juices from flowing."

Rawlins recommends starting with a prompt instead (see above), and then thinking, reacting to, and connecting things as you go.

3. "Data sponges" to Rawlins are people who take in or produce thoughts separately but "don't do both at the same time." He claims that "the best time to try to get things out is when things are going in," otherwise one becomes passive, and a good thinker (and writer) is reactive. Rawlins's advice to "data sponges" is to "practice your reacting skills" by learning to think in terms of going "from little, concrete things to big, abstract things" and by practicing making connections--as when "two previously unrelated bits in the brain meet."

4. The department meeting-construction worker's story illustrates Rawlins's point about making unlikely connections. He thinks that after he heard that faculty member speak, he "must have been checking everything that came into my brain against the faculty-meeting remark for a possible connection. Or perhaps I had opened a file in my mind labeled 'people who think in terms of those who belong and those who don't' and dumped anything related in there as it came along."

5. "The Head Principle says you can't predict what will connect with what." Mr. Head represents someone who made an astute and unlikely connection between two fields (aviation engineering and downhill skiing and tennis) and founded his success upon it.

6. Answers will vary to the first part of the question. Rawlins suggests that writers should begin with particulars and move to abstractions, because they should start with something they <u>know</u> and know about.

7. Answers will vary.

SIMPLICITY (p. 397)

William Zinsser

<u>Understanding the Essay</u>
1. Clutter consists of "unnecessary words, circular constructions, pompous frills and meaningless jargon." Zinsser calls it a disease because we are strangling ourselves with clutter in our written communication. Answers to the final part of the question will vary.

2. We can free our writing of clutter by stripping down every sentence to its cleanest components.

3. Answers will vary.

58

4. Writers must clear their heads by asking themselves, "What am I trying to say?" and "Have I said it?" These questions are important because if the answers are not clear, the writer has let some "fuzz" into the "machinery."

5. Zinsser uses the questions in paragraph 2 to get readers to identify with the problem of clutter. He blames the writer rather than the reader for the reader's failure to understand. This helps establish his main point, that writing should be simplified for the reader's sake.

6. According to Zinsser, "Clear thinking becomes clear writing; one can't exist without the other." Students should acknowledge that clear thinking translates to clear writing only through hard work, so it is possible to think clearly and not write clearly.

7. Answers will vary, but make sure that the analysis ties in to Zinsser's point that good writing cannot be cluttered.

WRITING FOR AN AUDIENCE (p. 404)

Linda Flower

Understanding the Essay
1. In her opening sentence, Flower states, "the goal of the writer is to create a momentary common ground between the reader and the writer."

2. When Flower refers to the "distance" between writer and reader, she means the difference in age, background, attitude, and the like that can stand in the way of successful communication. The first step in closing this gap is for writers to "gauge the distance" between themselves and their readers by analyzing the audience for whom they are writing.

3. Flower defines knowledge as "conscious awareness of explicit facts and clearly defined concepts" that "can be easily written down or told to someone else." Attitude, on the other hand, is more like an "image" or "loose cluster associations" (4). This distinction is important because "a reader's image of a subject is often the source of attitudes and feelings that are unexpected and, at times, impervious to facts" (5). Writers, therefore, need to be conscious of this distinction to bridge the "distance" between themselves and their readers.

4. Flower says "a good college paper doesn't just rehash facts; it demonstrates what your reader, as a teacher, needs to know--that you are learning the thinking skills his or her course is trying to teach" (9). Writers use knowledge rather than

just expressing what they know when they "meet the demands of an assignment or the needs of their reader" by reorganizing or rethinking their ideas.

5. Students' responses to this question may vary, though it seems apparent that Flower has made some conscious attempts to suit her essay to her college audience. In her discussion of needs, for instance, she focuses on writing done on a job and in college courses--both examples of the kinds of writing college students are concerned about.

CHAPTER 14: Thesis

THE DIFFERENCE BETWEEN A BRAIN AND A COMPUTER (p. 412)

Isaac Asimov

Understanding the Essay
1. By stating at the outset that he believes the "difference between a brain and a computer can be expressed in a single word: complexity," Asimov immediately informs his reader of where he is going with the comparison. There is no confusion about what ideas he will be pursuing in the essay, and he has placed his reader in a position of focus and preparedness.

2. Paragraph 3 restates Asimov's thesis: "Even the most complicated computer man has yet built can't compare in intricacy with the human brain." The opening statement implies that the brain is more complex than the computer, but in paragraph 3 the position is clarified.

3. The definition of "thinking" is important because the depth of the comparison between the brain and the computer relies on it. By some definitions, computers do indeed "think" in the same way that humans are said to "think." Being "programmed," in human and mechanical terms, means having certain limited capabilities. "Thinking," on the other hand, may be defined "in terms of the creativity that goes into writing a great play or composing a great symphony, in conceiving a brilliant scientific theory or a profound ethical judgment" (6).

4. As Asimov points out, the brain is composed of physical matter, of "cells in certain arrangements and the cells are made up of molecules in certain arrangements" (8). When he says "if anything else is there," he is probably referring to ideas about some spiritual or other nonmaterial element in human brain function. For example, humans are the only known animals to possess consciousness of self; does that consciousness have a physical basis? If so, where is it located? Asimov's argument hinges on the fact that the brain is made

of matter (as far as we know) and that the complexity of that matter can be duplicated in computers.

5. According to Asimov, a "complexity explosion" is a point at which the sophistication of something, like technology, advances exponentially on its own. In terms of computers, this may mean building a computer than can "design another computer more complex than itself. This more complex computer could design one still more complex and so on and so on and so on" (9). Asimov posits that if a "complexity explosion" in computers occurs, then someday "computers may exist that not only duplicate the human brain--but far surpass it" (10).

6. Asimov seems to take a positive view of the vision of a future world run by computers. He suggests that humans are, at least presently, poorer managers of the earth than a supercomputer might someday be. The final paragraph relates to the thesis in that it brings the complexity distinction between brains and computers to what Asimov suggests might be its ultimate conclusion.

THE ISSUE ISN'T SEX, IT'S VIOLENCE (p. 417)

Caryl Rivers

Understanding the Essay
1. Rivers cites evidence that images of violence against women are entering the mainstream media at a rapid rate. Without active response, she implies that these images will become more and more acceptable. Such stories as the AC/DC song that inspired a murderer in California also lend weight to her argument.

2. Rivers's thesis is that violence against women is greeted with silence. By writing the essay, she is both breaking that silence herself and encouraging others to join her.

3. "Sesame Street" teaches young people that television teaches them the truth. With this attitude, teenagers have a difficult time distinguishing between reality and fantasy in adult television shows and on MTV. The second part of the question is a matter of opinion.

4. Rivers cites the examples of one of her journalism students who was raped and murdered, two others who were raped, and another who was permanently injured as the result of an assault against her. These personal experiences show in part why she is interested in the issue, and they lend an air of authority to her argument.

5. Rivers is arguing that images of violence against women must be eliminated from the mainstream media and that such images should be condemned, not ignored.

6. Rivers proposes that women rock stars speak out against violence against women. She would like disk jockeys to boycott certain recordings, and she would like journalists, artists, critics, and parents to keep the issue alive rather than maintain their current silence. The second part of the question is a matter of opinion.

DEBATING MORAL QUESTIONS (p. 424)

Vincent Ryan Ruggiero

Understanding the Essay
1. Ruggiero's thesis is located in the fifth and last sentence of the opening paragraph. The author briefly presents the issue and the sides of the controversy in the first four sentences before taking a stand.

2. The examples Ruggiero uses to illustrate how impossible it is not to make value judgments are of Raoul Wallenberg's heroic sacrifice and the New York City mother's negligence toward her children. One might argue that these two examples are compelling; they appeal to the reader's emotions and morality in a way that makes them seem undeniably supportive of the author's argument.

3. Ruggiero insists that "we must judge" moral issues because morality is the foundation of the laws that create society, as well as the society that creates the laws. He gives two quick examples of the role of moral judgment in society.

4. By accentuating the similarity between modern and medieval cultural morality (asserting that the "only difference is our rejection of the idea that animals are responsible for their behavior" [6], the example of the medieval punishment of animals supports Ruggiero's position that, when it comes to judging moral issues across cultures, "the degree of difference has often been grossly exaggerated" (5). The author is trying to establish a case in favor of making cross-cultural moral judgments, because it strengthens his original argument that it is proper to make moral judgments in general.

5. Ruggiero's attitude toward these examples of Brazilian culture seems to be one of disagreement with the Brazilian moral value system. The reader can guess that the author does not approve of how women are treated in these two cases from Brazil because in paragraph 7, he clearly states, "we can say a society is acting

immorally by denying women their human rights" right before he cites the examples in paragraph 8. The rest of the answer may vary.

6. Ruggiero, in paragraph 9, takes his argument to its furthest point; he argues that "it is proper to debate moral issues" (1) even across cultures (7), he offers clear, compelling illustrations (8), and then he makes a general statement incorporating all his points in the concluding sentence.

CHAPTER 15: Organization

THE BOX MAN (p. 432)

Barbara Lazear Ascher

Understanding the Essay
1. Ascher's thesis is stated in the final line of the essay: "One could do worse than be a collector of boxes." Her main point has already been stated in paragraph 19, which is that the Box Man's chosen mode of living "declares what we all know in the secret passages of our own nights, that although we long for perfect harmony, communion, and blending with another soul, that this is a solo voyage." Paragraphs 1-8 depict the Box Man and his solitariness, from which (with the addition of other images) Ascher will draw her conclusions.

2. Ascher is trying to identify a little bit in her own way with the Box Man by recalling a book she read as a child in which "the young protagonists" lived lives of total freedom and self-sufficiency (9-10). The passage refers to the Box Man and also sets up the musings she will have next about how his life "is of his choosing" (12), and how he "is not to be confused with the lonely ones" (13).

3. "The lonely ones," Ascher implies, do not choose to be alone; unlike the Box Man who lives by his own terms, the lonely old women Ascher describes are victims of circumstance. By asking a question like "What will she do with the rest of the night?" (13) and stating simply "Not necessarily a lonely life except that 3 A.M. lights and television proclaim it so" (17), Ascher demonstrates what she means by "lonely." Ascher includes examples of "the lonely ones" to offer contrast with the Box Man, who, though alone, is not lonely.

4. Ascher writes that the "Box Man knows that loneliness chosen loses its sting and claims no victims" (19). Through her previous description of him and the examples of "the lonely ones," Ascher has already communicated the distinctions that choice makes in how one perceives one's solitariness.

5. In paragraph 20, Ascher asserts that as children and adolescents, we "stubbornly deny" our growing suspicion that life "is a solo voyage" (19). As evidence, the author offers what she presents as the typical progression from the childhood discovery that "our saviors, our parents, are strangers," to the adolescent "quest for the best friend" and the young adult hope of "true love." The rest of the answer will vary.

6. One kind of order Ascher seems to use is stream of consciousness, or a chain of associations. She sees the Box Man, thinks of the Boxcar Children, compares the Box Man with "the lonely ones," and expresses her conclusions. Her strategy, which was likely more complicated and finely crafted than pure stream of consciousness, is effective because it invites the reader to participate in the linked associations and follow Ascher's thoughts to their profound end, as if the reader were thinking them too.

7. Ascher seems to be writing this essay to a wide audience who, she may be assuming, share with her a sense of wonder at people who live solitary lives. Thus, she is probably not addressing homeless people like the Box Man or lonely old women. If her purpose is to highlight the distinctions between chosen and unchosen loneliness to make a grander point about the ultimate aloneness of each person, then her presentation is indeed effective.

CHINA'S ANTIDRUG TRADITION AND CURRENT STRUGGLE (p. 440)

Ling Qing

Understanding the Essay
1. Qing's major thesis is stated in the first paragraph: "To eradicate its harm, it is necessary for people all over the world to make a concerted effort" (1). His secondary thesis is located in paragraph 11, where he asserts that "China's own history and the present international antidrug struggle show that the spread of drug trafficking for enormous profits is a chronic malady of capitalism." The rest of the answer will vary but should recognize that the essay sounds very much like an appeal to the West and the United Nations to help fight harder against the rise in Chinese drug trade and drug abuse.

2. The first three paragraphs recount the story of Lin Zexu's anti-opium efforts, which culminated in the burning of 170 chests of opium (a patriotic gesture, according to Qing). The story illustrates part of the history of China's struggle with drugs and provides the background for the rest of Qing's argument.

3. The first part is the story described above, which introduces the topic Qing is going to address. The second part (4-7) lists four major reasons (three of them

statistical) why Qing feels the worldwide drug "situation is grim" (4). Third, Qing summarizes the history of opium use in China (8), discusses the drug problem in recent years (9), and reports on a current series of triumphs against the proliferation of drugs there (10). The fourth part argues that drug trafficking "is a chronic malady of capitalism" (11), and calls for greater global cooperation in ending the drug trade in China and everywhere.

4. Qing's transition from the first part to the second part is chronological; he moves from an incident in the past to "Today, unfortunately, narcotics are still polluting the world." The transition from parts two to three is like that in a report; Qing cites the statistics and then moves on to provide the historical overview in which to place those statistics. Between parts three and four, the transition is based on the author's argument; the author refers in part three to how "China is again
faced with an arduous and complicated struggle against drug abuse," and moves on in part four to link drug trade to capitalism and to Qing's call for a global solution.

5. The author's assertion that drug trafficking is linked to capitalism is based on statistics reflecting the prevalence of drugs in the United States and the United Kingdom, and the United Nations survey reporting that "narcotics rank second only to the munitions industry in value of traffic" (11). "Money," writes Qing, "smoothes the way for the passage of narcotics" (12), owing to corruption among officials. The rest of the answer will vary.

6. The last two paragraphs, though perhaps offering less "neat" endings for the essay than paragraph 13, attempt to demonstrate China's commitment to the eradication of the drug trade and its willingness to cooperate with other nations and the UN in the worldwide struggle.

WHY MEN FEAR WOMEN'S TEAMS (p. 448)

Kate Rounds

Understanding the Essay
1. Rounds hooks the reader with the first sentence: "Picture this." Next she challenges the reader by describing a TV sports scene that typically involves men--then directs, "Now imagine that the players aren't men" (2). Rounds is operating on the assumption that readers will not think of women when they read paragraph 1, so paragraph 2 hinges on challenging the reader's stereotypes. The rest of the answer may vary.

2. Rounds comes across as supportive of women's professional team sports. Her thesis, the last sentence of paragraph 2, uses the word _fantasy_ in a way that suggests that women's professional team sports is something she hopes for. Second, she refers to women "able to break through sexist barriers in golf and tennis" (4), so the reader knows Rounds recognizes and disapproves of sexism in professional sports. Third, in the last two paragraphs of the essay, Rounds's attitude is one of disappointment and sadness that the "prospects for women's professional team sports don't look bright" (21).

3. First Rounds uses an attention-getting device to capture the reader's interest (1-2). She presents the issue of gender bias in professional sports and provides some background on women's gains in golf and tennis (3-4). Then she goes into the history of sexism in women's sports and the efforts of various people to promote women's professional volleyball and basketball leagues (5-10). The author next turns to softball, baseball, and team tennis (11-15). Paragraphs 16-17 recount the history of the relatively successful women's baseball league that originated during World War II, and paragraphs 18-20 describe the current flourish of women's professional team sports abroad. Rounds concludes with paragraphs 21 and 22, which suggest that men fear women's teams because physically strong women are generally perceived by men as intimidating.

4. The main points of the essay all highlight various aspects of sexism and gender bias in professional sports: the lack of seriousness with which women athletes are regarded (3-4), the failure of organized attempts at creating women's professional sports leagues (5, 9-15), prejudice against lesbians and images of strong women (6-7), the fact that women's team sports have worked in the past (16-17), and the relative success of professional women's teams in Europe (18-20). Transitions include "It took a while" (4), "By contrast" (5), the implied emphasis on "does" in "What volleyball does have" (6), "The response . . . is" (8), and the repetition of "or something" as an opener to paragraph 13.

5. The "L word" is "lesbian." As Lindy Vivas points out in paragraph 6, mainstream American society "has problems dealing with women athletes and strong, aggressive females" who are ignorantly labeled categorically as lesbians. Rounds's purpose in quoting Vivas and others is to demonstrate how "image" in women's professional sports is much more important than in men's and that the same qualities glorified in male athletes are considered unattractive and unacceptable in women athletes.

6. In paragraphs 18-20, Rounds compares the success of women's teams in Europe with their failure in the United States to suggest that the United States is more prejudiced against women athletes and that it is more shortsighted in terms of the financial potential of women's professional sports. The essay concludes that

American society holds "deep-rooted sexual bias and homophobia" that profoundly discriminate against women athletes. The rest of the answer may vary.

7. Answers may vary.

CHAPTER 16: Paragraphs

THE ICEMAN'S SECRETS (p. 461)

Leon Jaroff

Understanding the Essay
1. The first sentence, "Women have inquired about the possibility of having his baby," is very provocative and compels readers to jump into the rest of the essay. The first eleven paragraphs introduce the discovery of the Iceman and the controversies surrounding it. Overall, it is an interesting, engaging, and informative beginning that clearly reveals the author's own fascination and enthusiasm.

2. The topic sentence of paragraph 4 is the first sentence about the "new insight into Stone Age society" that the Iceman's discovery has offered scientists. Specifically, the remainder of the paragraph lists the Iceman's arrows, clothes, medicine, haircut, and tattoos. The last sentence of paragraph 4 provides another example of what researchers might learn from the Iceman while simultaneously serving as a transition to paragraph 5.

3. The three paragraphs all hark back to the opening sentence of the second section, "A broad portrait of the Iceman and his times is gradually emerging from the tests and observations" (12). Paragraph 14 covers the Iceman's body hair and tattoos, while 15 addresses the Iceman's basic clothing, and 16 describes his cape, shoes, and cap. Actual student outlines will differ.

4. Paragraph 22 posits the general circumstances in which the Iceman may have met his death. The transition to paragraph 23 is the first sentence ("At some point . . .") that breaks the Iceman away from his group and suggests why and how he might have struck out on his own. Paragraph 24's topic and transition sentence, "It was late summer or autumn," suggests what the weather conditions might have been for that time of year and how the Iceman might have died. Paragraph 25 opens with an explanation of the hole in the back of the Iceman's head and continues with an idea of how the Iceman began to be preserved. Finally, paragraph 26 uses the transition sentence about how the Iceman was "tucked away in a deep 'pool' in the glacial stream" to lead into a discussion of the climatological conditions that made it possible for the Iceman to be uncovered.

5. Paragraph 28 describes the custody arrangement between Austria and Italy. Paragraph 27 reports that Austria's claim to the Iceman is technically invalid because he was found about one hundred yards inside the Italian border. Paragraph 29 outlines the Innsbruck (Austria) scientists' plan "to conduct as much research as possible" while they still have possession of the Iceman.

6. Essentially, the author is suggesting that the fight over who has the Iceman and what should be done with him is overshadowing the more important issues of what can be learned about him and how that knowledge might enhance the entire world's understanding of the Stone Age. The topic sentence of paragraph 30 lists several crucial kinds of information that the custody "bickering has seriously delayed," and the concluding sentence of the essay repeats what "a sad irony it would be if . . . the Iceman and his ancient secrets would be lost to human folly and politics."

7. Jaroff appears enthusiastic about, even fond of, the Iceman near the end of the essay, as he more or less calls for better management of and protection for the discovery. He cites several examples of how the "Iceman's appeal is universal" (31) and how experts are trying to maintain a sense of dignity and responsibility toward the Iceman (30, 32). Evidence that the Iceman was pillaged, poorly handled and transported, maimed, and fought over has led Jaroff to conclude that much of what the Iceman has to offer is being jeopardized by petty, unnecessary squabbling.

KNOCK WOOD (p. 475)

Paul Chance

Understanding the Essay
1. The first sentence of paragraph 10 is Chance's thesis statement: "True superstitions are activities that have no effects on events but exist because of coincidental rewards and society's prejudices." Certainly, Chance could have begun the essay with this statement, although it would have lessened the impact of the humorous and engaging introductory paragraph. He could have placed it at points throughout the explanation of Skinner's experiments and the findings of other psychologists, but they, too, might have been undermined in the way any story is ruined when the punch line comes too soon.

2. The topic sentences of paragraphs 5 and 7 are similar in that they both occur at the beginning of the paragraph, declare the paragraph topic, and provide transitions from the previous paragraph. The structure of the two sentences is different, in that the topic sentence of paragraph 7 begins with an adverbial clause and is therefore a bit more complicated and subtle. The supporting sentences in

paragraphs 5 and 7 provide examples that illustrate and clarify the points in the topic sentences.

3. The "prejudice" to which Chance refers is a societal prejudice or bias in favor of superstition. Chance's evidence for this bias consists of two examples of hypothetical accidents and generalizations about the survivors' reactions. Although the examples are not concrete, the situations "ring true," and most readers would probably agree and identify with the generalizations.

4. Chance opens the essay with a story about a "lucky pen" that he tells with some sarcasm (as in the admission that the pen "didn't have all the right answers, but with it I believed I could present my ignorance in the most favorable light"). At the end of the first paragraph, Chance declares that he "gave up all . . . superstitions, thanks largely to the work of psychologists" whose experiments and theories Chance is about to discuss. In the final sentence of the essay Chance repeats that he is "free of all such nonsense, and . . . happy to report no ill effects," but then adds "--knock wood." It is hard for a reader to tell whether Chance is joking about "knock wood," or whether, like the tongue-in-cheek sentence, "Of course, I no longer have any superstitions" (10), Chance is suggesting that he can't help but participate in superstitions, regardless of the scientific explanation for them.

5. Chance is saying that some superstitions may be based on real, practical issues; they are more like sensible procedures that either originated as or became superstitions. Paragraph 9 continues the scientific discussion of superstition by providing yet another aspect to the coincidental reward theory. The paragraph links the idea about societal prejudice in favor of superstition to Chance's thesis and conclusion.

6. Paragraph 10's topic sentence is also the author's thesis. Sentences 2 through 6 bring the thesis back around to the author's personal experience with superstition, which is how the essay began. The last sentence hints that the author, though firm in his scientific understanding of superstitions, still harbors a little bit of residual belief in them.

HOW TO MARK A BOOK (p. 481)

Mortimer Adler

<u>Understanding the Essay</u>
1. Adler's thesis--"Unless you do [write between the lines], you are not likely to do the most efficient kind of reading" and "marking up a book is not an act of

mutilation but of love"--is presented in the first and second paragraphs of the essay.

2. The topic sentence of each paragraph is the first sentence of the paragraph. Adler expands upon the specific point made in each topic sentence within the framework of each paragraph.

3. Writing in the book you are reading keeps you awake, helps you think a book through, and helps you remember your thoughts and the author's.

4. Adler lists seven devices, from underlining to writing in the margins. Answers to the second part of the question will be based on individual experience.

5. Adler does not have "a false reverence for paper, binding, and type--a respect for the physical thing." Instead he feels that possession of the "beauty" of a great book is not a matter of ownership. Words such as <u>beauty,</u> <u>soul,</u> and <u>rich</u> indicate Adler's general affection for books.

6. The first fourteen paragraphs outline all the reasons why readers ought to mark books. The last thirteen explain how to do it and what the consequences will be. But Adler assumes throughout the essay that he is talking to nonbelievers, so, in both sections of the essay, he addresses the unspoken objections of his readers.

CHAPTER 17: <u>Effective Sentences</u>

WHY I FEAR OTHER BLACK MALES MORE THAN THE KKK (p. 494)

Essex Hemphill

<u>Understanding the Essay</u>
1. Hemphill's attitude toward violence that blacks commit against other blacks is one of anger and frustration. Because in the essay he uses a personal experience to illustrate his argument, one might guess that he is writing the essay to express some of his negative feelings and share them with others. Hemphill's statements in paragraph 5 suggest that his target audience is black protesters who demonstrate against racism but ignore the problem of violence among blacks.

2. If one converted the last two sentences of paragraph 3 from questions to statements, they might read: "It is hard for many black Americans to acknowledge publicly the crimes blacks commit against other blacks. We excuse black misbehavior by hiding behind charges of racism." Hemphill's main idea is also communicated less directly in paragraphs 4 and 5.

3. The sentences in paragraph 1 are all relatively short; they create a sense of urgency. The longest sentence describes Hemphill's evening stroll to the market, reflecting the calm regularity of the event. The two short sentences about the $13 draw attention to how little money he had on him, how extreme the robbery was for such a small sum, and how senseless it would have been to die for $13.

4. Paragraph 3 is composed of two questions, two statements, and two more questions, all based on parts of Hemphill's main argument. The effect created by the questions is one of wonder, frustration, demand for change, and challenge to the people he is criticizing.

5. The structure of the first sentence in paragraph 4 is complicated but clear; the four commas around the adjectival clause ("where I now live") and the appositive ("Yong Chang") create several pauses, yet are used effectively enough that Hemphill's information is communicated. (The rest of the answer may vary.)

MIYOK, HEALTH FOOD FROM THE SEA (p. 498)

Kwon Byung-Rin

Understanding the Essay
1. Miyok is "the best quality" seaweed in Korea, according to the author. Miyok is a low-fat, nutritious plant that reportedly helps "in preventing and controlling diabetes, colon cancer, the cholesterol count in blood, and arterial sclerosis" (2). It is a traditional medicine used for blood purification and for women after childbirth (1). The rest of the answer may vary.

2. Byung-Rin seems to be promoting miyok; the beginning and the end of the essay both refer to how this wonderful food is still being cultivated today, and how its farmers "are more ambitious and put in much more care and heart in what they are doing than ever before" (12). The essay first discusses the health benefits of miyok (1-3), then outlines the history and geography of miyok cultivation (4-6) and current miyok growing procedures (7-10), then concludes with the best miyok producers and the above-mentioned final comments about the dedication of contemporary miyok farmers.

3. The topic sentence of paragraph 1 is the first sentence, which introduces a time of day, a place, and the subject of the essay (seaweed). The topic sentence of paragraph 2 is also straightforward and informative, but there is no setting--just a scientific description and categorization of miyok.

4. Byung-Rin uses short, descriptive sentences to describe both miyok and processes, but the author uses more quotations in analyzing miyok cultivation

practices, which results in a few longer sentences. The author's concluding paragraph contains only three sentences, two of which are particularly long in comparison with the rest of the essay.

5. Paragraph 9 is about the business of miyok cultivation in Kongsu Village. It lists how many families participate in the business, how much miyok they produce, and how big their sea farm is. Also included is information about how miyok is sold, wet or dry, and weather conditions that hamper the drying process. The last sentence of paragraph 9 is related to the first sentence because it is an important detail in the miyok business in the village.

6. As the main point is how beneficial miyok is and how it continues to be cultivated today after a long history of medicinal use, the final sentence of the essay sums up the author's enthusiastic endorsement by claiming that miyok today may be the best it's ever been.

I HAVE A DREAM (p. 505)

Martin Luther King, Jr.

Understanding the Essay
1. King tells his audience that even though blacks have not received the freedom and justice guaranteed by the Founding Fathers, they should go on working nonviolently for civil rights. His message for us is to keep working for the day when people will join together, as stated in the last paragraph of his speech.

2. King's organization begins with the least and moves to the most emotional elements of his appeal in a style identical to the evangelical preaching tradition from which he came. He begins with a simple greeting, then relates a bit of the history of blacks in America, which serves both as a context for the rest of his speech and provides the rationale for the march. In paragraphs 3-5, he outlines the purpose of the march, which will be a beginning of a calling-due of civil rights owed blacks. In paragraph 6, King warns the rest of America not to underestimate blacks' sense of urgency in the matter; then in paragraph 7, he warns blacks to refrain from violence in their fight for justice. In paragraph 8, King lists what blacks want that they do not yet have. In paragraphs 9 and 10, he offers a pep talk to the veterans of the struggle who may be weary. Then, beginning in paragraph 11, King begins probably the most famous section of the speech--the "I have a dream" repeated again and again as the chorus of his vision. The speech ends with the fulfillment of the vision in the ringing phrase, "we are free at last."

3. King uses parallel constructions in paragraphs 11-18 and 22-26. The parallel structures add dramatic flair to his speech and make it accessible to listeners, for

they enable important ideas to stand out. They are also rhythmical; the speech becomes almost like a song and is easy to listen to.

4. "We cannot turn back." "I have a dream today." "This is our hope." The short sentences give special emphasis to their content and add interest to the rhythm of the speech. If too many are included, the rhythm becomes choppy and difficult to follow.

5. The analogy is effective for King's argument because civil rights for blacks, like "paying up" a check, do not need to be justified. It is not only the law, it is the right and moral thing to do.

6. King's speech has endured because of the basic truth of its message and the lasting importance of that message to black Americans in particular and to the health of the nation in general. In addition, King's speech is rhetorically impressive and memorable.

St. Martin's